PRAISE FOR *LIKE BIRDS IN A CAC*

"This book is quite unique in the way that it com
history of Zionism, careful interpretation of the Bible, and firsthand, recent experience of everyday life for Palestinians living under occupation on the West
Bank. David Crump understands Christian Zionists extremely well because he
grew up as one, and because he reads and quotes what many Christian Zionist
leaders have been writing in recent years. My hope and prayer is that this book
will help American Christians of all kinds to wake up to the very significant
ways in which Christian Zionism has contributed—and continues to contribute—to this tragic conflict. They might then be more able to challenge their
government's policies."

—COLIN CHAPMAN, author of *Whose Promised Land?*

"*Like Birds in a Cage* is destined to become a standard text on Christian Zionism in the USA. With devastating precision, Dave Crump exposes the cancer-
ous nature of this deviant theology. For Evangelicalism to survive with any
credibility, it must repudiate the justification of apartheid and ethnic cleansing
in Palestine. Crump's book provides not only the diagnosis but also the cure."

—STEPHEN SIZER, Founder and Director, Peacemaker Trust

"This new volume by David Crump may be the most comprehensive critique
of Christian Zionism by an evangelical author to date. As a former 'insider,' his
unique perspective has delivered a tour de force by combining scholarly biblical exegesis of key texts with incisive theological analysis. His solid grasp of
the relevant political and historical context of the Israeli-Palestinian struggle
adds context and texture to this wonderfully written book. I hope this volume
will be widely read and reviewed across the evangelical spectrum by pastors,
biblical scholars, students, and perhaps most urgently, evangelical politicians."

—DON WAGNER, author of *Anxious for Armageddon*

"A keenly reasoned, comprehensive, full-frontal critique of Christian Zionism. Equally at ease interpreting Saint Paul, critiquing ideologies of privilege, deconstructing Israel's discriminatory legal regime, and narrating scenes of unarmed, tear-gassed villagers, David Crump mounts a formidable case against the troubling logic and deadly deployment of ethnocracy and territorial exceptionalism. This prophetic call to walk not *where* Jesus walked, but *as* Jesus walked, is more urgent now than ever."

—BRUCE N. FISK, Senior Research Fellow, Network of Evangelicals for the Middle East

Like Birds in a Cage

Like Birds in a Cage

Christian Zionism's Collusion in Israel's
Oppression of the Palestinian People

DAVID M. CRUMP

Foreword by Gary M. Burge

CASCADE Books · Eugene, Oregon

LIKE BIRDS IN A CAGE
Christian Zionism's Collusion in Israel's Oppression of the Palestinian People

Cascade Books
An Imprint of Wipf and Stock Publishers
199 W. 8th Ave., Suite 3
Eugene, OR 97401

www.wipfandstock.com

PAPERBACK ISBN: 978-1-7252-6957-6
HARDCOVER ISBN: 978-1-7252-6956-9
EBOOK ISBN: 978-1-7252-6958-3

Cataloguing-in-Publication data:

Names: Crump, David M., author. | Burge, Gary M., foreword.

Title: Like Birds in a Cage : Christian Zionism's Collusion in Israel's Oppression of the Palestinian People / by David M. Crump; foreword by Gary M. Burge.

Description: Eugene, OR: Cascade Books, 2021 | Includes bibliographical references and index.

Identifiers: ISBN 978-1-7252-6957-6 (paperback) | ISBN 978-1-7252-6956-9 (hardcover) | ISBN 978-1-7252-6958-3 (ebook)

Subjects: LCSH: Christian Zionism. | Israel—History. | Jewish-Arab relations.

Classification: BT93 C78 2021 (paperback) | BT93 (ebook)

10/22/21

Terry and I dedicate this book to Ayed, Ghada, Suhaib, Rewaida, Selma, Jude, and Qusai, who opened their hearts to us without limit; to everyone in both the Al-Azzeh and Amira families, who have made Aida Camp our home away from home; to Abu Abed, who shares his home with us in the Judean desert and takes us camping in the barren landscape he knows like the back of his hand; and to the many additional friends, Palestinian, Israeli, European, and American, whose paths have intersected with ours as we all benefited from the abundance of West Bank hospitality.

We continue to pray for the day when all Palestinians will finally be free to enjoy justice, equity, and self-determination in their own land, living in peace and equality with all citizens of Israel.

Contents

x   Contents

Foreword

The evangelical church has been examined from almost every angle in the last five years. From its political commitments to its deeper moral values, many have begun to wonder if the passions within this movement are still personal faith in Christ, exemplary moral leadership, orthodox theological convictions, and care for the poor. These are values evangelicals study in the Bible. Pundits marveled at evangelical voting behavior in the last two elections (2016, 2020), wondered at evangelical tolerance for less than excellent moral conduct among leaders, and began to see that political action had moved to some center stage in evangelical life since the 1980s.

While North Americans are keenly aware of this in our national elections, there is another dimension here that has slipped beneath the radar. Running through the evangelical world is a particular political commitment that is as unwavering as it is invisible to outsiders. It is Christian Zionism. This commitment is the perfect wedding (or the perfect storm) where a dubious reading of the Bible has wed itself to raw political interests in the Middle East. Most evangelical pastors know this problem instinctively: for some people, commitment to Israel ranks up there with commitment to Jesus. Pastors have told me that it would be safer to proclaim an error in the Bible than to openly criticize Israel. Or to doubt the claim that Israel is a divinely sanctioned country with unique privileges. Israeli leaders also know instinctively what messages they need to send to American evangelicals to secure cover for their national policies. As one Israeli leader remarked, Israel has more friends among American evangelicals than among Jews. This translates into enormous sums of money, political leverage in Washington, and an outcome in Israel that few American ever see.

David Crump's *Like Birds in a Cage* is perhaps the most complete analysis of Christian Zionism to date. Crump has credentials that every evangelical will recognize. His family was conservative evangelical (fundamentalist perhaps) and attended independent dispensationalist Bible churches. His Sunday school classes were decorated with those long charts illustrating the seven dispensations and always pointing to the present time and Israel. He was taught from an early age that Israel's miraculous appearance as a new nation in 1948 was a crucial sign that we were now living in the "end times," because Israel was key to God's fulfilment of biblical prophecy and the second coming of Jesus Christ. The Scofield Reference Bible and Hal Lindsay's *Late Great Planet Earth* were mainstays on his family's reading list.

While his church friends went to fundamentalist Bible colleges after high school, David attended the University of Montana. And here his worldview shifted. It was through InterVarsity Christian Fellowship that David began finding new heroes and new authors such as John Stott and J. I. Packer. At eighteen he was a convinced Christian Zionist. By twenty-five he believed that his evangelical background had betrayed him. He would earn a PhD in New Testament and become a highly respected scholar in biblical studies, eventually teaching at Calvin University in Michigan.

David never left classical evangelical faith. His role models were simply relocated to InterVarsity, where sincere faith is wed to deep commitments to social justice. Through his own careful study of the Scriptures he came to see that the Bible is being misused by a movement in evangelicalism called Christian Zionism.

This marvelous book is the culmination of David's forty years of reflection on how evangelicals succumbed to a teaching about the modern state of Israel that misrepresents the Bible. But more, this teaching has led to the oppression of millions of Palestinians in the Middle East. He is no amateur in this matter. This study is replete with resources showing that he is a first-rate biblical scholar who has decided to apply his advanced research skills on one topic that is compromising the faith of the church. He has also traveled to Israel and Palestine many times, even living for extended periods in refugee camps in the West Bank. It is also important to know that a critique of Israel does not mean that a writer hates Israel. Nor is the rejection of Zionism a sign that someone is antisemitic. Opponents of his view will say this but they are wrong.

Like Birds in a Cage will take you on a tour through the history of Christian Zionism and show how it emerged on the twentieth-century scene. You will learn its power in American politics and how its followers are easily manipulated to believe things about Israel that are untrue. Above all, David will model a thoroughgoing and compelling use of the Bible, unmasking interpretations that are as unscholarly as they are misdirected.

This book is a signal achievement by a senior biblical scholar. It deserves a close reading by anyone who is committed to Christ, desires to promote Christlike values in the world, and is open to rethinking the role of modern Israel in the American church.

Evangelicalism is today at a crossroads. Just as America is polarized, so too, evangelicals are polarized. Some are pulling the church into political theaters like we have never seen before. Other evangelicals are in despair about the whole mess—and when they see these political movements like Zionism upending good churches, their despair runs deeper. It is at times like this when the church desperately needs prophets like Dr. David Crump.

GARY M. BURGE, PhD
Dean of the Faculty
Professor of New Testament
Calvin Theological Seminary

Acknowledgments

I AM GRATEFUL TO a number of friends who have helped me bring this book to light and influenced its final shape. My friends Ayed, Mohammed, Glenn, Marla, Sharon, Scott, and Gene have all read different sections of the manuscript at different stages of development and provided helpful suggestions. Thanks, guys.

My friend Michael Thomson, now an acquisitions editor for Wipf & Stock, planted the original seed for tackling this project years ago. He also went through the manuscript with a fine-tooth comb, making a myriad of suggests that we discussed at length in several, long Skype sessions. Michael's editing is always a boon in improving my prose and focusing an argument. I am grateful for his patience, clearheadedness, practiced eye, and sympathy for my concerns. With Michael's help and encouragement, this is a far better book than it might otherwise have been.

Caleb Shupe oversaw the final copyediting, saving me from public embarrassment, and the reader from needless irritation, by catching my mistakes and inconsistencies before the manuscript went to print.

I am also grateful for the helpful feedback of my friend Suzanne McDonald, theology professor at Western Theological Seminary. Suzanne reviewed several chapters in the book's early stages of development. She offered helpful suggestions for strengthening my arguments, as well as much-needed encouragement to continue during one particular episode when I was doubting myself.

My thanks also go out to my friend, New Testament scholar Gary Burge, who graciously took time from his busy teaching and administrative schedule at Calvin Theological Seminary to read the final version of this manuscript. His encouragement, gentle critiques, and willingness to write the foreword have meant a great deal to me. Gary is a leader in the American evangelical church where he has often been a lone voice in advocating for truth, justice, mercy, and equality on behalf of the Palestinian people living in Israel and the Occupied Territories. Gary's three books engaging Christian Zionism from a non-Zionist perspective (see the bibliography), telling the stories of Palestinian suffering which are seldom heard by Western churchgoers, have made Gary an important trailblazer among evangelicals for the advancement of true justice in the Holy Land. Terry and I were delighted when he had the opportunity to visit our Palestinian family in the Aida Refugee Camp several years ago. And they loved having him.

Even the worthiest manuscripts will have little if any effect in the world if they are doomed to gather dust in the author's bottom desk drawer. Publishers with vision are essential to making a writer's thoughts available to the public. For a time, I imagined that gathering dust might be the fate of *Like Birds in a Cage*. I am deeply grateful, therefore, to the editorial team at Wipf & Stock for choosing to publish my book after so many others had declined. I believe they made a wise decision. I trust they will continue to agree.

Finally, as with every writing project, I am thankful to my wife, Terry, who is always my first editor. She has her own stories to tell about life in Israel and the West Bank. She has experienced it with me and can testify to the veracity of my descriptions about Palestinian life under military occupation.

Introduction

Confessions of a Former Christian Zionist

I AM A CHILD of American fundamentalism, a fundamentalism highlighted by the bold colors of dispensational theology[1] and Christian Zionist passion.[2] Christian fundamentalism was from the first a movement that sought to protect the boundaries of evangelical Christianity by affirming the "fundamentals" of the faith. It was born in the late nineteenth and early

1. Christian Zionism has been closely associated with a school of theology known as dispensationalism, which is distinguished by its "two-track" view of salvation history. According to dispensationalist thought, God has one salvation plan for Israel and another for the Christian church. When the leaders of Israel rejected Jesus of Nazareth as the Messiah, God's plan for the Jewish people was put on hold while God turned to a new work through the Christian church. Once God has completed his work with the church, punctuated by the physical translation of all Christians into heaven at the Rapture, he will restart the original, divine plan for national Israel. In this way, dispensationalism has provided a theological framework in which Christian Zionism could operate. A recent movement calling itself the "New Christian Zionism" (to be addressed in the chapters ahead) has tried to disconnect Christian Zionism from its historic dispensational ties, recalling the philosemitism of certain Puritan theologians and nineteenth-century evangelicals long antedating dispensationalism. However, whether new or old, Christian Zionism remains a loyal partner to Israel's political Zionism, even as it seeks to become more ecumenical in its choice of theological dance partners.

2. The word Zionism was coined by Nathan Birnbaum (1864–1937) in 1890. Broadly speaking, it refers to a movement advocating the Jewish people's return to Palestine. The branch of Zionism known as political Zionism went further than this by insisting on Jewish, political sovereignty over an ethnic Jewish nation of Israel. The sovereign, *ethnic* dimension is essential to political Zionism. We will discuss a few of the different types of early Zionism and their widely differing goals in chapters 3 and 4. However, we may note here that nineteenth-century, English-speaking Christianity had a considerable role to play in the early success of political Zionism's plans for a state called Israel; for a detailed examination of this history, see Lewis, *Origins*. Lewis amply demonstrates that "the earliest Zionists were Christian Zionists" (114).

twentieth centuries in reaction to the rise of theological liberalism in mainline protestant circles. It's also important to remember that fundamentalism as a movement reacted negatively to the social gospel movement—a movement concerned with linking the gospel to solving real-world problems. The legacy of fundamentalism's allergic reaction to the social gospel movement will reappear throughout this book.

Fundamentalism also proved to be reactionary toward early twentieth-century, cultural modernism. An array of new intellectual developments proved troublesome for those affirming the fundamentals, such as developments in modern science where Darwin and others affirmed the theory of evolution and concluded that the earth was billions of years old. Equally troubling were developments in biblical higher criticism which questioned the historical accuracy of the biblical narrative. Such cultural and intellectual forces caused many evangelical fundamentalists to feel that historic, Christian orthodoxy was under attack. From 1910 to 1915 a twelve-volume set of essays was published entitled *The Fundamentals: A Testimony to the Truth*. These volumes defended such historically orthodox doctrines as the virgin birth, the substitutionary atonement, the inerrancy of Scripture, the bodily resurrection of Jesus, and the importance of interpreting the Bible literally. Many fundamentalist voices also insisted on the need for a conversion experience of personal transformation, often referred to as a born-again experience. They and their followers came to be known as evangelicals.[3]

My mother was raised in a metropolitan, Independent Bible church proud of its long-standing membership in the IFCA, that is the Independent Fundamental Churches of America, an organization founded in 1930 for anti-organizational, fundamentalist congregations.[4] My father was converted as a teenage delinquent through a local Salvation Army basketball team. After serving in the Korean War, he returned to the States and met my mother at a USO club in Seattle.[5] Her church provided volunteers to help organize club activities. The two quickly married and set off for Los Angeles, California, where my father enrolled in the Bible Institute of Los Angeles, now called Biola University, hoping to become a church pastor. Studying at

3. See Carpenter, *Revive Us Again*; Marsden, *Fundamentalism*; Sandeen, *Roots of Fundamentalism*.

4. See a description at the organization's home page at https://www.ifca.org/page/who-we-are.

5. The United Services Organization (USO) was formed in 1941 by President Roosevelt. The Salvation Army, Young Men's Christian Association, Young Women's Christian Association, National Catholic Community Services, National Travelers Aid Association and the National Jewish Welfare Board all joined hands to provide entertainment and recreational opportunities for US combat forces at home and abroad.

Biola confirmed him in the ways of dispensational thinking which insisted that zealous Christian Zionism was the true heartbeat of biblical Christianity. Placing Christian Zionism at the center of genuine Christian faith is a long-standing practice in certain strains of English-speaking evangelicalism. As Donald Lewis explains in *The Origins of Christian Zionism*, "by the mid-1820s, belief in the restoration of the Jews to Palestine had become the litmus test of Christian orthodoxy."[6]

Thus was I predestined to become a Christian Zionist.

My father's brand of piety taught me that there were two types of people in the world who called themselves Christians: dispensationalists and liberals. A liberal was anyone who did not embrace the literal, historical accuracy of everything stated in the Bible (this view is often called biblical inerrancy in very conservative protestant circles), which included all the miracles, and most pertinently to this book, the establishment of modern Israel in 1948 as God's centerpiece for the end of history which would herald the second coming of Christ. Liberals were fundamentally deficient Christians. Since it was impossible for liberals to actually know Jesus, dispensationalism was the only theological game in town for anyone interested in real Christianity.

The way I was taught the faith, the principal outward sign of fundamentalist-dispensational devotion to Jesus was to express love and support for the Jewish people and the modern state of Israel. A fervent Christian Zionism and the accompanying admiration of all things Jewish summed up the entirety of a Christian's social consciousness. All liberal efforts at social activism within the church, whether it concerned the civil rights movement, anti-war activism, or equal rights for women, were invariably seen in the circles I grew up in as sinful worldly collaborations, or worse yet, a gateway drug to communism.[7] The truly Christian social conscience, therefore, focused its energies on defending Israel. After all, the Jews were God's chosen people; the state of Israel was God's golden child. Israel could do no wrong. Thus, Christians and Christian America were obligated to combat any and all forces that opposed the Jewish state, for whatever reason. After all, had God not promised Abraham, "I will bless those who bless you, and whoever curses you I will curse; and all the peoples on earth will be blessed through you" (Gen 12:3 NIV)? America's attitude toward Israel was the divine key to earthly blessings and national security.

6. Lewis, *Origins*, 79.

7. America was in the midst of the Cold War in constant contention with the Soviet Union. Conservative Christianity linked arms with conservative politics in seeking to thwart the ever-present threat of godless communism from invading American society. Israel was an important ally in this task.

I offer this description of my youthful religious background not as a reactionary recanting of my fundamentalist upbringing. Rather, I hope this background can help locate my criticisms of Christian Zionism against a larger story, and that this will help make sense of my personal journey from Christian Zionism to the fervent non-Zionist faith I espouse today. By no means have I abandoned all aspects of my upbringing. Certain elements of American fundamentalism continue to shape me to this day. I will forever value the importance of regular Bible-reading and prayer—what I learned to call a daily Quiet Time—taught to me by fundamentalist pastors and youth leaders. Although my views on the Bible and its divine inspiration have matured over the years, I still hold to the Bible as the unchanging authority, as God's reliable word of salvation to all humanity. As the Westminster Confession of Faith affirms, "The whole counsel of God, concerning all things necessary for his own glory, man's [sic] salvation, faith, and life, is . . . expressly set down in scripture."[8]

I became serious about my personal devotion to the Lord Jesus after a dramatic spiritual encounter during my sophomore year in high school. I immediately bought a large, black Scofield Reference Bible for my personal study.[9] I wanted a Bible with the largest margins possible for the notes, questions and observations I was certain to make in my daily reading. That Bible, with its scribbled marginal notes and uncertain underlining, sits in my office today. As any good dispensationalist knew, the Scofield Reference Bible was the only English version worth studying, since it offered both the King James translation, as well as Cyrus I. Scofield's extensive system of cross-referenced footnotes at the bottom of each page. Scofield's notes and commentary were an essential guide to explaining how dispensationalists should understand the Scriptures, fitting together the scattered puzzle pieces of God's plan for Israel, the church, and the end of the world.

My fundamentalist-dispensational moorings started to come loose during my college years. As a student at the University of Montana, I became involved with InterVarsity Christian Fellowship, a student-led organization centered around on-campus worship, small group Bible study, evangelism, and world missions. I was the only graduating senior in my church youth

8. See *Confession of Faith*, chapter 1, para. 6.

9. C. I. Scofield (1843–1921) was an early leader in the burgeoning fundamentalist movement, portions of which were popularizing dispensational theology in America. His reference Bible was published in 1909 and promptly established itself as the most widely read study-Bible in dispensationalist circles because of its extensive footnotes and commentary collating the biblical text with dispensational beliefs. In 1914 he founded the Philadelphia School of the Bible in Philadelphia, Pennsylvania (now Cairn University).

group to attend a state university. My youth leader once preached a sermon condemning Christian parents who allowed their children to attend "secular" universities. All of my church-going peers attended one of the numerous *Bible schools* or *Institutes* established by nineteenth-century fundamentalists in order to train *Bible believing* pastors in an environment free of the dangers of secular, modernist schooling.[10] Thankfully, my mother was a bit of a rebel who had attended the University of Washington and passed along an independent streak to her son.

At university my eyes were opened to the fact that Jesus Christ was also loved, worshiped, and served by a variety of people from a wide spectrum of Christian denominations—all of which were labeled as liberal in the fundamentalist church of my youth. I quickly discovered that it *was* possible to follow Jesus without being a dispensational fundamentalist. I began reading theology books published (primarily) by InterVarsity Press. They were good books written by well-educated and godly authors such as John Stott and J. I. Packer. Men who were self-avowed evangelicals, but were neither dispensationalists nor Christian Zionists.

How was this possible?

Perhaps the most important factor in my growing disillusionment arose when I subscribed to *Bibliotheca Sacra*, a theological journal published by Dallas Theological Seminary, the educational flagship of American dispensationalism. I suspect that my father had always hoped I would one day enroll at Dallas Seminary. It was considered the equivalent of an Ivy League education for anyone from my background. As my own formation grew more diverse, and more rigorous, it did not take long before *Bibliotheca Sacra* began to strike me as religious propaganda rather than honest scholarship. Most issues featured an article by then-seminary president John Walvoord; I found these to be especially troubling. Walvoord's circular reasoning was often expressed as some sort of Dallas Theological Seminary mantra: (1) the Bible must be interpreted literally (what I will call "literalistically" in this book); (2) anyone who does not read the Bible literally, as we do at Dallas Seminary, is a theological liberal; (3) both dispensational theology and Christian Zionism are the assured results of properly literal Bible reading; (3) therefore, the only place to receive a solid, Bible-based

10. Schools such as the Bible Institute of Los Angeles (founded in 1908 and launched Talbot Theological Seminary in 1952), Moody Bible Institute (founded in 1886 by fundamentalist preacher/evangelist D. L. Moody), Prairie Bible Institute (now Prairie College, founded in 1922), and Multnomah School of the Bible (now Multnomah University, founded in 1936) are examples of the institutions founded by American fundamentalism in its efforts to train pastors and to protect its young people from the threats of modernism.

theological education is Dallas Theological Seminary, where you will be schooled in these fundamentalist-dispensational truths.

Even at the tender age of twenty I could see that Walvoord's syllogism was *Bibliotheca Baloney*. I never applied to Dallas Seminary.

The final breach with my Christian Zionist upbringing occurred as I sat reading the Bible on the edge of my bed one early Montana morning. By this point, my disaffection with dispensationalism had progressed to the point where I had set aside my Scofield Bible and replaced it with a simple, unannotated New International Version (NIV). I had been focusing my daily readings on Paul's Letter to the Romans. On this particular morning, I read the apostle's words in Romans 4, explaining how God's promises to Abraham (the biblical progenitor of the nation Israel) were now fulfilled in the life of anyone who had faith in Jesus Christ:

> So then, he [Abraham] is the father of all who believe but have not been circumcised, in order that righteousness might be credited to them. . . . Therefore, the promise comes by grace and may be guaranteed to all Abraham's offspring—not only to those who are of the law but also to those who are of the faith of Abraham. He is the father of us all. (Rom 4:11b, 16 NIV)

I will never forget the impact those verses had on me that day. It was like a bolt out of the blue. My upbringing taught me to read the Bible literally, to accept its "plain sense" meaning. Well, the plain sense meaning of Romans 4 became as clear to me in that moment as it is to me today.[11] I am a gentile, not a Jew, yet Paul declares that Abraham became my father the moment I believed in Jesus. Why had I never seen this before? My mental wheels began spinning furiously. Who, then, were the biblical Israelites? Who were the descendants of Abraham? Paul seems to redefine Abraham's descendants in terms that have nothing to do with ethnicity or physical descent. If being a descendent of Abraham was no longer equated with being born into a Jewish family, but rather was now extended to those who had faith in Jesus Christ, what did this mean for my Zionist upbringing?

I recall thinking to myself: If this is true, and since the Apostle Paul says it, I will accept it as true, then why do so many in the church invest so much time and energy in defending the biblical endtime significance of a Jewish state reoccupying an ancient homeland? Why waste money on prophecy conferences, learning to "read the signs of the times," speculating about the "mark of the beast" (see Rev 13:16–18), and looking for signs of

---

11. Naturally, like so much else in the field of biblical studies, my understanding of Romans 4 is hotly contested among New Testament scholars. For a collection of differing interpretations, with authors' mutual critiques, see Bird, *Four Views*.

the anti-Christ (1 John 2:18, 22; 4:3; 2 John 1:7), all of it revolving around God's unfulfilled plan for ethnic Israel? None of it made any sense. Paul said that the children of Abraham were now reconstituted by the gospel of Jesus Christ. Romans 4 was the beginning of the end of my Christian Zionism. Just as my exposure to the breadth of world Christianity terminated my fundamentalism.

Of course, the proponents of Christian Zionism have ways of defending their interpretation and would seek to sweep aside my youthful conclusions on the plain sense of Paul's logic in Romans 4. In spite of their apologetics though, the more I studied the more convinced I became that Christian Zionism was fundamentally wrong. My father's college graduation gift to me was a copy of Lewis Sperry Chafer's eight-volume *Systematic Theology*. Chafer was the founding president of Dallas Theological Seminary and one of the patriarchs of American dispensationalism. I faithfully carried these books with me for years, and read them intently. Yet, in my estimation, Chafer compared poorly to the other theologies I explored at the time; works such as John Calvin's *Institutes*, John Bright's *The Kingdom of God*, and the works of German theologian Emil Brunner.[12] The more I studied for myself, the more convinced I became that fundamentalism, dispensationalism, and Christian Zionism were all wrong.

INVESTIGATING ISRAEL'S MODERN STORY

After years of graduate school and a busy pastorate, I eventually became a professor of New Testament studies at Calvin College in Grand Rapids, Michigan. Every semester I taught a course entitled "An Introduction to the Bible and Theology." The course covered the history of ancient Israel along with the origins and development of the Old and New Testaments. The intent was to help students see the canonical arc of salvation history, beginning with Abraham and concluding with Jesus Christ. I was conversant with the Jewish side of this story through the second century AD but had never given much attention to the relevance of that ancient history to the modern story of the nation-state of Israel.

I knew well the official Zionist story line advanced by the Israeli government and repeated verbatim by advocates of Christian Zionism—modern Israel's birth in 1948 was a divine miracle; the meager, ill-equipped Zionist forces were like a modern David confronting a gigantic Goliath in the numerous Arab armies hoping to extinguish the fledgling state; Israel is

---

12. Especially Brunner's *The Christian Doctrine of God* and *The Christian Doctrine of Creation and Redemption*.

now the lone beacon of democracy in the Middle East. However, I also knew that all countries craft their own national mythologies. Certainly, Israel was no different. America and Israel both view themselves as God's "exceptional" nation. I began reading widely about the history of Zionism, Israel's founding in 1948, the conduct of that war, and the political, social, and cultural consequences of political Zionism in the modern Jewish state.[13] I quickly discovered the works of several Jewish, Israeli historians often referred to as *The New Historians*, whose research has rewritten the conventional story of modern Israel. Their works—careful histories by Benny Morris, Ilan Pappé, Avi Shlaim, and Simha Flapan—figure prominently in this book, for they extensively document a tragic history, long buried beneath Israeli government propaganda, that diverges widely from the conventional Zionist story line. I then discovered another group of professional historians—people such as Walid Khalidi, Rashid Khalidi, and Michael Palumbo—who criticized the New Historians by revealing how even they (with the exception of Ilan Pappé) had limited the scope of their research and not gone far enough in exposing the truth about Israel's brutality against the Palestinians.[14]

All Christians everywhere must be committed to the truth, however painful. Yet, for whatever reason, Christian Zionist literature continues to ignore the research of the New Historians' and many others, clinging instead to the old mythologies of Zionist, Israeli nationalism. During the late 1970s to late 1980s, vast quantities of official, state documents, including collections of private papers and political party documents, were declassified by the Israeli government as the official, thirty-year secrecy period elapsed. A treasure trove of new documentation emerged covering the seminal years immediately before and after Israel's Declaration of Independence (1948), including the dramatic events of Israel's war with the surrounding Arab states (1947–49), and the origins of the Palestinian refugee problem.[15] Anyone genuinely interested in understanding the emergence of modern

13. Morris's book, *Birth*, and Shlaim's *Iron Wall* were the initial eye-openers in my pilgrimage toward a better understanding of Israel's modern history.

14. A concise discussion of this issue appears in Palumbo, "What Happened to Palestine?"

15. Several of the New Historians have discussed the historical significance of this declassification and how their subsequent research has superceded a great deal of the standard, Israeli history writing which did not have access to this material; see Flapan, *Birth of Israel*, 3–12; Morris, *1948 and After*, 1–48; Pappé, *Making*, vii–ix; Rogan and Shlaim, *War for Palestine*, 2–7; Shlaim, *Israel and Palestine*, 54–61. Pappé has also discussed the deeply entrenched tendency of past Israeli historians, many of whom participated in the events they wrote about, to produce historical works in service to the patriotic agenda of the Zionist nation-state; see his "Critique and Agenda" and "Vicissitudes."

Israel would find it difficult to overestimate the importance of this extensive historical work based on previously secret archives. In comparison to the nationalistic, Zionist histories that came before, Simha Flapan insisted that the newly opened archives "swept away the distortions and lies that have hardened into sacrosanct myth" among Israel's supporters.[16] Similarly, Ilan Pappé has concluded that "the newly available material has served to demolish many myths and misconceptions" about Israel and the Palestinians.[17] Yet, Christian Zionist writers continue, by and large, to ignore the work of the New Historians, the Khalidis, Palumbo, and others for ideological reasons explored in the chapters ahead.

VISITING ISRAEL/PALESTINE MYSELF

In the summer of 2009, I had the chance to take a summer study leave in Israel. While staying in the Old City of Jerusalem, I took the opportunity to see for myself the current living situation of Palestinians in both Israel and the West Bank. Was it as oppressive as described by the critics of the Israeli government? Two tours of east Jerusalem and the West Bank convinced me that Israel's critics were telling the truth. My first tour through east Jerusalem was conducted by members of the *Israeli Committee Against House Demolitions* (ICAHD) who explained the oppressive policies that kept Palestinian Israelis living in ghetto-like neighborhoods lacking the most basic public services in cinderblock houses frequently destroyed by government officials.[18] My second tour was with members of an Israeli veterans' organization called *Breaking the Silence*. They took my group to the Hebron area of the West Bank.[19] The leaders of this tour were former members of the Israeli Defense Forces (IDF) who had once been stationed in the area we were visiting. They carefully explained Israel's systematic, armed oppression of the Palestinian people by taking us to the places where they had served and then described for us (as eyewitnesses) how and why the Palestinian villages lay in ruins while the neighboring Jewish settlements prospered and thrived.[20]

16. Flapan, *Birth of Israel*, 4.

17. Pappé, *Making*, viii.

18. ICAHD uses volunteer labor to rebuild the demolished homes of Palestinians being displaced in order to make way for the expansion of Jewish development projects. For information about ICAHD and its work see the website at https://icahd.org/.

19. For information about *Breaking the Silence* see the website at https://www.breakingthesilence.org.il/about/organization.

20. I will revisit the significance of these two organizations and the tours that they offer in the chapters ahead.

I returned from Israel filled with a deep sense of sorrow and shame. My church heritage, blinded by its misinformed commitment to both Christian and Israeli Zionism, had long turned a blind eye while providing financial and political support to the wholesale subjugation of an entire people in Israel/Palestine. The status quo was utterly unacceptable. I knew that I had to become involved in working to somehow change this unconscionable situation. I simply could not believe that Jesus Christ would sanction the rampant, commonplace injustices I had seen with my own eyes.

As we eventually became empty nesters, my wife and I decided to offer ourselves as volunteers in one of the Palestinian refugee camps in the West Bank. We found a number of Palestinian-led NGOs (non-government organizations) that welcomed international volunteers. We wanted to live with a Palestinian family and share in their daily lives. We expected to pay our way in order not to become a financial burden. We wanted to be under the direction of local Palestinian, not Western, leadership, and I believe the Lord answered our prayers by putting us somewhere that has become our home away from home. Whenever we visit, we live with a beautiful, extended family who have become precious to us. My wife and I return to the West Bank as often as we can afford the airfare. The personal stories contained in this book arise from our lived experience in a refugee community suffering under Israeli military occupation.

I am writing this book to share with you the things that I have learned in my journey away from Zionism toward a more faithfully Christian response to the realities of modern Israel and the plight of the Palestinian people. I am now a convinced NON-Zionist Christian. Whenever I refer to anti- or to non-Zionism throughout this book, I have in mind a *theological position* that contains a specific *political application*. The brand of anti-Zionism presented here—which is hardly unique to me[21]—criticizes two different but closely related issues. First, when I use the words anti-Zionist or non-Zionist, I am criticizing any religious claim making the establishment of ethnic, national, territorial Israel a biblical imperative. I reject Zionist assertions that the Bible teaches that modern, secular Israel stands in direct continuity with the Old Testament descendants of Abraham, or that Israel's reoccupation of the land is the necessary precursor to the return of Christ and the Father's recreation of a new heavens and a new earth (Rev 21–22). The second issue I have in mind concerns morality; namely, the failure of Christian discipleship that I am convinced generally accompanies Christian Zionism. As citizens of the kingdom of God, a multiethnic, global

---

21. See the works by Alexander, Burge, Chapman, Robertson, Raheb, Ruether, Sizer, and Wagner in the bibliography.

community seeking to imitate the life Jesus in this world, the Zionist ethno-cratic state of Israel is not something that God's people can support.

THE ROAD AHEAD

Chapter 1 begins with matters of biblical interpretation and the fulfilment of Old Testament prophecy. How can Zionists and non-Zionists read the same passages but arrive at opposite conclusions as to the meaning of those texts? Answering that question will introduce the importance of reading scripture canonically. Reading the Bible holistically requires that we follow in the apostles' footsteps and adopt their two-stage method of interpreta-tion: we first read from front to back, from the Old Testament to the New, but then, like the apostles themselves, we must learn to reread the canon from back to front, seeing the Old Testament through New Testament eyes. Neither testament is privileged above the other, but both are read as only one part of the larger canon.

Chapters 2, 3, and 4 survey the rise of both Christian and Jewish Zi-onism, giving special attention to the appearance of political Zionism in the European context of nineteenth-century, ethnic nationalism. The un-fortunate alliance between Christian Zionism and Jewish political Zionism, rather than any of the alternative forms of Zionism available at the time, sets the framework for the church's engagement with the Israel-Palestinian conflict today.

Intermittent chapters throughout the book describe the daily experi-ences of the people living in the Occupied Territory known as the West Bank. Chapters 5, 9, 10, 11, and 17 contain eyewitness accounts describing Palestinian life under Israeli military rule and the systematic dehumaniza-tion that results for everyone involved. Rather than segregate these accounts into a separate "story section," I hope that their dispersal throughout the book, cheek to jowl with more rigorous sections of investigation, will help the reader to remember that theological and political theorizing about Israel-Palestine has real-world consequences for the people who live there.

Chapters 6, 7, and 8 excavate the unwarranted assumptions and arbi-trary "rules" of interpretation that control the way Christian Zionists read the Bible. By looking at several New Testament passages, I illustrate how these specious rules and erroneous assumptions distort Scripture in consis-tent, predictable directions that ensure Zionist outcomes.

Christian Zionists believe that biblical Israel is characterized by three essential features: ethnicity, nationhood, and territory. Chapters 12, 13, 14, and 15 unfold by examining each of these characteristics in turn from both scriptural and real-world perspectives. Thus, chapters 12 and 13 dissect the significance of Israel's ethnic nationalism; especially, its claim to be a uniquely Jewish nation-state: a Jewish ethnocracy with different levels of citizenship segregating Jews from non-Jews. Chapters 14 and 15 then focus on the various ways in which territorial control—Jewish dominance over Israeli real-estate—cements Israel's status as an ethnocratic state working hard to preserve its heritage as a settler colonial enterprise fulfilling an ancient biblical mandate.

Chapter 16 confronts the inevitable accusations of "the new anti-semitism" which intentionally confuse the politics of anti-Zionism with the racial animus of historic antisemitism. The seeds of this confusion were sown in the earliest days of political Zionism when its founders described European antisemitism as both an incurable gentile pathology as well as political Zionism's greatest ally. While Christian Zionists do well to warn against the dangers of genuine antisemitism, their sympathies for this new, specious form of antisemitism only puts them at loggerheads with the Old Testament prophets who criticized Israel freely and often.

Finally, chapters 18 and 19 attempt to stir Christian Zionists from their cultural captivity to the American and Israeli mythologies of national exceptionalism. The Christian's primary allegiance is always to the kingdom of God which should never be confused with any particular nation-state.

I know there is a lot to unpack here. So, let's get started.

Chapter 1

Unravelling the Zionist Ball of String

CORNERSTONE CHURCH OF SAN Antonio, Texas is the deeply conservative home base of America's most influential advocate for Christian Zionism: Pastor John Hagee. For Hagee, Christian support for the Zionist state is a non-negotiable, doctrinal issue. He even includes a mandate requiring personal support for the state of Israel into his church's doctrinal statement, linking the defense of Israel with the never-ending fight against antisemitism.[1]

With a church congregation of over twenty thousand people and an international broadcasting empire, Pastor Hagee has proclaimed his own version of the prosperity gospel for over fifty years—God blesses those who bless Israel.[2] Since founding the nine-million member organization, *Christians United for Israel* (CUFI), which claims to be the largest pro-Israel lobbying organization in America, Hagee also claims to have given over fifty million dollars to the country.[3] Scanning the roster of Israeli government officials who spoke at Hagee's annual CUFI Summit in 2020 would appear to endorse Hagee's claim. How else can one explain the personal presentations

1. See the Hagee Ministries home page at https://www.jhm.org/Who-We-Are.
2. "Hagee's Prosperity Gospel," 2.
3. "Hagee's Prosperity Gospel," 2.

provided to Cornerstone Church by Israel's Prime Minister Benjamin Netanyahu, Israel's President Reuven Rivlin, the Minister of Defense Benjamin
Gantz, and other luminaries too numerous to list?

As Hagee Ministries demonstrates, Christian Zionism has become
a flamboyant and politically compelling battle standard for conservative
Christianity throughout the English-speaking world. Defending the modern state of Israel as God's chosen nation, providentially reclaiming the
promised land in 1948 in fulfilment of biblical prophecy, thereby preparing the way for the second coming of Jesus Christ (including, perhaps, the
rapture, the tribulation, and the battle of Armageddon),[4] is almost as dear
to the heart of many conservative Christians as belief in the resurrection
of Jesus and mom's apple pie. For many adherents of Christian Zionism, to
dispute any of these beliefs is to be ranked among the heretics.

Belief in something as complex as Christian Zionism is both easier
and much more common than understanding its complexity. The truthfulness of most heartfelt convictions are commonly self-evident only to the
true believer. Life teaches us that one person's self-evident conviction can be
another person's muddled confusion. How can we find mutual understanding with those on the opposite side of the fence? How can a Zionist and
someone decidedly unpersuaded by their ideology fruitfully engage each
another? Asking questions and listening with an open mind is a good place
to start. What is the evidence, for and against, the contending positions?

Learning to understand the mind of those who disagree with me,
working to see a question from someone else's vantage point, is an important
step in understanding why we believe the things we do. More importantly, it
also helps to clarify whether or not we should maintain our current beliefs
or entertain an alternative. Without such honest engagement and reflection
on perspectives that challenge our own, we are always in danger of simply
repeating ideas passed along to us by others, believing what everyone else
believes because we have never been exposed (in an honest, unbiased fashion) to the likely alternatives.[5]

Such a process must always begin with ourselves, and I am talking
about my own theological journey. I have already noted that I was born and
raised in a fundamentalist branch of American Christianity where Christian
Zionism was considered essential to being an orthodox believer. This sort
of fundamentalism drew a hard line between genuine Christians and im-
posters espousing false doctrine, and genuine Christians were Zionists just

---

4. For clarity, the first half of this rather ponderous sentence is my basic definition
of Christian Zionism.

5. See Jacobs, *How to Think*.

like me, my parents, and my church. Rejecting the affirmation that Israel was resurrected as a nation in keeping with God's promises to Abraham, and paving the way for Christ's return, was tantamount to rejecting belief in Jesus, full stop.

The surety with which I embraced this Zionist form of Christian faith was also my problem.[6] Alternative voices were never allowed a hearing. If the odd visitor did manage to raise her voice in defense of a different perspective, her arguments could not be taken seriously, nor honestly.

UNRAVELLING THE FIRST STRAND

Christian Zionism is not the confession of one single thing to believe. Rather, it is a complicated mix of different, interwoven beliefs and influences interacting with one another like some sort of chemical soup. At the root of the matter are theological assertions involving biblical interpretation, which is why there will be some sustained attention to the Bible in this book. However, it is not just a matter of how one reads Bible texts. There are other important strands of thought, especially historical research, that make up Christian Zionism. These must also be addressed. Like an old ball of string plucked from the kitchen junk drawer, this untangling may seem to be a lengthy process, but the untangling is necessary if we are to offer a credible response.[7]

It is not surprising that all parties to the Christian Zionist debate argue that their way of reading Scripture is the right way. Thus, Christian Zionists typically insist that their reading method (or *hermeneutic*) is the only acceptable method because it is the only truly *objective* or *literal* method

6. I am not suggesting that all Christian Zionists are ill-informed people who only believe what they are told. I will interact with numerous, scholarly Christian Zionists in the course of this book, all well-versed in defending their positions. However, Christian Zionism is the distinguishing characteristic of many American evangelicals and fundamentalists. A great many of these churchgoers become avid supporters of Israel simply because they inhabit a religious atmosphere pervaded with Zionist ideology, which typically includes the derision of other voices. I hope that these folks will read this book.

7. Yes, all the players in this debate claim that theirs are the truly biblical answers to these questions. However, even though I insist that my interpretations are truer to the New Testament writers' original intentions (yes, I also believe in the importance of authorial intent, as I will explain in the pages ahead), I will not insist, as many Christian Zionists do, that my way of reading scripture is somehow more honorable or that it reflects a higher regard for biblical authority. At this point in the discussion, the issues at stake are methodological, not moral or spiritual. Those concerns will arise at a later stage in our argument.

of interpretation.[8] *Literalistic interpretation* is the basic keystone to Christian Zionist Bible reading.[9] The implication is that alternative, non-Zionist readings, such as those presented in this book, fail the test of literalness and objectivity because they either (a) reject the objective historicity of the events described throughout the Old Testament story line and/or (b) reject the literal meaning of the words inscribed on the pages of Scripture.

The debate over interpretive methods, however, is not actually about whose readings of the Bible are more objective or more literal. The more relevant question is: *whose interpretations are most appropriate?* That is, whose interpretations are most coherent with the textual cues embedded in the literature? This search for the most appropriate reading is not a subjective quest directed by personal preferences or subjective bias; it is not determined by political correctness or the latest social trend. Rather, the most appropriate reading is always indicated from within the text itself. As we will see, many New Testament uses of the Old will appear to us as unexpected *rereadings*—some might even say misreadings—of the Old Testament text. Richard Hays, professor emeritus of New Testament at Duke University, has thoroughly examined this aspect of biblical interpretation in his important book, *Echoes of Scripture in the Letters of Paul*. Hays notes how characteristically the Apostle "Paul repeatedly interprets Scripture in ways that must have startled his first audience." For instance, Paul's quotation of Psalm 19:4 in Romans 10:18 transforms the psalmist's mediation on creation's heavenly testimony to the glory of God into a divine indictment against those Jews who reject the gospel. Another example is Paul's reference to Exodus 17:6 in 1 Corinthians 10:4, where a bruised rock gushing fresh spring water for the Israelites wandering in the wilderness becomes a preview of the new life available to believers in Christ.[10]

8. See Blaising, "Biblical Hermeneutics," 79–105. Blaising offers to begin "a discussion about proper interpretation with those who believe proper interpretation is possible and achievable, who believe it is both possible and necessary to speak objectively about of the story of the Bible, its narrative plot, its themes, its claims and its theology. . . . [My] claim is that the view being presented here [i.e., Christian Zionism] is a right reading of the text and that the alternative view is wrong" (79–80). Note the important gem tucked into Blaising's assertion about who is right and who is wrong. Proper interpretation sides with those who "speak objectively" about Scripture's narrative. The implication is that those who are wrong, like me, reveal their wrongheadedness by their failure to read the Bible *objectively*. This frequent Zionist concern for an objective reading, which is really a synonym for a literalistic reading of the text, will be discussed at length in chapters 6 and 7.

9. Sizer, *Christian Zionism*, 108–23, offers an historical survey of this literalistic method of interpretation.

10. See Hays's discussion of these examples and more in *Echoes*, 1–2.

Christian Zionist readings, for all their stress on a literal interpretation, cannot account for the creative and surprising ways that New Testament writers consistently reread the Old Testament in light of Jesus Christ and his earthly ministry. The problem is that *Christian Zionist interpreters prejudge what the fulfilment of a biblical promise must look like because "fulfilment" is defined according to their preconceptions of what constitutes objectivity and literalism.* However, the interpreter's responsibility is not to prejudge the acceptable parameters of a text's possible meanings but to allow the text to speak for itself with its own accent, however foreign that accent may sound to our untutored ears. To borrow again from Professor Hays:[11]

> Paul's citations of Scripture often function not as proofs but as tropes: they generate new meanings by linking the earlier text (Scripture) to the later (Paul's discourse) in such a way as to produce unexpected correspondences, correspondences that suggest more than they assert.

Recognizing Scripture's authority as a guide to faith and life, as Christians have done through the centuries, must include recognizing and accepting scripture's own methods of interpreting itself. Scholars nowadays refer to this as *intertextuality*, that is, noting how the canonical texts interact with each other.[12] Literal, historical readings provide only the first step toward understanding, creating a platform for the many different, biblical authors to converse among themselves, conducting a canonical conversation that is often unexpectedly creative.

READING SCRIPTURE TWICE

The Old and the New Testaments stand in a symbiotic relationship to each other. The light of biblical interpretation shines in both directions, first directing us from the Old to the New, and then projecting backward from the New onto the Old (as illustrated in the examples below). Learning to read and interpret twice, looking in both directions, is the key to biblical, canonical understanding.[13]

Reading Scripture twice is not an arbitrary methodology but has been the practice of the church since its inception. Please note that I am not

---

11. *Echoes*, 24. A trope is the umbrella label covering any figurative use of a word or expression, such as metaphor, simile, metonymy, etc. In literature, trope also refers to a conventional plot device.

12. See Hays's discussion of intertextual interpretation in *Echoes*, 14–24.

13. For another example of this, see McKnight, *Reading Romans Backwards*.

giving priority to the New Testament at the expense of the Old, nor do I presuppose the existence of "a canon within the canon."[14] Those approaches would be instances of circular reasoning, that is, highlighting the evidence that best confirms a previously held conviction. What I am proposing, on the other hand, is an inductive approach to interpreting the Bible. An inductive method first observes the evidence at hand, giving close attention to the ways in which parts of Scripture interpret other parts, and then, on the basis of those observations, formulates an appropriate conclusion.

When we examine the original contexts of those Old Testament passages cited by New Testament writers as evidence for Jesus' Messiahship, we find that the proof of their fulfilment is more apparent in the New Testament eating than it is in the Old Testament pudding. "Fulfillment" for the New Testament writers was defined *by their experience of Jesus' teaching about the kingdom of God, his ministry, crucifixion, and his resurrection.* Thus, the old covenant narrative arc about God's faithfulness to Israel is now fully interpreted only by reading backward through the lens of the new covenant realized in Jesus and in his gospel of grace.[15]

Two, brief examples will help to illustrate this point.

Matthew's Gospel tells a unique story about King Herod's plan to murder a newborn child in Bethlehem rumored to be the claimant to his throne (Matt 2:13–18). An angel warns Joseph of Herod's impending plot, instructing him in a dream to flee with Mary and Jesus into Egypt where

14. Believing in a canon within the canon describes a method of interpretation where the preferred parts of Scripture are allowed to minimize or to erase the significance of other parts of Scripture that the interpreter believes are less meaningful. For a representative example of these common Christian Zionist accusations, see Vlach, *Church*. Vlach lists the "interpretive priority of the New Testament over the Old" and "belief in nonliteral fulfillments" of Old Testament promises as hermeneutical distinctives of non-Zionist Bible reading (84–85). However, as is also common in Christian Zionist literature, Vlach discusses these issues as if they were *a priori* beliefs imposed onto scripture. By framing the debate in this way, Vlach (and others like him) misunderstands and thus mischaracterizes what non-Zionist Bible readers, at least those like myself, are doing. It is a good example of what happens when we mistakenly assume that our opponent thinks like us. Since Christian Zionist interpretation begins with fundamental assumptions about what Scripture can and cannot do, they assume that all non-Zionists must be thinking in the same way. I believe this mistaken assumption is one of the reasons the pro-Zionist/non-Zionist debate becomes so intractable. Pro-Zionist interpreters are looking in the mirror. Seeing only their own reflection, they approach every non-Zionist argument as if it were constructed like one of their own. Thus, they continually miss the point.

15. Richard Hays explains this reciprocal dynamic between Old and New very well in his concise study, *Reading Backwards*. I make a similar argument in my book, *Encountering Jesus*. My original title for this book, had the publisher agreed, was something along the lines of "Doing Theology Backwards."

they are to wait for further instructions. Matthew interprets these dramatic events as the fulfilment of Hosea's words, "Out of Egypt I have called my son" (Hos 11:1).[16]

In their original context, however, Hosea's words have nothing to do with a coming messiah. Neither do they describe God's plan for rescuing Israel's deliverer from a life-or-death situation by sending him to find safe-haven in Egypt. In fact, Hosea 11:1 does not look to the future but to the past. The prophet offers a historical reminiscence assuring Israel that despite their impending punishment at the hands of Assyria, divine judgment is not the last word on God's attitude toward them. So, the Lord reminds Israel of their miraculous exodus out of Egypt. Israel remains God's "firstborn son" (Exod 4:22–23), the beloved child rescued from Egyptian bondage (Hos 11:1). In similar fashion, God promises one day to rescue Israel from Assyrian captivity:

> "When he roars,
> his children will come trembling from the west.
> They will come trembling
> like birds from Egypt,
> like doves from Assyria.
> I will settle them in their homes," declares the Lord.
> (Hos 11:10–11 NIV)

Hosea's words look forward to a time when God will rescue Israel from Assyrian captivity.[17] His words *literally* have nothing to do with a future messiah; they provide an encouraging, historical reminiscence. Furthermore, in Hosea God's son (Israel) is miraculously delivered *out of* Egypt. Whereas, in Matthew God's son deliberately flees *into* Egypt. For Hosea, Egyptian slavery was a paradigm of the son's *enslavement*. For Matthew, Egypt becomes a safe haven offering *protection* for God's son. If Matthew's intent was to draw a prophetic parallel to Jesus' eventual return to Israel from Egypt, he could have easily quoted the prophet at that point in his story (Matt 2:19–23). But that is not what he does. Apparently, drawing literal connections was not uppermost in his mind. Matthew was more interested in *depicting Jesus as God's final instantiation of obedient Israel*. It is the parallel between ancient Israel and Jesus of Nazareth, both serving as "God's son," that leads Matthew to draw from the Old Testament prophet.

---

16. I have also discussed Matthew's reinterpretation of Hosea in *Encountering Jesus*, 17–18, 26–27; also see Hays, *Reading Backwards*, 38–42.

17. Interestingly enough, a deliverance that never occurs for the northern kingdom of Israel as it did for the southern kingdom of Judah.

It is not hard to understand why, to the best of our knowledge, no pre-Christian interpretive tradition had ever understood Hosea 11:1 as a predictive, messianic text. Discovering an episode from the Messiah's biography in Hosea 11 was an unprecedented, Matthean innovation made possible by the Evangelist's gospel-inspired imagination as he reread the Old Testament from back to front, rethinking retrospectively. Whether Matthew's use of Hosea qualifies for anyone's definition of literal, objective interpretation is irrelevant. What matters is observing how Matthew actually makes use of Hosea. The Gospel writer shows us that he understood Jesus of Nazareth to be the long anticipated, real-world exemplar of the covenant faithfulness that God had expected from his people, Israel.

Yet, in spite of all this, Christian Zionists such as Barry Horner survey Matthew's citation of Hosea 11:1 as an example of literal, prophetic fulfillment. Despite the many, noticeable contextual shifts introduced by Matthew's curious use of Hosea's words, Horner nevertheless remains faithful to his literalistic bona fides, insisting that "the literal interpretation of Hosea stands . . . Matthew did not reinterpret Hosea; he simply understood Hosea as fulfilled."[18] While it is true that Matthew quotes Hosea as one of his ten "fulfilment citations,"[19] what Horner and others fail to recognize is that Hosea's fulfilment occurs only by way of Matthew's *obvious reinterpretation.*[20]

18. Horner, *Future Israel*, 197–98. Also see Blaising's vague paragraph on Hosea 11:1 and Matthew 2:15 affirming Hosea's literal fulfilment while evading any mention of the specific issues involved in "Israel and Hermeneutics," 157.

19. See Matt 1:22–23 (Isa 7:14); 2:15 (Hos 11:1); 2:17–18 (Jer 31:15); 2:23 (Isa 11:1?); 4:14–16 (Isa 23–9:1); 8:17 (Isa 53:4); 12:17–21 (Isa 42:1–4); 13:35 (Ps 78:2); 21:4–5 (Isa 62:11; Zech 9:9); 27:9–10 (Zech 11:12–13; cf. Jer 32:6–15). Donald Hagner's commentary, *Matthew 1–13*, speaks for the majority of Matthean scholars today when he observes: "These quotations represent Matthew's own creative interpretation of his narrative (liv) . . . the most difficult challenge of these quotations for the modern reader is to understand the hermeneutical basis upon which the majority of them rests. Although the word 'fulfill' is used, the quoted texts themselves are as a rule not even predictive of future events (lv). . . . What needs to be stressed is that these quotations are not to be understood as prooftexts that would in themselves persuade, for example, Jews who had rejected the gospel. The quotations have as their foundation Christological convictions—they are, indeed, christocentric. They take as their *starting point* that Jesus is the one promised by the OT scriptures . . . their compelling power is only evident to those who have been confronted with the fact of the risen Christ" (lvi). In other words, Old Testament "fulfillment" appears only when we read scripture from back to front with the eyes of faith.

20. R. T. France also explains the widely held insight, "As usual, Matthew's Christological interpretation consists not of exegesis of what the text quoted meant in its original context, but of a far-reaching theological argument which takes the OT text and locates it within an over-arching scheme of fulfillment which finds in Jesus the end point of numerous prophetic trajectories"; see *Gospel of Matthew*, 81. France has not imposed a controlling methodology, but states his conclusion based on careful

For the Evangelist, who knew Jesus to be Immanuel, the man in whom "God had come to dwell with us" (Matt 1:23) as God had dwelt with Israel in the land of Canaan; who knew Jesus to be the son of David, the son of God (Matt 1:17–25) this constellation of covenantal, redemptive themes recast Hosea's ancient words into a new frame of reference. A uniquely Christian interpretation emerged in the light of Christ's accomplishments that made the very real, objective, historical contradictions irrelevant in light of God's actual fulfilment. Time and again we will see similarly unexpected results due to the New Testament authors' way of rereading the Old Testament backward, peering through the lens of a gospel-inspired imagination.

My second example is, perhaps, the most surprising. Isaiah 53 provides the classic, Old Testament prediction forecasting the Messiah's redemptive suffering and death. As the prophet declares:

> He was pierced for our transgressions,
>   he was crushed for our iniquities;
>   the punishment that brought us peace was upon him,
>   and by his wounds we are healed.
> We all, like sheep, have gone astray,
>   each of us has turned to his own way;
> and the Lord has laid on him the iniquity of us all. (Isa 53:5–6 NIV)

However, the traditional Christian reading of Isaiah 53 faces a major problem: to the best of our current knowledge, there were no pre-Christian interpretive traditions that read Isaiah 53 as the description of a suffering, dying messiah whose death held atoning value.[21] Finding a crucified savior in the beautifully pathos-laden poetry of Isaiah 53 is a uniquely New Testament discovery. Jesus had literally appeared as the Messiah no one expected.[22] In fact, no one had ever noticed a crucified, resurrected messiah anywhere in the Old Testament until certain disciples of Jesus, men like Simon Peter, reexamined those words and *interpreted their significance in the light of what they already believed Jesus had accomplished.* Because Peter learned to read backward, he was able to explain how Jesus had become Isaiah's Suffering Servant:

observation of Matthew's evidence. It becomes obvious that enforcing preconceptions about literalistic interpretation will inevitably blind the reader to both the New Testament's own method of interpretation and the message being conveyed.

21. See my lengthier discussion of the issues at stake in finding predictions of Jesus' suffering, death and resurrection in the Old Testament in *Encountering Jesus*, 21–24; also, Wright, *Jesus*, 588–91, who aptly concludes, "There was no such thing as a straightforward pre-Christian Jewish belief in an Isaianic 'servant of YHWH' who, perhaps as Messiah, would suffer and die to make atonement for Israel or for the world" (591).

22. See my extended treatment of this claim in *Encountering Jesus*, 19–45.

He committed no sin, and no deceit was found in his mouth. (Isa 53:9)

When they hurled their insults at him, he did not retaliate; when he suffered, he made no threats. . . . He himself bore our sins in his body on the tree, so that we might die to sins and live for righteousness; by his wounds you have been healed. (1 Pet 2:22–24 NIV)

The book of 1 Peter offers a quintessential example of retrospective interpretation par excellence.

WHY IT MATTERS

So, what bearing does this trek through biblical interpretation have on our understanding of Christian Zionism? We have noted already that Zionists insist they are reading the Bible literally and objectively. Unfortunately, however, this illusory standard of objective literalism then precludes the sort of readings I have described because they do not fit into the predetermined, Zionist script.[23]

Tragically, for certain extreme Zionists, loyalty to their preferred method of literalistic interpretation is more important than loyalty to Christ. For instance, Daniel Juster, a leader in the strongly pro-Zionist, Messianic Jewish community, condemns the intertextual approach to Scripture reading that I have demonstrated above. In response to such readings, Juster insists that[24]

no one reading these [Old Testament] passages could come up with any anticipation of such a [non-literalistic, retrospective] meaning. Jewish people especially find such interpretations to be perverse and offensive. Were this really the teaching of the New Covenant Scriptures, Jewish people would be duty bound to reject the New Covenant Scriptures as false Scriptures that did not cohere with previous revelation.

Sadly, the more things change, the more they stay the same; especially when it comes to the necessities of spiritual illumination and surrendering to Jesus the Messiah. How ironic it is that, in spite of their insistence on Scripture's divine authority, many Christian Zionists refuse to accept the

23. Actually, they do not ignore the method I have described here as much as they discount it. It is criticized as an unacceptable "spiritualizing" or "transcendentalizing" process that not only detracts from Scripture's authority but smells of latent antisemitism; see Blaising's use of such pejorative labels in "Biblical Hermeneutics," 80, 85, 97.

24. Juster, "Messianic Jew," 76.

New Testament's own interpretive keys. Mr. Juster goes even further astray by sanctioning the hard-heartedness of those who have yet to believe in Christ. The New Testament demonstrates that God fulfills his promises with unforeseen twists, turns, and surprises. If we can accept the New Testament's message on its own terms, we will discover, not that God is fickle in surprising us as he does, but that God's perspective is infinitely more expansive, gracious, and creative than ours will ever be.

Chapter 2

Diving into History

THE ZIONIST CONQUEST OF Palestine was the final chapter in a long story of Western colonialism extending its supposed civilizing grip throughout the underdeveloped world.[1] At the close of World War I, the newly established League of Nations placed Palestine under the control of a British mandatory government, a system of oversight that allowed preeminent colonial powers like Great Britain, France, and Belgium to maintain a semblance of colonial control over foreign territories. Thus, in a new, purportedly post-colonial era, political Zionism's territorial designs on Palestine were allowed to slip in under the wire with the help of Great Britain. Palestine was designated as a Class A Mandate (as were all territories formerly controlled by the Ottoman Empire), meaning that the mandatory power (Great Britain) was theoretically responsible to shepherd the native people toward self-determination and national independence—but, of course, in ways that benefited the geopolitical interests of the mandatory power. Palestine was the only Class A Mandate where this goal of national (i.e., Palestinian) self-determination was never pursued due to Great Britain's prior commitment to the Balfour Declaration, promising the Zionist movement "a national home for the Jewish people" in Palestine.

1. See Kattan, *From Coexistence*, 44–63, 121–45, 187–89, 253–55; Erakat, *Justice for Some*, 25–26, 34–38, 39.

At this point, it is worth recounting some of the key historical events that proved most influential in shaping the way this story unfolds. This will help provide context for the discussion ahead. History is a continuum. The present and the future never lose connection to the past. Understanding that past is essential to grasping how we got to where we are today.

In February of 1896, Austro-Hungarian journalist Theodor Herzl published his Zionist manifesto, *The Jewish State*, calling for a secular, Jewish nation exercising sovereignty over its own territory. He appeared to be unaware of the long history of evangelical Christian Zionism working toward the same goal in Great Britain (see chapter 3). A few decades later, in November of 1917 during the First World War, the British government issued a public statement, known as the Balfour Declaration, supporting the establishment of *a national home* for the Jewish people in Palestine. In a letter from the British government to Lord Rothschild, who was financing early Jewish settlements in Palestine, the declaration stated:[2]

> His Majesty's government views with favour the establishment in Palestine of *a national home* for the Jewish people, and will use their best endeavours to facilitate the achievement of this object, it being clearly understood that *nothing shall be done which may prejudice the civil and religious rights of existing non-Jewish communities in Palestine*, or the rights and political status enjoyed by Jews in any other country. (emphasis mine)

Lord Balfour, like many of his political contemporaries, had strong evangelical Christian roots with deep Zionist sympathies.[3] In the years ahead, British leaders will often need to remind Zionist leaders that the promise of "a national home" in Palestine was never a promise that all Palestine would be handed over as their Zionist, Jewish state. Nor could the expanding Zionist community ever justify the brutal ways in which they ignored the "civil rights" of native Palestinians—naturally, neither the British nor political Zionists gave any consideration to Palestinian *national* rights in their own land.

---

2. It would be hard to find a document more expressive of the imperialistic colonizer's sense of superiority and entitlement. As an English cabinet member in 1919, the former prime minister, Arthur Balfour, wrote a memorandum stating, "In Palestine we do not propose even to go through the form of consulting the wishes of the present inhabitants of the country. . . .The four great powers are committed to Zionism, and Zionism . . .[is] of far profounder import than the desires and prejudices of the 700,000 Arabs who now inhabit that ancient land." See Edward Said's discussion of the Balfour Declaration in *Question of Palestine*, 16–17.

3. Lewis, *Origins*, 1–5.

After World War I, from July 24, 1922, to May 15, 1948, the League of Nations authorized the British Mandate over Palestine, entrusting Great Britain with the responsibility of governing Palestine and implementing the promise of the Balfour Declaration. During this period, on November 29, 1947, the United Nations adopted Resolution 181 calling for the partition of Palestine into two states, one Jewish and one Palestinian, with an international zone embracing Jerusalem and Bethlehem. The vote for partition led to a brief civil war between Palestinian and Zionist paramilitary forces that lasted from November 29, 1947, to May 15, 1948. In December of 1947 Sir Alan Cunningham, British High Commissioner at the time, reported to London on "the spontaneous and unorganized" Arab demonstrations opposing the UN decision. "The weapons initially employed were sticks and stones and had it not been for Jewish recourse to firearms, it is not impossible that the excitement would have subsided and little loss of life been caused," he said.[4] This outbreak marks the beginning of the process of Palestinian ethnic cleansing by Jewish forces and, thus, the Palestinian refugee crisis.[5] To illustrate the lopsidedness of this phase of the contest it is noteworthy that Palestinian fighters never conquered a single Jewish settlement.[6]

During this civil war, on April 9, 1948, history records the Deir Yassin massacre, the most well-known of the many massacres committed by Jewish (in this case, Irgun) militias against Palestinian villagers.[7] The estimates as to the number of villagers killed at Deir Yassin range from one to two hundred, including the elderly, women, and children. Homes were demolished with grenades as residents fled; many were killed by shrapnel and collapsing debris. Women were raped before being shot. Thirty infants were among the victims, many stabbed.[8] Word of the slaughter spread rapidly. Palestinians now began to flee in terror before approaching Jewish forces.

---

4. Palumbo, "What Happened to Palestine?," 5. For a history of Cunningham's tenure in Palestine, see Golani, *Palestine between Politics & Terror, 1945–1947*.

5. By May 15, 1948, three hundred fifty thousand Palestinians had already become refugees. By the end of the war that figure would climb to seven hundred fifty thousand, according to UN estimates. During this period, Zionist forces concentrated on conquering land and destroying Palestinian villages (nearly 350 villages by October) *within the territory designated for a Palestinian state* in the UN partition plan; see Pappé, *Making*, 96–99.

6. Morris, *1948*, 400. Morris (an Israeli Jew and committed Zionist) also states that "in truth, the Jews committed far more atrocities than the Arabs and killed far more civilians and POWs in deliberate acts of brutality in the course of 1948" (405).

7. Pappé, *Ethnic Cleansing*, 258, accounts for between thirty-one to thirty-seven such massacres committed by Zionist forces during the war.

8. See the accounts in Morris, *Righteous Victims*, 207–9; Pappé, *Ethnic Cleansing*, 90–91.

Just over one month later, on May 14, 1948, David Ben-Gurion public-ly read Israel's Declaration of Independence (from British rule), proclaim-ing the establishment of a Jewish state in "the land of Israel." Significantly, the Declaration does not delineate the borders of the new Jewish state; an anomaly that remains to this day. The next day, on May 15, 1948, Britain declared the end of its mandate over Palestine and began to withdraw its troops after years of shepherding the new state into the light of day and battling against Zionist militia-terrorist organizations such as the Haganah, Irgun, and the Stern Gang. Thomas Suárez's thoroughly researched book, *State of Terror: How Terrorism Created Modern Israel*, has established the crucial role played by Zionist terrorist organizations, working throughout the Middle East and Europe, in persuading Great Britain to leave Palestine.[9]

Following this declaration, from May 15, 1948, to January 1949, Israel found itself at war with surrounding Arab states. In light of Israel's Decla-ration of Independence; its military takeover of large areas intended for a Palestinian state by UN resolution 181; the stories circulating of numerous Zionist massacres; and the growing flood of Palestinian refugees flowing into neighboring countries, five Arab countries—Egypt, Iraq, Jordan, Leba-non, and Syria, all with generally small, ill-equipped armies—announce their plans to invade Palestine. Israel engaged with only three of these na-tions and was predictably victorious.[10] In fact, the English commander of the Jordanian Arab Legion dubbed the 1948 war the "Phony War."[11]

Nearly twenty years later, from June 5–10, 1967, Israel went to war with Egypt, Jordan, and Syria in what became known as the *Six Day War*, winning a quick, decisive victory. Israel seized the Golan Heights from Syria, the Gaza Strip and Sinai Peninsula from Egypt (though the Peninsula was eventually returned), and the West Bank (including east Jerusalem with

9. Northampton, MA: Olive Branch Press, 2017.

10. Jordan's Arab Legion was the only military force posing a real threat to Israel. However, Jordan's leader, King Abdullah, eager to annex the West Bank to his desert kingdom, had entered into secret negotiations with the Zionist leadership. They agreed to let Abdullah have the West Bank, while he agreed that his army would not leave that area or confront Israeli forces (though there were encounters around the Old City of Jerusalem); see Shlaim, *Collusion Across the Jordan*. At the last moment, Lebanon chose not to participate in the attack and never sent troops as originally planned. The remain-ing three armies were each small, inexperienced, poorly equipped, badly trained, and utterly unprepared for the task they were sent to perform. Israel's victory was a forgone conclusion. Contrary to Zionist mythology, Israel was the superior force in this conflict, whereas the Arab states (only recently independent and freed from their own foreign, mandatory governments) were collective underdogs from the beginning. For extensive discussion and documentation, see Morris, *Righteous Victims*, 215–49; Morris, *1948*, 180–263; Pappé, *The Making*, 102–34.

11. Pappé, *The Ethnic Cleansing*, 128.

the Old City) from Jordan. The continuing refugee crisis was compounded as three hundred thousand Palestinians fled their homes in the West Bank (many for the second time) and one hundred thousand Syrians evacuated the Golan Heights.[12]

The final fruit produced by Zionist activity between 1920 and 1967 was the forceful eviction of the vast majority of resident Palestinians from their ancestral homes by a well-equipped, Zionist military determined to sweep the land of Palestine clean of as many Arabs as possible. The special oddity of Zionist settler colonialism (see chapters 3 and 14) is characterized by its unilateral declaration that these primarily European (Ashkenazi), Jewish settlers had a more primal claim to the land of Palestine than the brown-skinned native Palestinians they fought to replace.[13] While the Puritans may have honestly believed that they were God's new covenant people predestined to build a New Zion in Massachusetts Bay, no Puritan ever had the temerity to insist that he was also more indigenous, more native, more wedded to the American landscape than the local people who had greeted his arrival. However, this ethnic assertion of primogeniture is the racial pretext at the heart of the political Zionist story line.[14]

Contrary to the popular Zionist mythology, the land known as Israel-Palestine[15] was not the proverbial "land without a people waiting for a people without a land."[16] Long before the state of Israel came into existence

12. Morris, *Righteous Victims*, 302–46; Segev, *1967*.

13. Settler colonialism is a specific form of colonialism that seeks to replace and/or eliminate a region's native population and replace them with a new, invasive society of foreign settlers. For a discussion of Zionism as a form of colonialism, see Rodinson, *Israel, a Colonial-Settler State?*; also Kattan, *From Coexistence*, 21–26, 52–54; Erakat, *Justice for Some*, 23–60, 216–18, 255n12; Shafir, *Land, Labor*. Khalidi, *Iron Cage*, tells the story of how Great Britain's mandatory regime consistently undercut Palestinian efforts for national self-determination and, thereby, laid the groundwork for the defeat of Palestinian forces in the 1947–49 war.

14. Primogeniture is the feudal right of succession belonging to the first born.

15. The strip of land sandwiched between Syria to the north and Egypt to the south was first written about as "Palestine" by the Greek historian Herodotus in the fifth century BC. This book is not concerned with the moment at which this area's inhabitants first identified themselves as Palestinians, but with the fact that historic Palestine had long been inhabited by the descendants of ancient residents by the time Zionist immigrants began to colonize the region. These indigenous people would eventually call themselves Palestinians.

16. Hirst credits the Zionist writer Israel Zangwill as coining this famous phrase in his article "The Return to Palestine"; see *Gun*, 139. However, Lewis provides numerous examples of Lord Shaftesbury (1801–85), an English evangelical, politician, philanthropist, social reformer, and ardent proponent of the Jewish resettlement of Palestine under British auspices, describing Palestine as "an empty land" or "a county without a nation" that has been waiting for "a nation without a country"; see *Origins*, 121, 140,

this particular piece of Middle Eastern real estate, bordered on one side by the Mediterranean Sea and by the Jordan River on the other, was known as Palestine, a region populated by a healthy collection of indigenous peoples with ancient roots. Israeli Prime Minister Golda Meir infamously insisted, in 1969, that "there was no such thing as Palestinians." This is but one instance of the many attempts that Zionists have made to erase the history of this native people, blotting them out of existence. Meir went on to say:[17]

> When was there an independent Palestinian people with a Palestinian state? . . . It was not as though there was a Palestinian people in Palestine considering itself as a Palestinian people and we came and threw them out and took their country from them. They did not exist.

Golda Meir knew as well as anyone that the collective consciousness of human societies, based upon shared culture, common history, and long-term residence on a shared land, did not begin with the rise of Western nationalism, as her Zionist word-game presumes. The land of Palestine has always been home to many intertwining rivulets of people descended from ancient occupants and invaders. People like the Egyptians, Hittites, Phoenicians, and Philistines, together with more recent residents such as the Greeks, the Romans, and eventually the Crusaders, have all mixed and coexisted with the remnant of Israelites, then Jews (who were not above some mixing themselves), to form an evolving, yet continuous, population of native inhabitants. The land has never been empty.

When the region became a largely Arab and Muslim territory at the end of the seventh century another genetic stream was added to this mix. Undoubtedly, many of the earliest Muslim converts were Jews and Christians doing what they could to survive. Even David Ben-Gurion, prominent Zionist leader and Israel's first prime minister, recognized this ethnographic certainty and advertised it widely in the years prior to the Arab Revolt of 1936–39. In his book *Palestine, Past and Present*, published in 1918, Ben-Gurion argued that the native Palestinians were descendants of those sixth-century Jewish converts to Islam. In that, he was almost certainly partially correct.[18] However, Ben-Gurion's imagined history, in which all Palestinians were the descendants of Jewish converts, was as mythical as Golda Meir's

---

144–45, 151–52, 162, 187, 199, 205, 319. This particular piece of Zionist mythology, first among both Christian and then Jewish circles, is a prime example of projection and its role in Zionist wish fulfilment.

17. "Golda Meir Scorns Soviets," A15; also see Kimmerling and Migdal, *The Palestinian People*, xxvi–xxviii.

18. Teveth, *Ben-Gurion and the Palestinians Arabs*, 30–32.

story about Palestinian non-existence. Like so many populations around the world, Palestinians were and are undoubtedly a complex, genetic swirl of the peoples that made up their history. Their genetic and cultural heritage contained varying degrees of ancient Jewish and non-Jewish lineages from peoples who have lived in the land called Israel-Palestine longer than any-one can remember. This is no different than most Americans whose genetic history is a mish-mash of the cultures that made the new world their new home.

SETTING THE FOUNDATIONS

Unfortunately, the average American is rarely exposed to the many Palestin-ian voices who would tell their stories of living in a land occupied by Zionist settler colonialists. Living in a society marked by racial separation, Jewish-only neighborhoods, military occupation, ethnic identity cards, designated living areas, travel barriers, checkpoints, random searches and arrests is normal fare for Palestinians living in Gaza, the West Bank, and even Israel proper.[19] Would perceptions of Palestinians change for more Americans if stories of everyday Palestinians robbed of their homes, made refugees in the land of their birth, and daily denied basic human rights could be heard in an unbiased way? This book intends to hear the voices of such aggrieved Palestinians. The Palestinian people are not accidental victims inadvertently harmed in the fog of war. Rather, Christians and all people of conscience need to understand that the tragedy of Palestinian trauma is that it results from deliberate policies fueled by political Zionist ideology.

The earliest generations of Zionist settlers laid the groundwork for everything that was to follow until reaching its climax in 1949. They made no bones about the need to remove Palestinians from their homes before their new Jewish nation could exist. The necessity of "population transfer" was regularly discussed in private and occasionally in public. To cite only one example, Menahem Ussishkin (1863–1941), a leading Zionist figure

---

19. Professor Israel Shahak, of the Hebrew University in Jerusalem, got to the heart of the matter when he wrote, "By any standard, the State of Israel must be considered a racist state"; see "Racism and Discrimination in Israel," cited in Hirst, *Gun*, 89. Shahak (1933–2001) was a survivor of both the Warsaw Ghetto and Bergen-Belsen extermina-tion camp. He was professor of organic chemistry at Hebrew University in Jerusalem and headed the Israeli League for Human and Civil Rights from 1970 to 1990. His point, and mine, is not to say that every individual Israeli is a racist. Rather, Shahak is accusing *the State* of Israel of *official, state-sanctioned racism* in its creation and enforce-ment of policies, laws, and social structures that entrench systematic discrimination against Palestinians.

and head of the Jewish National Fund, published an article in the Jerusalem daily newspaper *Daor Hayom* (April 28, 1930) reminding his Hebrew readers to remain diligent in their Zionist objectives:[20]

> We must continually raise the demand that our land be returned to our possession. . . . If there are other inhabitants there, they must be transferred to some other place. We must take over the land. We have a greater and nobler ideal than preserving several hundred thousands of Arab *fellahin*.

Ussishkin's article illustrates the racist, colonial mentality animating many of the early Zionist leaders, all of whom were from Europe, who generally viewed the people of the Near East as backward, believed in their own racial superiority, and eagerly benefited from the political and military assistance provided by the British empire, global imperialists *par excellence*.

Moshe Dayan (1915–81) was born into a Zionist settler family and raised on the first kibbutz established in a region that would eventually become part of Israel.[21] Dayan grew up to become one of Israel's most legendary military and political leaders who would play an important role in the 1948 war. In a 1969 interview with the Israeli daily newspaper, *Haaretz*, he candidly described the consequences of Zionist settler colonialism:[22]

> Jewish villages were built in the place of Arab villages. You don't even know the names of these Arab villages, and I don't blame you, because these geography books no longer exist. Not only do the books not exist, the Arab villages are not there either. . . . *There is not one single place built in this country that did not have a former Arab population.*

Not one single place where Arabs were not replaced by Jewish settlers. Let that sentence sink in.

---

20. Quoted in Masalha, *Politics of Denial*, 14. *Fellahin* was the commonly used word for an Arab farmer. For extensive discussions of Zionist appeals to (and eventual implementation of) forced population transfer, see Masalha, *Expulsion of the Palestinians*; Morris, *Righteous Victims*, 138–44; Morris, *Birth*, especially the chapter entitled "The Idea of 'Transfer' in Zionist Thinking Before 1948"; Pappé, *Ethnic Cleansing*, esp. 61–72.

21. Many of the early Zionist settlers were socialists or communists. A kibbutz was a communal farming settlement where all property was held in common and the profits were collective property reinvested into the community.

22. *Haaretz*, April, 4, 1969 (emphasis mine). This is a frequently cited quotation; see Hirst, *Gun*, 347.

ERASING THE INCONVENIENT

The erasure of native Palestinians from both the land and the memory of modern Israel began decades before the official outbreak of war in 1948. The prominent Israeli historian, Benny Morris, a staunch Zionist himself, as well as Haifa University professor, Benjamin Beit-Hallahmi both describe Israel's massive displacement of native Palestinians as the nation's founding act of "original sin."[23] Tragically, Israel's sinful work of eliminating all things Palestinian has always been and continues to be a potent ingredient of many Zionists' political strategy. This philosophy gave impetus to Jewish colonization as well as military conquest and the national militarization of Israeli society that followed. The coldhearted results include the misleading signs posted for tourists to read in a public square that render invisible the Palestinian people whose historic roots to these places have been severed.

Israel was host to 3.6 million tourists in 2017, most of them undoubtedly intent on visiting one of Jerusalem's most popular religious sites: the Western Wall (also known as the Wailing Wall among Christians, or the al-Buraq Wall among Muslims), such as can be seen today, is a tenuous remnant of the second Jewish temple constructed by Herod the Great as a monument to his rule, and the very temple that Jesus of Nazareth is said to have visited in the Christian Gospels.

Walking among the labyrinthine cobblestone streets woven throughout the bustling Muslim Quarter in the Old City, every visitor to the Western Wall passes along the same ancient corridor. It is habitually lined with shopkeepers and young Israeli soldiers armed with semi-automatic rifles. Approaching the street's terminus, visitors climb a final limestone stairway leading upward to a sunlit passage through a thick stone wall separating the Muslim from the Jewish Quarter of the city. Beyond this opening, far off to the left, is the Western Wall, a sixteen-hundred-foot-long retaining wall buttressing the west side of the Temple Mount. It serves as the eastern

---

23. Beit-Hallahmi, *Original Sins*, 168; Morris, "New Historiography," 20, originally published in *Tikkun*, November/December, 1988. Whereas Beit-Hallahmi is straightforward in making his charge, Morris offers his accusation in a more circumspect way. Referring to the debate surrounding his research demonstrating Israel's direct responsibility for the Palestinian refugee problem, he says, "If the Arab contention is true—that the Yishuv had always intended 'transfer' and in 1948 systematically and forcibly expelled the Arab population from the areas that became the Jewish state—then Israel is a robber state that, like young Jacob, has won the sympathy and support of its elders in the West by trickery and connivance and the Palestinians are more or less innocent victims. If, on the other hand, the Israeli propaganda line is accepted—that the Palestinians fled 'voluntarily' or at the behest of their own or other Arab leaders—then Israel is free of original sin."

edge of a five-acre square, neatly paved with off-white flagstones, called the Western Wall Plaza.

Not too many years ago, every visitor passing through this gateway linking the Arab and Jewish Quarters would have noticed a prominent sign describing a romantic—and entirely fictitious—background to the scene laid out before them. After noting the Roman destruction of the second Temple in 70 AD, the sign declared, "For one thousand, nine hundred years the wall was deserted but the sight of its stones was engraved on every Jewish heart. Zionism brought back the Jewish people."[24] While such plaques present themselves as educational, they are finally nothing more than Zionist propaganda, giving the impression that there was no history, no people, no claim to this place until the repatriation of Jewish people to the land.

For one thousand, nine hundred years the Wall was deserted but the sight of its stones was engraved on every Jewish heart.

Zionism brought back the Jewish people from around the globe to the ancient Western Wall where mourners lamented the sorrow of exile, and celebrated the return of

Historical commentary for tourists that was once posted near the entrance to the Western Wall Plaza. It has since been replaced. Photo taken by the author.

The Western Wall was not deserted before Zionism returned the Jews to Jerusalem, however. When Israeli soldiers occupied the Old City in the 1967 Six Day War, what is now the Western Wall Plaza was the bustling center of a centuries-old community in the Magharibah (Moroccan) Quarter of the city. It was home to a sizeable Palestinian village of some one hundred thirty-five families, approximately one thousand people. On June 11, 1967, under the cover of night, the entire village was flattened, bulldozed to the ground. All one thousand inhabitants were made homeless refugees before sunrise. Those who lived long enough to flee were the lucky ones; many fled

---

24. I have a photo of this sign, taken around 2010–12. It has since been replaced by another from the city's ruling rabbi instructing visitors about the Wall's sanctity as a place of prayer.

as the walls of their homes toppled around them. One elderly woman was discovered buried in the rubble. She died soon afterwards.[25]

This most sacred of Israeli tourist attractions, drawing Jewish and Christian pilgrims from around the world, is living testament to the crimes of political Zionism.[26] First, is the historic crime of ethnic cleansing against the indigenous people already inhabiting this place; and second, is the ongoing crime of "memory-cleansing," of denying Palestinian existence, of selling a Zionist fable to an unknowing public about an empty, deserted land waiting to be settled, civilized, and paved over with off-white flagstones.

The story of modern Israel is a story about Palestinian suffering. Like every Western, settler colonial enterprise, the nation of Israel was born in cruelty and bloodshed. The convergent ideologies of colonialism and Jewish ethnocracy (see chapter 12), intertwined as they are in political Zionism, share the same goals: Jewish colonists must subdue or confine the native population in order to monopolize territorial, social, and political power. The colonial march of Western history has left a number of vivid examples in its wake. The European settlement of North America, Australia, New Zealand, South Africa, and Israel all proceeded by way of ruthless ethnic cleansing, which is the standard purchase price for the ethnic dominance of colonial settlers. The story is as heart-breaking as it is common. Whether white, European settlers were eradicating Native Americans from the western frontier, Aborigines from Australia, Zulus from South Africa, or Palestinians from Palestine, asymmetrical warfare, slaughter, displacement, confinement, and racial segregation are the typical tools of settler colonial movements that gauge their "success" by the metrics of ethnic domination over occupied territory.

The history of modern Israel is no different. In fact, the British Foreign Secretary, Ernest Bevin (1881–1951), once compared the Zionist "expulsion of the Arabs" to "the expulsion of the Indians in America."[27] The Jewish state's ethnocratic dominance over non-Jewish "outsiders" is not a mistake or an unfortunate mishap. It is the victorious, national expression of explicit, political Zionist aspirations. It is a story of displacement, forced removal at

25. For an eyewitness description of the village's destruction from Uzi Benziman, a journalist for the Israeli newspaper *Haaretz*, see Tibawi, "Special Report," 180–89. The village's destruction is also described in Segev, *1967*, 400–402. Segev, an Israeli journalist, concludes that those who carried out the demolition "had no interest in the fate of the 135 Arab families who became the victims of these [Zionist] longings." He describes the death of the elderly woman discovered beneath the ruins of a wall (400–401).

26. See chapter 4 for an introduction to a few of the major differences among of the various sorts of Zionism.

27. Segev, *One Palestine, Complete*, 493n.

gunpoint, destroyed villages, and war crimes. All of it performed by Zionist soldiers and settlers like Moshe Dayan, many of whom had fled European oppression in the hopes of building a new life for themselves in a land called Palestine. It is also a story that Israel's ruling elites continue to work very hard to bury or to expunge from the historical record. Israeli journalists continue to publish disturbing accounts of government efforts to reclassify and block access to millions of official documents (many previously declassified) held in the state archives documenting Israel's historic war crimes.[28]

While the first draft of history may be written by the victors, subsequent redrafts can expose those darker historical corners that the victors hoped to hide. Israel's vast, public relations machinery, a conglomerate of government agencies operating under the auspices of the National Hasbara Headquarters, has been extremely successful, especially in Western media, in keeping those dark corners covered and erasing Zionist crimes from public memory.[29] That cover-up must be exposed, not least because it has blinded the Western, Christian church as well as many other people of conscience to the dark underbelly of the story of modern Israel.

BROKENNESS HEAPED UPON BROKENNESS

"In sin did my mother conceive me," laments the Old Testament psalmist (Ps 51:5 KJV).[30] These words have become a foundational proof text for the Christian doctrine of original sin, the belief that all people, regardless of race, creed or color, are born with an inherent inclination to disobey God and do wrong. Perhaps, one of the clearest displays of this human predilection for evil is revealed in the tortured rationalizations devised by victimizers as they try to justify their own sins of abuse.

It is almost a truism that one of the dark twists in human nature is that many who have suffered abuse evolve into abusers themselves. Rather

---

28. See Hazkani, "Catastrophic Thinking"; Goldman, "Classified"; Aderet, "Activists"; Cook, "Why Israel Is Blocking."

29. *Hasbara* is the Hebrew word for "explanation"; it is also commonly translated as "propaganda." The NHH oversees a number of government information/propaganda agencies, including the National Hasbara Forum, the Ministry of Public Diplomacy and Diaspora Affairs, the Ministry of Tourism, the Jewish Agency for Israel, and the IDF Spokesperson Division. For a fuller account of the relationships between these government "explanation" agencies and Israel's extensive investment in curating a positive, public image, see "Hasbara Apparatus." Also see Blumenthal, "Israel Cranks Up the PR Machine"; Scheindlin, "Against 'Hasbara.'"

30. In most cases my biblical quotations will come from the New International Version (NIV).

than blossoming into empathy as one might hope for a person who has suffered, many who have been victimized paradoxically emerge as the next generation of victimizers. The English poet W. H. Auden memorialized this all-too-human process in his poem, "September 1, 1939":[31]

> What huge imago made
> A psychopathic god:
> I and the public know
> What all schoolchildren learn,
> Those to whom evil is done
> Do evil in return.

Many of the Jewish immigrants who settled in Palestine were fleeing violent displacement from their homes in Europe, the Soviet Union, and elsewhere. They were victims of antisemitism searching for a new life free of ancient, racist threats. Yet, many of these very fugitives would brandish a new type of antisemitism that targeted their equally Semitic, indigenous neighbors. Sadly, being the victims of European antisemitism prepared many Zionist settlers to become antisemites themselves, mistreating local Palestinians with impunity.

The Jewish author Ahad Aham, described by David Hirst as "the conscience of early Zionism,"[32] lamented as early as 1891 how this all-too-human tendency

> has produced in them [Jewish immigrants to Palestine] that inclination to despotism that always occurs when the servant becomes the master. They treat the Arabs with hostility and cruelty, unscrupulously depriving them of their rights, insulting them without cause, and even boast of such deeds; and none opposes this despicable and dangerous inclination.[33]

Time has not changed the situation.

What moral logic can derive from the heartbreaking stories of European persecution—violent antisemitic pogroms;[34] impoverished Jewish emigrants searching for a new home—the justification for the brutal eviction of hundreds of thousands of Palestinians by Zionist paramilitary forces in the war of 1947–49? Yet this is what happened. Western imperialists employed poor Jewish settlers, often coerced by Zionist thugs to serve as the tip of

---

31. I discovered Auden's poem while reading Jacobs, *The Year of Our Lord 1943*, 3.
32. *The Gun*, 143–44.
33. *Am Scheideweg* (Berlin, 1923), vol. I, p. 107; cited by Hirst, *The Gun*, 144.
34. The officially sanctioned, organized destruction of an ethnic group.

an imperialist spear.[35] Although everyone in this multi-generational story of abuse deserves a measure of sympathy, victims-turned-victimizers remain victimizers with their victim's blood in turn staining the promised land.

ENTER THE CHRISTIAN ENABLERS

Though Christians follow a Messiah who sympathizes "with our weaknesses" (Heb 4:5) and therefore ought to be sensitive to such suffering, they all too often reveal how they are equally subject to the perversions of original sin, and blithely contribute to the pain of the Palestinian people.[36] If we are to untangle the scriptural morass that has led to the destructive ideology of Christian Zionism, we will need to read the Bible with care to remove the twisted scriptural underpinnings of Christian Zionism. It is a crucial task as the triumphalist ideology of Christian Zionism makes the American evangelical church into political Zionism's greatest cheerleader, financier, and all-around global enabler. It is worth pausing to consider an analogy from psychology.

Abusers attract dysfunctional enablers that in turn share in the guilt of an abuser's crimes. Enablers become enablers because they choose, consciously or not, to make themselves selectively blind, periodically deaf, and morally obtuse to the suffering inflicted on the victims. The evangelical church has perfected its role as political Zionism's Western enabler, dutifully serving Israel's political interests, just as the United States now serves a role previously filled by the British. In adopting this role, American evangelicals have numbed themselves into a moral stupor when it comes to all things Israel and the Palestinians. The evangelical church has trained itself to ignore the systematic racism, dehumanization, and collective punishment of an entire group of people at the hand of "God's chosen nation." Furthermore, the US government does little if anything to restrain Israel's inhumane treatment of Palestinians, in part due to the influence of evangelical voters and their mega-church leaders. Year after year the United States supplies Israel with $3 to $4 billion in foreign aid, while conveniently ignoring the many national traits that make Israel look more and more like apartheid South

---

35. After the war, Zionist agents were located throughout the European camps for displaced persons in order to "recruit" Jewish emigrants for relocation to Israel. People were strongly discouraged from emigrating to any other country and denied assistance if they would not cooperate. The Zionist methods of persuasion were often coercive and dishonest; see Segev, *1949*, 108–16; Segev, *Seventh Million*, 128–39.

36. See Compton, *End of Empathy*.

Africa—a situation that will not change until our government is pressured from within to adopt a new policy.[37]

The largest, most powerful pro-Israel lobbying block in the United States is the evangelical church,[38] exerting tremendous political influence in combination with the pro-Zionist group AIPAC (the American Israel Public Affairs Committee) and other pro-Zionist lobbying groups.[39] Organizations such as the International Fellowship of Christians and Jews, Christian Friends of Israel, Christian Friends of Israel Communities, Christians United for Israel, and others like them provide unquestioned support for the racist policies of political Zionism while funneling hundreds of millions of dollars to Israel each year.

A growing volume of Christian financial aid is also helping to fuel the illegal multiplication of Jewish, colonial settlements in the Occupied Territory known as the West Bank, sometimes called Judea and Samaria by Zionist advocates of Israel's territorial expansion. With every dollar spent, American evangelicals are deliberately helping Israel to commit ever-expanding war crimes. That is, the crime of population transfers into territory acquired through warfare, a crime that Western nations—under the leadership of the United States—first defined as a crime at the Geneva Convention. This Convention was attempting to offer a civilized response to Nazi Germany's efforts to coopt neighboring territories by relocating population groups.[40] The Convention's goal was to rally the international community

37. See Carter, *Palestine Peace Not Apartheid*.

38. Approximately 25 percent of Americans identify themselves as evangelicals; that's about eighty-two million people.

39. See Mearsheimer and Walt, *Israel Lobby*.

40. During the Second World War, Adolf Hitler undertook ethnic cleansing in parts of eastern Europe. He then resettled these areas with ethnic Germans, planning to incorporate the newly settled territories into an expanded German state. For only one example, nearly one hundred twenty-two thousand Poles were expelled from German occupied Pomerania in 1939–40. They were replaced by one hundred thirty thousand ethnic Germans who were resettled in place of the former Pomerania population. German settlement expansion in eastern Europe was a part of Hitler's "Germanization" program, referred to as *Generalplan Ost* (the GPO); see Ahonen et al., *People on the Move*, especially 26–42. The complete text of *Generalplan Ost* is available at http://gplanost.x-berg.de/gplanost.html. The close parallels between the Nazi plans to "Germanize" eastern Europe and the political Zionist plans to "Judaize" Palestine are both remarkable and chilling. After the war, the Geneva Convention declared that such population transfers by the victors into territory conquered during warfare were illegal. Israel first violated this part of international law in 1948–49 when it conquered 50 percent of the territory allotted by the United Nations for a Palestinian state. Israel now continues its violation of international law in the West Bank, which Israel captured from Jordan during the 1967 war. The West Bank has remained under military occupation ever since, hence its identification as Occupied Territory. Article 49, paragraph 6

in standing against future tyrants like Adolf Hitler, ensuring that Nazi-like land grabs would never again go unpunished.

For all of the Religious Right's complaints about the church's need for greater political influence, when we examine this area of US relations with Israel, an arena where conservative Christianity has garnered significant political leverage, what is that influence being used to accomplish? *The aiding and abetting of a criminal enterprise.* Settler colonialism is alive and well in Israel today with American suffrage. It appears in the expansion of illegal, Jewish-only settlements into territory occupied as the spoils of war by the Israeli army. In other words, American evangelicalism is helping to finance political Zionism's flagrant imitation of Nazi Germany. Even worse, this malicious theft of another people's territory is justified by a Christian Zionist ideology that claims to stand on scripture.

This misbehavior must stop.

Here evangelical religious convictions coincide perfectly with the full-throated propaganda of political Zionism. In fact, the core value of Zionist story-telling shines most brightly in the long-standing, concerted effort to justify Israel's forcible removal of as many Palestinians as possible by pleading that "we Jews were here first; or at least, this used to be our land before it was theirs." When political Zionism is not denying the existence of Palestinians, as it does at the Western Wall Plaza, this insistence that Palestine was/is theirs by right of previous occupancy (and divine promise) becomes the bedrock rationale for excusing Israel's settler colonial crimes against humanity. That "we were here first" message becomes Israel's get-out-of-jail-free card ensuring that American evangelicals remain devout Zionist allies, never bothering to scratch beneath the shallow surface of Israel's nationalistic, patriotic cover stories.

---

of the 1949 Geneva Convention IV says, "The Occupying Power shall not deport or transfer parts of its own civilian population into the territory it occupies." Article 85(4)(a) of the 1977 Additional Protocol I adds that "the transfer by the Occupying Power of parts of its own civilian population into the territory it occupies" is a serious breach of the protocol. Article 8(2)(b)(viii) of the 1998 Statute of the International Criminal Court states that "the transfer, directly or indirectly, by the Occupying Power of parts of its own civilian population into the territory it occupies" is a war crime. See https://ihl-databases.icrc.org/customary-ihl/eng/docs/v2_rul_rule130. Robert Nicholson's chapter "Theology and Law" in McDermott, *New Christian Zionism*, 249–80, provides an astonishing example of confusion, misrepresentation, and specious hair-splitting in his attempt to justify Israel's Judaizing settlement programs. For a careful, detailed analysis demonstrating the illegality of Israel's occupation, see Finkelstein, *Gaza*, 367–408.

AWAKENING A DORMANT CONSCIENCE

Certain readers will object that my arguments in this book are offensive. Some will even go so far as to call them antisemitic. Perhaps the outrage at these arguments is simply misplaced. Yes, these are harsh realities that call for costly changes. Though truth is often costly, it must never be intimidated by those who have either been lulled to sleep by apathy or corrupted by their own self-interests. Scripture describes these sorts of people as "having consciences seared as with a hot iron" (1 Tim 4:2 NIV).

When Scripture is read carefully and in context, we discover that a characteristic tenor to Scripture's voice is its consistent defense of the oppressed; its condemnation of every oppressor; and its insistence upon justice in every relationship. Ideology, on the other hand, describes and normalizes the ruling ideas of the powerful. Ideology constructs a system of thought that justifies society's misuse of power, defends the abusive status quo, and works to convince those who suffer that their pain is unavoidable, inevitable, even justifiable—which is precisely what Christian Zionism does as it defends Israel's oppressive, Zionist policies today. This is why I will often refer to Christian Zionism as an *ideology* rather than a *theology* throughout this book. A calloused conscience is always more amenable to a hospitable ideology than it is to a truly biblical theology.

What is truly offensive is the way so many in the church have trained themselves to turn their backs on the downtrodden and the despised. Too many Christians imitate the priest and Levite in Jesus' parable of the Good Samaritan (Luke 10:25–37). We see the Palestinian people being beaten and robbed, thrown into a ditch by Israel's inhumane policies, and then we close our eyes, shuffle off to the other side of the road and hurry on past, afraid that we might actually notice a crime in progress.

After Cain murdered his brother, Abel, the Creator ominously warned, "What have you done? Listen! Your brother's blood cries out to me from the ground" (Gen 4:10 NIV). Whatever the cries of human bloodshed may sound like, the Holy Land surely rattles heaven's gates day and night with the lament-laden chorus of blood-born screams rising before God's throne. My hope is that this book will faithfully relay these cries and help the church honestly face what the biblical witness makes clear: that God hears such cries and calls for the church to respond with justice and love.

Chapter 3

The Origins of Political Zionism

LORD ASHLEY SHAFTESBURY (1801–85) was a leading figure among nineteenth-century British evangelicals who exercised tremendous influence as a politician and social reformer. He was also a staunch Zionist who urged Great Britain to fulfil its "destiny" as imperial benefactor to Jews around the world, a benefaction he believed must eventually include a Jewish homeland. In this respect, Lord Shaftesbury was not only an English evangelical but also a man of his age reflecting the cultural influence of European Romanticism's primordial vision of restoring "ancient peoples" to the lands of their forefathers.[1] In fact, by the mid-nineteenth century "the doctrine of the inalienable right of the Jews to Palestine, their restoration, and the role that Britain there acquired, became a commonplace. . . . It was an essential component of the British understanding of Palestine."[2] By the 1860s, several colonization efforts were underway in the region spearheaded by Britain and Germany.[3]

As a leading advocate for the rebirth of a sovereign Jewish nation, under the protective wings of British imperialism, Shaftesbury unwittingly disseminated a thoroughly fictitious story line about the Jewish people and

---

1 Lewis, *Origins*, 92; Scholch, "Britain in Palestine," 42, 44–48.

2. Scholch, "Britain in Palestine," 48.

3. Scholch, "Britain in Palestine," 48–52.

their promised land. His message consisted of three points, all the unwitting creation of his own wishful thinking. First, he contended that all Jewish people shared the same blood as members of a unique ethnic group. Second, he argued that the land of Palestine was a wasteland nearly devoid of inhabitants. Third, he declared that the majority of Europe's Jews were eager to emigrate and resurrect their ancient nation in the empty lands of Palestine.[4] The reality however was that Palestine was far from empty, as Jewish Zionists would eventually discover for themselves. Lord Shaftsbury also failed to understand that the vast majority of British and European Jews had little if any interest in emigrating to Palestine.[5] Whether Jewishness was a matter of religious practice or ethnicity was also a contested issue throughout the Jewish community, as we will see. However, these three Zionist figments of Shaftesbury's pious imagination became important ingredients of nineteenth- and early-twentieth-century British evangelicalism. Once popularized, this evangelical mythology provided much-needed political leverage for Jewish Zionism's persistent lobbying for a British-sponsored national charter.[6]

Great Britain had always been political Zionism's preferred partner for creating its new homeland.[7] Britain was a parliamentary democracy with a history of relatively mild expressions of antisemitism (compared to Russia and Eastern Europe) and a sizeable Jewish, immigrant population. Many Jews had thoroughly assimilated to English society and risen to positions of great wealth and political power. As the poor supplicants knocking at England's door, Zionist leaders understood that they needed well-connected, well-heeled advocates and benefactors if they ever hoped to achieve their dreams. Lobbying Great Britain's Jewish community and political elites was a crucial part of the political Zionist strategy.

Prior to World War I, Palestine was an integral part of the Ottoman Empire. The sultan in Constantinople held the key to any settlement in

4. Lewis, *Origins*, 4–5, 16, 45–47, 50, 92, 115, 120–21, 139–40, 144–45, 151–54, 157, 160–63, 166, 173, 183–89, 199, 205, 319, 334–36, has amply demonstrated how Shaftesbury's misunderstanding of these "facts on the ground," as today's political Zionists would say, shaped his advocacy for Christian Zionism. Shaftesbury's erroneous views were largely influenced by evangelical, Jewish-Christian ministers and missionaries who were themselves fervent Zionists.

5. See Oren, *Power*, 274; Schneer, *Balfour Declaration*, 110; Alam, *Israeli Exceptionalism*, 4, 20–21.

6. Lewis, *Origins*, documents how widely evangelical religion had penetrated the British upper class, including its politicians and parliamentarians. Lord Shaftesbury and his circle of friends exerted significant influence in the politics of their day.

7. As Herzl admitted, "From the first moment I entered the Movement, my eyes were directed toward England"; quoted in Alam, *Israeli Exceptionalism*, 95.

Palestine. Theodor Herzl traveled to the Ottoman capitol city several times to meet with the sultan hoping to convince him of the economic benefits a growing Jewish colony in Palestine would bring to his empire. But they were never able to reach a mutually agreeable plan. The sultan had no interest in fostering a Jewish state within the borders of his empire.[8] Finally, accepting defeat in Constantinople, Herzl immediately turned his focus to London.

While Zionist organizations had been growing in England and Europe, the majority of Jews remained indifferent or even hostile to the new movement.[9] The vast majority of Jewish emigrants (from eastern and central Europe) were seeking new lives in western European countries, America, or Canada, if possible. Few were interested in moving to Palestine. As historian Jonathan Schneer explains,[10]

> Prewar [WWI] indifference to Jewish nationalism was widespread . . . Few wished to deny their Jewish heritage, but few wished to assert it by joining a utopian movement, populated, as they thought, by dreamers and visionaries.

No one could have anticipated the dramatic transformation brought by the First World War.[11] The Ottomans entered the war by siding with Germany, which immediately caused Britain and its allies to turn their imperial attentions to the Middle East.[12] Protecting the Suez Canal was vital to the British economy and the maintenance of its empire.[13] The prospects of a German-Ottoman alliance threatening British troops in Egypt or cutting off its only land route between the Mediterranean and the Red Sea (and to India) were unacceptable. Without going into unnecessary detail, political Zionist leaders suddenly found British government officials eager to hear their plans for a Jewish colonizing project in Palestine, a new colonial state that would help to opposed the Axis powers and safeguard British interests in the Middle East.[14]

Before the war was over, England and France had already begun negotiations behind closed doors over how they would divide the former Ottoman Empire between themselves and cripple Turkey's future influence.

8. Lacqueur, *History*, 100, 108, 112–18.

9. Lacqueur, *History*, 96; Schneer, *Balfour Declaration*, 111. In 1897 the German Rabbinical Council, together with other Jewish leaders, protested against Zionist plans to hold their first Congress in Munich; Alam, *Israeli Exceptionalism*, 222n8.

10. Schneer, *Balfour Declaration*, 110.

11. Schneer, *Balfour Declaration*, 111.

12. Schneer, *Balfour Declaration*, 131–33.

13. Schneer, *Balfour Declaration*, 33.

14. Schneer, *Balfour Declaration*, 125–26.

Zionist leaders like Chaim Weitzman were also promising the financial support of world Jewry to Britain's war effort if London would commit to supporting Jewish immigration, land ownership, and colonial settlement in Palestine.[15] With a number of sympathetic and pragmatic leaders now sitting in the British war cabinet, political Zionists finally received the endorsement they had been waiting for—the Balfour Declaration.[16]

British evangelicals were not the only nineteenth-century Zionists shaped by the ethnic nationalist visions of Romantic philosophy. The arrival of Jewish emancipation in eighteenth/nineteenth-century Europe sparked an internal debate over Jewish self-definition, a debate that Romantic, ethnic nationalism would eventually address by way of political Zionism.[17] Prior to the late eighteenth/early nineteenth century, Jewishness was uniformly defined as a *religious* identity (with hereditary roots) requiring a life of Torah obedience and submission to Abraham's God.[18] Rabbi Shimon Schwab (1908–95), a German rabbi who emigrated to the United States to escape the Nazis, was representative when he wrote, "There was within Judaism only one interpretation of Jewish purpose, history and future that was considered authentic. Loyalty to the Law of God was life's ultimate purpose for every individual."[19] The influential Israeli rabbi, Yeshayahu Leibowitz (1903–94), based his longstanding criticisms of political Zionism (and its

15. Schneer, *Balfour Declaration*, 125–26. Weitzman and others were exploiting common Jewish stereotypes about a monolithic Jewish population controlling global finance. Robert Cecil's marginal notation on a Foreign Office document illustrates the power of this mythology when he wrote, "I do not think it is possible to exaggerate the international power of the Jews." Zionists also warned British leaders that they were being courted by Germany which hoped to acquire Jewish financial support for their war effort against Britain; Schneer, *Balfour Declaration*, 343–45, 366. Lord Balfour also believed that Britain could secure the support of America's Jewish community (many of whom had emigrated from Germany) by supporting the Zionist cause; Oren, *Power*, 360. Schneer concludes, "The Balfour Declaration sprang from fundamental miscalculations about the power of Germany and about the power and unity of Jews" (345).

16. See chapter 2.

17. Laqueur, *History of Zionism*, 3–39, offers a survey of European emancipation and its effects; Rabkin, *Threat from Within*, 5–41, expands his survey to include the opposition of religious Jews against assimilation, secularization, and political Zionism, aspects of the story that are typically omitted from official Israeli histories of the state.

18. Liebman and Don-Yehiya, *Civil Religion*, 227–29; Rabkin, *Threat from Within*, 5–10; Ram, "Zionist Historiography," 98–101; Sand, *Jewish People*, 72; Sussman, "Jew," 372–75; Zeitlin, "Names," 372, 373–74, 376–77.

19. From the book *Heimkehr ins Judentums* (*Homecoming to Judaism*) (New York: n.p., 1978; original German edition published in Frankfurt, 1934); cited by Rabkin, *Threat from Within*, 6.

occupation policies) on the fact that "until the end of the eighteenth century no one ever questioned this [religious] identification."[20]

Arising from the European Enlightenment, Jewish Emancipation would bring several revolutions to the Jewish communities of Europe. One of those revolutions was political Zionism. Emancipation ushered in the demise of Jewish ghettos as well as increased integration into non-Jewish society, promising legal equality, integration, and citizenship rights to all Jews in the countries where they resided. Many took the prospects of social equality as an opportunity to assimilate themselves into the national, social, and typically Christian, world in which they lived. But cultural assimilation often meant the demise of Jewish religious practices as emancipated Jews became increasingly secularized. The resulting crisis of secularized Jewish identity was a large factor in creating the social environment into which political Zionism was born. Eventually, every assimilated Jew had to answer the question "What makes a Jew a Jew once she no longer practices the Jewish religion?"[21] This question became especially pressing for those who discovered, as many did, that neither Jewish emancipation, assimilation, nor secularization could extinguish antisemitism.

Political Zionism entered into this fray by declaring itself the irreligious answer to the question of Jewish identity, replacing the traditional, religious definition of Jewishness with its new *ethnic nationalist* definition. In this respect, political Zionism was only one among a number of tribal, blood, and soil nationalisms that arose throughout Central and Eastern Europe at the time, all bearing the indelible stamp of nineteenth-century Romanticism. Poland, Hungary, Italy, and the Balkan states[22] also saw the rise of Romantically inspired nationalist movements where the psychic bonds of an "organic" national unity were fabricated by mythical histories of ethnic identity and a unifying cultural heritage embedded in the primordial past of an ancient homeland. To some degree, Europe's Romantic dreams of tribal nationalism sprung up in reaction to the liberal, civic nationalism

---

20. Leibowitz, "Religious Significance," 215.

21. Orr, *UnJewish State*, traces the history of this debate within Zionism with special emphasis on the hypocrisy of Israel's political debates over the definition of Jewish nationality. Orr describes, with copious documentation, how the *secular, irreligious* leaders of political Zionism finally had no choice but to fall back on the *religious* features of Jewish identity as they shaped Israel's citizenship laws; see especially 5, 20–21, 37, 105, 111–17, 129, 137, 148–50, 157, 172, 186–206, 215, 218, 237. For more on the long-standing antagonism between religious (especially orthodox) Judaism and political Zionism, see Laqueur, *History of Zionism*, 407–13; Rabkin, *Threat from Within*; for the more recent debate, see the collection of essays in Karcher, *Reclaiming Judaism* and Shatz, *Prophets Outcast*.

22. Orr, *UnJewish State*, 28.

represented by the American and French Revolutions. Liberal, civic nationalism called for collective loyalty to the shared values of equality and
personal liberty as the heart of national consciousness, ideals that tribal
nationalism openly rejected.[23]

The originators of political Zionism were generally assimilated, secularized Jews long parted from whatever religious upbringing they may have
once enjoyed. In fact, all of the movement's early leaders were thoroughly irreligious and secularized.[24] As David Ben-Gurion (Israel's first prime minister) confessed, despite his penchant for quoting the Old Testament, "I don't
personally believe in the God it postulates . . . I am not religious, nor were
the majority of the early builders of Israel believers."[25] For them, Zionism
was a new secular religion ready to redeem world Jewry from its Diaspora
slumbers. As Yakov Rabnik, history professor at the University of Montreal,
puts it: "Jewish nationalism came to substitute for Judaism."[26] Filling the
self-conscious void in Jewish identity created by secularism demanded that
the infant political movement "invent a new meaning of Judaism—Jewish
nationality."[27] In effect, political Zionism's offer of a new Romantic nationalism to European Jews, now *ethnically defined*, emerged as a secularized,
tribal religion offering cohesion and hope to those who had stopped hoping
in Abraham's God.

Jewish religious leaders predictably condemned the new Zionist movement as heresy. Israeli historians Charles Liebman and Eliezer

---

23. For a good introduction to the formative influence of European Romanticism
on political Zionism and the significant differences between Romantic, organic nationalism, on the one hand, and liberal, civic nationalism, on the other, see Sand, *The Invention*, 46–54, 252–62; Sternhell, *Founding Myths*, 10–16, 52–59.

24. Laqueur, *History of Zionism*, 309, 408–9; Orr, *UnJewish State*, 6, 50, 101, 161,
172, 175, 182; Rabkin, *Threat from Within*, 2–10. Israeli historians, Liebman and Don-
Yehiya, *Civil Religion*, 194, raise the pertinent question: "How can one ascribe a central
role in redemption to a movement composed primarily of nonreligious—in many
cases, antireligious—Jews?"

25. Cited from the *Jewish Virtual Library*, in Davis and Coffman, "Political Zionism," 25.

26. Rabkin, *Threat from Within*, 25.

27. Ram, "Zionist Historiography," 100. I will use the words nation, nationality, and
ethnicity as synonyms, following the definitions of Walker Conner in *Ethnonationalism*, xi: "Nation connotes a group of people who believe they are ancestrally related.
Nationalism connotes identification with and loyalty to one's nation. . . . It does *not*
refer to loyalty to one's country." The changing lexigraphical relationships between the
words race, ethnicity, nation, and people need not concern us. As for the irreligious,
often atheistic, attitudes of early Zionist leaders, see Laqueur, *History of Zionism*, 309,
408; Orr, *UnJewish State*. 6–7, 50–51, 90–91, 101, 161–62, 172, 175, 182; Rabkin, *Threat
from Within*, 7, 9, 25–26.

Don-Yehiya offer a litany of condemnations from Jewish religious leaders in their book, *Civil Religion in Israel: Traditional Judaism and Political Culture in the Jewish State*.[28] To offer two examples, rabbi Elḥanan Bunim Wasserman (1875–1941), an important leader in the Lithuanian synagogue, was representative of all religious leaders at the time when he warned that "Zionism is a particularly dangerous form of idolatry because it was devised by Jews who rebelled against God."[29] Rabbi Shulem ben Schneersohn was more specific in pointing out that "they [Zionists] think nationalism has replace religion, and is the best means for the preservation of society."[30]

Theodore Herzl's political Zionist manifesto, *The Jewish State* (published in 1896), is a direct product of this Romantic atmosphere as political philosophy mingled with the many disappointments of Jewish Emancipation. After coming to the conclusion that Europe would never allow the Jews to integrate themselves into gentile society as equal partners, Herzl boldly declared that all Jews were "one people" united, first, by blood and, second, by the worldwide plague of antisemitism. He was not alone in insisting that antisemitism was a universal psychosis that permanently, inexorably afflicts all gentiles everywhere for all time.[31] The plague's only cure, he argued, was massive Jewish emigration back to the land from which they originated. Born as it was of such disappointment, Herzl's ethnocentric vision was as cynical and fatalistic as it was naively Romantic.[32]

Unfortunately, Herzl's formative embrace of an organic, tribal nationalism, centered as it was around the mystical union of "blood and soil," will forever flag political Zionism's historical kinship to the National Socialist party and Nazi Germany's Third Reich.[33] For the fact of the matter is that both political Zionism and Nazism were drinking from the same well, inspired by the same Romantic movement that encouraged mythical, nationalistic dreams for restoring the ancient union of *blood and soil* throughout Europe. For National Socialists, this meant a German fatherland inhabited

---

28. University of California, 1983; see 185–94.

29. Liebman and Don-Yehiya, *Civil Religion in Israel*, 187. I quote the authors' summary of the rabbi's argument.

30. Liebman and Don-Yehiya, *Civil Religion in Israel*, 187.

31. Herzl, *Jewish State*, 43–45, 47–54.

32. Lucien Wolf, a Jewish anti-Zionist leader in London, opposed the efforts of Chaim Weitzman to gain British support. Schneer, *Balfour Declaration*, 120, explains, "he judged Zionism to be a creed of anti-liberalism and despair, precisely because it rejected assimilation on the grounds that 'anti-Semitism is unconquerable.'"

33. For an analysis of the historical development and effects of Romantic, ethnic nationalism in Europe, including the rise of German National Socialism, see especially Mosse, *Crisis of German Ideology*; Smith, *Continuities of German History*, 170–233.

only by the descendants of Hitler's mythical Aryan race. Political Zionists similarly dreamt of a Jewish fatherland inhabited only by descendants of the biblical patriarchs, Abraham, Isaac, Jacob.

While it may be surprising for many today to learn about the shared intellectual heritage that associated political Zionism and Adolph Hitler, when the Nazi party came to power in the early 1930s the ideological connections were self-evident and readily acknowledged. In fact, the Zionist Federation of Germany welcomed the Nazi Nuremburg Laws that were intended to segregate Jews (identified by ethnic heritage) from the non-Jewish, German population. One of the organization's leaders, Georg Kareski, composed a document addressing leaders of the German Reich in 1933. He explained the basic affinities shared by political Zionism and National Socialism:[34]

> Zionism believes that a rebirth of national life, such as is occurring in German life . . . must also take place in the Jewish national group. . . . Our acknowledgement of Jewish nationality provides for a clear and sincere relationship to the German people and its national and racial realities . . . because we, too, are against mixed marriage and are for maintaining the purity of the Jewish group. . . . Only fidelity to their own kind and their own culture gives Jews the inner strength.

When Germany's Nuremburg Laws were issued in 1935 Kareski pointed out that they seemed "entirely to conform with this [Zionist] desire for a separate life based on mutual respect [between Germans and Jews]" as espoused by Germany's Zionist Federation.[35]

Kareski was not a lone voice. In 1934 German Zionist rabbi, Dr. Joachim Prinz, published a book titled *Wir Juden* (*We Jews*) celebrating Hitler's rise to power and his defeat of liberalism (recall Romanticism's hostility toward liberal, civic nationalism). He wrote:[36]

> A state built upon the principle of the purity of nation and race can only be honoured and respected by a Jew who declares his

34. Brenner, *51 Documents*, 43–44. Israel today continues to prohibit mixed marriages in the state. Only religious marriage ceremonies are allowed in Israel, and they require couples to adhere to the same faith. While mixed marriages do exist, couples must have their wedding ceremonies outside the country. Cyprus is a favorite destination.

35. Brenner, *51 Documents*, 156. Brenner's book documents the wide variety of efforts made by different Zionist leaders to collaborate with the Nazis, in their own self-interests, of course. Not everyone agreed with these efforts, especially as Hitler's antisemitism became more widely understood.

36. Shahak, *Jewish History*, 85–86 (emphasis original). Fortunately, Rabbi Prinz soon saw Hitler more clearly. He fled to the United States in 1937, eventually becoming vice-chairman of the World Jewish Congress.

belonging to his own kind. . . . For only he who honours his *own* breed and his *own* blood can have an attitude of honour towards the *national will of other nations*.

The diversity of Zionist leaders who sought to collaborate with Nazi Germany demonstrates the powerful ideological connection they shared, a connection rooted in their common commitment to tribal, ethnocentric, blood-and-soil nationalism.

THE CREATION OF ZIONIST HISTORIOGRAPHY

Political Zionism quickly constructed its own school of historiography in order to manufacture the ideal past required for its blood-and-soil ideology. Members of this new school appear to have used the same conjuring spells as Lord Shaftesbury insofar as their story line tells the same tale of an ancient, ethnically distinct, Jewish nation eternally wedded to its native soil. This new historical narrative was manufactured by selectively stitching together imagined scenarios cut from only the most useful bits of Israelite and Jewish history.[37] A key ingredient included disparaging, even ridiculing, Jewish life in the Diaspora. For instance, a repentant ex-Zionist, Hayim Greenberg, confessed that "there was a time when it used to be the fashion for Zionist speakers (including the writer) to declare from the platform that 'to be a good Zionist one must first be somewhat of an anti-Semite.'"[38] Greenberg's confession reflects his acknowledgment that for Zionist ideology, Jewish blood separated from Jewish soil could only result in weakness, passivity, corruption, and degradation[39]—the antithesis of the new "muscular" Jew that Zionism intended to construct in a future Jewish homeland. Thus, demeaning Jews living in the Diaspora (or the *Galut*, the Exile) quickly became an important element of Zionist rhetoric. "A hatred of the diaspora and a rejection of Jewish life there were a kind of methodological necessity for Zionism."[40] Describing "exiled Jews in terms that at times resembled those of the most rabid anti-Semites" became normalized.[41] For instance, A. D. Gordon (1856–1922), an early leading light in political Zionist circles,

37. For a detailed discussion with numerous examples, see Ram, "Zionist Historiography," 91–106; Sand, *Invention*, 100–115.

38. Quoted by Brenner, *51 Documents*, 123; he is citing Greenberg's article "The Myth of Jewish Parasitism," in *Jewish Frontier*, March 1942.

39. Liebman and Don-Yehiya, *Civil Religion in Israel*, 37.

40. Sternhell, *Founding Myths*, 49. Zeev Sternhell was a professor of political science at Hebrew University in Jerusalem until his death in 2020.

41. Sternhell, *Founding Myths*, 47.

described the Jewish people as "sick and diseased in body and soul . . . we are a parasitic people. We have no roots in the soil; there is no ground beneath our feet. . . . We in ourselves are almost nonexistent."[42] David Ben-Gurion (1886–1973), Israel's first prime minister, went so far as to describe "Diaspora Jewry" as "'the dust of humanity' since it could not experience full national-human existence."[43]

One of the masterminds behind this new brand of Zionist historiography, drawing the different strands of rhetoric together into a consistent narrative, was Ben Zion Dinur (1884–1973), professor of Jewish history at Hebrew University in Jerusalem and a founding member of the Land of Israel Association for History and Ethnography (in 1923).[44] Appointed Israel's Minister of Education and Culture from 1951 to 1955, Dinur implemented a nationwide education curriculum that shapes both Israeli and Christian Zionist public opinion to this day. As Uri Ram, a sociology professor at Ben-Gurion University, explains in his article, "Zionist Historiography and the Invention of Modern Jewish Nationhood," Dinur "performed a paradigmatic revolution in Jewish historiography" by inventing a new, politically correct story line for the Jewish people.[45] Dinur constructed this new narrative through his single-minded quest to provide political Zionism with its "ancient roots," as required by Romantic, blood-and-soil nationalism.

Dinur's book, *Israel and the Diaspora*, clearly spells out his organic, nationalist vision for Israeli Zionism. He repeatedly asserts that even after their Dispersion (which he curiously dated from the Arab conquest of Palestine, perhaps to stir the flames of Israel's anti-Arab sentiments) "the unity of the Jewish people still remained complete and unbroken. . . . Even in dispersion the nation formed a distinctive organic entity."[46] The centerpiece of this

42. Quoted in Sternhell, *Founding Myths*, 47–48.

43. Cited in Liebman and Don-Yehiya, *Civil Religion in Israel*, 88, quoting Ben-Gurion's *Like Stars and Dust: Essays from Israel's Government Year Book*, 185.

44. Of course, Dinur did not create this Zionist historiography *de novo*. He built upon the work of important predecessors, specifically Heinrich Graetz (1817–91), Moses Hess (1812–75), Simon Dubnow (1860–1941) and Yitzhak Baer (1888–1980); see Sand, *Jewish People*, 71–81, 87–95, 100–107. In describing Dinur's work, Sand says, "If Graetz was responsible for the foundation and scaffolding of the retroactive construction of the Jewish nation, Dinur laid the bricks, hung the beams, and fitted the windows and doors" (104).

45. Ram, "Zionist Historiography," 97. Of course, all historical writing is affected in one way or another by the historian's presuppositions, whether tacitly or overtly. The issue here is Dinur's production of a supposedly historical narrative for the explicit purpose of propagandizing the public for the goal of enhanced social control. This is the goal of nationalistic civil religion. It is not the work of a legitimate historian. It is also a common feature of tribal nationalism.

46. Dinur, *Israel and the Diaspora*, 47; for the Diaspora beginning with the Arab

organically unified Jewish community (in Diaspora) was its "revolt against the *Galut*."[47] He described this unifying urge as a nationalist revolt characterized by "all the accumulated energy of their [the Jews] ardent yearning 'to rebuild their own Land and to be rebuilt in it.'"[48] Despite the fact that only a small minority of Jews supported political Zionism prior to Israel's postwar establishment, Dinur depicts it as a widespread, unifying movement that gave rise to "the new, defiant type of Jew."[49] Dinur's description of this new breed of militant, "muscular Jew" reconquering the land of Palestine further displays both his embrace of blood-and-soil nationalism as well as his deployment of that ideology to justify his goal-directed reconstruction of Jewish history.[50] He writes, "The true significance of the resettlement [of the land] was that *the acquisition of the soil was intimately tied to a complete renewal of social and psychological experiences. [It] could be accomplished only through laying bare the basic instincts which bind man to the soil and which are hidden in the recesses of his being.*"[51] Curiously, Dinur never offers any empirical evidence to substantiate his many sweeping psychological claims about the "organic unity" or "the basic instincts" "hidden in the recesses of his being" driving the Jewish collective to be reunited with its native soil. But this is not unusual. Ideologies frequently flourish through the hopes of dispirited people who find dreams more compelling than reality and evidence less meaningful than faith.

---

conquest, see 3, 6, 66–67.

47. Dinur, *Israel and the Diaspora*, 86–87, 141, 145–46.

48. Dinur, *Israel and the Diaspora*, 141, 145.

49. Dinur, *Israel and the Diaspora*, 143.

50. Rabkin, *Threat from Within*, 10, describes political Zionist historiography as "this teleological version of history."

51. Dinur, *Israel and the Diaspora*, 170 (emphasis mine).

Chapter 4

All Zionisms Are Not Alike

A FRIEND OF MINE, who happens to be Jewish, once asked if my criticisms of the Israeli government and its policies toward Palestinians were rooted in a more visceral rejection of Zionism itself. His question implied that I may need to examine myself, to see if my true motivation was an antisemitic opposition to Jewish statehood, to Jewish national independence. I understood the reason for my friend's question and appreciated his challenge, but I was also struck by the way Israel's unilateral claim to be the Jewish nation-state for all Jews everywhere has muddied the waters when it comes to discussing antisemitism and anti-Zionism (see chapter 16).

Many people do not realize that the modern, Zionist state of Israel does not represent the totality of all historic forms of Zionism. It represents only one: a brand called *political Zionism* (see chapter 3). Alternatives to political Zionism had their advocates in the past, but they all lost out in the early struggle for national supremacy. In modern parlance, *Zionism* has become a shorthand reference for *political Zionism*, though most people do not realize it. I tried to explain these things to my friend, hoping to clarify that my criticisms of Israel were actually criticisms of political Zionism specifically, not the more general aspirations of Jewish, national independence.

I hope that he believed me.

In chapter 1, I began to offer a corrective to the standard Christian Zionist approach to Scripture and described in its stead an appropriate method of biblical interpretation arising from the biblical texts themselves. That was the first strand in the Christian Zionist ball of string. Examining the second strand requires excavating the specific nature of modern Israeli political Zionism and its relationship to Christian Zionism within the church.

While Jewish Zionism has never been monolithic, it possessed a much greater breadth of both ideological and methodological diversity in the past than it displays today. Sadly, the constraints of historical development have sharply narrowed the range of possibilities for Israel's modern political establishment. Ideas have consequences, especially when held by people doggedly determined to create a new world. Bad ideas can have especially bad consequences when they justify ethnically based behaviors, including ethnic separation, discrimination, population transfers, and the construction of an ethnic national identity rooted in the maintenance of an ethnic majority. Not all forms of historic Zionism endorsed the vision of an ethnic majority/superiority that created and sustains the state of Israel as we know it today. However, the more humanitarian streams of liberal, inclusive Zionism, such as *cultural Zionism* which remained open to the growth of a bi-national arrangement with native Palestinians, eventually lost the battle for Israel's future, falling before the conservative, colonial forces fighting for a Jewish nation-state built on ethnic purity.[1]

Christian Zionists, who offer their undying support to the Israeli government, ought to have at least a basic understanding of the particular brand of Zionist ideology pervasive in Israel today. Supporting a movement blindly is frankly irresponsible, but this is what happens in many evangelical quarters today with their support of Zionism. When one supports a charity or an organization, is it not wise to do some research to see how they spend their money, to learn what it is used for? Is the money actually spent in the way the organization promises? Christians should be asking if their donations are financing something in harmony with Christian morality. Christian Zionists need to understand the sorts of Israeli policies they are underwriting with the large sums of money and consistent political support they offer up to Israel.

1. For a discussion of cultural Zionism, see Avishai, *Tragedy of Zionism*, 45–66. Avishai explains that "the cultural Zionists were more secure in their Jewish identity than people like Herzl" (45). They were not interested in building a nation-state but in securing a "homeland" where Jewish culture could flourish as the growing community built schools, farms, publishing companies, and other Jewish institutions throughout Palestine. As Avishai summarizes, "cultural Zionists perceived the Jewish predicament, not from what was ominous about the Gentile world, but from what was most compelling about the Jewish tradition" (47). Jeff Halper argues for the establishment of a new, decolonizing, cultural Zionist movement today; see his *Israeli in Palestine*, 293–300.

Given the nature of this book, we will have to be content with a brief survey; we simply cannot explore all the complexities in the history of the Zionist movement.[2] In the past, there have been different philosophical expressions of Zionist convictions. The central theme of these various expressions centered on the construction of a sovereign Jewish community (not necessarily a nation-state), preferably in the land of Palestine, determining its own future. Within that common goal, however, there was a spectrum of Zionist opinions on how that future community ought to be created, constituted, governed, and how it ought to relate to the native people already living in Palestine. It is enough for our purposes to categorize the competing strains of Zionism under two headings: (a) those who wanted to build *a Jewish nation*, and (b) those who wanted to build *a nation for Jews*. Although those two phrases sound deceptively similar, the different models for nation building they describe stand worlds apart.

FIGHTING FOR A JEWISH NATION

On November 10, 1975, the United Nations General Assembly passed Resolution 3379 by a vote of seventy-two to thirty-five (with thirty-two abstentions).[3] This controversial Resolution, which was finally rescinded in December of 1991, caused offense by stating "that Zionism is a form of racism and racial discrimination," ranking it among such historic sins as "colonialism and neo-colonialism, foreign occupation . . . [and] apartheid." Naturally, Israel's government and its international supporters were outraged; many insisted that the resolution was antisemitic, an insult to all Jews everywhere.

Why would the same international body that had played a positive, essential role in Israel's creation make such a radical about face and condemn the new nation only twenty-seven years later? It is important to note that the resolution did not condemn Israel, Jews, or Judaism. It could only be seen as "antisemitic" by those who mistakenly equate Zionism with Judaism.[4] Reso-

---

2. See Avishai, *Tragedy of Zionism*; Laqueur, *History of Zionism*; Sofer, *Zionism*.

3. The complete text of Resolution 3379 may be found at https://unispal.un.org/DPA/DPR/unispal.nsf/0/761C1063530766A7052566A2005B74D1. Ben Norton points out that the crucial factor in determining a member nation's vote was its own history as either a perpetrator or a victim of colonialism. He writes, "The countries that voted against the resolution were primarily colonial powers and/or their allies. The countries that voted for it were overwhelmingly formerly colonized and anti-imperialist nations." Norton provides a world map to illustrate this point; see Norton, "US and Israel Rewrite History."

4. This all-too-common but false equation will be examined in chapter 16.

lution 3379 specifically condemned Zionism, which is a political ideology, not a religion, a people, or a nation-state. Furthermore, the resolution did not condemn all possible expressions of Zionism, but only the specific brand of Zionism that had firmly grabbed the tiller of Israel's ship-of-state since the outbreak of war in 1947.

That prevailing strain of Zionism, which precipitated the United Nation's condemnation, is a particular Zionist subspecies known as *political Zionism* that has been powerfully influenced by another subspecies called *revisionist Zionism*.[5] For all practical purposes, the contemporary form of political-revisionist Zionism has ruled the roost of Israeli *Realpolitik* ever since the nation's founding. And even though many of Israel's earliest political leaders identified themselves as *labor Zionists*, because of their sympathies for Marxist and socialist ideals, the on-the-ground strategies adopted by these leaders (men such as the labor Zionist leader, David Ben-Gurion) for (a) acquiring as much territory as possible while (b) relocating or "transferring" the local Palestinian population elsewhere reflected revisionist priorities.[6] The distinguishing principles of political-revisionist Zionism were always made clear by its founding fathers.

First, both Theodor Herzl (the founder of political Zionism) and Vladimir Jabotinsky (the founder of revisionist Zionism) were open about the fact that large-scale Jewish immigration from (primarily eastern and central) Europe for resettlement in the land of Palestine would *define Zionism as a settler colonial project*, eventually to be sponsored by the British Empire. In 1902, Herzl traveled to London in order to appeal to Nathaniel Meyer Lord Rothschild, a man unsympathetic to Zionist aims who held a

5. Political Zionism was fathered by Theodor Herzl (1860–1904) who believed that immediate political action was necessary if Jews were ever to have their own homeland. Herzl opposed the alternative strains of religious Zionism and cultural (or practical) Zionism, which believed that a new Jewish homeland would develop eventually as the result of patient, diligent adherence to Jewish religious devotion and/or Jewish cultural development, respectively. Revisionist Zionism was launched by Vladimir (Ze'ev) Jabotinsky (1880–1940) who feared that his political Zionist contemporaries were too willing to compromise on Zionist fundamentals. He wanted to "revise" earlier compromises made with Great Britain by political Zionist leaders which reduced the territory available to Zionist settlement. The revisionists wanted all of Transjordan as well as Palestine. Jabotinsky insisted that his revisionism was the true heir to Herzl's political Zionism. For the beginnings of political Zionism, see Vital, *Origins*, 233–370. For a discussion of political and cultural Zionisms, see Avishai, *Tragedy of Zionism*, 22–66; for discussions of Jabotinsky and Revisionist Zionism, see Laqueur, *History of Zionism*, 338–83; Sofer, *Zionism*, 199–223.

6. For the origins and distinctives of labor Zionism, see Avishai, *Tragedy of Zionism*, 67–98; on labor Zionism's adoption of revisionist tactics under the leadership of David Ben-Gurion (1886–1973), see Shlaim, *Iron Wall*, 16–22.

seat on the Royal Commission investigating the growing westward migration of eastern European Jews. Herzl described their encounter in his diary: "I . . . said: 'I want to ask the British government for a colonization charter. . . . I want to found a Jewish colony in a British possession.'"[7] As we saw in chapter 2, Herzl's book *The Jewish State* openly anticipates Zionism's need for European, imperial assistance in dealing with unhappy, displaced Palestinian natives. Jabotinsky was equally forthright. In 1924, he published an article explaining his "programme" in simple terms. It "is not complicated," he wrote. "The aim of Zionism is a Jewish state. The territory—both sides of the Jordan. The system—mass colonization."[8] Any honest appraisal of today's Israel must begin here. Israel is the final expression of European, settler colonialism intent on bringing Western civilization and culture to the Oriental world by replacing an indigenous population with European settlement, just as white settlers in the American West replaced Native Americans.

Second, for Jabotinsky, an eventual Zionist nation-state must include *the whole of Palestine*, including the Transjordan territory east of the Jordan River (now the country of Jordan).[9] This was his "revision" of Herzl's original vision. Jabotinsky was a maximalist in every respect. He always opposed any partition plan that would divide the land of Palestine between Jews and Palestinians.[10] In his view, the Jewish people deserved exclusive control over all of British Mandate Palestine. Even though later labor Zionists were more pragmatic, eventually agreeing to the international partition plan, their expansionist ideals saw partition as only the first step in a process that (hopefully) would allow them to control more and more territory. It is no accident that Israel's Declaration of Independence omits any reference to Israel's borders. To this very day Israel is the only nation in the world that has never declared where its final borders will be.

Third, both revisionist and political Zionists emphasized that Jews could only be secure in a sovereign nation where they, the Jews, were a sizable majority of the population. On December 3, 1947, Ben-Gurion spoke

---

7. Laqueur, *History of Zionism*, 120.

8. Laqueur, *History of Zionism*, 353; see pp. 347–49 for additional descriptions of Jabotinsky's belief in the need of "mass colonization."

9. For this and the following points, see the outline of issues from Jabotinsky's *Basic Principles of Revisionism* (London, 1923) in Laqueur, *History*, 347–48. Most Zionists eventually abandoned the idea of occupying the country of Jordan. However, the expansionist stream of thought continues to express itself in the occupation of the Golan Heights, the West Bank, and Gaza, as well as the rapid proliferation of all-Jewish settlements throughout the West Bank.

10. Shlaim, *Iron Wall*, 11.

to a gathering of senior members of his Mapai political party. Explaining his worries over the "demographic needs" of the future Jewish state and the problems posed for a Jewish majority by the UN Partition plan, Ben-Gurion remarked, "Only a state with at least 80% Jews is a viable and stable state."[11] Almost one year later, in October 1948, the official Zionist Transfer Committee confirmed Ben-Gurion's earlier demographic calculations by insisting that the eventual Palestinian population of the Jewish state should not exceed 15 to 20 percent.[12] Political Zionism could only succeed by creating *a Jewish nation-state*. Although a remnant of Palestinians may be allowed to remain after the war, they must always be kept to a minority so as never to challenge Jewish dominance.

Fourth, revisionists viewed themselves as realists in that they insisted on the inevitability of rule by force and Arab hostility. Jabotinsky viewed a Zionist state in Palestine not as a Jewish "return" to the homeland but as a colonizing "offshoot or implant of Western civilization in the East." Consequently, "Zionism was to be permanently allied with European colonialism against all the Arabs" in the region.[13] This would only be possible through armed force. Jabotinsky wrote two foundational articles describing his vision for an *Iron Wall* of Jewish military might that would both defend the immigrant community and teach "the Arabs" that a Zionist state was there to stay. Interestingly enough, he never begrudged the Palestinian's the right to resist their colonization. As the historian Avi Shlaim notes, Jabotinsky calmly "pointed out that since no native population anywhere in the world would willingly accept an alien majority," Zionism was forever obliged to enforce its colonial rule through the barrel of a gun. Eight years after Israel's founding, David Ben-Gurion affirmed Jabotinsky's forecast when he candidly remarked, "Why should the Arabs make peace? If I were an Arab leader, I would never make terms with Israel. That is natural. We have taken their country."[14] Jabotinsky's foresight is an important corroboration of the many claims made by Palestinian leaders at the time who explained that Arab hostility toward Zionist settlement was not the result of antisemitism but of Arab resistance to the perpetuation of European colonization and British imperialism so clearly expressed in the Balfour Declaration.[15]

11. The entire speech is published in Ben-Gurion's book, *In the Battle*, 255–72, quoted in Pappé, *Ethnic Cleansing*, 48, 269n19.

12. Masalha, *Expulsion of the Palestinians*, 199.

13. Shlaim, *Iron Wall*, 12.

14. Cited in Alam, *Israeli Exceptionalism*, 39, 227n1; from Goldman, *Jewish Paradox*, 99.

15. For abundant testimony to this attitude, see Jacobsen and Naor, *Oriental Neighbors*, 2, 19–20, 25, 31, 48, 49, 81, 121–49. The fact that Zionist settlers were European,

Thus, the modern state of Israel sprouted and grew to maturity in the hothouse of an ethnically biased, settler colonial, expansionist, militaristic expression of political Zionism. The country's *de facto* Constitution takes the form of numerous "Basic Laws" which have codified these political-revisionist distinctives.[16] For instance, the Basic Law on "Human Dignity and Liberty" explains "the values of the State of Israel as a Jewish and democratic state," specifying that these rights apply to "Jewish nationals."[17] As we will see, however, in a Jewish state only Jews can qualify for all the democratic benefits of "Israel nationals."[18] The obvious contradiction at the heart of Israel's "democracy" is that it defines its citizenry in ethnic terms. This results in an unresolvable oxymoron that haunts Israeli society to this day. It is not accidental that no Israeli law explicitly protects the right to equality and freedom from discrimination. In effect, all non-Jews, Palestinians in particular, remain second-class citizens within their own country. As a Jewish state, an ethnocracy, Israel offers democracy only to its Jewish citizens. Evidence of this fact is made available to outsiders by an Israeli organization called *Adalah: The Legal Center for Arab Minority Rights in Israel.* As a part of its mission to defend Israeli Palestinians against systemic discrimination, it has created an online database cataloguing over sixty-five Israeli laws that discriminate (either directly or indirectly) against Palestinian citizens in Israel as well as Palestinian residents of the Occupied Territories (the West Bank and Gaza).[19]

Ashkenazi Jews, distinct from the indigenous, Sephardi Jews long resident in Palestine, helps to explain the intractable nature of this problem. The earliest Palestinian protests, which included many native Sephardi/Arab Jews, were anti-Zionist not antisemitic events. There is a difference between the two, though pro-Zionist apologists prefer to ignore the distinction. Early Zionist leaders interpreted the hostilities in Palestine through a European lens ground and polished by the long history of Western antisemitism. By imposing their paradigm of European antisemitism onto the challenge of Palestinian anti-Zionism, Zionist leaders misunderstood Palestinian motives and deepened the antagonism between the two peoples. It is a classic example of cross-cultural miscommunication; see Jacobsen and Naor, *Oriental Neighbors*, 4, 22, 25–26, 31, 49, 72.

16. Israel has never adopted a national Constitution, despite the fact that its admission to the United Nations in 1949 was predicated on its doing so.

17. Find the full text at https://www.mfa.gov.il/MFA/MFA-Archive/1992/Pages/Basic%20Law-%20Human%20Dignity%20and%20Liberty-.aspx.

18. See chapter 14 as well as the detailed explanation in Davis, *Apartheid Israel*, 88–108. Davis is a Jewish resident of Israel, a professor of anthropology, a civil rights activist and past vice-chairman of the Israeli League for Human and Civil Rights. He explains that "the State of Israel does not have one single universal citizenship for all of its citizens. Rather, informed by the dominant ideology of political Zionism, the Knesset legislated a schedule of four classes of citizenship based on racial discrimination . . . representing another form of apartheid."

19. See https://www.adalah.org/en/content/view/7771.

The legal foundation for Israel's policies of national, ethnic discrimination was constitutionally enshrined by the 2018 Basic Law, "Israel—The Nation-State of the Jewish People."[20] This most recent Basic Law begins by declaring:

a. Israel is the historic homeland of the Jewish people in which the State of Israel was established.

b. The state of Israel is *the nation-state of the Jewish people* in which it fulfills its natural, religious, and historic right to self-determination.

c. The fulfillment of the right of national self-determination in the State of Israel is *unique to the Jewish people.*

Imagine how we would reconsider America's beginnings if the founding fathers had drafted a Constitution that defined the fledgling colonies as an exclusively WASP nation. That is, only White, Anglo-Saxon Protestants could ever enjoy all the rights enshrined in the Constitution. Of course, the United States has its own shameful history of long denying equal rights to women, African Americans, Native Americans, and others. Completing that work of national equality is far from finished. But imagine the constant paranoia stirred up by a government that continually focuses its energies on safeguarding its "democratic values" exclusively for America's WASP majority. Then imagine reading unsettling newspaper articles, on a regular basis, about the growing "Jewish threat," or "Italian threat," or "Negro threat," all components of the ever present "demographic threat" eating away at the country's WASP majority because the Jews, Italians, or Negros were having too many children. For some that scenario may sound like a science fiction story (or everyday experience, perhaps) but it is, in fact, everyday life in Israel.

THE ZIONIST ALTERNATIVE NEVER ATTEMPTED

Jabotinsky was not the only Zionist leader to oppose the idea of partitioning Palestine into sections, one for Jews and the other for Palestinians. Another strain of Zionism called Ha-Shomer Ha-Tza'ir founded in 1924 also rejected partition, but their anti-partition principles were very different from Jabotinsky's. Rather than believing that Jews alone should control all of Palestine, they believed that Jews and Palestinians should share the land together as equals. As the Zionist historian Sasson Sofer explains, "Ha-Shomer Ha-Tza'ir advocated a bi-national state based on political parity

---

20. Read the full text at https://www.jpost.com/Israel-News/Read-the-full-Jewish-Nation-State-Law-562923 (emphasis mine).

between the two nations of the Middle East."[21] Here was a Zionist vision, not of a Jewish nation but of *a nation for Jews*, as well as for everyone else; a nation that would not be ruled by an ethnic majority but by "a multitude of equals," to quote the Jewish philosopher Martin Buber.[22] At the Twelfth Zionist Congress (September 1921) Buber presented his party's (called Hitachdut) platform arguing for Jewish coexistence with the Arabs of Palestine. The paper declared that Zionism's goals "will not be achieved at the expense of other people's rights. By establishing a just alliance with the Arab peoples, we wish to turn our common dwelling-place into a community that will flourish . . . bring[ing] each of these peoples unhampered independent development."[23] Buber's bi-national proposal, in league with the bi-national efforts of Ha-Shomer Ha-Tza'ir and Brit Shalom, was echoed in similar Palestinian efforts to construct a bi-national agreement with the Zionist community—contrary to the Zionist mythology of implacable Palestinian hostility and antisemitic rejectionism. In 1922 an organization known as the Palestine Arab Executive composed a draft proposal, offered through British authorities acting as mediators, describing how all of Palestine could become an independent state with proportional voting for all its citizens and a representative legislature composed of both Jews and Palestinians.[24] The proposal was immediately rejected by Chaim Weizmann (then president of the World Zionist Organization, later the first president of Israel) and other political Zionist leaders.

During the 1930s two more groups emerged that shared in this vision of a bi-national, democratic coexistence for both Jewish immigrants and native Palestinians. They were called Kedma-Mizraha and the League for Jewish-Arab Rapprochement and Cooperation. All together these diverse streams, composing what I will call "Unity Zionism," were labeled the Ihud (Unity) party. Such Ashkenazi Jewish luminaries as Albert Einstein, Judah Magnes (the first president of Hebrew University in Jerusalem), Martin

21. Sofer, *Zionism*, 168; for a history of the Ha-Shomer Ha-Tza'ir movement see 160–78.

22. Sofer, *Zionism*, 351.

23. Mendes-Flohr, *Land of Two Peoples*, 61. For a history of the Zionist efforts for creating a bi-national Palestine, see Flapan, *Zionism and the Palestinians*, 163–89.

24. For more details on this Palestinian suggestion, see Flapan, *Zionism and the Palestinians*, 70. As Flapan observes, "[Chaim] Weizmann [1874–1952, president of the Zionist Organization and the first president of Israel] and the Zionist Organization [founded in 1897 at the instigation of Theodor Herzl and the First Zionist Congress in Basel, Switzerland] were militantly opposed to the setting up of representative institutions in Palestine which they regarded as inimical to hopes for a Zionist state. . . . Weizmann opposed both a bi-national state and self-government [for Palestinians], explaining that *democracy was not appropriate for backward peoples*" (71, emphasis mine).

Buber, Gershom Scholem (both professors at Hebrew University), insisted that some form of co-fraternity between Palestine's immigrant, Ashkenazi Jewish community and its native Palestinians (which included "Oriental" Sephardi, Mizrahi/Arab Jews) was the only possible way forward for any brand of Zionism worthy of the Jewish people.[25] As a result, the Ihud movement also opposed all plans for transferring Arabs out of Palestine in order to make way for a Jewish majority.

According to the Ihud movement, political Zionism's uncritical adoption of European nationalism as their ideological template was a tragic mistake. Because of this mistake, Judah Magnes believed that "Zionism had usurped Judaism and accorded pre-eminence to politics." He further warned that establishing a Jewish state by force would ensure that it "would simply be another pagan country."[26] In a 1929 letter to Chaim Weizmann, Magnes argued that a "policy of cooperation is certainly possible and more hopeful of achievement than building up a Jewish Home (National or otherwise) on bayonets and oppression. Moreover, a Jewish Home in Palestine built up on bayonets and oppression is not worth having."[27]

While Martin Buber was not as opposed to nationalism as Magnes, he remained the preeminent voice of conscience opposed to political-revisionist Zionism, constantly condemning the injustices of Zionist territorial expansion. Buber lamented that "our historic return to our country has entered by the wrong gate." His article on "Hebrew Humanism" predicted that "by contrasting Hebrew humanism with the nationalism of empty existence . . . the Zionist movement has to decide if it is to be nationalist-egoist or nationalist-humanist. If it decides to be nationalist-egoist, it will suffer the same fate as all empty nationalism."[28] Sadly, the Zionist leadership chose to remain thoroughly egoist. With prophetic insight, Buber warned

25 The native Jewish community in Palestine had long coexisted with their Muslim and Christian neighbors. Sometimes *Sephardi* is specifically used to designate the descendants of Jews expelled from Spain in the late fifteenth century (together with Spain's Muslim population) who then migrated across North Africa into the Middle East and Asia Minor. The term *Mizrahi* is also used for the descendants of indigenous, Jewish communities resident in North Africa and the Middle East. Sometimes the two terms are confused and used synonymously. These subsets are also known as Oriental or Arab Jews, demonstrating that the common distinction made between "Jews" and "Arabs" in Palestine is inaccurate and confusing. It can also become a word game intended to highlight the European racial heritage of the *Ashkenazi* Jewish settlers who came from Europe to colonize Palestine and displaced the native Arabs, whether Muslim, Christian, or Jew. On the history of the Ihud movement, see Sofer, *Zionism*, 337–56.

26. Sofer, *Zionism*, 342, 345.

27. Goren, *Dissenter in Zion*, 277.

28. Sofer, *Zionism*, 350.

that Israel's future was doomed to endless conflict, war, and bloodshed if it continued on its current course. Furthermore, this violent future would be entirely of its own making.

Different Ihud leaders suggested various political options for a bi-national confederation of two states within a shared country or republic, several plans offered by Sephardi leaders, as well as Judah Magnes, suggested an independent, bi-national Palestine be integrated into a Federation with neighboring Arab states.[29] Unfortunately, none of the options were taken seriously by the leaders of political-revisionist Zionism, who were intent on the formation of an ethnocratic state for Jews alone. We do know that Ihud principles would never have allowed for a nation dependent on the maintenance of a perpetual Jewish majority. Instead, they would have guaranteed equal rights for all, whoever they might be, whether a majority or a minority in the land of Palestine/Israel. As the Israeli journalist-historian, Tom Segev, has written, these proponents of bi-nationalism "confronted Zionist ideology with its conscience . . . [they] brought to the fore the contradiction between the national aspirations of the Zionists and the standards of universal morality they aspired to."[30] That political contradiction, and the many deceits required to camouflage its reality, haunts the Jewish nation-state to this day.

I know that defenders of Israel's current state of affairs will argue that the Ihud movement's vision was naïve; that it refused to recognize the depth of Palestinian hostility toward the Jewish settlers coming to Palestine. But cavalier dismissals of an option never seriously attempted do not pass the smell test. Critical second-guessing about what the Palestinian response may or may not have been to a serious offer of democratic coexistence in a shared land, had the scheme been supported by Zionism's most important leaders (from both the local and immigrant communities), only serves as an empty bluff by those who either lack imagination or are committed apologists for the *status quo*. Such negativity also ignores an abundance of historical evidence suggesting that the local Palestinian population would have been positively disposed to sharing the land with the growing Jewish community had serious efforts been made in that direction. Historians Abigail Jacobson and Moshe Naor explore this story of Jewish/Arab coexistence—and its unrealized potential for peace in the region—in their book, *Oriental Neighbors: Middle Eastern Jews and Arabs in Mandatory Palestine*. Their account describes the long-standing friendship and cooperation that

29. Jacobson and Naor, *Oriental Neighbors*, 40, 45, 66.
30. Segev, *One Palestine*, 409.

existed between Arab Jews, Christians, and Muslims prior to the arrival of Zionist, Ashkenazi settlers from Eastern and Central Europe.

We will never know what Israel might have become under Ihud/Unity leadership because it was never tried. What we do know is that there was once a strain of Zionism whose leaders, in all likelihood, would have agreed with the United Nation's Resolution 3379. Because they embraced the Old Testament prophetic heritage of Jewish ethics, they condemned in advance any Israeli law reducing Palestinian Israelis to second-class citizens. They wanted to tear down, indeed, they would never have constructed, Jabotinsky's *Iron Wall* of separation in the first place. Like the prophets themselves, these leaders speak to us from the grave, excoriating the Basic Laws that enshrine Israel's status as a Jewish state where only the Jewish majority is guaranteed democratic rights to freedom and equality before the law.

Zionism began as a thoroughly secular movement, so it is not surprising that a secular perspective on power politics and ethnic nationalism proved victorious in the game of hardball politicking played so shrewdly by David Ben-Gurion and his political Zionist comrades. But the testimonies of men (and women) like Magnes, Buber, and others speak volumes to the Christian church, for we give lip-service to sharing the same prophetic heritage. Surely, of all people, those who claim to follow Jesus Christ as citizens in the kingdom of God ought to feel themselves, not only weighed down but supremely *obligated* by the moral gravity of Jeremiah's injunction, "Do what is just and right. Rescue from the hand of his oppressor the one who has been robbed. Do no wrong or violence to the alien, the fatherless or the widow" (Jer 22:3 NIV).

The point of my question at the opening of this chapter about UN Resolution 3379 and its condemnation of Israeli Zionism has now been answered. We must now ask why so many in the Christian church continue to offer their loyal support to the most brutal, discriminatory expression of Jewish Zionism, the political-revisionist Zionism ruling over Israel today?

Chapter 5

In the Camp We Are Birds

THE RUBBER BULLET TORE through Mohammed's face, leaving a trail of ripped flesh and crushed bone as it smashed into his right cheek bone and lodged beneath his eye, fracturing his skull.[1] Actually, rubber bullet is a misnomer. It suggests something pliable that might bounce off a hard target. Not so! Think instead of hardened, rubberized plastic wrapped around a steel core, either a cylinder or a sphere, the size of a large marble. The exemplar I keep on my office desk, as a reminder of their destructive power, is a black cylinder encircled by two, slightly raised ribs.

When this type of projectile—fired at a muzzle velocity of one hundred meters per second—meets human flesh, it does not bounce. It penetrates, mangles and shreds. The "bullet" tumbles and spins erratically as it passes through the body, leaving a trail of destruction in its wake.[2] Israeli research-

---

1. In future stories I will change people's names in order to protect their identities. In this case, when I told Mohammed that I would not use his real name, he insisted that I should not only use his name but include his address and phone number, as well. Obviously, I have not gone that far, but his given name is Mohammed. As a well-known photojournalist, his story was widely covered by the international press; see the articles with photographs at Activestills, "PHOTOS"; "Palestinian Photographer Shot in Face"; Purkiss, "Journalist Shot"; Robbins, "Shooting the Messenger."

2. For detailed descriptions of the military ammunition used by Israel's military against Palestinian civilians, see the November 2000 report written by Physicians for Human Rights: "Evaluation of the Use of Force." The PHR investigation concluded that

ers should have consulted with Mohammed or the many Palestinians who have died from rubber bullet wounds before announcing that they are "safer than live rounds and inflict only superficial damage."[3]

Mohammed is an award-winning filmmaker and photojournalist who was born and raised in the Aida Refugee Camp located on the northwestern outskirts of Bethlehem. Aida is one of three refugee communities, including the Al-Azzeh and the Dheisheh Camps, scattered throughout the town of Jesus' birth. All are densely populated with nowhere to expand but up. Most homes are multi-story affairs, with the eldest son typically laying claim to the next layer of construction. Aida's five thousand five hundred residents are crowded cheek-to-jowl in cinderblock high-rises built by their owners on twenty-five acres of land tucked between Rachel's Tomb on the east and Israel's looming Separation Wall, built to hug the camp's northern and western boundaries.

Like every other Aida resident, Mohammed is the descendant of refugees forced to abandon their original homes in the rolling hill country that stretches from Jerusalem south to Hebron. Their exodus was only one of the many turbulent streams of human suffering that eventually merged into the swelling river of refugees fleeing before Zionist military units in 1947–49. Whereas, Zionist leaders described these events as their War for Independence, the surviving Palestinians called it al-Nakba—Arabic for The Catastrophe.

Mohammed's grandparents had grabbed their children and ran for their lives with nothing more than the clothes on their backs and whatever else they could carry, hoping to escape the advancing Jewish army. The invading soldiers occupied and confiscated Palestinian homes, public buildings, farmlands, orchards, vineyards, businesses and everything else the local people were forced to leave behind, often at a moment's notice. Between four hundred to five hundred villages were wiped off the map by Israeli soldiers.[4] By the end of the war in 1949, at least three quarters of a

---

Israel regularly resorts to the illegal use of military force against Palestinians. They also concluded that soldiers regularly aim for the head or face, a fact confirmed by years of Palestinian experience.

3. See "Doctors Urge Rubber Bullet Ban."

4. Morris, *Birth*, 342, first established the number of four hundred destroyed villages; subsequent investigations suggest a higher number. Pappé, *Forgotten Palestinians*, 19, puts the figure at five hundred; see Khalidi, *All That Remains*; Abu-Sitta, *Palestinian Nakba*. Extensive demographic information on the destroyed villages and their displaced residents, complete with maps, archival documents and oral histories are publicly available at Palestine Remembered (https://www.palestineremembered.com/), the *Palestine Land Society* (http://www.plands.org/en/home), and *The Nakba Files* (http://nakbafiles.org/). Morris has documented the extensive evidence from Zionist sources

million refugees were struggling to survive in makeshift tent cities throughout Lebanon, Syria, Jordan, the Gaza Strip, and the area known as the West
Bank. All of them were waiting for their chance to return home. They were
the fortunate survivors. Many Palestinian civilians were not so lucky.

Like every community center in a refugee camp, the Lajee Center (one
of several community centers that offer educational classes and sporting activities for young people) teaches the younger generation not to forget their
history or the suffering endured by their ancestors.[5] Such remembrances on
the part of the oppressed is not unusual. Jews worldwide rightly memorialize the Holocaust, and Israel's political DNA codes Holocaust memorial into
a justification of its Zionist ideology.

Mohammed contributes to the Lajee Center by offering classes in
photography and filmmaking so that future generations of Palestinian
photographers, journalists, and film-makers will continue to document life
under Israeli military occupation. His office is located on the second floor.
A large sliding glass door opens onto a small balcony overlooking one of the
camp's main streets. This street is also the main entry point for the Israeli
soldiers and military vehicles that frequently enter the camp unannounced,
wreaking havoc. I have photographed these incursions myself a number of
times, watching Israeli soldiers fire indiscriminately into the neighborhood.
Generally, no explanations are given. Certainly, nothing is communicated
to camp residents. Public statements may say something about Palestinian
violence, but I have never seen any provocation for these violent intrusions.

On the morning of April 8, 2013, Mohammed happened to be working for the Palestine News Network when another band of Israeli soldiers
walked into the Aida camp, automatic weapons at their shoulders, announcing their arrival by firing tear gas and rubber bullets into the vacant streets
and alleyways. Mohammed picked up his new Canon 600D with a 50–250
mm zoom lens, opened the sliding glass door, and stepped onto the balcony
to photograph whatever would unfold.

---

showing that both the Palestinian population transfer and the destruction of Palestinian villages were deliberate strategies and not merely the "accidents" of war; see *Birth*,
39–64, 313–17, 344–60; on the earliest stages of confiscating abandoned Palestinian
lands, including their resettlement with Jewish immigrants, see 360–413; for the common figure of seven hundred fifty thousand refugees, see 589. Morris, a Jewish-Israeli
historian living in Israel, concludes that "(population) transfer was inevitable and in-
built into Zionism" (*Birth*, 60).

5. *Lajee* is the Arabic word for refugee. The reader can find the center's home page
at http://lajee.org/. For information on the history and composition of Aida Refugee
Camp, see https://www.unrwa.org/where-we-work/west-bank/aida-camp and https://
en.wikipedia.org/wiki/Aida_Camp.

The balcony where Mohammed was standing when he was shot in the face by an
Israeli soldier. Photo by the author.

Israeli soldiers ordering Mohammed to go back inside.
Photo by Mohammed al-Azzeh.

The new year in the Aida camp had begun tragically. January and February saw funeral processions carrying the bodies of three boys (ages twelve, fifteen, and sixteen) shot and killed by Israeli soldiers (possibly these soldiers) on that very street.[6] All three were targeted by Israeli soldiers with live ammunition and *safer* rubber bullets. One was killed by a bullet which pierced his chest; the others with bullets to their heads. None of the boys were holding a weapon, unless you count the boy who may have thrown a rock.

6. Greenberg, "Fatal Shootings"; Purkiss, "Teenager Shot"; Sherwood, "Palestinian Deaths"; Toogood, "Two Youths."

**Israeli soldier shooting down the street in Aida Refugee Camp.
Photo by Mohammed al-Azzeh.**

One of the soldiers approached Mohammed standing some thirty-five feet away at ground level. He aimed his rifle and shouted to Mohammed (rather ironically) to "go home."

Mohammed asked, "Why? I am only taking pictures."

Now more soldiers started shouting to Mohammed, "Go inside! Go inside!"

Mohammed replied, "No, I will not go. As you have a gun and shoot at children, I have a camera—and I'm taking pictures—I do nothing to you."

As the soldiers became more threatening, Mohammed finally stepped back into his office. When he turned to close the sliding door, a fortuitous movement that may have saved his life, the soldier closest to him fired. Mohammed's head felt as if it were exploding with fire. Crumpling to his knees, feeling like he would pass out while a warm trail of blood ran down his cheek and neck, Mohammed yelled for help. A friend in the Lajee Center ran upstairs and helped Mohammed struggle down the stairs and to the front door. They shouted to the soldiers that they were coming out, but repeatedly, as they tried to exit, the soldiers peppered the door with a volley of bullets, forcing the men to remain inside. This continued even as Mohammed's friend shouted, "Let us out! He is bleeding to death! You have killed him! You've killed him!"

Fortunately for them both, like most doors in Aida, the Lajee Center's entrance is an iron door that undoubtedly shielded them from further injury.

Eventually, after repeated cries for an ambulance, the soldiers allowed them to leave. Making their way to a neighbor who owned a car, Mohammed was rushed to the hospital where he immediately underwent one of many surgeries.

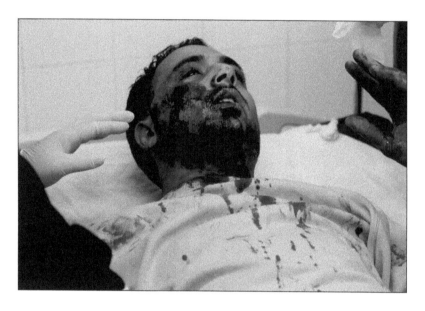

Mohammed laying in a hospital bed.
Photo courtesy of Mohammed al-Azzeh.

The story of a journalist shot in the face while doing his job received extensive coverage in both local and international news outlets. Perhaps the most poignant interview occurred when an Al Jazeera reporter spoke with Mohammed's mother as she sat beside her son's hospital bed, his swollen head heavily wrapped in thick white bandages. "My son was not violent," she said.

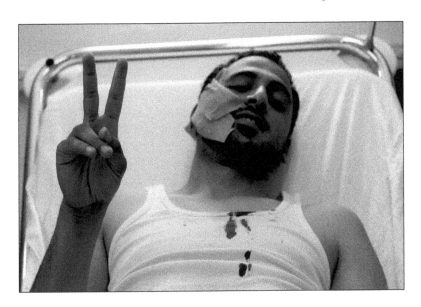

Mohammed bandaged waiting for the doctors.
Photo courtesy of Mohammed al-Azzeh.

"All he did was try and photograph the confrontations in the camp and this is what he gets in return? In the camp, we are birds. From time to time, they take a shot at us for practice."[7]

THE FACTS OF LIFE UNDER MILITARY RULE

Mohammed's story is not at all rare or unusual.[8] Just the opposite. The stories I share in this book are only a sampling of the many accounts that I have witnessed, heard, and recorded over the years, and there are many more

7. See Purkiss, "Shot, Hunted." I will continue with the next phase of Mohammed's story in chapter 11.

8. Though it is impossible to find exhaustive records on the numbers of Palestinians injured each year by Israeli soldiers, two good sources are: the *B'Tselem: Statistics* website, https://www.btselem.org/statistics; *B'Tselem* offers statistical reports on Palestinian fatalities, property destruction, detainees, prisoners, and travel restrictions in the Occupied Territories. A second resource is the statistics page created by *If Americans Knew* at https://ifamericansknew.org/. *If Americans Knew* compares Palestinian vs. Israeli injury rates demonstrating the excessive, disproportionate use a force applied by the Israeli army. Of course, government authorities always have an official explanation justifying these kinds of attacks. I am not suggesting that there is no such thing as a violent Palestinian or that soldiers are never attacked, but Western media coverage rarely, if ever, offers an honest description of the Palestinian situation.

beyond those I can attest to first hand. No Palestinian family in the West
Bank is immune to Israeli military action, especially those who live in one of
the nineteen registered refugee camps.[9] Many families have multiple stories
to tell; stories about night raids, home invasions, sleeping children pulled
from their beds and taken without a word, random searches (always without
a warrant or explanation), property destruction, homes demolished, tear
gas, bullet wounds, beaten faces, broken bones, endless waiting at army
checkpoints, unannounced road closures, land confiscation, arrest and imprisonment without charges, and of course death.

In Aida Camp, visits by Israeli soldiers regularly include bursts of gunfire using both live ammunition and rubber bullets, typically aimed at the
dozen or so adolescent boys who rally spontaneously to throw rocks and
harass the intruders. The soldiers fire dozens of tear gas canisters into the
narrow streets, onto the rooftops and the solitary playground that is often
filled with small children. I have watched a friend's home movie of children,
mothers, and grandmothers engulfed by an encroaching white fog as they
run from the soldiers pelting their swing sets and merry-go-round with tear
gas shells. Residents who forget to shut their windows not only find clouds
of tear gas billowing throughout their homes, but hot gas canisters bounc-
ing across the living room floor or ricocheting off the bedroom walls. In
2014, a forty-four-year-old Aida mother named Nuha Katamish died from
an asthma attack triggered by aggressive tear gassing. She had recently given
birth and was sitting in her own living room.[10]

9. According to the UNRWA (United Nation Relief and Works Agency) website, as
of December 31, 2016, there were 809,738 registered Palestinian refugees in the West
Bank. One quarter of them live in nineteen different refugee camps, with the rest living
in West Bank towns and villages; see https://www.unrwa.org/where-we-work/west-
bank. According to the Palestinian Authority's Population Registry, as of 2018 the total
Palestinian population in the West Bank was approximately three million; see Berger
and Koury, "How Many?"

10. For a more extensive description of Katamish's death and the frequent IDF attacks on the Aida refugee camp, see Al-Orzza and Hallowell, *Forced Population Transfer*, 25–28; Beiler, "Palestinians Mourn Woman"; Cohen and Khoury, "Palestinians";
"Israeli Tear Gas."

Israeli soldiers shooting tear gas and rubber bullets into Aida Refugee Camp, for no apparent reason. Photo by the author.

Soldiers shooting tear gas in the streets, without provocation. Photo by the author.

Firing tear gas into the narrow streets where children play. Photo by the author.

The source of these attacks is the adjacent military base located on the other side of the Annexation Wall. The IDF (Israeli "Defense" Forces) have their own private entrance to the camp through a massive, sliding steel barrier installed within the wall. I have watched it operate many times. In October 2015, an Israeli Jeep equipped with sizeable loudspeakers drove into the camp. Blaring through the loudspeakers, a soldier broadcast this message:[11]

> Inhabitants of Aida, we are the occupation's army. If you continue to throw stones, we will continue to shoot gas, until you die; the children, the adults, the elderly, the dying. Everything. We do not want to leave any of you alive. . . . We will shoot gas until you die: on your homes, on your families, brothers, sons, everything.

11. See Al-Orzza and Hallowell, *Forced Population Transfer*, 28. I have watched a video of this announcement filmed by an Aida resident at the time. Friends have also confirmed the translation from Arabic into English. The soldiers were also holding a young man captive and threatened his public execution in the camp.

The tall, sliding door in the background is a part of the Separation Barrier bordering Aida Refugee Camp. It serves as the IDF entrance for military vehicles and personnel, allowing soldiers to come and go as they please. Notice the tear gas and teenagers being shot at. Photo by the author.

Palestinian victims of Israeli violence simply do not have access to any effective legal means either to combat the abuse they experience or to seek legal restitution because they live under military rule. The vast majority are not citizens of any country.[12] They are a stateless people governed by Israeli military law; more specifically, they are "governed" by a version of the Defense (Emergency) Regulations of 1945.[13]

The Defense (Emergency) Regulations of 1945 were first adopted in September of that year by the British government then ruling over mandatory Palestine (from 1920 to 1948) under the auspices of the League of Nations. In response to the Arab Uprising of 1936–39 and the increasing levels of chaos created by Zionist terror-organizations attacking British targets,

12. Pappé, *Biggest Prison on Earth*, xxvi, 102. When Israel conquered the West Bank in 1967 (previously governed by Jordan), Israeli citizenship was offered only to Palestinian residents of East Jerusalem. Most of them rejected the offer for obvious reasons. All other Palestinians were excluded.

13. The full text of the Defense (Emergency) Regulations of 1945, as amended in 2011, is available at http://nolegalfrontiers.org/military-orders/milo29ed2.html?lang=en, and the Israeli-Palestinian Conflict Database at https://ecf.org.il/media_items/1472.

Palestinian citizens, and any Jew who refused to cooperate with their bloody methods, the British government imposed a form of military dictatorship over the entire population of Palestine.[14]

Naturally, Zionist leaders were justly critical of this imposition of military rule over their community, and they protested vigorously. In 1946, the Hebrew Lawyers Union declared that:[15]

> The powers given the ruling authority in the Emergency Regulations *deny the inhabitants of Palestine their basic human rights.* These regulations *undermine the foundations of law and justice* . . . they institute a regime of *arbitrariness without any judicial supervision.*

Similarly, Jacob (Ya'akov) Shimshon Shapira, who would eventually become Israel's first attorney general, wrote that:[16]

> The established order in Palestine since the Defence Regulations is *unparalleled in any civilized country. Even in Nazi Germany there were no such laws* . . . only in *an occupied country* do you find a system resembling ours. . . . It is our duty to tell the whole world that the Defence Regulations passed by the government in Palestine *destroy the very foundation of justice* in this land. It is a mere euphemism to call the military courts "courts." To use the Nazi title, they are no better than "Military Judicial Committees Advising the Generals." *No government has the right to draw up such laws.*

Another outspoken critic, Bernard Joseph (Dov Yosef), destined to become Israel's minister of justice, asked:[17]

14. On Zionism's widespread use of terrorism, not only in mandatory Palestine but throughout Europe, with extensive primary source documentation, see Suárez, *State of Terror*; also Morris, *Righteous Victims*, 147–48, 161, 171, 174, 179–81. The most active paramilitary (i.e., terrorist) groups were the Irgun and Lehi, also known as the Stern Gang. Menachem Begin was an important leader in the Lehi. He would go on to become Israel's prime minister from 1977 to 1983. Both the Irgun and Lehi were splinter groups that separated from the Haganah, the primary underground Jewish paramilitary organization. Yet, Suárez shows that the Haganah was not above using terrorist tactics themselves. During the Arab Revolt, Zionist paramilitary groups collaborated with the British by forming a "Colonial Police" which received British military training and then helped to attack Palestinians and destroy property. Within a decade, the Irgun and Lehi would turn around and use the same tactics against their British trainers; see Schoenman, *Hidden History*, 28–30.

15. Cited in Schoenman, *Hidden History*, 75 (emphasis mine).

16. *Ha-Praklit*, February 946, 58–66; cited in Suárez, *State of Terror*, 128 (emphasis mine).

17. Cited in Davis, *Apartheid Israel*, 128 (emphasis mine).

Are we all to become victims of *officially licensed terrorism?* . . .
In a country where *the administration itself inspires anger, resentment, and contempt for the laws,* one cannot expect respect for
the law. *It is too much to ask of a citizen to respect a law that
outlaws him.*

When the Zionist armies finally stood victorious over mandatory
Palestine, the Jewish people were liberated from the unjust British yoke
imposed by the Emergency Regulations.[18] But for the estimated one hundred sixty thousand Palestinians remaining in the land, British military rule
was simply replaced by Israeli military rule. On October 21, 1948, David
Ben-Gurion (the provisional Prime Minister and Minister of Defense) reaf-
firmed the British Emergency Regulations, which gave "unlimited control
to the military government over the Palestinian community."[19]

Consequently, for the next seventeen years, until 1966, Israel openly
maintained two separate legal systems applying two different sets of laws:
civil law for Jewish citizens and military law for Palestinians.[20] Jews went to
civil courts and stood before civil judges knowing that they had civil rights
and legal protections. Palestinians, on the other hand, continued living under the draconian military laws of the British Emergency Regulations—the
very same laws that Zionist leaders had previously condemned as unjust,
uncivilized, typical of an occupied people, "officially licensed terrorism,"
and unworthy of any citizen's respect. After 1966, when Israel declared the
military regime to be terminated, the Emergency Regulations covertly remained in place behind the scenes. Enforcement was merely shifted from
military personnel to the civilian police force and the General Security Service (GSS). The two-tiered system of legal inequalities remained in place.[21]

The Zionist "war for independence" never intended to found a *state
for Jews* as well as for others. Its sole purpose had always been the establishment of an exclusively *Jewish state* as we saw in chapter 3. There would be
no offer of an equal share of liberty and civil rights to the Palestinian people
still living in the newfound nation. The Zionist victory merely perpetuated
Palestinian oppression in areas almost entirely designated by the United
Nations as an Arab state. All Palestinians, simply by virtue of their being

18. Mandatory Palestine was the geopolitical area established between the years of
1920 and 1948 in Palestine under the terms of the Mandate for Palestine.

19. Pappé, *Forgotten Palestinians,* 49.

20. For detailed discussions of Israel's two separate legal systems and the various
ways in which it is used to exclude Palestinians from obtaining equal citizenship in
Israel, see Davis, *Apartheid Israel,* 94–108; White, *Palestinians in Israel,* 8–21.

21. Jiryis, *Democratic Freedoms,* 27–33, 43–45, 95; Bäuml, "Israel's Military Rule,"
123–27.

Palestinians, were viewed as enemies of the newly founded state.[22] Israel's Declaration of Independence, proclaimed on May 14, 1948, promised to "ensure complete equality of social and political rights to all its inhabitants," was but one more politically expedient document written with an eye to satisfying the United Nations and the rest of the international community.[23] Israel's High Court of Justice ruled in 1950 that the Declaration of Independence had no constitutional authority. In other words, it offered only the hollow promise of equality for Palestinians remaining in Israel. A decade later the Court further explained that the civil liberties promised in the Declaration of Independence were neither automatic nor universal but applicable only as determined by Israel's courts and legal system. In fact, the language of equal rights was included "primarily to make it possible for other countries to recognize Israel," particularly at the United Nations.[24] Palestinian lived experience has never reflected the noble aspirations proffered in the document, not least because the Declaration itself defines Israel as an exclusively Jewish state. After 1949, Israel's resident Palestinians continued to appear before military courts that applied military law which ensured that they had no guarantees to the civil rights or legal protections enjoyed by their Jewish neighbors.

A brief summary of only a few of the procedures justified by the Emergency Regulations will provide some insight into their punitive effects on Palestinian daily life within Israel.[25] Regulation number 109 allows the military governor to expel the entire population from any area he chooses. Number 110 permits the governor to place anyone under arrest and have them brought to a police station at any time without a warrant or explanation. Regulation number 111 permits "administrative detention," meaning that Palestinians can be arrested and held for an unlimited period of time

22. This attitude continues today, reappearing in the frequent warnings about "the demographic threat" posed to Israel by its growing Palestinian population; see Cook, *Blood and Religion*, 109–22; Pappé, *Ethnic Cleansing*, 248–56. The frenzied public discussions of comparative birth rates between Israel's Jews and Palestinians is remarkable. For only one example, see Gideon Levy's condemnation of this worry in "The Threat." Imagine the (very legitimate) uproar that would ensue if the US government began monitoring Jewish birth rates because it was worried about the dangers of "too many Jews."

23. For an English text of Israel's Declaration of Independence, see Laqueur and Rubin, *Israeli-Arab Reader*, 81–83; also https://mfa.gov.il/mfa/foreignpolicy/peace/guide/pages/declaration%20of%20establishment%20of%20state%20of%20israel.aspx.

24. Jiryis, *Democratic Freedoms*, 77.

25. See Pappé, *Forgotten*, 51–53; *Biggest Prison*, xviii–xix. For a more extensive summary of the many ways in which the Regulations are used to strip Palestinians of their rights to property, free speech, a free press, and freedom of movement, see Schoenman, *Hidden History*, 74–76.

without explanation or trial. Regulation number 125 allows the government to impose military rule over any piece of territory or real estate it chooses, declaring it closed to the (Palestinian) public. In October 1948 the newly formed Israeli Cabinet issued a new Emergency Regulation, called the Cultivation of Fallow Land Act, authorizing the Agricultural Minister to transfer all Palestinian lands abandoned during the war over to Jewish settlers. Thus, when the war was over, the surviving owners would return to their property only to discover that Israel had labelled them "absentees." During their absence, all "absentee property" had magically become Jewish property.[26]

The Israeli government exploited the people's instinct for self-preservation by confiscating their homes and fields while they were fleeing from the horrors of war. Such regulations sanctioned the ongoing confiscation of Palestinian lands and properties, wholesale population transfers, and the destruction of Palestinian villages long after the conclusion of the war in 1949.[27] Of the three hundred seventy new Jewish settlements created between 1948 and 1953, three hundred fifty of them were established on Palestinian-owned land seized by the government for Jewish development. By 1954, over one-third of Israel's Jews lived or worked on Palestinian absentee property.[28]

Even though the Emergency Regulations were ostensibly suspended (while covertly maintained) within Israel in 1966, they were publicly resurrected for the newly acquired Occupied Territories in June of 1967 after the Six Day War. The victorious Israeli forces found themselves occupying nearly six thousand square miles of new territory located in Gaza to the

26. Robinson, *Citizen Strangers*, 35–36. For an extensive description of the all-pervasive oppression of Palestinian Israelis created by the Emergency Defense Regulations see 29–67. Israel's extensive theft of Palestinian land by means of absentee property laws and the labeling of certain Palestinians as absentees, even as "present absentees," will be discussed in chapter 14.

27. Pappé, *Ethnic Cleansing*, 220. Pappé remarks that "as late as 1956" Israel's government Committee for Arab Affairs "seriously advocated plans for the expulsion of the 'Arabs' from Israel. Massive expulsions continued until 1953. The last village to be depopulated at gun point was Umm al-Faraj, near Nahariyya. The army went in, drove out all the inhabitants and then destroyed the village. The Bedouin in the Negev were subjected to expulsion up to 1962. . . . Had it not been for some liberal-minded Israeli politicians who objected to the schemes, and the Palestinian minority's own steadfastness . . . we would long ago have witnessed the ethnic cleansing of the 'remnant' of the Palestinian people now living within the borders of the Jewish state. . . . The appropriation of Palestinian lands by the government continued from the 1950s onwards under the auspices of the JNF [the Jewish National Fund]."

28. Robinson, *Citizen Strangers*, 47. The rightful owners were rarely, if ever, compensated for their loss.

southwest, the Golan Heights to the North, the eastern portion of Jerusalem (including the Old City), and the territory known as the West Bank, effectively extending the whole of Israel's eastern border to the Jordan River. All of this land, including its Palestinian population of 1.1 to 1.5 million people, had previously been excluded from the Jewish state by the 1949 Armistice Agreement that ended the Arab-Israeli war. However, during those six days of fighting, three hundred fifteen thousand (or more) Palestinians were made into refugees, many for the second time.[29] The Palestinian refugee crisis of 1947–49 dovetailed with these land seizures. This was no coincidence or accident, for the territorial and ethnic goals of political Zionism had never changed. Thus, Israel's military operations unfolded accordingly, using tactics very similar to the 1947–49 strategies of population transfer, home demolition, raising entire villages, and the expropriation of Palestinian land and resources. In time, the Palestinian people would describe the tragedies of the 1967 war as an-Naksa—Arabic for "The Setback."

The Israeli government had long been preparing for such an annexation. It had anticipated the occupation of the West Bank for many years. Already, in September 1948, David Ben-Gurion had urged the provisional Zionist government overseeing the war to launch an attack on the West Bank, thereby adding historic Judea and Samaria to the successive territorial gains extending far into the area originally designated for a Palestinian state by the UN partition plan.[30] Three and a half years before the outbreak of the Six Day War, in December 1963, General Chaim Herzog had already been appointed the West Bank's military governor.[31] His appointment as military governor was the result of organizational meetings held in Jerusalem the previous summer preparing for Israel's takeover of the West Bank and Gaza. The plan's code name was the Shacham Plan. Its official title was "The Organization of Military Rule in the Occupied Territories."[32] The imposition of the Defense (Emergency) Regulations of 1945 over these newly occupied regions was the plan's key component. The same unjust military rule that had governed the Palestinian community living inside of Israel was now imposed on the Palestinians living in Gaza, the Golan Heights and the West Bank.

No sooner had the Six Day War ended than the Jewish settlement of the West Bank commenced; first in East Jerusalem where Palestinians were expelled from portions of the Old City in order to make way for Jews; then

---

29. Pappé, *Biggest Prison*, 45.

30. From David Ben-Gurion, *War Diaries*, Sept. 26, 1948; cited in Flapan, *Birth of Israel*, 48.

31. Morris, *Righteous Victims*, 336–37; Segev, *1967*, 458.

32. Pappé, *Biggest Prison*, xiv–xv.

incrementally further and further into the West Bank itself. All of it at the expense of Palestinian families whose lands were taken from them for the development of new Jewish-only communities—all of which are illegal un-der international law as we saw in chapter 2. The Jewish settlers brought their Israeli citizenship, civil, and legal rights with them. They continued to be governed by Israel's civil laws despite the fact that they no longer lived in Israel. Only now the Palestinians were governed by military law in their own homeland. Only the Palestinians appeared in military courts to be judged by military officers for offenses only they could commit because they alone were now occupied. The old two-tiered legal system was back with a vengeance.

Benny Morris, professor emeritus of history at Ben-Gurion University and a staunch Zionist himself, describes the legacy of these military courts "as a dark age in the annals of Israel's judicial system."[33] Although Israeli authorities insisted that theirs was an "enlightened occupation," Morris de-scribes it as something "radically different. Like all occupations, Israel's was founded on brute force, repression and fear, collaboration and treachery, beatings and torture chambers, and daily intimidation, humiliation, and manipulation."[34] Ilan Pappé, another of the original New Historians, for-merly a history professor at the University of Haifa who now teaches at the University of Exeter, agrees. He describes the West Bank and Gaza as a vast, open-air "mega-prison" housing 1.5 million inmates.[35] As a man intimately familiar with his nation's history, Pappé explains that the official decisions undergirding the construction of this territorial prison were "the inevitable outcome of Zionist ideology and history . . . decisions [that] reflected the consensual Zionist interpretation of the past and present reality of Palestine as an exclusive Jewish State. . . . The only way of challenging the decision taken [in 1967] was by questioning the very validity of Zionism itself."[36]

THE MORE THINGS CHANGE, THE MORE THEY STAY THE SAME

Though many things have changed over the years in Israel's relationship with the West Bank, the suffocating authority of military rule has never been lifted. Mohammed, his family and every other Palestinian resident of the Occupied Territories are reminded every day of how quickly Israeli troops will resort to violence. Their attacks serve as a tactical reminder that

33. Morris, *Righteous Victims*, 341.
34. Morris, *Righteous Victims*, 341.
35. Pappé, *Biggest Prison*, xix, xxvii.
36. Pappé, *Biggest Prison*, xxi–xxii.

Palestinians have no control over their lives. Even when Israel appears to offer the Palestinians a measure of independence and self-determination, it proves to be another illusory act of kabuki theater. When it comes to the Palestinian people, Israel demonstrates again and again that it is unashamed to betray the very democratic principles it claims to espouse.

Three particular developments in the West Bank must be mentioned, however briefly, before we can conclude this chapter. These are (1) the West Bank's division into three zones of governance, (2) the rapid increase of Jewish-only settlements, and (3) Israel's construction of the "Separation Wall."

As a result of the Oslo II Peace Accords in 1995, the West Bank was divided into three different administrative regions, Areas A, B, and C.[37] Area A makes up 18 percent of the West Bank, centering on eight Palestinian cities such as Bethlehem and Ramallah, although East Jerusalem is not included. Area A was supposedly handed over to the complete control of the Palestinian Authority (known as the PA, the presiding Palestinian government in the West Bank).

Area B comprises 22 percent of the West Bank and is focused around four hundred forty of the smaller Palestinian villages. Here local governance is divided between the Palestinian Authority's responsibility for civil control and Israel's maintenance of military, security control.

Area C contains 61 percent of the West Bank, which includes all of the land surrounding Areas A and B. Areas A and B consist of small, isolated islands of real estate that make a map of the West Bank look like a kidney-shaped piece of Swiss cheese. Area C, on the other hand, has contiguous borders, which means that the people who live there—primarily Jewish settlers—are able to travel and visit one another without leaving Area C. Palestinians, on the other hand, living in the isolated islands that make up Areas A and B, must travel through Area C, with its military check points controlling Palestinian traffic, whenever they wish to visit another community. Area C encompasses all of Israel's Jewish-only settlement blocks in Palestinian territory, as well as the vast majority of the West Bank's natural resources and open, undeveloped land. A major portion of this open space consists of agricultural land belonging to Palestinian families now excluded from Area C and confined to Areas A and B.

---

37. For an introductory description of these territorial divisions, see https://en.wikipedia.org/wiki/West_Bank_Areas_in_the_Oslo_II_Accord; Frisch, "Knowing Your ABC." For a brief description of the division's negative effects on Palestinian development planning, see *B'tselem*'s web page at https://www.btselem.org/planning_and_building; for maps of the division boundaries, see https://www.researchgate.net/figure/Map-of-Areas-A-B-and-C-after-Oslo-II_fig1_276258691 and *Al Jazeera America*'s page at http://america.aljazeera.com/multimedia/2014/7/west-bank-security.html.

Despite the pretense of offering incremental self-rule to the Palestinian people, this tripartite subdivision of the West Bank has merely entrenched Israel's control under the guise of a peace process. For instance, the city of Bethlehem is squarely located in Area A where all security issues are supposedly handled by the Palestinian security forces. Yet, the Israeli army maintains an outpost on the city's border from which they regularly send armed units to invade, not only the city's three refugee camps, but the city itself. Armed soldiers man the numerous sniper-towers built into the Separation Wall that overlooks Bethlehem's northern boundary. I have already described the violent intrusions of Israeli soldiers into the Aida camp. Israel's draconian military rule continues throughout the whole of the West Bank in every Area, regardless of the Oslo Accord's diplomatic niceties.

The second development rapidly changing Palestinian life in the West Bank is the growth of Jewish-only settlements. An Israeli organization, *B'Tselem: The Israeli Information Center for Human Rights in the Occupied Territories*—winner of the 2018 Human Rights Prize of the French Republic—tracks Jewish settlements in the Palestinian territories. According to their research, by the end of 2017 there were more than two hundred Jewish-only settlements scattered throughout the West Bank, housing more than six hundred twenty thousand Israeli citizens building their homes (many with government funding and subsidies) on land expropriated (a fancy word for stolen) from Palestinians.[38] In December of 2018, Israel's government approved the construction of one thousand four hundred fifty-one new housing units in these West Bank settlements with another eight hundred thirty-seven units planned for the near future.[39] By early 2019 another four thousand four hundred sixteen new housing units were approved for construction within the Jerusalem municipality, with a large share of that growth occurring in East Jerusalem neighborhoods located on West Bank occupied land.[40]

B'Tselem's report on Israel's ongoing settlement of the West Bank concludes, "The settlements are the single most important factor in shaping life in the West Bank. Their destructive impact on the human rights of Palestinians extends far beyond the thousands of hectares, including farmland and grazing areas, that Israel appropriated from Palestinians in order to build them."[41]

38. See the extensive discussion of the growth of the settler movement and its effects on the Palestinian people at https://www.btselem.org/settlements; for various responses to *B'Tselem*'s winning of the Human Rights prize, see Harkov, "B'Tselem"; Levy, "Netanyahu."

39. Berger, "Israel Approves."

40. "Israel Approves More than 4,000 New Settlement Units."

41. One hectare equals approximately two and a half acres.

Another prominent feature of the settler movement's "destructive impact" on Palestinian lives appears in Israel's construction of an extensive network of Jewish-only roads connecting Jewish-only communities to one another and to Israel. This is yet another construction project that consumes more and more Palestinian land, while also separating more Palestinian villagers from their neighbors as well as from their historic agricultural properties. Meanwhile, Palestinian drivers are left to travel on less direct, narrow, more roundabout roads that are poorly maintained due to the Palestinian Authority's consistent lack of funds.[42]

The third important West Bank development has been the construction of Israel's four-hundred-forty-mile-long Separation Barrier, an obvious descendant of Jabotinsky's vision for an Iron Wall separating Zionist Israel from its Arab neighbors as we saw in chapter 3. Although the Wall/Barrier was begun in 2002 under the pretext of keeping Palestinian terrorists out of Israel, over 85 percent of the Barrier snakes its way far into the West Bank, extending well beyond Israel's eastern border known as the "Green Line," originally drawn to separate Israel from the West Bank after the Armistice Agreement in 1949.[43] If Israel's conquest of the West Bank after the Six Day War had erased the Green Line's political significance, then Israel's Separation Wall has erased its on-the-ground, territorial significance once and for all.

Following a serpentine course that squiggles its way far into the West Bank while swallowing up Jewish settlements and illegally annexing even more Palestinian land, the Separation Barrier (which I prefer to call the Annexation Wall) will leave the residents of some one hundred fifty Palestinian communities stranded, permanently cut off from their traditional farmlands. Thousands more will be trapped between the Green Line to the west and the Separation Wall to the east, with neither a home in Israel nor access to their family property beyond the Wall. If the Wall adheres to its originally proposed route, it will annex nearly 12 percent of the West Bank to the Israeli side of the Barrier.[44] During the final days of his 2019 reelection campaign, Prime Minister Benjamin Netanyahu promised that, should he be reelected (as he was), he would officially extend Israel's territorial sovereignty over all of the land now engulfed by the Separation Wall, all of the

42. Israel's government collects West Bank taxes on behalf of the PA, and then regularly refuses to hand the money over for distribution.

43. See B'Tselem's report on the Separation Barrier at https://www.btselem.org/separation_barrier.

44. For detailed reporting of the Wall's demographic effects, together with color-coded maps, see https://www.btselem.org/separation_barrier/statistics and https://www.btselem.org/download/separation_barrier_map_eng.pdf.

Jewish settlements on that land, and all settlements remaining beyond the Wall.[45] The controversy sparked by Netanyahu's pronouncement merely disguised the fact that Israel already exercises *de facto* control over 100 percent of the Occupied Territories.

We can see that the historic problems of land theft, discrimination, segregation, military threats, denial of ownership, and home demolitions all continue to play a vital role in twenty-first-century Zionism's determined pursuit of Israel's nationalistic goals within the Occupied Territories: acquire more land for Israel by hook or by crook, with as few Palestinians remaining as possible.

When I sit with Palestinian friends in Aida, enjoying the cool night air, talking at the kitchen table as we share another pot of tar black, Arabic coffee, finely ground with a sprinkling of cardamom seeds, I sometimes ask how they manage to remain hopeful in the midst of their seemingly hopeless circumstances. Without exception, these descendants of Palestinian refugees that I have come to know and love are the most hospitable, generous people imaginable. Even as more and more are taken from them, they remain sacrificial in their kindness to outsiders.

The last time I asked my question, I was met with teary eyes and a soft, low voice. "What else can we do but hope?" I was told. "If we give up hope, we have nothing but despair."

45. Sales, "Netanyahu's Promise."

Chapter 6

Making the Right Assumptions

Immersing oneself in Christian Zionist literature, especially works that focus on Zionist biblical interpretation, may engender a nagging sense of futility in non-Zionist readers. Studying books on this topic, the same shopworn arguments are paraded out again and again. I suspect that Christian Zionist writers likely feel similarly when they encounter their critics. It is not surprising that each side in this debate is firmly entrenched in its own assumptions and biblical interpretations. The back-and-forth argumentation suggests an intractable exegetical and political debate with both sides deeply entrenched.[1]

What is less common in the biblical debates in this literature is an analysis of the foundational, interpretive and theological assumptions that undergird the way Christian Zionists read the Bible.[2] That is what this chapter will undertake.

1. Exegesis is the process of explaining what a text means. I agree with those Christian Zionists who insist that biblical interpretation begins by using the grammatical-historical method. That is, understanding the original language, literary genre, and historical context are fundamental requirements for understanding an ancient text like the Bible properly. As I will explain, however, I disagree with Christian Zionists in the way that they use the grammatical-historical method to constrain the possibilities of how the New Testament writers were able to use the Old.

2. Hermeneutics is the theory of interpretation that one applies to the work of exegesis. It concerns both the most appropriate methods for understanding the ancient

Every human being is a living, breathing bundle of assumptions, conscious and unconscious, stated and unstated. We are influenced and molded by our environment, upbringing, and life history. By the time we reach maturity, each human psyche finds itself configured by a laundry list of beliefs, convictions, and prejudices that help us conform us to the society in which we live while also helping us to distinguish ourselves as individuals. Consciously or not, these inherited presuppositions guide our lives and choices. None of us can eliminate all of our cultural conditioning, nor would we want to. The best we can manage is work to become as self-aware as possible, identifying our assumptions and testing them, working to change them if we come to recognize that they are false, unhelpful, or destructive.

Of course, not all assumptions need to be changed. Appropriate, warranted assumptions are not only beneficial but absolutely essential to a well-lived life.[3] They help to align us with the way things are. For example, each morning I wake up and crawl out of bed assuming that my wife loves me. That assumption is based on forty-plus years of marital experience. If my wife becomes cross with me, I interpret her reprimand in light of my basic assumption that she loves me and has my best interests at heart. This is a warranted assumption that helps my life be ordered in a way fitting both reality and experience.

On the other hand, inappropriate, unwarranted assumptions can be damaging because, in one way or another, they distort both the individuality and the sociability that God intends for our lives.[4] For example, if I assumed that all non-Caucasians are inherently inferior to white people, I would be harboring an unwarranted, racist assumption about other human beings who are all created in the image of God. It is both costly and damaging to maintain such prejudices. Racists miss out on celebrating the splendor of a multiracial, multiethnic humanity. The unwarranted beliefs that fuel prejudice alienate and harm other divine image bearers. Our history shows that such beliefs were and are used to justify violence against

---

biblical text, as well as the theory of application that derives contemporary, practical significance from the meaning of that ancient text. Good examples of non-Zionist Biblical interpretation—with variations among themselves—may be found in Davies, *Gospel*; Wright, *Climax*; Brueggemann, *Land*; and three important books by Burge: *Jesus and the Land*; *Who Are God's People?*; *Whose Land? Whose Promise?*

3. A warranted claim or assumption is one that is supported by evidence.

4. An unwarranted claim or assumption is one that lacks evidence and is, therefore, illegitimate. I have learned the most about my own unwarranted life assumptions by talking with people trained in the field of cognitive behavioral therapy. I suggest investigating this field of psychology to learn more about the role of warranted and unwarranted assumptions in our lives. The way we read the Bible cannot be separated from the way we shuffle through this maze called life.

other people. When these assumptions infect the church, they shatter fellowship, and those clinging to them fail in showing mercy and grace, to the detriment of many. Illegitimate assumptions are not just misguided, they are often destructive.

POSITIVE OUTCOMES AND THEIR MISUSE: RESISTING ANTI-SEMITISM

Zionists interpreters regularly highlight the ever-present danger of anti-semitism. This is, perhaps, the most important contribution that Christian Zionism offers to the contemporary, evangelical-fundamentalist church. Sadly, not only is this particular brand of racism a continuing problem in American society, but during Donald Trump's tenure as president we have seen an upsurge in antisemitic incidents around the world.[5] Writers such H. Wayne House and Craig Blaising provide an important service to the entire church by reminding us of the sordid, shameful periods of history when Christians led the way in attacks against the Jews, vilifying them as "Christ-killers."[6]

Unfortunately, the value of these important convictions against antisemitism are often overshadowed by the ways Christian Zionists repeat fallacious redefinitions of antisemitism proclaimed by Israeli propaganda in the service of political Zionism. A good example of this problem appears in the title of Barry Horner's book, *Future Israel: Why Christian Anti-Judaism Must Be Changed*. Horner's work embodies the political ideology and the rhetorical strategy used by political Zionism. The public relations mission of such propaganda is to convince the world that Israel remains a perpetual victim.[7] Horner thus confuses the nation of Israel with the whole

---

5. For example, see the report from *Human Rights Watch* on the growth of antisemitism throughout Europe, Cossé, "Alarming"; also Roache, "Surge."

6. House, "Church's Appropriation," 77–110; Blaising, "Theology of Israel and the Church," 85–100.

7. See Burg, *Holocaust Is Over*. Burg is an Israeli businessman and politician who was the first Speaker of the Israeli Knesset born in Israeli territory after the 1948 war. His book is a moving expose about the damaging social consequences of Israel's collective Holocaust remembrance. He laments the various ways in which Israel's memorializing of the Holocaust has "resulted in perpetual hysteria. . . . Propaganda tells us that we await total destruction or salvation, with nothing in between" (56). "Israeli victimology prospers. . . . We must always feel like perpetual victims and must always sacrifice to avoid responsibility for the reality that we face" (128). Shlomo Sand, history professor at the University of Tel Aviv, offers a similarly mournful confessional and social critique in his book, *How I Stopped Being a Jew*. He laments the rise of "the Holocaust industry" with its institutionalized control over "the specificity, exclusiveness, and total

of Judaism. Such writing, secure in its unwarranted presuppositions, then goes on the offensive accusing anyone who criticizes Israel, particularly in its treatment of Palestinians, of being an antisemite. Mitch Glaser, a professor at Talbot School of Theology, is especially adamant in this regard in his article, "The Dangers of Supersessionism," where he repeatedly accuses anti-Zionists who criticize Israeli policies of fomenting (whether explicitly or implicitly) antisemitism within the church.[8] Professor Glaser and others never seem to consider alternatives in decrying antisemitism. For instance, much more could be done to combat antisemitism if Zionist writers corrected their own erroneous conflation of Judaism with the state of Israel and instead educated the Christian church, clarifying the differences between Jews, Judaism, and Zionism. What Christian Zionists must do is come to terms with the reality that the secular state of Israel deserves criticism for its systematic, long-term mistreatment of the Palestinian people. Calling out such abuses is not antisemitic but is being faithful to a vision of biblical justice.

When those who defend Israel, at all cost, equate Israel with all Jews and Judaism they are making a logical error, specifically, a *category mistake*. In this case, items from one category (the ethnic/religious categories of Jewishness and/or Judaism) are lifted out and placed into a completely different category (the political nation-state category of Israel) as if they were perfectly interchangeable. They are not. World Jewry and Israel are not interchangeable, as the many anti-Zionist Jews in this world will loudly tell you.[9] The pro-Israel lobbyists in the United States invoke this form of verbal hocus-pocus in their partisan efforts to silence Israel's political critics. Horner's book—and a great deal of other Christian Zionist writings—are guilty of such category confusion, often wedded to a schismatic, fundamentalist agenda. The implication that Horner and other Christian

---

national ownership of suffering . . . with the objective of maximizing the painful past in order to accumulate capital" (62). For more on this important subject, see Finkelstein, *Holocaust Industry*.

8. See Glaser, "Dangers," where he says that Christian anti-Zionism "gives Christians a negative view of the Jewish people and provokes anger toward Israel" (114); it has "charged the evangelical Christian atmosphere with a negative view toward Israel that has spilled over to the Jewish people as a whole" (115); Christian anti-Zionism can "lead to presenting Israel and the Jewish people in a fiercely negative light" (116).

9. For only a few examples of anti-Zionist Jews, both secular and religious, see Rabkin, *Threat from Within*, as well as the anti-occupation organizations *Jewish Voice for Peace*, and the religiously orthodox, Haredi groups like Neturei Karta and Satmar Hasidism; see Ravitzky, "Ultra-orthodox."

Zionist authors infer is that non-Zionist theologies that critique this brand of Christian Zionism are also, by definition, antisemitic.[10]

We will return to a deeper study of such Zionist thinkers (in both their Jewish and Christian expressions) and their accusations of antisemitism later in the book. It is worth noting for now that Christian Zionism is deeply embedded in the apologetic agenda of Israel's powerful political Zionist ideology. Whereas Jesus insists that his "kingdom is not of this world" (John 18:36), Christian Zionism continues to forge a theological apologetic for political Zionism's ultra-nationalism.[11]

SUPERSESSIONISM AND THE ENDURING SIGNIFICANCE OF THE ABRAHAMIC COVENANT

Another positive contribution offered by Christian Zionist thought has been its focus on the enduring significance of Paul's teaching about the Abrahamic covenant, including the importance of Israel in Romans 9–11, a text which many, including myself, understand as the climax of the book. Historically, supersessionist theology (see the discussion below) often claimed that God had rejected Israel as punishment for the nation's rejection of Christ. Consequently, all of God's covenantal promises have been transferred from the Jews to the gentile church. Michael Vlach's point that supersessionists believe that "national Israel has somehow completed or forfeited its status" as God's people is an apt description of what far too many Christians have believed.[12] Wayne House also laments (quite rightly) the ways in which supersessionist thinking has sometimes nurtured Christian antisemitism. "Gradually the church turned hostile to the Jewish people and . . . the church began to reject Jewishness itself as well as the Jew."[13] Thus, highlighting Paul's explanation in Romans 11:11–32 about *the temporary nature of Israel's hard-heartedness toward the gospel is a valuable emphasis*

---

10. For example, see Horner, *Future Israel*, 3: non-Zionists are described as holding "to an *anti-Judaic* belief denying that modern Israel has any eschatological future in *national* and *territorial* terms" (emphasis mine); furthermore, any type of non-Zionism amounts "to the same basic *denigration of the Jews* and ultimately of national Israel" (emphasis mine).

11. Before anyone accuses me of suggesting that the kingdom of God is only "spiritual" or "other-worldly" with no practical relevance to real-world politics, I encourage you to read my book *I Pledge Allegiance*, as well as Yoder, *Politics of Jesus* and *The Priestly Kingdom*.

12. Vlach, *Church*, 27.

13. House, *Church's Appropriation*, 103.

provided by Christian Zionism to the entire church, offering a much-needed antidote to the temptations of Christian antisemitism.[14]

Romans 9–11 powerfully addresses (and corrects) the ancient Christian tendency to write the Jewish people out of salvation history. This theology has been labelled either *supersessionism* or *replacement theology* because it maintains that the (gentile) Christian church has replaced or superseded the Jews as God's covenant partner. After providing a theological rationale for why the good news of Jesus' Messiahship has found a more ready acceptance among gentiles than among Jews, Paul reminds gentile believers in the Roman church "not to be conceited: Israel has experienced a hardening in part until the full number of the gentiles has come. And so all Israel will be saved" (Rom 11:25–26 NIV). This is not the place to wrestle our way through the various, competing interpretations of these three chapters and their importance to the rest of Paul's Roman letter.[15] It is enough for our purposes simply to note Paul's affirmation of the continuing significance of God's covenant with Abraham. To boastful gentile Christians imagining that they now have the upper hand over the Jews, Paul insists that the Jews "are [still] loved on account of the patriarchs, for God's gifts and his call are irrevocable" (Rom 11:28–29 NIV). The apostle to the gentiles maintains that the Father of our Lord Jesus Christ has not forgotten his ancient, covenant commitment to the descendants of Abraham, Isaac, and Jacob. We may wish that the apostle had provided a more detailed, elaborate explanation of what he meant by this statement—I certainly wish he had—but one thing is clear: no one should proclaim that God has closed the door on the Jews and moved on to care only for an exclusively gentile church.

Christian Zionism understands this important point. To their minds, supersessionism is Enemy Number One, posing a dangerous doctrinal trap for the evangelical community. A recent book on the subject, *Israel, the Church and the Middle East: A Biblical Response to the Current Conflict* explains that its purpose is to "challenge the Supersessionist drift of the modern Church."[16] One contributor warns that "Supersessionism is on the rise today and capturing a new generation of adherents," as if supersessionism were the latest version of the false gospel excoriated by Paul in his Letter to the Galatians (1:6–9).[17] If the term supersessionism is meant to refer specifically to *ethnic* replacement, then this is a much needed warning.

14. See Hoehner's exposition in "Israel in Romans 9–11," 145–67; also see Saucy, *Progressive Dispensationalism*, 246–63.

15. A useful introduction to this debate is Compton and Naselli, *Three Views*; I also recommend Wright, *Climax*, 231–57.

16. Bock and Glaser, "Introduction," 12.

17. Glaser, "Dangers," 101.

But it can also become the problem. When Christian Zionists define their supersessionist enemy they typically confuse a variety of different perspectives as if they were identical and all equally supersessionist. Yet, many of their targets insist that they are not supersessionists at all. A few examples will illustrate the point. Gerald McDermott, a professor emeritus at Beeson Divinity School, describes supersessionists as believing "the Church has replaced the Jews as the inheritors of all the biblical promises concerning Israel."[18] Note McDermott's emphasis on ethnic replacement. Craig Blaising, professor at Southwestern Baptist Theological Seminary, repeats McDermott's definition, categorizing it as "ethnic supersessionism" in which God is believed permanently to have rejected the entire Jewish race in order to ensure that "the church . . . is a Gentile reality."[19] H. Wayne House shifts his supersessionist focus from ethnicity to nationhood (without clarifying what he means by "nation") when he describes replacement theology as the belief that "the church has replaced national Israel as the recipient of God's blessings . . . [because] the church has fulfilled the terms of the covenants given to Israel, which they rejected."[20] House's reference to "national Israel" rather than "the Jews" signals the centrality of Israeli-Jewish *nationalism* in Christian Zionist theology. Not only do Christian Zionists (rightly) oppose the idea of ethnic Jewish rejection; they (mistakenly) insist that God's faithfulness to the Jews must include a restored, Jewish nation-state in Palestine.

Throughout church history, there have been voices that espoused a racial form of supersessionism, claiming that God has forever withdrawn his grace from the Jewish people, making way for an exclusively gentile church.[21] Such racist supersessionism is, indeed, a form of theological antisemitism that raises its ugly head nowadays only among the most marginal,

18. McDermott, *Israel Matters*, 2.

19. Blaising, "Theology of Israel," 86. Many of these definitions depend on the work of R. Kendall Soulen who distinguished three forms of supersessionist thinking: economic supersessionism, punitive supersessionism, and structural supersessionism; see Soulen's work, *God of Israel*, 29–31. Blaising says that ethnic supersessionism is his rebranding of Soulen's punitive supersessionism. Also see Vlach, *Church*, 17–39, as well as his more popular treatment of the subject in *Has the Church Replaced Israel?*, 9–17.

20. House, "Church's Appropriation," 78. Remember that not all nations define themselves ethnically, and many citizens of Israel today are not Jews. Strictly speaking, a "nation" is a "self-differentiating ethnic group"; see Connor, *Ethnonationalism*, 40. However, nation is often confused with "state" in common usage even though they are different things. Connor, *Ethnonationalism*, 40, defines a state as a social group sharing a common territory "organized under common political institutions." Unfortunately, the two words are regularly confused; see Connor's section on "Terminological Confusion," 90–117. It is not always clear which concept is intended when Christian Zionist literature uses the word nation.

21. See McDermott, "History of Supersessionism," 33–44.

extremist, right-wing sects. However, when alluding to the role ethnic su-persessionism has played in church history, Christian Zionists commonly gather up *all* anti/non-Zionist views building a case of guilt by association, painting any and all supersessionism as racists. *Voila!* A crucial shift has taken place, yet many readers will not detect this sleight of hand. The legitimate theological questions surrounding supersessionism and Zionism have been eclipsed by spurious moral questions about antisemitism.[22]

Benjamin Merkle, a professor at Southern Baptist Theological Seminary, provides a good example of a non-Zionist writer attempting to help the conversation move forward by clarifying the issues at stake:[23]

> My view is *not* a form of replacement theology. The church does not *replace* Israel. Rather, God *incorporates* the church into his people through their union with Christ. Replacement theology states that one group is out (Jews) and another is in (Gentiles/ the church). My view is that both groups can be in if they believe in Christ.

Still, too many Christian Zionist writers proceed without making the slightest effort to acknowledge the valuable nuances offered by writers like Merkle. In fact, Horner goes so far as to explicitly reject all such distinctions outright. He insists:[24]

> Whatever the terminology that is used concerning this perspective, whether replacement theology, supercessionism, fulfillment theology, transference theology, or absorptionism, they all amount to the same basic denigration of the Jews and ultimately of national Israel.

The bulk of Christian Zionists, like Horner, reason by painting everything in black and white, arguing that if you question secular Israel, you denigrate Jews and Judaism.[25] Everyone is either a Christian Zionist or an

---

22. Reader beware. My Christian Zionist critics will try to dismiss this point by insisting that theology cannot be separated from its moral implications. I wholeheartedly agree. But that is not the issue here. I am not ignoring theology's moral value. I am pointing out the immorality of slandering others with accusations of antisemitism through sloppy thinking and scurrilous innuendo.

23. Merkle, "Typological Non-Future-Mass Conversion," 205.

24. Horner, *Future Israel*, 3.

25. Rydelnik also insists that, regardless of the label, whether it is called replacement, expansion, or fulfilment theology, it all boils down to "the basic categories of supersessionism"; see his essay, "Hermeneutics," 70. Similarly, Blaising notes, as a representative of the so-called "New" Christian Zionism, without a hint of dissention, that "it should not be surprising that economic supersessionism has been criticized as anti-Semitic"; see "Theology of Israel," 87; recall Soulen's three different categories

antisemite, whether they realize it or not. I am reminded of my father's fundamentalist belief that everyone in the church was either a dispensationalist or a liberal.

THE FOUNDATIONAL ASSUMPTION: LITERALISTIC INTERPRETATION

Christian Zionism stands or falls with its dogged insistence on an exclusively literalistic interpretation of the Bible.[26] In pursuit of this literalist meaning, Christian Zionists use fairly standard grammatical and historical methods of interpretation, that is, a proper grasp of the texts' original languages is undertaken along with a study of the original historical settings. Most responsible interpreters do the same. Such linguistic and historical study of a text is meant to lead readers to grasp how a given text's original recipients would have understood it for themselves. Simple common sense has an important role to play in this process, ensuring that the words of the Bible "are allowed to stand according to their plain and obvious sense."[27] The literal, "common sense understanding" becomes the only acceptable understanding.[28] Michael Vlach is typical when he insists that "Old Testament texts, as understood within their historical-grammatical contexts, must be the starting point for understanding God's plans for national Israel."[29] This

---

of supersessionism discussed in note 20. Larsen describes supersessionism as "a view that has regrettably fueled anti-Semitism across the centuries" after collapsing ethnic supersessionism into a generalized supersessionism, see "Celebration," 307.

26. Sizer, *Christian Zionism*, 108–23, offers a helpful survey of the Zionist insistence on literalistic interpretation.

27. Horner, *Future Israel*, 187. For a defense of the grammatical-historical method and the recovery of authorial intent, see Vlach, *Church*, 185–88; Blaising, "Israel and Hermeneutics," 154–55.

28. Larsen, "Celebration," 308.

29. Vlach, *Church*, 124; also see Vlach's responses to his debate partners in Compton and Naselli, *Three Views*, 22, 146–47, 213–15. Similarly, Bock writes, "Nothing in what lies ahead has been altered from what the OT declared . . . we never lose what God committed himself to do in the teachings of the OT"; see "Biblical Reconciliation," 171. See also the writings of John Feinberg and Charles Rylie who are key voices in Christian Zionist theology. Vlach authoritatively quotes from Feinberg's essay, "Systems of Discontinuity," saying, "If an OT prophecy is made unconditionally to a given people and is still unfulfilled to them even in the NT era, then the prophecy must still be fulfilled to them . . . Progress of revelation cannot cancel unconditional promises" (76). One of the several unexamined hermeneutical assumptions here, aside from the insistence on literalism, is the presumption that one part of the biblical canon is not allowed to place conditions on another part of the canon, such that the promises are not truly unconditional after all.

likewise pertains to the prophetic passages regarding Israel and the land; only a strict literalism will do.

Some examples will help to clarify the centrality of literal interpretation for creating the Christian Zionist vision of both contemporary history and the future. Darrell Bock, a professor at Dallas Theological Seminary, provides a characteristically literal reading of Old Testament prophecy when he explains the future significance of Isaiah 2:2–4.[30] The prophet writes:

> In the last days
> the mountain of the Lord's temple will be established
> as chief among the mountains;
> it will be raised above the hills,
>   and all nations will stream to it.
> Many peoples will come and say,
> "Come, let us go up to the mountain of the Lord,
>   to the house of the God of Jacob.
> He will teach us his ways,
>   so that we may walk in his paths."
> The law will go out from Zion,
>   the word of the Lord from Jerusalem.
> He will judge between the nations
>   And settle disputes for many peoples. (Isa 2:2–4 NIV)

On the basis of this text, Bock describes a future where all the nations of the world will live in peace as they flock to the reconstructed temple in Jerusalem in order to worship Yahweh, the one, true God and the father of the Lord Jesus Christ. The truth of God's holy scriptures will be universally recognized, and all people everywhere will look to the nation of Israel for instruction in how to live lives pleasing to God. Bock insists, "Literally, the Torah will go out from there. Torah in this context is about God's will and ways . . . Cases will be settled among nations there . . . The picture is of world peace . . . This reconciliation to peace involves all the nations and Israel is at its center."[31]

Mark Saucy, a professor at Talbot School of Theology, offers another example of such literalistic interpretation of the prophet Isaiah in his

30. Bock, "Biblical Reconciliation," 177–78.

31. Bock, "Biblical Reconciliation," 177. McDermott concurs, saying that God wants "to impress" the world through the manner of Israel's national redemption. He further insists that "God deals with the nations *through* Israel (emphasis original). In their relationship to Israel, the nations in some mysterious way come into contact with the God of Israel. They respond to God and are judged by God in this *secret relationship*" (emphasis mine); see McDermott, "History of Supersessionism," and "Implications and Propositions," 44, 328.

contribution to the book *The People, the Land and the Future of Israel.* Isaiah 49:6 says, "I will also make you [Israel] a light for the Gentiles, that you may bring my salvation to the ends of the earth." Saucy explains this text as describing how all the people of Israel will one day turn to Jesus as their Messiah, at which point "the nation of Israel [is given] a mission as a light to the nations to bring them deliverance (Isa 49:6). Under the patronage of Messiah, Israel would fulfill this mission from a position of *cultural supremacy*."[32] In other words, the world will eventually come to universal faith in Jesus Christ by observing the overwhelming, irresistible "cultural supremacy" of an Israeli Utopia where perfect justice, mercy, righteousness, and international human community are all miraculously achieved in literal fulfilment of Old Testament prediction. It is not difficult to see that a good deal of Christian Zionism's adulation for the state of Israel draws from their belief that today's Israel is tomorrow's Utopia *in nuce.*

Christian Zionists' single-minded, biblical literalism excludes from the outset any possibility that a New Testament author might reinterpret an Old Testament promise in such a way as to alter its literalistic fulfilment. Zionist writers simply state that "the New Testament [never] reinterprets or changes the original meaning of Old Testament texts, especially those that address eschatological issues regarding Israel."[33] Yet, we have already examined several passages (see chapter 1) where such reinterpretations take place. Zionists, however, tend to ignore such discussions. Some have tried to legitimize their position by concocting a new theological principle, that of *antecedent theology.* Although interpreters through the ages know nothing about this "principle" of antecedent theology, Zionists use it to claim that "the Old Testament needs to guide the understanding of the New Testament, and not vice versa."[34] In other words, the Bible can only be read literalistically from front to back.

But Zionists have a problem here. In enacting a principle which denies that the Bible should ever be reread from back to front, they have to ignore or explain away the many occasions where New Testament writers do just that, rereading the Old Testament in retrospect, and reapplying God's promises in non-literal ways that the original audiences could never have imagined.[35] Reliance upon "antecedent theology" is actually a clear instance where a baseless assumption, one that ignores pertinent evidence, is imposed upon

32. Saucy, "Israel as a Necessary Theme," 178 (emphasis mine).

33. Valch, *Church,* 123; also 185–87.

34. Rydelink, "Hermeneutics of the Conflict," 71.

35. For two classic works exploring this phenomenon, see Ellis, *Paul's Use of the Old Testament*; Juel, *Messianic Exegesis.*

the biblical text in order to uphold a closely held ideological conviction. This leads otherwise capable scholars to offer specious proof-texts that mislead the unwary reader. This sort of failure to entertain contrary evidence is something we may expect in the realm of political propaganda, but it is very disappointing when cutting corners on clarity and evidence drifts into the work of biblical scholarship.

THE DANGERS OF COGNITIVE BIAS

Detecting the assumptions of others is always a tenuous affair. Not that it is impossible. Returning to an earlier example, if someone consistently refers to other ethnic groups in demeaning, disparaging terms, then it is safe to assume that you are dealing with a racist. Rarely will a racist identify themselves as such. The evidence of their behavior, though, is sufficient to detect their assumptions. Sometimes you can judge a book by its cover.

However, it is also easy to get things wrong. All of us are prone to making skewed judgments about the assumptions of others because of something philosophers like to call cognitive bias. For our purposes it is enough to understand that cognitive bias is the tendency to assume that other people think about issues in the same way that we do. Human beings naturally gravitate toward groups that hold important beliefs in common. We gravitate toward people who generally reason the way we do, who share our perspectives on life. In time, subconsciously perhaps, we tend to assume that all rational people think the way we do.

Have you ever been in conversation with someone you just met at church, or the Kiwanis club, or a local volunteer organization who quickly began a political monologue assuming you wholeheartedly agree with them? How do you break into the conversation to disabuse them of that bias? I confess that I sometimes enjoy the disillusioned facial expressions that appear when I burst their bubble. This new friend was displaying *cognitive bias* by assuming that your mind worked like theirs because you shared a common interest or association.

As Christian Zionists are candid about their own foundational assumptions and the governing role those assumptions play in shaping their exegetical conclusions, they regularly begin their arguments with non-Zionist, biblical interpretation by pointing to what they believe are the erroneous assumptions distorting non-Zionist Bible reading. Christian Zionists affirm that literally interpreted Old Testament passages constrain any New Testament writer from changing, reinterpreting, or reapplying the original meaning of an Old Testament text as understood by Christian Zionist grammatical-historical and literalistic reading. Consequently, Christian Zionists assert, based on these assumptions, that no New Testament writer ever reinterprets an Old Testament promise in such a way as to alter its original, literal significance and eventual fulfilment.

In this way, Zionist apologists express their cognitive bias by assuming that all non-Zionist Bible readers must impose their interpretive presuppositions upon the text in the same way they do. Non-Zionist interpreters, then, must be characterized in such a way that their method of interpretation can be explained away. For instance, Vlach offers three headings that he believes are the primary Christian non-Zionist assumptions: "(1) belief in the interpretive priority of the New Testament over the Old Testament; (2) belief that national Israel is a type of the New Testament church; and (3) belief in nonliteral fulfillments of some Old Testament texts."[36]

Vlach is correct in identifying these three perspectives as important elements in non-Zionist interpretation: the so-called "interpretive priority" of the New Testament when reading the Old; understanding that Israel is sometimes used as a "type" that may figuratively represent the New Testament church;[37] and observing that the New Testament frequently explains the nonliteral fulfillment Old Testament texts. But Vlach's Zionist framing of the role these three perspectives play in non-Zionist interpretation misconstrues their significance. These are not governing assumptions used to guarantee a desired interpretive outcome. Rather, all three of these convictions are conclusions that follow from observing how New Testament authors interpret the Old Testament. They are not the result of *a priori* commitments to allegorical method, typology, or a spiritualizing bent toward universalism. Christian Zionists allow their literalist presuppositions to control—even to censor—their own biblical interpretation. They then unwittingly expose their own cognitive bias by assuming that non-Zionist Bible readers are similarly controlled by the "presuppositions" listed above. Unfortunately, Vlach and his compatriots fail to recognize that the three underscored beliefs are not presuppositions that determine non-Zionist conclusions, but are conclusions derived from straightforward, careful reading of the New Testament.[38]

---

36. Vlach, *Church*, 84–85, with citations; see his extended discussion on 84–120, 158–85. Vlach has repeated his arguments in *Has the Church?*, 79–107.

37. Typology describes the relationship between an Old Testament character or event, called a "type," that foreshadows an eventual fulfilment in its New Testament "anti-type."

38. I am not claiming that no non-Zionist has ever fallen into the trap of allowing a governing presupposition to censor or to predetermine the permissible interpretation of Scripture. Of course, this can happen, just as everyone is equally prone to cognitive

Christian Zionists often impute additional assumptions to non-Zionists. For example, some suggest that non-Zionist ways of reading the Bible are due to the influence of Marxist liberation theology and theologically liberal universalism.[39] Others posit a devotion to medieval methods of "spiritualizing" a text's meaning through allegory.[40] Others accuse their opponents of perpetuating a Marcion-like dismissal of Old Testament authority.[41] Still others describe non-Zionist thinking as a new form of Gnosticism directed by a philosophical aversion to material embodiment and ethnic specificity.[42] Gerald McDermott declares that "the New Christian Zionism proposes that the scandal of Zionism is the twenty-first-century version of the scandal of particularity"![43]

---

bias in one form or another. My current proposal arises from simply observing the nature of the contemporary debate.

39. Tooley, "Theology and the Churches," 203–7, 216–19; Benne, "Theology and Politics," 246–48; Horner, *Future Israel*, 100.

40. House, "Church's Appropriation," 82.

41. House, "Church's Appropriation," 219; Vlach, *Church*, 158–59.

42. Horner, *Future Israel*, 45, 246, 313–18; Larsen, "Celebration," 304; McDermott, "Implications and Propositions," 324–25; McDermott, "What is the New Christian Zionism?," 29; McDermott, *Israel Matters*, 11, 110. The point of origin for this accusation appears to be Soulen, *God of Israel*, 57–80. Soulen bases his argument in an examination of the theologies of Immanuel Kant and Friedrich Schleiermacher, noting their supersessionist interest in divorcing a rationalist, universal understanding of Christian theology from all things Jewish, including the historical particularity of a Jewish Jesus. Unfortunately, both Soulen and those Christian Zionists who follow in his footsteps fail to distinguish (a) the philosophical foundations undergirding Kant's and Schleiermacher's supersessionist aversion to the scandal of Jewish particularity and (b) the biblical, exegetical foundations of the contemporary non-Zionism represented by this book. It is worth noting that Soulen is a systematic theologian whose book is devoid of any biblical interpretation. He also fails to note the long history of European antisemitism embedded in eighteenth- and nineteenth-century German theology and higher criticism. This is a significant oversight. For a study on the influence of antisemitism in the development of German theology see, Gerdmar, *Roots of Theological Anti-Semitism*.

43 Bock, "How Should the New Christian Zionism Proceed?," 313; McDermott, "Implications and Propositions," 324–25; McDermott, *Israel Matters*, 113–14, 116. Lessing's essay, "On the Proof of the Spirit and of Power," in *Lessing's Theological Writings*, offers a rationalist's discussion of the difficulties faced by modern people when they are asked to wager their eternal destinies on the debatable "truth" of an historical event or individual. Lessing states, "If no historical truth can be demonstrated, then nothing can be demonstrated by means of historical truths. That is: *accidental truths of history can never become the proof of necessary truths of reason*" (53, emphasis original). Lessing believes that he cannot accept historic, Christian orthodoxy because of the "ugly, broad ditch, which [he] cannot get across" (55). The ditch is created by "the accidental" nature of historical truth and, thus, history's inability to demonstrate "the universal truths of reason." In effect, Lessing argues that believing in the gospel of Jesus Christ and Christ's status as universal truth is asking him to embrace a category mistake, i.e., contingent

The offense of particularity was classically expressed by the rationalist thinker Gotthold Lessing. He asserted that the universal truths of reason cannot be expressed through the contingent particularities of mundane, temporal existence, including the story of a Jewish man named Jesus of Nazareth. However, what Lessing asserts no orthodox Christian can accept. This Zionist attempt to confuse (a) the rejection of modern Israel's right to the holy land with (b) the denial that God has revealed eternal truth in the course of history (and implicitly a denial of the incarnation) is what logicians call a category mistake of epic proportions. It is an attempt to identify the non-Zionist rejection of secular Israel's theological significance with a rationalistic, anti-historical reading of Scripture. This is utter nonsense.

One of the earliest scholars to make a similar appeal to the scandal of particularity is W. D. Davies in his book, *The Territorial Dimension of Judaism*. Concerning modern Israel's occupation of the land, Davies writes: "Just as Christians recognize 'the scandal of particularity' in the incarnation, in Christ, so for many religious Jews . . . there is a scandal of territorial particularity in Judaism."[44] He later connects this "territorial scandal" to the rationalist objections against Jewish claims of a peculiar status as God's chosen people.[45]

We should notice, however, that Davies is pointing out the two different ways in which the same rationalistic, philosophical challenge is mounted against *both* Christian *and* Jewish theology, since both religions believe that God has revealed himself in history. Just as Christianity faces a Christological offense of particularity—how can an individual human being reveal divine truth for all humanity?—so Judaism faces a territorial offense of particularity—how can an obscure piece of real estate belonging to an "elect" nation be the centerpiece of God's saving activity for all humanity? Davies's comparison has nothing to do with competing interpretive conclusions based on different ways of reading Scripture, whether they are Zionist

---

historical truth and the universal truths of reason are distinct categories of truth. We cannot leap from one to the other. Here are the philosophical origins of the so-called "scandal of particularity." Modern thinkers are scandalized by the claim that a historical individual named Jesus of Nazareth is the Savior of the world and the only path for knowing God. It hardly needs pointing out that describing Zionist ideology as the "new scandal of particularity" is in fact a scandalous attempt at rhetorical overreach, not to mention sloppy thinking, exceeded only by the attendant, offensive accusation that non-Zionists are the new rationalists scandalized by the historical particularity of divine revelation. For a good discussion of the various, evasive confusions embedded in Lessing's arguments and the very helpful, theological dissection of Lessing performed by Søren Kierkegaard, see Crites, *In the Twilight of Christendom*, 58–95.

44. Davies, *Territorial Dimension*, 85.

45. Davies, *Territorial Dimension*, 87.

or non-Zionist. Thus, in accusing non-Zionists of succumbing to the scandal of particularity, Christian Zionists move far beyond Davies's argument. They also commit another category mistake by confusing a philosophical argument with a disagreement over how to responsibly interpret the text. The debate between Christian Zionism and Christian non-Zionism has nothing to do with belief in divine revelation. Neither is there any disagreement over whether such revelation can occur in the details of historical contingency. Rather, we are talking about *a difference of opinion* over the biblical necessity of *one specific* particularity—whether or not national Israel must reoccupy the land. Making the acceptance of an abusive, secular, modern Israeli state the litmus test for Christian orthodoxy is problematic in the extreme. Accepting this one particularity in a long sequence of successive particularities (consider the particular contingencies of the biblical story line moving through Abraham, Isaac, Jacob, Moses, Joshua, and so on that together compose salvation history) cannot serve as the ultimate litmus test for a scholar's recognition that God acts in history. It simply is neither charitable nor accurate to impose this artificial standard as the way to measure the integrity of any biblical interpreter.

Each of these unmerited accusations is an example of the logical fallacy known as *ipse dixit*, or an argument of assertion. For none of the writers who make these charges ever provides anything resembling a cogent argument, complete with evidence of conceptual or literary dependence from one source to another, in order to support their claims. We should recall that asserting something does not make it so.

PAUL'S REINTERPRETATION OF HOSEA

As the proof is in the pudding, we conclude this chapter by returning to another example of the unexpected ways that the New Testament uses Old Testament prophecy, illustrating once again the problems with Vlach's misconstrual of non-Zionist observations. We previously examined how the Gospel of Matthew reinterprets Hosea 11:1 (see chapter 1). Now we turn to Paul's reinterpretation of Hosea in his Letter to the Romans.

Speaking to the ten tribes of Israel prior to their Assyrian captivity, the prophet Hosea warned the idolatrous, covenant-breaking northern kingdom of God's imminent judgment.[46] But he also promised that Israel's exile

46. The twelve tribes had become divided into two kingdoms following the death of Solomon. The ten tribes of the northern kingdom were called Israel, while the two tribes of the southern kingdom were called Judah.

would be followed by their eventual redemption. In Hosea 1:10b and 2:23, the LORD describes this judgment and its future reversal:

> In the place where it was said to them, "You are not my people," they will be called "sons of the living God." . . . I will show my love to the one I called "Not my loved one." I will say to those called "Not my people," "You are my people." (NIV)

In Paul's Letter to the Romans, the apostle looks to Hosea for an authoritative explanation of God's gracious inclusion of believing gentiles (by faith in Christ alone, without adherence to the Law) within the same covenant family as believing Jews like himself. Paul surprisingly finds his explanation in Hosea 1:10b and 2:23. He writes:

> What if he did this to make the riches of his glory known to the objects of his mercy, whom he prepared in advance for glory—even us, whom he also called, not only from the Jews but also from the Gentiles? As he says in Hosea:
> "I will call them 'my people' who are not my people;
>   and I will call her 'my loved one' who is not my loved one,"
> and,
> "It will happen that in the very place where it was said to them,
>   'You are not my people,'
>   they will be called 'sons of the living God.'" (Rom 9:22–26 NIV)

Paul puts Hosea to work at a completely unexpected task. He reinterprets the prophet's words by applying them, not to repentant Israelites as Hosea intended, but to repentant gentiles now joining the Christian community. In Hosea, those who are first rejected as "not my people" and then restored as "my people, children of the living God" were the idolatrous tribes of the northern kingdom. But in Romans, God's restored people are transposed into idolatrous gentiles who are now embraced through their faith in the gospel of Christ. So stark is Paul's reinterpretation of Hosea's original intent that commentator C. H. Dodd remarked, "It is rather strange that Paul has not observed that this prophecy referred to Israel."[47] Strange indeed. I suggest, however, that the strangeness is due not to Paul's failure to understand Hosea, but to his inspired reinterpretation and the unprecedented application Paul makes of the prophet's words.

It would be difficult to find a more compelling example of why it is important to read the whole of Scripture twice: first, from front to back, and then from back to front, just as Paul has done in light of the newness of the Gospel. Concluding that the New Testament does indeed often reinterpret

---

47. Dodd, *Epistle of Paul*, 172.

the Old after rereading it in retrospect does not require a prior commitment to "New Testament priority." Nor are these conclusions due to artificially imposing nonliteral readings onto texts that would otherwise yield literalistic results. Observing the plain sense of Paul's use of Hosea in Romans 9 does not require a latent distain for Old Testament authority, or a philosophical prejudice in favor of universalism, liberalism, or allegorical spiritualizing. Rather, *it is the straightforward result of simple observation*, allowing the text to speak for itself as opposed to inventing creative ways to ensure that the New Testament always reads from a predetermined, literalistic script.

It is remarkable to observe the lengths to which Christian Zionist authors will go in their efforts to avoid such straightforward conclusions when they do not fit with their literalistic presuppositions. For instance, Ray Pritz, formerly a professor at Hebrew University in Jerusalem, says that Paul uses Hosea in order to show that God's remnant of faithful Israelites "will include some gentiles," which is a handy way of avoiding the fact that Hosea does not say anything about either a remnant or gentile inclusion.[48] Similarly, Barry Horner and David Rudolph (a professor at The King's University) both ignore Paul's surprising reinterpretation altogether. Instead, they focus on the geographic reference in Hosea's phrase "in the place it was said to them."[49] Asking about the location of "the place" in question is certainly appropriate, but it also avoids the larger question of what Paul has done with the prophet's words.

Fred Zaspel and James Hamilton, both professors at Southern Baptist Theological Seminary, correctly highlight Paul's theological emphasis in Romans 9 on divine sovereignty as God selects whomever he chooses to become his beloved people, whether Jew or gentile. But as they note Hosea's allusion to the Abrahamic promises in Genesis 22:17, they go on to say, "So Paul sees the Gentile inclusion as *analogous* to that of rebellious and rejected Israel. . . . *There is little question that in Hosea's prophecy Israel is in view*, but it seems that . . . [Paul] opens the door for *extending* the prophecy to Gentiles also."[50] However, their description of Paul's reading as an analogy and extension of Hosea's message deflects attention away from the most apt descriptor of what is happening—Paul is reinterpreting Hosea in light of the experience and reality of Christ. Paul is *not* describing an analogy to or an extension of Hosea's words to Israel but their *reapplication to an entirely different subject*. Paul reinterprets Hosea's original meaning and

---

48. Pritz, "Remnant of Israel and the Messiah," 70.

49. Horner, *Future Israel*, 231; Rudolf, "Zionism in Pauline Literature," 192.

50. Zaspel and Hamilton, "Typological," 104–5 (emphasis mine). See Vlach's equally evasive suggestions in *Has the Church?*, 103–4.

reapplies his words to a new group of people. The prophet's original concern for rejected Israel is replaced by Paul's concern for the previously rejected gentiles. Hosea's promise that God will one day restore Israel to the covenant is replaced by Paul's awareness that gentiles (who have never enjoyed a covenant relationship with God) are now also saved by grace through faith.[51]

Paul's surprising use of Hosea 1:10b and 2:23 occurs within the broader context of his argument in Romans 9–11, in a context where he defends the continuing importance of Israel's relationship to the Abrahamic covenant. This should prevent anyone from suggesting that Paul is advancing ethnic supersessionism. Neither am I doing so anywhere in this book. The point at issue has nothing to do with supersessionism or replacement theology. Rather, this is a simple observation about one instance of the New Testament's reinterpretation of the Old, where the Apostle Paul rereads the biblical canon backward, from back to front with his gospel-inspired imagination. This apostolic reading method is now normative for all God's people. As Colin Chapman warns, "Christians today do not have the liberty to interpret the Old Testament in any way that appeals to them." All of Scripture must now be read through the "lens of Jesus Christ" with "the eyes of the apostles."[52]

SCRIPTURE MUST BE ALLOWED TO SPEAK FOR ITSELF

My purpose in this book is not to enter ongoing, exegetical debates surrounding the numerous, intertextual biblical passages that turn on the question of reinterpretation. Rather, I have offered examples—very clear examples, in my view—where both Matthew and Romans reinterpret passages from Hosea by drawing out applications—fulfilments, if you will—that only make sense in light of the life and ministry of Jesus Christ. I believe a compelling case can be made for the careful, open-minded reader to discover that such rereading and interpretation in retrospect is very common, even normative, throughout the entire New Testament. The two texts we discussed, Matthew 1:14–15 and Romans 9:24–26, are but two examples among many.

My objective in this chapter and the next is to examine Christian Zionist presuppositions and how those presuppositions affect Zionist biblical

---

51. Using the word "replaced" in this context is not evidence of replacement theology. I am not affirming ethnic or economic supersessionism. I have not said that Jews are now replaced by a wholly gentile church. I am only noting an exegetical, linguistic fact evident in a specific text; a fact that ought to appear obvious to anyone not constrained by inappropriate hermeneutical presuppositions.

52. Chapman, *Whose Promised Land?*, 172, also 125.

interpretation. I have begun by focusing on the most fundamental of those presuppositions: literalistic interpretation directed by the grammatical-historical method. I share Christian Zionism's high regard for the grammatical-historical method. I share their goal of working to clarify, as best we can, the original meaning of a text for its original audience. But we differ in how to proceed in allowing the New Testament authors to read and to apply the Old on their own terms. Our presuppositions must always remain open to being reworked whenever evidence undermines their credibility. In the realm of science, such adjustments are called a *paradigm shift*. For instance, Albert Einstein's theory of relativity and quantum physics caused a paradigm shift when Einstein's calculations led physicists to abandon the previously ruling model of Newtonian physics.[53] I am arguing that Christian Zionism must make such a paradigm shift, for its presuppositions muzzle the biblical text, preventing the New Testament writers from speaking for themselves.

Christian faith is demonstrated by following the Holy Spirit whose work in salvation history is nothing if not surprising. Paul reminds his readers of God's mysterious ways in Roman 11:33–34:

> Oh, the depth of the riches of the wisdom and knowledge of God!
>> How unsearchable his judgments,
>> and his paths beyond tracing out!
> Who has known the mind of the Lord?
> Or who has been his counselor?

This chapter hopefully clarifies one way in which Christian Zionism empowers fallen human nature in its self-serving quest to control scripture's message. Let us rather humble ourselves before heaven's unsearchable decisions made by an unknowable mind, leading us along untraceable paths.

---

53. See Kuhn, *Structure of Scientific Revolutions.*

Chapter 7

Bad Assumptions Lead
to False Conclusions

CHAPTER 6 BEGAN TO expose the faulty foundational presuppositions that form the basis of Christian Zionist biblical interpretation. We discovered that Zionism's presuppositional starting point is a single-minded devotion to literalistic interpretation, especially of the Old Testament, generated by the grammatical-historical method of exegesis. This a priori commitment to Old Testament, prophetic literalism and its modern-day application, yoked to an ideologically driven defense of the modern state of Israel as God's chosen nation, is buttressed by a cluster of intersecting, secondary assumptions that all contribute to the architecture of Christian Zionist thinking. My goal in this chapter is to peel away these secondary assumptions, typically expressed as "rules" of interpretation, highlighting their dependence on the prior assumption of interpretive literalism. We will see that the errors of the faulty taproot infect the logical (or illogical) extensions that grow out of it. Unfortunately for Christian Zionists, the whole theological structure becomes a proverbial house of cards constructed of one flawed assumption on top of another.

The first assumption related to Christian Zionist claims that all Scripture must be read literalistically is revealed in the *ex cathedra*[1] proclamation

1. This Latin phrase originally referred to decisions and pronouncements delivered

that the New Testament never modifies the "plain sense" of the Old. As we saw in chapter 5, this is commonly referred to as the rule of antecedent theology. Christian Zionists seem to be in lockstep on this point. Paul Feinberg, former professor at Trinity Evangelical Divinity School, argues that "the sense of the OT text must be determined within its historical and cultural setting, and that sense is determinative for the NT fulfillment."[2] Michael Rydelnik, professor at Moody Bible Institute, concurs: "the Old Testament needs to guide the understanding of the New Testament, and not vice versa."[3] In a similar vein, Charles C. Rylie, of Dallas Theological Seminary, insists that "new revelation cannot mean contradictory revelation. Later revelation on a subject does not make the earlier revelation mean something different."[4] As Christian Zionists argue, in what sense can biblical revelation be called revelatory if there is not a literal, one-to-one correspondence between the details of the Old Testament expectation and the claims of New Testament fulfilment?[5]

The rule of antecedent theology is another tool for assuring Zionist results while ignoring Scripture's inconvenient details. This is not an evidence-based conclusion derived from careful, inductive Bible study. Rather, Christian Zionists merely declare this to be the case. Thus, they blatantly beg the question by assuming what they declare and then declaring what they assume. By whose authority should we accept these claims as true? The unfortunate result is that so-called antecedent theology flattens the beauty and complexity of intertextual, canonical, biblical interpretation.

Neither should we accept the claim that a "different" interpretation, as may be found in the way the New Testament interprets the Old, is necessarily a "contradictory" interpretation. Furthermore, the reductionism of Zionist interpretation weakens any understanding of revelation that corresponds to the texts as we have them. We saw earlier (chapter 1) that Jesus appeared as the Messiah no one expected. This decisive revelation alone

---

by the Pope. Today it is often used more broadly to describe an authoritative declaration, typically beyond question, without justifying evidence or argument. Logicians describe such pronouncements as *ad verecundiam* or *ipse dixit* statements.

2. Feinberg, "Hermeneutics of Discontinuity," 127.

3. Rydelnik, "Hermeneutics of the Conflict," 70–71. For earlier, formative discussions of the importance of antecedent theology for Christian Zionism, see Feinberg, "Systems of Discontinuity," 76–77; Feinberg, "Hermeneutics of Discontinuity," 116, 120, 128.

4. Rylie, *Dispensationalism*, 84; cited in Vlach, *Church*, 127; also see Vlach's explanation in "Non-typological," 66.

5. Feinberg, "Hermeneutics of Discontinuity," 118, 120, 128.

undercuts easy, one-to-one correspondence theories about the nature of promise and fulfilment within Scripture.

Unfortunately, Christian Zionist interpretation ignores, or outright denies, the idea that revelation unfolds gradually through the canon, made most complete in Jesus. Their literalistic and positivistic approach flattens thematic developments and intertextual elaborations by simply outlawing them from the start. Actually, Christian Zionism's idiosyncratic laws for acceptable Bible reading are a thoroughly modern construct, derived from a set of concerns far removed from the Scriptures themselves. The Christian Zionist emphasis on the priority of plain, literal meanings, common sense interpretation, and a quasi-scientific, empirical approach to biblical interpretation are all deeply rooted holdovers of nineteenth-century fundamentalism's romance with a philosophical school known as Scottish Common-Sense Realism, which emphasized the reliability of sense perception in conveying the reality of other objects.[6]

These Zionist declarations remind me of the children's book *There's No Such Thing as a Dragon,* by Jack Kent. It's a story about a boy who wakes up one morning with a small dragon in his bed. As he moves through the day, he continually tries to draw his mother's attention to the colorful dragon following him everywhere. The mother has only one response, "There is no such thing as a dragon!" But with each motherly denial, the dragon grows a bit larger until the family's house is nearly destroyed. Only then will the mother recognize what the boy has always seen—a very real dragon. I have never met a dragon, but I have met many Bible readers who take refuge in dogmatic pronouncements, refuse to keep an open mind, and will not take account of evidence that is plain as day to others.

---

6. For an introduction to this philosophical tradition and its deep influence on American fundamentalism-evangelicalism, see Marsden, *Fundamentalism,* 14–16, 55–62, 112–16. We need not be aware of all the historical influences ineluctably molding our research into a particular shape. Yet, the telltale signs of historical influence can be clear, nonetheless. American fundamentalism took Scottish Common-Sense Realism as their justification for applying a "scientific," supposedly empirical, method to biblical interpretation and theology. It was also their way of finding a contemporary foothold allowing them to go toe-to-toe with the threats of modernism and scientism. Christian Scripture was seen as a historical-literary world analogous to the natural world. The same empirical method that "guaranteed" predictable, reproducible results in the natural sciences could also be applied to Bible study and the theological sciences. The grammatical-historical method of exegesis became the literary, scientific method of choice. Reality is subject to uniform categorization, which does not change. What you see is what you get, every time in every place. This is the intellectual heritage of Christian Zionism. It also reveals how deeply rooted is American fundamentalism-evangelicalism in the modernist, scientific worldview.

Another assumption, working in coordination with the rule of antecedent theology, is the rule of double fulfilment.[7] In this case, if the New Testament asserts the non-literal fulfilment of an Old Testament text, that non-literal fulfilment is interpreted as only the first fulfilment; a second fulfilment-event is still anticipated so that the Old Testament promises to Israel will still have a literalistic realization in the future. As John Feinberg, professor at Trinity Evangelical Divinity School asks, why shouldn't the New Covenant fulfilment of the Old "have one application to the church now plus a further application to national Israel in the future?"[8] Feinberg's hypothetical question all-too-conveniently provides the perfect setup for activating his additional assumptions regarding literalistic interpretation and antecedent theology.

David Larsen, professor at Trinity Evangelical Divinity School, cavalierly invokes "the law of double reference" to account for Paul's unexpected interpretation of Hosea 2:23 in Romans 9:25.[9] Larson feels no need to grapple with Paul's reinterpretation of Hosea. Rather, he simply invokes the "law" of double fulfillment, creating an academic-sounding justification for his Christian Zionist reading while ignoring the New Testament writers' assertion that the new covenant fulfilment of God's promises to Israel occur in the life of Christ and his church. The terminology we find in Zionist Christian literature describes an approach to Bible reading that does not naturally arise from the text. Having come up with terms like "antecedent theology" and "the law of double fulfillment," Christian Zionists then deploy the terminology as if it arises from the text or as if Christian readers have always thought this way. Neither is the case. Rather, these readings sustain the specter of an Old Testament, national Israel as the all-important goal of biblical theology. Sadly, this is then put to the service of defending a nation with a terrible track record of ethnic prejudice and abuse.

The next assumptions Christian Zionists bring to reading Scripture concern the nature of the state of modern, secular Israel. This third assumption requires an unquestioned identification of the modern state of Israel with the Old Testament descendants of Abraham, Isaac, and Jacob. Modern, secular Israel equals biblical Israel. Everything the Bible says to Abraham's ancient descendants is also being said today to the contemporary

7. Feinberg, "Systems of Discontinuity," 77, 81; Feinberg, "The Hermeneutics of Discontinuity," 118–19, 127–28.

8. Feinberg, "Systems of Continuity," 68.

9. Actually, Larsen does not mention either of these texts specifically, but his claim that "Hosea 1–2 . . . refers to Israel's historical experience but also applies to Gentile conversions" can only be a reference to Paul's citation from Hosea in Romans 9; see Larsen, *Jews, Gentiles*, 51. See the previous discussion of these texts in chapter 6.

nation-state squeezed between the Mediterranean and the Jordan River. This point is critical, and we will return to it in greater detail. Suffice to note for now that this presumption is deeply implicit in Christian Zionist readings of Scripture.

Finally, Christian Zionists assume that whenever Israel is mentioned in Scripture, it always denotes "an ethnic, national, and territorial (ENT) reality," whether or not those characteristics are mentioned in the text.[10] Thus, there is a near universal commitment to understand the word "Israel," anywhere in the Bible, as always denoting (a) a distinct, identifiable ethnic/racial group, (b) possessing a divine right to a corporate, national existence, (c) exercising national sovereignty within the bounds of the territory promised to it by God.[11] These three elements make up the Zionist trifecta for Israel's existence, past, present, and future.

However, as non-Zionist authors regularly point out, establishing the priorities of (1) Jewish ethnic distinctiveness with (2) the creation of an ethnically defined nation-state that (3) exercises Jewish sovereignty over the Old Testament promised land, is *not* a self-evident part of New Testament teaching. Occasionally, an unusually candid writer will admit as much, as when Michael Vlach confesses, "Granted, *there is no undisputed New Testament verse* that explicitly states 'Israel will be restored to its land and have a special service to the nations.'"[12] But, then, the rules of antecedent theology and double fulfilment are always available to supply covertly the required, Zionist meanings and implications that the New Testament never states overtly.

Zionist assumptions about the Bible and Israel are thus deeply intertwined. Inserting the rules of antecedent theology or double fulfilment or the necessity of an ethnic, national, and territorial Israel as precursors to actually reading the text is akin to the proverbial shop owner placing a thumb on the scale, skewing each sale in his favor. These supposed rules of biblical interpretation prop up the artifice of Christian Zionist ideology. They also explain away the actual text of the New Testament when it does not meet their agenda. Ironically, Christian Zionist readings of the Bible finally render any New Testament affirmation on the importance of ethnic, national, or territorial Israel completely moot. As John Feinberg asks, "If God makes

10. Blaising, "Theology of Israel," 85; see also 87, 89, 90–92, 96–97, 99.

11. For further examples, see Feinberg, "Systems of Discontinuity," 72–73; Larsen, *Jews, Gentiles*, 25, 231, 289; Horner, *Future Israel*, 183, 188, 224, 291, 298, 309; Vlach, *Church*, 37–38; Zaretsky, "Israel the People," 39, 44; Jelinek, "Dispersion and Restoration," 235.

12. Vlach, *Church*, 203 (emphasis mine). Mentioning Israel's "special service to the nations" is another way of referring to the importance of Jewish ethnicity (E) in defining its nationhood (N).

a point once (the OT), why must he repeat it in the NT for it still to be true and operative?"[13] The answer, of course, is, God doesn't, unless the New Testament brings a New Word from the LORD, as Christians historically have affirmed.

The Old Testament promises to Israel define the Christian Zionist reading of the New Testament to such a degree that Zionists must shoehorn an ethnic, national, and territorial Israel into any relevant New Testament text.[14] Muting the witness of the four Gospels and the New Testament letters, Christian Zionists will not recognize that God brings about a surprising fulfillment, reconstituting the people of God around Christ's kingdom, which is both in continuity and in discontinuity with the Old Testament promises. Instead, constrained by their antecedent presuppositions, that whatever came first must literalistically interpret what follows, and bound by their law of double reference, the New Testament vision of the kingdom of God being defined by the outpouring of the Spirit on all who believe—well, this must play second fiddle to the return of secular Israel at all costs. Tragically, the Palestinian people end up paying the brunt of that cost.

By insisting that the biblical canon may *only* be read literalistically from front to back—*never* from back to front in the light of Christ, as it was read by the New Testament authors—Christian Zionism conveniently shelters itself from the questions and contradictions that otherwise arise from the dearth of New Testament evidence in support of their Zionist vision. The New Testament's uniform failure to reassert God's old covenant intentions for an ethnic, Jewish state in the land of Palestine is handily overcome by superimposing a preexisting vision of a national, ethnic, territorial Israel whenever, wherever the need arises by hook or by crook. But, of course, this leaves unanswered a hauntingly crucial question. Why were the New Testament authors so consistently incapable of clearly expressing what they actually meant?

---

13. Feinberg, "Systems of Discontinuity," 76.

14. One of the objectives of the so-called New Christian Zionism is to bolster both the academic integrity and the exegetical competence of Zionist argumentation. McDermott, *New Christian Zionism*, offers a collection of essays written by ten different Zionist apologists. The book's cover displays a prominent Star of David with a cross in its center, advertising the importance of Christian Zionism to the Jewish-Christian movement known as Messianic Judaism. Though I cannot offer a detailed book review here, I will say that I am struck with how much of the Old Christian Zionism remains unchanged within the New. I am also surprised at the regularity of arguments that depend on the logical mistakes of special pleading, circular reasoning, and *non sequiturs*, especially in the chapters presenting biblical and theological arguments. I am afraid that the New Christian Zionism has not overcome the charge of shoehorning ENT Israel into places where it cannot fit.

Christian Zionists justify their arbitrary, self-serving rules by describing them as essential safeguards against the ever-present dangers of "uncontrolled subjectivity in the interpretive process."[15] They also appeal to the importance of protecting God's character, for if God is to remain faithful and worthy of our trust, then his promises must always be literally fulfilled exactly as Zionist interpreters understand them.[16] We have already seen how the New Testament authors *do*, in fact, reinterpret and reapply Old Testament texts in light of the new covenant work of Christ (chapters 1 and 6). We have seen that this is not about my own or any non-Zionist reader's subjective interpretation. Rather, this is a matter of the New Testament apostolic witness whose interpretation did in fact reread the Old Testament from back to front in the light of Jesus' earthly ministry now fulfilling all of God's promises, however unexpectedly.[17]

We will take a look at two additional passages (in this chapter and the next) that illustrate how Christian Zionist readings are not only unwarranted by the text, but actually do great harm to the New Testament.

THE SINAI COVENANT, ISRAEL, AND THE CHURCH

In Exodus 19 we discover a new chapter in the life of a battered people. The descendants of Abraham have labored for generations as an enslaved minority swallowed up by the Egyptian empire. Eventually, a deliverer is given to them. His name was Moses, and he announced that he was sent by Yahweh, the God of their father Abraham, to lead them out of Egyptian bondage into the promised land of Canaan. After escaping Pharaoh's army through the raucous Red Sea, all the people gathered at the foot of Mount Sinai. Here they are invited into a new relationship with the God of Abraham, a relationship defined by what we now call the Sinai Covenant. Unlike the unilateral promises of the preceding Abrahamic covenant, promises guaranteeing Abraham both land and descendants (Gen 12:1–3; 15:5–7; 17:4–8; 22:17–18), the Sinai covenant is a bilateral agreement with obligations levied toward the Israelites.[18] The Sinai Covenant's conditionality is immediately made evident in the "if . . . then" clause of the opening sentence.

15. Larsen, *Jews, Gentiles*, 22, 191.

16. Feinberg, "Hermeneutics of Discontinuity," 128; Larsen, *Jews, Gentiles*, 22, 200, 288, 325.

17. For more on this important distinction, see my book *Encountering Jesus*, 15–45, 71–112.

18. Genesis 17:9–14 adds a decidedly conditional clause to this otherwise promissory covenant with Abraham. Every male child must be circumcised on the eighth day in order to remain within the covenant. In other words, God's covenant offers

Here is the introduction to this new, reciprocal covenant as it appears in the Greek version (known as the Septuagint or the LXX) of Exodus 19:5–6:[19]

> *If* you listen closely to my voice and observe my covenant, *then* you shall be to me a special people above all nations. For the whole earth is mine. But you shall be to me a king's priesthood and a holy nation. (my translation)

The Sinai covenant did not alter the fact that Israel remained a chosen nation in keeping with God's covenant with Abraham. However, the Sinai covenant predicated being God's special people on "listening closely to God's voice and observing the [Sinai] covenant." Only then would they be God's "royal priesthood and holy nation." But the Old Testament story line is tragic and mercurial. Consider how often the prophets lament in calling Israel out of idolatry; how many times we read denunciations of Israel's covenant breaking; how often we hear warnings of impending divine judgments. God persistently calls his unruly people back to repentance. However, Israel is eventually deported, twice, into foreign lands for not responding to the "if, then" of Sinai and the warnings of the prophets. Readers may fairly ask if the promises described at Sinai were ever actualized, for Israel had not fully lived into its vocation as God's people in the world.

This intriguing question about Israel's rebelliousness and the offerings of the Sinai covenant creates an evocative backdrop to the citation of Genesis 19:5–6 appearing in 1 Peter 2:9–10:

> But you are <u>a chosen race</u>, *a king's priesthood*,[20] *a holy nation,* <u>a people destined for vindication</u>, that you may declare the praises of the one who called you out of darkness into his marvelous light. Once you were not a people, but now you are the people of God; once you had not received mercy, but now you have received mercy (my translation).

Peter's description of the ethnically diverse, Jewish/gentile[21] Christian communities spread throughout Asia Minor (1 Pet 1:1) draws from both

---

conditional promises to Abraham's descendants.

19. I am translating the Greek Septuagint (LXX) text of Exodus 19:5–6 because this is the Old Testament version used throughout 1 Peter, including 2:9–10.

20. J. H. Elliott offers compelling evidence for translating this phrase as "royal residence and priestly community" rather than the traditional rendering of "royal priesthood"; see *1 Peter*, 435–38, 443–55. Referring to an earlier publication by Elliott, Kelly adopts Elliott's translation in his work, *Commentary*, 96–98. However, I am finally persuaded by Michaels's arguments against Elliott in favor of his own translation in *1 Peter*, 108–9, which I follow here.

21. Vlach attempts to defend the view that Peter is writing to an exclusively Jewish

the language of the Sinai Covenant we just looked at (Exod 19:6) as well as the prophet Isaiah's promises to rebellious Israel after it has eventually been restored through the mercies of God (Isa 43:20–21 LXX). My translation of 1 Peter *italicizes* the words drawn from the "if . . . then" clause of Exodus 19 and underlines those phrases taken from Isaiah 43. That way one can see immediately in 1 Peter which are the additional declarations in verse 10 about those who were once "not a people" becoming "God's people." We discover that it is the same language taken from Hosea 2:23 that we noted Paul quoting in Romans 9:24–25 (see chapter 6)

Peter's application of the promises given to Israel (Isa 43:20–21; Hos 2:23) to the New Testament followers of Jesus Christ appears to have been a common way of reading the prophets (and the rest of the Old Testament) among the earliest Christians. Paul and Peter both reread the Old Testament in light of the New Testament work of Jesus. For each of them, the prophet's hopes for a restored Israel turning from "not a people" into "God's people," a "chosen race," and "a people destined for vindication" are now being realized in the communities of Jesus followers, Jews and gentiles, meeting in the homes of elders or other early Christian leaders. Nowhere does Peter suggest that this spiritual renewal of Jews and gentiles alike through faith in Christ is only a provisional or a penultimate stage in the process of God's plan for salvation. Rather, he assures these early communities that now "you are the people of God." The exalted status offered conditionally to Israel in the Sinai Covenant is now realized for 1 Peter among the followers of Christ. The former "if . . . then" of Exodus 19 has become a "you are" for 1 Peter. These ethnically mixed communities now are *a* chosen race (note the singular; not *races*), a king's priesthood, a holy nation, a people destined for vindication. Peter's point is plain. The ancient covenantal promises originally offered to the wandering people of Israel at the foot of Mount Sinai are now fulfilled, through the resurrected Jesus, for all who gather around him in obedient discipleship. The multilingual, multiethnic, transnational church of Christ

---

audience; see *Has the Church Replaced?*, 147–48. In this way he hopes to avoid the problem (for him) of applying Old Testament covenant promises to Christian gentiles. But it seems impossible that Peter could have ever warned a community of Jews to stop "conforming to the evil desires you had when you lived in ignorance" (1:14), or that they "have spent enough time in the past doing what pagans choose to do—living in debauchery, lust, drunkenness, orgies, carousing and detestable idolatry" (4:3; cf. 1:18). These verses are *prima facie* evidence that the recipients of Peter's letter included formerly pagan gentiles. We can presume a Jewish presence as well for several reasons: (1) it is the general New Testament pattern to assume that Christian communities included both Jews and gentiles; (2) we know that synagogues existed throughout these regions of Asia Minor; (3) Peter's abundant use of Old Testament citations presumes some familiarity with Israel's sacred texts.

has been "incorporated into God's ancient covenant people and share the heritage of ancient Israel."[22]

Peter, along with Paul, completely redefines what it means to be counted as people of God. It is not by observation of Torah or circumcision. Peter calls all believers in Christ, Jews and gentiles alike, to be the people of God's covenant by their participation in Christ's New Covenant blessings. God is now fulfilling in this new Christ-centered group of believers the hopes expressed in the covenant made with Israel at Mount Sinai. Throughout the Old Testament, the place of Israel as the covenant people defined the nation's claim to uniqueness. That Israel knew the living God demonstrated that Israel was in covenant with the living God. Every other epithet applied to Israel, chosen race, king's priesthood, or holy nation, derived from their participation in God's covenant with them.

Peter's belief, a belief he shared with the Apostle Paul, was that faith in Jesus now made Christian disciples genuine members of God's covenant community. For the Jewish disciples of Jesus, the promises made to Israel at Mount Sinai were completely, finally fulfilled in the ministry of Jesus, with all believers receiving the Spirit in his name. Two New Testament scholars who have done significant work on the text on 1 Peter, John Elliott and J. Ramsey Michaels, both rightly point out that 1 Peter 2:9–10 never ascribes the titles "Israel" or "new Israel" to the church.[23] Yet, 1 Peter does recognize the church as the Covenant People, joining with the Old Testament faithful. Salvation in 1 Peter is now centered on the work of Jesus Christ, something even the prophets were pointing toward:

> Concerning this salvation, the prophets, who spoke of the grace that was to come to you, searched intently and with the greatest care, trying to find out the time and circumstances to which the Spirit of Christ in them was pointing when he predicted the sufferings of the messiah and the glories that would follow. It was revealed to them that they were not serving themselves but you, when they spoke of the things that have now been told you by those who have preached the gospel to you by the Holy Spirit sent from heaven. (1 Pet 1:10–12)

1 Peter thus depicts a situation where what is accomplished in Christ was foretold and yet unexpected: "even angels long to look into these things" (v. 12). Israel's promises were for this time, when God's covenant people would be reconstituted with both Jews and gentiles. This salvation is the same salvation promised by the prophets, and yet it is completely redefined

---

22. Elliott, *1 Peter*, 443.

23. Elliott, *1 Peter*, 113, 411, 419, 435, 443, 447; Michaels, *1 Peter*, liv, 13, 107.

as effected by the sacrifice of Christ and the gift of the Holy Spirit. Peter, a Galilean Jew, embraces this new multiethnic vision of God's people as something he had not anticipated, as is also demonstrated by his surprising vision of the unclean animals in the book of Acts (10:9–48).[24]

Naturally these observations won't track with Christian Zionists. The irony is that even though they take the posture of advocating a literal approach to Scripture, these observations on 1 Peter 2:9–10 flow quite naturally from a literal, plain-sense meaning of Peter's words. Regardless, Zionist interpreters who give attention to 1 Peter have found ways to make this text conform to Zionist talking points. They typically point out that:

First Peter never calls the church "Israel" or the "new Israel" as if to displace the Jewish community (a point also noted by Elliott and Michaels).[25] Further, they argue that applying Israel-terminology to gentiles does not mean that gentiles become a part of Israel, much less replace Israel. Instead, the language may be an example of analogy or typology, i.e., the church is *like* Israel in *some* respects; it is not necessarily intended to prove identity, i.e., the church *is* the new Israel.[26]

If 1 Peter is applying the Sinai language to the church by way of analogy, then the future remains open for a literal (double) fulfilment of that same language to an ethnic, territorial nation-state.[27]

If 1 Peter 2 is saying that God's election of ethnic, national Israel has been "annulled," then "God's promise and faithfulness are clearly at stake," and Peter's promises to the church are meaningless.[28]

Finally, since 1 Peter never describes the church as fulfilling the national, political, or territorial promises made to Old Testament Israel, this passage cannot negate the future, literal fulfilment of those promises describing Israel's central role in the coming, messianic kingdom.[29]

It is not difficult to recognize the heavy seasoning of Christian Zionism's unwarranted assumptions reflected in each of these critiques. Like Don Quixote, several of these arguments stubbornly tilt at nonexistent windmills. Zionists argue that 1 Peter does not define the church as the new

24. I accept the traditional claims of Petrine authorship for this letter (see the opening phrase in 1:1). For arguments in defense of this position, see Elliott, *1 Peter*, 118–20.

25. Saucy, "Israel and the Church," 249; Saucy, *Case*, 206; Glenny, "Israelite Imagery," 179; Vlach, *Church*, 179; Vlach, *Has the Church?*, 149–50.

26. Saucy, "Israel and the Church," 249; Saucy, *Case*, 207; Glenny, "Israelite Imagery," 181–83; Vlach, *Church*, 178; Vlach, *Has the Church?*, 149–50.

27. Saucy, *Case*, 207; Glenny, "Israelite Imagery," 184–85.

28. Glenny, "Israelite Imagery," 185.

29. Saucy, "Israel and the Church," 251–52; Saucy, *Case*, 208–11; Glenny, "Israelite Imagery," 187.

Israel, nor does this passage argue that gentile Christianity replaces the Jews. However, as noted above, non-Zionist interpreters do not necessarily read 1 Peter that way either. From that silence, however, Zionists will erroneously conclude that 1 Peter stands on their side of the debate. The rigidity of their assumptions precludes the possibility of a non-Zionist theology that does not embrace an ethnic-replacement supersessionism. Zionist interpretation is thus tethered to the manufacture of straw men arguments and inevitable *non sequiturs* that prop up unwarranted conclusions that simply do not fit the evidence.

Christian Zionists' obsession over the question "Who is called Israel?" leaves them blind to the actual question posed in 1 Peter: "Who are members of the covenant?" For ancient Israel the covenant was the basis of its identity. Israel could be Israel only because of God's covenant. Every privilege, every calling Israel could claim flowed directly from their covenant identity. Therefore, as *the central point of 1 Peter 2:9–10* is the fact that these Jesus followers are now God's covenant people, Christian Zionist arguments about the church being merely analogous to Israel rather than being designated the new Israel are irrelevant disputes arising from concerns that have nothing to do with the interests of 1 Peter.[30]

---

30. For whatever reason, 1 Peter is not interested in further clarifying the relationship between the Christian church and unbelieving Jews outside the church. The reference in 1:18 to his readers' redemption "from the empty way of life handed down from your forefathers" can have equal relevance to both Jewish and gentile believers in Christ (compare Gal 4:3–5, 9–10; Col 2:20–23). Peter deploys Ps 118:22 against "those who do not believe" (2:7–8) in the same way that Jesus used this verse to confront hostile Jewish leaders (Matt 21:42–46; Luke 20:17–19). Jesus warned them against foolishly rejecting "the stone made to become the capstone." Obviously, the Savior's opinion about both himself and those Jews who rejected his Messiahship remained unchanged for the apostle. Perhaps Peter was sympathetic toward Paul's assessment of Israel's relationship to the church (Rom 9–11). The gospel of Jesus Christ is now separating the true Israel from the false (Rom 9:6–9) with two vital innovations: (1) new covenant membership is defined by faith in the resurrected Jesus and (2) believing gentiles enter this covenant in the same manner as believing Jews. If this is the case, it *may* explain Peter's clear attribution of ancient Israel's covenant status to the New Testament church without ever designating the church as "Israel" (compare Paul's emphasis on Israel's continuing, salvation-historical uniqueness in Rom 9:4–5; 11:11–12, 28–32). The new covenant has so thoroughly redefined the nature of God's people that using the title "Israel" would only raise more questions than it answers. In any case, for whatever reasons, 1 Peter chooses to give more attention to the pastoral concerns raised by the churches' present suffering than he does to disentangling the theological questions raised by Old Testament Israel's relationship to the New Testament messianic community. As Elliott explains, "The honorific epithets of ancient Israel are simply appropriated and applied to the messianic community without further comment. The believers are not said to constitute a 'new people' but, rather, are declared the eschatological realization of Israel as God's elect and holy people. . . . However, it is now through faith rather than biological membership in

Christian Zionism's presuppositions are clearly setting the framework of their objections and suggested solutions. While they insist on a wooden literalism, that literalism is only upheld if the text follows a one-to-one correspondence theory of promise-fulfilment pointing to a literal nation-state of Israel, now identified as secular Israel. But the author of 1 Peter literally does not read Israel's promises that way. Instead, he reads them literally as having been transformed by the work of Christ. It is especially ironic for Zionists to insist on the future occupation of the promised land as essential to God's promise while reading 1 Peter, for this letter offers one of the New Testament's clearest voices insisting upon *the landlessness* of God's covenant people in this post-advent world.

Christian Zionists insist that, since the Christian church is a transnational community with no territorial ties or claims to a specific geography, it cannot be the fulfilment of God's promises to Israel since those promises include the occupation of Middle Eastern real estate. However, rejecting the premises of *antecedent theology* and *double fulfilment* will go a long way toward correcting that misplaced addiction to territoriality. Peter's adoption of Israel's Old Testament story line for describing the New Testament church includes his rendering of the Christian community, Jews and gentiles alike, as "exiles/strangers scattered throughout" the world (1:1). God's new covenant people are participating in the status of the old (remember 2:9–10). Thus, despite the fact that Peter is almost certainly writing from Rome, he greets his fellow disciples from "Babylon" (5:13), the ancient empire that swallowed up and regurgitated the people of Israel in 586 B.C. Like Israel throughout its exile and dispersion, the apostle and the Christian church as a whole have become strangers (1:1; 2:11) and aliens (1:17; 2:11) in this world, traveling as refugees through a fleeting, ephemeral terra firma (1:3–6, 22–25; 4:7; 5:1) that can never provide a true or lasting homeland for God's people. The flip side of God's election is estrangement from this sinful world. As with ancient Israel, the disciples' foreignness is born of their place in the covenant. As displaced outsiders, recognizably distinct from their nativist neighbors, it is not surprising that followers of Jesus will necessarily share in their Lord's sufferings (2:4–8, 20–25; 4:1, 12–19), unjustly enduring personal pain, including the social discrimination commonly inflicted by the world's majority onto the unusual Other (1:6; 3:9–17; 4:12–19; 5:8–10).[31]

---

the house of Jacob"; see *1 Peter*, 447; also 97, 113, 315, 411, 419, 443; similarly, Michaels, *1 Peter*, 95–96, liv–lv, 112–13.

31. Christian Zionists frequently dismiss my reading of 1 Peter by labeling it as "dualistic," embracing an earthly/heavenly, material/spiritual bifurcation of reality. They then set themselves up as the fearless defenders of a genuinely material salvation, in contrast to non-Zionist "spiritualizers" hostile toward a particular people (Israel)

In the midst of Peter's emphasis on Christian suffering in an alien world, the author never hints at holding a territorial wild card up his sleeve. *All* of God's people are *entirely* and *permanently* estranged from this current, earthly domicile. That estrangement encompasses all disciples of Jesus, Jew and gentile. There are no exceptions. First Peter never suggests that God holds out an exception clause for certain Jews, as if to say, "Well, there *is* a small slice of this world that will be an earthly residence, a 'homeland' for *some* of God's people." Nor does 1 Peter suggest a two-tiered perspective on the salvation of Abraham's descendants, as if Jewish Christians (together with believing gentiles) will experience a landless redemption; whereas those Jews who persist in rejecting Jesus as their Messiah will nonetheless experience a "landed" redemption by possessing their own territorial nation-state.[32] First Peter's distinctive theology of participation, a participation in both the story of Israel and in the life of Jesus, would be twisted beyond recognition by this sort of Christian Zionist teaching.

We can recognize these arguments for what they really are: tendentious attempts to impose Christian Zionist ideology onto uncooperative Scripture. This is not exegesis (reading meaning out of the text); it is eisegesis (reading meaning into the text) born of ideological commitments and the refusal to admit that the biblical text is plainly saying something very different from what Christian Zionists require of it.

---

redeemed in this material world (the state of Israel). It is obviously one of Christian Zionism's more far-fetched defenses. My reading of 1 Peter has nothing to do with anyone's dualism. Rather, it is entirely eschatological, as is the rest of the New Testament. Peter encourages his audience by reminding them that one day Jesus will return for them. Upon his return, this cosmos will be remade into "a new heaven and a new earth"; a new cosmos, thoroughly material, free of sin, and never-ending.

32. I find it odd that Christian Zionists never explicitly address the relationship between these two different sets of Jews, Christian and non-Christian. (Or, if they do address it somewhere, I have failed to grasp it). Does God's unique plan for ENT Israel include Jewish Christians, including those continuing to live in the Diaspora with no interest in immigrating to Israel? If God's plan for ENT Israel is distinct from God's plan for the church—a belief shared by both dispensationalists and the so-called New Christian Zionists—then where does that leave Jewish members of the Christian church, especially those in the Diaspora? To leave the church, the body of Christ, requires renouncing faith in Jesus, whether or not Zionists will admit to this. Must Christian Jews apostatize before participating in God's plan for Israel?

Chapter 8

The Church Is an Entirely New Person

NEW TESTAMENT SCHOLAR MARKUS Barth, son of the eminent theologian Karl Barth, invested much of his life in building bridges between Jews and Christians. Three of his books, *The People of God*, *Jesus the Jew*, and *Israel and the Church*, all offer important contributions to this religious, theological dialogue. In his commentary on the New Testament book of Ephesians, Barth observed that Paul's[1] explanation of Jewish-gentile relations "says things about the peace between Israel and the gentiles, and about the relationship between Israel and the church, which have no equal in the New Testament."[2] Barth's apt assessment is a reminder that biblical texts must always be allowed to speak for themselves. Interpreters must tame whatever harmonizing impulses accompany their theological bias.

Looking at Ephesians 2:11–22 offers a second opportunity, following the previous study of 1 Peter 2, to see how Christian Zionist presuppositions can distort the plain sense of Scripture. I mention the challenge of illegitimate harmonizing because the distinctive lessons of Ephesians 2:11–22 are

---

1. I accept the traditional claim of Pauline authorship for the Letter to the Ephesians (see 1:1; 3:1). For two vigorous defenses of this position, see Barth, *Ephesians 1–3*, 36–50; Hoehner, *Ephesians*, 2–61.

2. Barth, *Ephesians 1–3*, ix.

often overlooked by interpreters. Too many of them rush headlong into Ephesians by reading it in light of Paul's teaching about the people of God as presented by the fig tree metaphor in Romans 11:11–24 with its natural, pruned, and ingrafted branches. This confusion of Ephesians with Romans allows such readers to maintain a characteristically Zionist separation between Israel and the church. However, Ephesians 2 highlights an issue not found in Romans 11—Oneness. Through their shared faith in Christ, believing Jews and gentiles become *One New Person*, not separate branches grafted into the same tree, but One.

Ephesians 2: 11–22	Romans 11: 11–24
11 Therefore, remember that formerly you who are gentiles by birth and called "uncircumcised" by those who call themselves "the circumcision" (which is done in the body by human hands)— 12 remember that at that time you were separate from Christ, excluded from citizenship in Israel and foreigners to the covenants of the promise, without hope and without God in the world. 13 But now in Christ Jesus you who once were far away have been brought near by the blood of Christ.	11 Again I ask: Did they stumble so as to fall beyond recovery? Not at all! Rather, because of their transgression, salvation has come to the Gentiles to make Israel envious. 12 But if their transgression means riches for the world, and their loss means riches for the Gentiles, how much greater riches will their full inclusion bring!
14 For he himself is our peace, who has made the two groups one and has destroyed the barrier, the dividing wall of hostility, 15 by setting aside in his flesh the law with its commands and regulations. His purpose was to create in himself one new humanity out of the two, thus making peace, 16 and in one body to reconcile both of them to God through the cross, by which he put to death their hostility. 17 He came and preached peace to you who were far away and peace to those who were near. 18 For through him we both have access to the Father by one Spirit.	13 I am talking to you Gentiles. Inasmuch as I am the apostle to the Gentiles, I take pride in my ministry 14 in the hope that I may somehow arouse my own people to envy and save some of them. 15 For if their rejection brought reconciliation to the world, what will their acceptance be but life from the dead? 16 If the part of the dough offered as first fruits is holy, then the whole batch is holy; if the root is holy, so are the branches.
19 Consequently, you are no longer foreigners and strangers, but fellow citizens with God's people and also members of his household, 20 built on the foundation of the apostles and prophets, with Christ Jesus himself as the chief cornerstone. 21 In him the whole building is joined together and rises to become a holy temple in the Lord. 22 And in him you too are being built together to become a dwelling in which God lives by his Spirit.	17 If some of the branches have been broken off, and you, though a wild olive shoot, have been grafted in among the others and now share in the nourishing sap from the olive root, 18 do not consider yourself to be superior to those other branches. If you do, consider this: You do not support the root, but the root supports you. 19 You will say then, "Branches were broken off so that I could be grafted in." 20 Granted. But they were broken off because of unbelief, and you stand by faith. Do not be arrogant, but tremble. 21 For if God did not spare the natural branches, he will not spare you either.
	22 Consider therefore the kindness and sternness of God: sternness to those who fell, but kindness to you, provided that you continue in his kindness. Otherwise, you also will be cut off. 23 And if they do not persist in unbelief, they will be grafted in, for God is able to graft them in again. 24 After all, if you were cut out of an olive tree that is wild by nature, and contrary to nature were grafted into a cultivated olive tree, how much more readily will these, the natural branches, be grafted into their own olive tree!

Authors, let alone apostolic authors, are not obligated to repeat themselves, only saying what they have said before. This is all the more so in the case of Paul who wrote letters occasioned by various circumstances, crafted to answer different questions from a range of audiences. The American philosopher and poet, Ralph Waldo Emerson, remarked that "a foolish consistency is the hobgoblin of little minds, adored by little statesmen and philosophers and divines."[3] The Apostle Paul's mind was anything but little, and the Spirit that inspired his writing certainly has no sympathy for hobgoblins. Paul's Letter to Ephesus is not his letter to the church in Rome. Keeping this fact in mind, I will focus on only three issues at the heart of Paul's weighty lesson explaining how faith in Christ transforms believing Jews and gentiles alike into something entirely unprecedented and different from both. Together they become One New Person, a single entity called the Church.

We begin with verse 17 by delving into Paul's allusion to the Old Testament prophet Isaiah. In Isaiah 57:19 the prophet extends the LORD's offer of peace and reconciliation to the scattered people of Israel. Those who remain "near" in the land, as well as those who are "far off," dispersed throughout the world, are both told that they have not been forgotten:

> "Peace, peace, to those far and near," says the LORD. "And I will heal them." (NIV)

Paul alludes to this text from Isaiah, with a nod to Isaiah 52:7 as well, when he writes:

> And he came and preached the good news of peace to you who were far off and peace to those who were near. (my translation)

As we saw earlier in Paul's quotation of Hosea 2:23 in Romans 9:24–25, the apostle once again reinterprets and reapplies the prophet's message. The far and the near are no longer two different groups of Israelites but are now believing gentiles, who used to be far from God, and believing Jews, who were nearer to God but required Christ's redemption, nonetheless. As we will see, God's intention was always to create a New Humanity composed of Jews and gentiles alike recreated into One New Person.

Circling back to verse 11 and following, we see that Paul reminds non-Jewish members of the Ephesian church about their previously dire state of spiritual poverty as uncircumcised gentiles. The litany of pejorative statements in 2:11–13 provides an interesting corollary to 1 Peter's focus on the centrality of covenant membership in 1 Peter 2:9–10. Paul offers his readers

---

3. From his work, "Self-Reliance," 7.

a retrospective interpretation of their spiritual condition prior to meeting the resurrected Jesus. Once again, we see how faith in Jesus reinterprets the past, both collectively and individually. Even though they did not realize it at the time, due to their exclusion from God's covenant with Israel (v. 11), gentile Christians had previously been (v. 12):

1. *Separated from Christ.* The Messiah came out of faithful Israel; thus, in being separated from Israel, gentiles were separated from the expectation of their Savior.

2. *Excluded from citizenship in Israel.* God had constituted Israel as his people. Uncircumcised gentiles stood outside this theocratic community.

3. *Aliens/foreigners to the covenants of promise.* Paul describes the flip side of 1 Peter's alien/stranger coin. After faith in Christ, all believers become foreigners in a strange world; before faith in Christ they were foreigners to God's covenants and, thus, alienated from God (also v. 19).

4. *Without hope and without God in the world.* As we saw in 1 Peter, exclusion from the covenant means exclusion from God's presence. The gentiles remained godless even as they worshiped their many deities.

Paul's appraisal of the gentile condition prior to Christian faith and membership in the church is firmly rooted in the priority of Israel's place in salvation history. The history of Israel is crucial to both the birth of the church and to Christian self-understanding. Without a faithful Israel there would have been no apostles, no Paul, no Peter, no Jesus of Nazareth, no resurrection, no ascension, no redemption. Consequently, if I were reading Paul's Letter to the Ephesians for the first time, I might imagine that God's solution for gentile alienation must involve drawing them close to Israel and into its covenants. I would be wrong. Paul begins to explain God's good news for gentile believers in verse 13:

> But now in Christ Jesus, you who were once far away have been brought near by the blood of Christ. (my translation)

The question is, to what or to whom are gentiles brought near by the blood of Christ? Zionist commentators generally understand this verse to say that gentile Christians are drawn near to Israel, sharing in Israel's covenant blessings through faith in Jesus.[4] They reach this erroneous conclusion by assuming that Paul's logic unfolds in a simple point/counterpoint

---

4. Horner, *Future Israel*, 272–73; Vlach, *Church*, 181–82; Vlach, *Has the Church*, 152–54. Hoch, "New Man," 108, 113, 126–26, says that gentiles are brought near to both God and Israel.

progression. But that is not how Paul's argument proceeds, as a careful reading of the text will demonstrate. As Paul's argument progresses, he clearly
states that the sacrificial blood of Christ brings believing gentiles *near to
God* (vv. 16, 18–19, 22)—a final, divine destination that comes as no surprise to those who remember that intimate, personal relationship with God
was always the goal of the covenant.

Unfortunately, however, a faulty Zionist interpretive assumption gives
rise to a thoroughly polemical Zionist conclusion: although the (gentile)
church may come close to Israel and share in its blessings, the church neither becomes a part of nor replaces Israel. The church and Israel are never
confused, meaning that they both retain their own separate roles in God's
plan.[5] Drawing upon the usual Zionist presumptions of literalism, antecedent theology, double fulfilment, and the necessity of an ethnic, nationalist,
and territorial Israel, the fact that Ephesians does not confuse Israel and
the church is assumed to mean that an ethnically distinct, national Israel,
independent of the Christian church, still has a separate role to play in God's
plan for redeeming the world.[6]

We see again how the Zionist concentration on ensuring that the
church and Israel are never confused continues to bear its predictable, unwarranted fruit. Harold Hoehner, of Dallas Theological Seminary, in his fine
commentary on the Greek text of Ephesians, criticizes, quite rightly in my
view, an argument put forward by a well-known Reformed commentator
by noting, "This theory should not be taken seriously for it is an example
of theology controlling exegesis rather than exegesis controlling theology."[7]
Yet, what is good for the goose is surely good for the gander. Reformed commentators are not the only Bible readers who can force their theology onto
scripture and make a mess of interpretation.

A closer reading of Ephesians will show that Paul had an entirely different motive for not confusing the church with Israel. And that motive
had nothing to do with safeguarding ethnic, national Israel's unique role in
God's future plans.

So, what does Paul have to say about the relationship between Israel
and the church in Ephesians 2? Paul does not confuse the church with Israel
because they both are transformed by Christ into something entirely new

---

5. Saucy, "Israel and the Church," 253; Vlach, *Church*, 181–82; Vlach, *Has the
Church*, 152–54. McDermott attempts to thread the needle by inventing a new category
with a new nomenclature. He says—again, *ex cathedra*—that gentile Christians become
"associate members" of Israel; see *Israel Matters*, 27–28, 125.

6. Saucy, "Israel and the Church," 254–57; Hoch, "New Man," 118; Horner, *Future
Israel*, 242, 269, 274; Vlach, *Church*, 183.

7. Hoehner, *Ephesians*, 358.

and different; something that has never been seen before; a new community "whose privileges transcend those of Israel."[8] Now we have arrived at the heart of Paul's argument (vv. 14–16):

> For he [Christ] is our peace, the one who has *made both one* and destroyed the dividing wall of partition, having abolished in his flesh the hostility, the law of commandments expressed in regulations. He did this in order that he might *create the two in himself into one new person,* thus making peace, *reconciling both in one body* to God through the cross, putting the hostility to death in himself. (my translation)

Paul repeats the central point of this passage three times in the space of three verses. Christ's death produced a transformation, creating One New Person from the previously distinct identities of Jews and gentiles. In emphasizing the new Oneness of all believers in Christ, Paul is not describing the "collapse," "dissolution," "eradication," or "deterioration" of ethnic differences, as certain authors fear.[9] Paul never required Jews to stop

---

8. Lincoln, *Ephesians*, 139.

9. Hardin, "Equality in the Church," 228, 229, 231, 232. Dr. Hardin's essay contributes to a Zondervan publication, entitled *Introduction to Messianic Judaism*, presenting this movement to an evangelical audience. It is not my intention to discuss this important movement or its theology here, but a few remarks are required. Hardin's analysis of Galatians and Ephesians 2:14–18 is in keeping with the other biblical scholars who contribute to the book in his emphasis that Jews, members of the people of Israel, remain a distinct *ethnicity* in the New Testament who retain their distinctiveness as members of the Christian church. Hence, his emphasis on no "collapse" or "dissolution" of ethnic differences in the church. In this regard, the entire volume illustrates the close association of Messianic Judaism with Christian Zionism; see especially Cohen's chapter, "Messianic Jews in the Land of Israel." I find several features of "Messianic Jewish" New Testament interpretation, using Hardin as one example, to be problematic in that it resembles the Zionist methods criticized in this book. The greatest problem is the consistent tendentiousness of Messianic Jewish interpretations, which renders their arguments unpersuasive. A major problem in Hardin's essay is the fact that he never defines what he means by "ethnicity," a not uncommon issue; for a discussion of this and the confusion that results see Connor's chapter on "Terminological Chaos" in *Ethnonationalism*, especially 100–103 on ethnicity. I adhere to the original, more limited definition of ethnicity as *a group characterized by common descent.* Hardin, on the other hand, appears to follow the more amorphous (American sociological) usage where ethnicity refers to *a group with a common sense of identity* based in shared cultural traditions, whether religious, social, or historical (real or imagined). Political Zionism exploits the word's ambiguity, as required for its arguments. Hardin's arguments indicate that he seems to define ethnicity as a matter of a group's *religious practices.* But it is unclear to me how Paul would understand Jewish believers in Jesus to maintain their distinct religious habits (i.e., their ethnicity) while worshiping together with gentiles, who are not required to become Jews (i.e., adopt Jewish religious practices), as the One New Person created in Christ. (I take it as a given that most, perhaps all, of Paul's churches were

identifying as Jews, for example. But those ethnic-religious distinctions, especially insofar as they served to divide people from each other, sometimes
in open hostility, have been disempowered by the redeeming, reconciling
work of Christ.

The fact that Paul finds three different ways to repeat his formulation
of "two into one" indicates that we must take the outcome of this redemptive
metamorphosis, resulting in One New Person, with all seriousness. In the
church, neither Jew nor gentile remain what they previously were. Their
prior distinctions have been transcended. Through their shared incorpora-
tion into Christ (v. 16) they are made into something new, not merely some
sort of amalgamation of the two. This One New Person is not a "syncretistic
mixture of Jewish and Gentile elements."[10] Nor is it "a uniform mass of . . .
Christians who would not remember their Jewish or Gentile origin."[11] A
more apt analogy would be the caterpillar that metamorphoses into a butterfly. There is continuity from the one to the other, but the butterfly is a
completely new creature. The scientist who wonders when the butterfly will
give up flying and return to crawling like the caterpillar it once was has
failed to understand the meaning of metamorphosis. The old is gone; the
new has come. There is no going back.[12]

According to Ephesians, that law of the covenant, which was intended
to build a fence around God's covenant people, was the principle instigator of
Jewish-gentile hostility.[13] "Abolishing that law with its commandments and

mixed bodies composed of Jews and gentiles together). Note that the Zionist concern
for keeping Israel/Jews separate and distinct is equally emphatic for Messianic Judaism
(at least for the contributors to the Zondervan volume) as it is for Christian Zionism,
even if for somewhat different reasons. Furthermore, if maintaining the distinctives of
gentile ethnicity is equally important (as Hardin and others claim it is), and ethnicity
is defined by religious practices (as Hardin's arguments imply), then Paul appears to
be blessing religious syncretism for his gentile converts. What would this look like?
The other possibility is that Hardin (and others) are relying on (unwittingly or not) the
terminological confusion attached to the word ethnicity in order to say one thing about
Jewish ethnicity and something very different about gentile ethnicity.

10. Barth, *Ephesians 1–3*, 310.

11. Barth, *Israel and the Church*, 31.

12. Lincoln, *Ephesians*, 139–51, provides a good analysis and description of the
significance of Paul's insistence on the unique creation of One New Person at the cross.
As he notes, "v. 19 does not simply take up where v. 13 left off with a straightforward
reversal of the Gentiles' previous relationship to Israel. Verses 14–18 show that what
produced the reversal in the Gentiles' status was of such a nature as to relativize the
earlier categories and even shed a different light on what appeared to be Israel's status"
(145–46).

13. In light of verses 14–15, Lincoln convincingly argues that the "dividing wall"
abolished by Christ is not a reference to the barrier excluding gentiles from the Jerusalem temple precincts, but the law itself. See his description, citing ancient sources, of the

regulations" (v. 15) removed the catalyst behind Jewish-gentile antagonism and separation, "the dividing wall of hostility" (v. 14). Old Jewish identity markers, circumcision, territory, food laws, all are made insignificant to the goal of belonging to God's people through the work of Christ. Thus, Christian Zionist commentators who focus on the importance of ethnic distinctions between Jews and gentiles (whether faithful to Jesus or not), and the necessity of national Israel reoccupying the promised land fail to grasp the full measure of Paul's teaching here.

Naturally, Christian Zionist interpreters have their justifications for downplaying the significance of Christ's creation of Jew and gentile into One New Person at the cross. Their arguments generally follow one of two variations on a theme. First, Christ's "one new man" is said to describe a spiritual, "salvific unity" that does not erase the ethnic and functional distinctions between Jews and gentiles.[14] Under this rubric, Paul emphasizes that Jews and gentiles alike discover salvation by faith in Christ alone. But to this is quickly added the proviso that sharing in the same means of salvation does not erase the functional distinctions between the two groups. Secondly, even while acknowledging Paul's language of oneness, many Zionists explain this oneness as a "new union" between the Jews and gentiles. In other words, it is not the dissolution of twoness into oneness, but an inter-ethnic union like an interracial marriage. Naturally, such a voluntary union permits both parties to maintain in their distinctiveness while offering worship to the same Savior.[15]

Galatians 3:28 is a favorite Zionist proof-text brought into the argument in order to buttress this dissimulation of Pauline oneness into a cooperative, spiritual union. Paul writes, "There is neither Jew nor Greek, slave nor free, male nor female, for you are all one in Christ Jesus" (NIV). This sentence from Galatians is then used as a template for understanding

---

mutual animus between Jews and gentiles that could be stirred up by Torah observance, which could include separation from gentiles; *Ephesians*, 141–43. The oral tradition could be described as a "fence" around the law (m. 'Abot 1.1–2; 3.18). In describing the law, the *Letter of Aristeas* (second century BC) says, "our lawgiver . . . *fenced us about* with *impenetrable palisades* and with *walls of iron* to the end that we should mingle in no way with any of the other nations, remaining pure in body and spirit . . . so that we should not be polluted nor be infected with perversions by associating with useless persons, he has *fenced us about* on all sides with prescribed purifications" (139, 142); see Lincoln, *Ephesians*, 141.

14. Saucy, *Case*, 162; Saucy, "Church," 126; Vlach, *Church*, 182; Vlach, *Has the Church?*, 153–54.

15. Saucy, "Israel and the Church," 254–56; Hoch, "New Man," 116–18, 120, 123–24; Saucy, *Case*, 161–62, 167; Horner, *Future Israel*, 273; Vlach, *Has the Church?*, 154; Blaising, "Biblical Hermeneutics," 88–89; Blaising, "Theology," 96.

Ephesians 2. The argument goes like this: obviously, Paul's description of becoming "one in Christ Jesus" in Galatians 3 does not erase ethnicity, gender, or a slave's legal status. Paul admits that these identity markers continue to exist. Thus, Ephesians 2 must be making the same point as Galatians 3. Becoming One New Person, therefore, cannot undo the functional distinctions between Jews and gentiles in God's plan of salvation. After all, Paul continues to write about Jews and gentiles!

Once again, however, the Zionist commitment to protecting ethnic Israel blinds them to Paul's actual point and prevents them from embracing the full measure of Paul's metaphor. Obviously, becoming a member of the church does not strip an individual of her unique, cultural background, much less her gender.[16] Paul is certainly not depicting the One New Person as a bland, unisexual, homogenized entity. Rather, Paul is driving home the practical significance of Christ's "abolishing of the law" (v. 14); namely, *ethnic, gender, political, social, national, and territorial distinctions no longer define God's ongoing redemptive work of making one new people in the image of his Son in this post-advent era of salvation history.* Israel's special status and identity has been subsumed within the identity of Jesus as the firstborn of God's New Humanity. Christ's work on the cross brings about a kingdom that is no longer dependent on a Jewish nation to accomplish its earthly destiny.

THEOLOGY, IDEOLOGY AND MORALITY

God's people are called to untangle themselves from this corrupted, fallen world with its hostile divisions, tribal rivalries, and the endless bloodletting unleashed by the evils of systemic sins, including those of racial segregation and ethnic-religious nationalism. God's people abandon their calling whenever the church embraces such malignant attitudes toward others. Embracing ethnic and religious nationalism denies the meaning of Jesus' sacrifice and the efficacy of his redemptive work for all humanity. The American evangelical church betrays its God-given status as a part of Christ's One New Humanity whenever it pays obeisance to the tin-plated idols of nationalism, militarism, American exceptionalism, or political

16. Barth, *Israel and the Church*, 31, makes the crucial point when he says that Paul's continued references to Jews and gentiles "is not to segregate the formerly Jewish from the formerly Gentile members of the church by stressing and defending some inalienable values of each one's previous existence, but to glorify the justification by grace and faith alone."

Zionism.[17] Any ideology that places a singular national, ethnic, religious, territorial identity centerstage in its quest for cultural and political dominance—whether American, Israeli, South African, Hutu, or Serbian—is not only anti-Christian, it is fueled by the spirit of the anti-Christ. The letters of John warn us that "many anti-Christs" have gone out into the world (1 John 2:18, 22; 2 John 7). Their message may begin with denying "that Jesus is the Christ who came in the flesh," but the book of Revelation spells out the ever-expanding spheres of ungodly distortion emanating from such false teachers (Rev 13:11–18). The antichrists of this world also serve as the prophets of imperialism, warfare, oppression, greed, and economic exploitation creatively reinvented by every temporal power (including the United States and Israel) who mimic the evils of ancient Babylon. They are earthly kingdoms that grow as anti-kingdoms, and God promises to destroy them all (Rev 18).

In theory there is no theological reason for Christian Zionists to withhold their criticisms of Israel's historic mistreatment of the Palestinian people. However, Christian Zionism continues to offer its carte blanche endorsement of the Israeli government and its unjust policies toward Palestinians, as it continues to share in the partisan blindness of political Zionism. This is why Christian Zionism is at least as much a political ideology as it is a Christian theology, more so when it continues to neglect the plight of the oppressed in the land.

My perspective in this book is neither antisemitic nor pro-Palestinian, labels that have become increasingly trite ways for Zionists to dismiss those voicing substantive disagreements. Rather, the position I espouse here is pro-Jesus, pro-gospel, pro-kingdom of God, pro-Christianity, pro-justice, and therefore pro-humanity. There is a serious deficiency of conscience in those who reflexively protest fair and legitimate corrections to their myopic moral sense. It is inexcusable for Christian Zionism consistently to gloss over and, in some cases, even to applaud Israel's ongoing crimes against humanity, at times even denying them outright in spite of overwhelming evidence.

This Protestant branch of Christian Zionism is a living denial of what Christ is doing in making One New Humanity through the church. Evangelicals who gleefully continue their tacit, and often financial, support for the secular Zionist state of Israel act as cheerleaders and co-criminal financiers for the daily trampling of Palestinian human rights. Many of these Palestinians are our brothers and sisters in Christ, fellow members of God's One

---

17. See my book, *I Pledge Allegiance*, for deconstructions of American exceptionalism, political partisanship, nationalism, and militarism as these idols confront the reality of God's kingdom in this world.

New Humanity. Not only does their daily suffering go unredressed, they are fundamentally betrayed by their fellow Christians in the American (and sometimes English and European) evangelical church. Whenever Palestinians lift their voices in meager, impoverished efforts to plead their cause, to tell their stories and to remind the world that they, too, bear the Image of God, they face the rancor not only of their Israeli Zionist overlords, but of their ill-informed Christian brothers and sisters in the West.[18] Theirs is an unjust suffering born of human selfishness and greed, for all expressions of ethnic-religious nationalism, whatever their motivations, are anathema to the kingdom of God.

Christian theology always has real-world implications. Every theology contains an ethic, whether implicit or explicit. To ignore ethics is to debase theology. Any theology that condones immorality and violence—such as occurs on a daily basis in Israel, Gaza, the West Bank, and the many Palestinian refugee camps scattered throughout the Middle East—and denies the One New Humanity created by Christ's sacrificial death is a not a Christian theology but a ghastly caricature. The enduring example of theological immorality took root in the German Christian church with its embrace of Nazi ideology in the 1930s–1940s.[19] The historical lessons to be learned from the German church's surrender to the blood-and-soil nationalism of Nazi ideology should be obvious to all. "The Nazis managed to create a moral universe where racism and brutality were approved, even encouraged. The German people behaved accordingly. Anti-Semitism and eugenics were morally good, while racial integration and opposition to the state were morally evil."[20] Today, political Zionism continues this age-old trick of collective, social manipulation. Because of this, tackling the illogical arguments and faulty exegesis put forward by Christian Zionism are the ethical obligations of every Christian who has some influence on the spiritual maturity of others in the church. Christian Zionism creates a veritable obstacle course of scriptural pitfalls and moral booby traps waiting to cripple the unwary disciple who ventures into the Zionist labyrinth.

A representative example of the immoral ethos created by Christian Zionist thinking appears in the book, *Israel, the Church and the Middle*

---

18. For only one example, see Glaser's partisan attack on the attempts made by Palestinian Christians to tell their side of the story and foster mutual understanding with Christian Zionists in the West through such events as the biennial "Christ at the Checkpoint" conferences, sponsored by Bethlehem Bible College (https://www.facebook.com/christatthecheckpoint/), and the "Kairos Palestine Document" in "The Dangers," 106–13.

19. See my discussion of the German Christian church in *I Pledge Allegiance*, 104–13.

20. Crump, *I Pledge Allegiance*, 108.

East.[21] Mitch Glaser, president of Chosen Peoples Ministries, contributes a chapter to this volume entitled, "The Dangers of Supersessionism." The entire chapter is riddled with an explicit rejection of Paul's lessons from Ephesians 2:11–22, expressed with an unfortunate petulance. I offer one example among many:[22]

> In effect, supersessionism nails shut the coffin of Jewish cov-
> enantal existence for all eternity. This viewpoint is a major im-
> pediment to reconciliation and peace between Arab and Israeli
> believers in Israel. Additionally, there is a deep concern that
> the anti-Christian Zionists [*sic*] is damaging the image of Israel
> within the church and causing [young evangelicals] to have a
> poor attitude toward Israel. . . . We must ask ourselves whether
> or not peace between Palestinian and Messianic Jews is even
> possible with one side believing that Israel lost her theological
> right to exist. . . . True reconciliation is only possible when Pal-
> estinian evangelicals and anti-Christian Zionists show respect
> for those who believe the Jewish people are God's chosen people
> and that the land was given to the Jewish people by covenant.

The chapter smacks of an unsavory sense of entitlement expressed with ideological truculence overlaid with a veneer of theological conviction. Glaser says that he would be happy to be reconciled with non-Zionist broth-ers and sisters in Christ *as long as* they first adopt his Zionist point of view. The central meeting point for Christian fellowship in Glaser's theology is his brand of Zionism. The Christian obligation to live out the truth of God's One New Personhood does not register. Jewish-Israeli exceptionalism ap-pears to take precedence over the Oneness of all God's people. Glaser simply ignores the plight of the Palestinians, including those who share his Chris-tian faith, rather than condemn Israel's continuing crimes against them. Glaser is one of a new generation of Christian Zionists who give lip service to raising concern over Israel's "supposed" mistreatment of Palestinians, but never find anything specific to criticize—at least in print. There appear to be no public records of such Zionists taking a stance against any specific Israeli act of injustice. They always hedge their rhetorical bets by referring only to Israel's unspecified, "alleged" offenses.[23] Their ongoing silence proves

21. Numerous examples of similar sentiments could be cited from Christian Zionist literature.

22. Glaser, "Dangers," 111.

23. Glaser, "Dangers," 107, 109, 112, 117. For additional examples of feigned concern that never sees an Israeli crime worth criticism, see McDermott, *Israel Matters*, 116, 119, 128–29, and Horner, *Future Israel*. Horner allows that "*some* of these charges *may* be justified" [emphasis mine: notice both his prevarication and diminishing of the number

that their unspecified, theoretical objections are merely another form of Zionist distraction. Instead of taking up the challenge of living out the new reality created by Christ's forging of One New Person at the cross, Glaser and company make Christian unity dependent upon the requisite display of "respect" that he believes he deserves from those who reject his Zionist ideology. I trust and pray that there are more conscientious, yet unpublished, Zionists somewhere in the church.[24]

Fortunately, Paul's description of the Christian church as a New Creation was taken with complete seriousness by many followers of Jesus in the earliest centuries of the church. The second-century apologist, Aristides, described Christians as "the third race" because of their distinctive, unifying beliefs and behaviors, which set them apart from all others. His second/third-century document called the *Letter to Diognetus* offers a moving description of what this third race, Paul's One New Person, looks like when Christians actually live in time and space so as to obey their ascended Lord as citizens of God's kingdom on this earth:[25]

---

of incidents worth consideration] while adding that Israeli explanations would certainly "shed new light" on the accusations (53), implying that the "new light" would almost certainly exonerate Israel's actions. The volume edited by McDermott, *New Christian Zionism*, is also representative of this recent attempt at expressing a more "conscientious" Zionism ostensibly willing to criticize Israeli behavior. For instance, McDermott admits that his allegiance to Israel "certainly does not mean that Israel is always right or that it has never been unjust in its dealing with other nations" (328); yet *the New Christian Zionism* regularly condemns anyone who dares to criticize Israel's policies toward Palestinians, while never offering a single criticism of its own, and repeatedly referring to Israel's "supposed injustices" against Palestinians! One can be forgiven for taking the New Christian Zionism's claims of even-handedness with a huge block of salt. For further examples, see McDermott, "Introduction," 12, 28; Tooley, "Theology," 197–219; Benne, "Theology," 245–48. However, by far the book's most flagrant misrepresentation of Israel's attitude toward Palestinians appears in the chapter written by Shadi Khalloul, "Theology and Morality," 281–301. Khalloul insists that Israel never discriminates against its resident ethnic groups by appealing to his own experience as an Aramean/Syriac Christian citizen of the state. This shocking chapter is the most egregious of the many distortions, misrepresentations, and falsehoods scattered throughout the book. What neither Khalloul nor the book's editor acknowledge—whether from ignorance or outright deception—is that Israel classifies all Aramean/Syrian Christians *as a distinct ethnic group all its own, completely separate from Palestinians*. As an Aramean Christian citizen of Israel, Khalloul's experience bears no resemblance to the daily life of Palestinians living in Israel, to say nothing of those living under Israeli military occupation in Gaza and the West Bank. I find it more than ironic that the book's one chapter explicitly addressing "morality" is also its more deceptive.

24. Thankfully, I have found a rare exception to this Christian Zionist, humanitarian double-talk in Larsen, *Jews*, 165, 214, 326, 328–31, where Israeli crimes are singled out and criticized.

25. See chapter 5 of Lightfoot's translation at http://www.earlychristianwritings.com/text/diognetus-lightfoot.html.

> They dwell in their own countries but simply as sojourners. As
> citizens, they share in all things with others, and yet endure all
> things as if foreigners. Every foreign land is to them as their
> native country, and every land of their birth as a land of strang-
> ers. . . . They are in the flesh, but they do not live after the flesh.
> They pass their days on earth, but are citizens of heaven. . . .
> They love all, and are persecuted by all.

The writer is not describing incidental traits but deliberate practices of
Christian disciples who understood that their old, worldly ideologies must
be replaced by a new life in Christ unfolding within the kingdom of God.
I am afraid that Christian Zionism—with its sacralizing of blood and soil;
its atavistic promotion of ethnic-religious nationalism; and its clutching at
ancient real-estate acquired at the expense of human lives—would be utterly
unrecognizable to the Christian community described for Diognetus.

But change is possible. Miko Peled is an IDF (Israeli Defense Forces)
veteran and a son of the well-known Israeli general Mattityahu Peled. General Peled fought in Israel's wars of 1947–49 and 1967. After Miko's niece
was killed in Jerusalem by a suicide bomber in 1977, he began a journey of
personal discovery and reconciliation. He movingly describes that journey
and its outcome in his best-selling book, *The General's Son: Journey of an
Israeli in Palestine.*[26] Beginning with an evening discussion group composed
of Israelis, Americans, Palestinians, Muslims, and Jews, he listens to Palestinians (who had become his friends) tell their family stories of suffering,
displacement, and homelessness. He reflects, "I was fully convinced that
with my background I knew more than anyone else about this aspect of the
conflict."[27] He quickly learned that he was wrong.

Miko's brother, a political science professor at the University of Tel
Aviv, advised him to read the histories written by the New Historians,
which he did. He also continued to befriend and to listen to more and more
Palestinians. This journey of exploration, he explains, "was a rude awaken-
ing for me. . . . The willingness to accept another's truth is a huge step to
take. It is such a powerful gesture, in fact, that contemplating it can make
you want to throw up. At first, I felt like a baby learning to walk, realizing
little by little that it was okay to let go of the comfort of holding onto what
I 'knew' to be true."[28]

Today Miko Peled travels the world, often with Palestinian friends and
coworkers, talking to people about the crimes of political Zionism and the

26. Just World Books, 2016.
27. Peled, *General's Son*, 141.
28. Peled, *General's Son*, 141–42.

importance of pressuring Israel (especially through the BDS movement) to become a genuine, liberal democracy for all the people living between the Jordan River and the Mediterranean Sea.

Sometimes, the things we "know" to be true are not true. Because he was willing to face this possibility, today Miko Peled is a living testament to the transformative power of open-mindedness, a passion for the truth, and the value of learning to love people, including our enemies, more than we love ideology, dogma, or revenge.

Chapter 9

Daily Life under Military Occupation

FRIDAY MORNING IN NABI SALEH

MY WIFE AND I stepped off the well-worn bus that had taken us to a small Palestinian village twelve miles northwest of Ramallah, the hub of Palestinian government (such as it is) in the West Bank. This was our second trip together to Israel and the West Bank, where we had the good fortune of living with a Palestinian family that had turned Bethlehem into our home away from home. One of our goals on this trip was to participate, as best we could, in local Palestinian efforts at openly resisting Israel's military occupation, which is their right under international and humanitarian law.[1] Life in

1. See Erakat, *Justice for Some*, 179, "Colonized people have the right to use force in pursuit of their self-determination," citing the International Committee of the Red Cross, Protocol Additional to the Geneva Conventions of 12 August 1949, and Relating to the Protection of Victims of International Armed Conflicts (Protocol I), 8 June 1977, art. 1(4). The UN Security Council has also consistently "rejected [Israel's] pleas of self-defense because, under international law, it could not defend territories it illegally occupied"; Erakat, *Justice for Some*, 189. For a wider analysis of Israel's manipulation of international law (a process called "lawfare") in order to "legalize" its occupation and its war against resistance, see Erakat, *Justice for Some*, 175–210. Also see Quigley,

Bethlehem, the birthplace of Christianity's Prince of Peace, was anything but peaceful. We witnessed frequent, violent attacks on unarmed people by Israeli soldiers, and heard the accounts of even more frequent night raids which typically ended with someone being thrown into the back of truck and taken away without a word of explanation. Some of our own friends in the neighborhood had been arrested in this way. We were witnessing first-hand how incessantly stressful, uncertain, and dangerous daily life could be for Palestinians living under military occupation.

During our first visit to Bethlehem, we had remained in the refugee neighborhood doing volunteer work at a local community center. This time we wanted to stretch our wings and see what Israel's military occupation looked like in other communities. We heard about a weekly Friday dem-onstration in a village north of Bethlehem named Nabi Saleh. So, early one Friday morning we hooked up with a friend, an independent photojournal-ist, and walked to the nearest bus stop. We did not know what to expect.

The bus took us up a narrow, dusty road and dropped us off at a small village, seemingly in the middle of nowhere. It was still morning, but we could already feel that it was going to be another hot day. The village looked abandoned. We decided to explore a bit as we waited. We soon discovered an ancient two-roomed building with an explanatory stone plaque saying that it had been erected during the Mamluk period (1250–1517 AD) in honor of a Muslim prophet named Saleh (Nabi means prophet, hence the village name), one of the five prophets named in the Koran. Saleh's career as a prophet conversely mimicked the biblical prophet Jonah. Saleh was sent to preach Mohammed's new religion to the pagan, Arab tribe of Thamud. Tradition says that the Thamuds rejected Saleh's message and were annihi-lated by Allah.

We then returned to the village center and sat down on a bench sur-rounded by shade trees. We waited. White houses constructed of concrete and limestone, adjacent to small garden plots and courtyards encircled by chest high concrete walls, all blended together into the whitish dust stirred up by the morning breeze. As early Friday prayers finally concluded, vil-lagers began to appear. Soon we were joined by some twenty-five people, primarily women and children with a handful of international supporters who came, like us, to link arms with the beleaguered residents of this village.

Nabi Saleh sits atop one of the rolling hills that overlook the fertile Raya valley. At the bottom of Nabi Saleh's hilltop, tucked into the bottom of

---

Case for Palestine, 189–97, for the consistent support provided by international and humanitarian legal bodies favoring the inalienable right of all peoples subjugated by an outside (colonial) power to resort to violence, if necessary, to secure their right to self-determination.

the valley, is a freshwater spring known as Ein Al-Qaws. For as long as any villagers can remember, the Raya Valley, the spring, the opposite hill facing Nabi Saleh, and a good deal of the land stretching to the southwest had all belonged to several families living in the area.

Not anymore.

In December of 1978 the Israeli government issued Military Order 28/78 unilaterally annexing 170 acres of Nabi Saleh's land by declaring it a closed military zone.[2] The designation is deceiving, however, for in the West Bank closed military zones are seemingly closed only to Palestinians. Order 28/78 was no different and it included provisions for the construction of a new Jewish colonial settlement on this very same piece of "closed land." This government sanctioned settlement would eventually be called Halamish. By bureaucratic fiat the residents of Nabi Saleh, the land's legal owners, were excluded from their own property and its essential water supply, while Israeli military orders paved the way for another illegal Jews-only colonial block defiantly facing them from across the valley.

Interestingly, Halamish was born in the same year that Israel implemented its "Drobles Plan," named after Matityahu Drobles, head of the World Zionist Organization Department for Rural Development.[3] The plan's official title was "Master Plan for the Development of Settlement in Judea and Samaria 1979–1983." Its rationale was blunt and to the point:[4]

2. Israeli government takeover of Palestinian land, even when privately owned, by means of military orders has been common practice both within Israel itself and in the Occupied Territories; for more on this problem, see chapter 14. For case studies of Nabi Saleh, Ein Al-Qaws, and the ongoing dispute with the neighboring Halamish settlement, see Tabar and Bari, *Repression of Non-violent Protest*; Baumgarten-Sharon, *Show of Force*; and United Nations, *How Dispossession Happens*, 15–18, complete with photographs and a map of the area. The reference to military order 28/78 appears on 27n43. For a broader discussion of Israel's policy of land confiscation, see Pappé, *Forgotten Palestinians*, 126–34. Under Israeli law all confiscated land automatically becomes Israeli state land (whether within Israel or in the Occupied Territories [de facto Israel]) and is placed under the control of one of Israel's several para-state agencies, such as the World Zionist Organization, the Jewish National Fund (JNF), or the Israel Lands Authority (ILA). The charters of these agencies, enforced as legally binding by the government, each demand that all land "*must be held in perpetuity for the exclusive benefit of the Jewish people.*" Consequently, they are closed forever to Palestinian use; see Tilly, *Beyond Occupation*, 117–20.

3. The World Zionist Organization was initiated by Theodor Herzl at the First Zionist Congress in 1897. Its goal is to promote Zionism and to serve as an umbrella organization for Zionist groups around the world.

4. Tilly, *Beyond Occupation*, 207 (emphasis mine); for more on the Drobles Plan also see 202, 255n180, n181, 257n225.

The civilian presence of Jewish communities [in the Occupied Territories] is *vital for the security of the state*. . . . There must not be the slightest doubt regarding *our intention to hold the areas of Judea and Samaria forever*. . . . [Land] should be *seized immediately for the purpose of settlement* in the areas located among and around the population centres [such as Ramallah] . . . in this period everything will be decided on the basis of *the facts that we create* in these Territories.

Several crucial assumptions governing the heart of political-revisionist Zionism are candidly embedded in this declaration. First is the notion that *the mere presence of Palestinians* poses a "security threat" to Israel. Second is the commitment to "create facts"—the more common phrase is "facts on the ground"—in the West Bank, ensuring that Israel will "hold the areas of Judea and Samaria forever." Those facts on the ground are the continual expansion of Jewish colonization into Palestinian lands, despite all international protests, opposition, and condemnation. Israeli policymakers commonly describe this continuous multiplication of Jewish settlements, typically planted in regions with high numbers of Palestinian residents, in both Israel and the Occupied Territories, as their *Judaization* program.[5] Daniel Reisner, former head of the Israel Defense Force's international law department, is quite candid in explaining Israel's "legal rationale" for this Judaizing of the land through colonization: "If you do something for long enough, the world will accept it."[6] In short, might makes right. And might infused with callousness and a stubborn indifference to the needs of others makes for the exponential increase of Jewish settlements throughout Occupied Palestinian Territory. In the worldview of political Zionism, Israeli security is strengthened through the multiplication of Jewish colonies because an increase in Jews creates a lower percentage of Palestinians. Here the central concern of political-revisionist Zionism is laid bare—*Israel is a nation-state for Jews only*. Thus, *any* non-Jewish population "threatens" Zionist Israel's ethno-national existence, especially when those non-Jews occupy land that Israel wants for itself. That land must be "redeemed" from

5. "Judaization" is the Israeli government's own label for its strategic management of new Jewish settlements, placing them in areas (such as Galilee, the Negev, and the West Bank) with a large Palestinian population but comparatively few Jews. The goal is to dilute the Palestinian presence with a Jewish majority that will fragment the Palestinian population and prevent the expansion of their communities; see Abu Hussein and McKay, *Access Denied*, 86–87, 190; Jabareen, "Controlling Land," 251, 259–60; Lustick and Berkman, "Zionist Theories," 43–44. For details about the Israeli government's illegal siphoning of government funds to settler groups for the Judaization of east Jerusalem, see Cheshin et al., *Separate and Unequal*, 211–24.

6. Shehadeh, "Op-Ed: Israel's New Settlement Law," 1.

non-Jews and "purified" by Jewish replacements, a national strategy that Israeli university professor, Oren Yiftachel, describes as "a product of the nationalist, expansionist logic of *purified ethnic space*."[7] In the world of political-revisionist Zionism, where outside criticism is often caricatured as the latest antisemitic step toward another Holocaust,[8] the need for such de-mographic policies appears self-evident. Every newborn Palestinian poses an existential threat to the ethnic paranoia intrinsic to the ethnically based, hegemonic Zionism ruling Israel.

The Jewish-only settlement of Halamish across the valley from Nabi Saleh.
Photo by the author.

The seizure of Nabi Saleh's land and resources by the Halamish colony is only one example of the unrelenting encroachment felt by Palestinians all throughout their homeland. Furthermore, Halamish was founded by members of an extreme, messianic, ethnic nationalist group named Gush Emmunim (the Block of True Believers) who are emphatic, and sometimes violent, advocates for Israel's annexation and settlement of the entire West Bank, which they prefer calling Judea and Samaria.[9] Though its official boundaries encompass over six hundred twenty acres, since the year 2000 these rapacious colonizers have unofficially expanded their borders even

7. Yiftachel, *Ethnocracy*, 190 (emphasis mine). Yiftachel is professor of geography and urban studies at Ben-Gurion University.

8. See chapter 16.

9. For more on the radical (and sometimes violent), ethno-nationalist philosophy of the Gush Emmunim movement, see Selengut, *Our Promised Land*; Zertal and Eldar, *Lords of the Land*; Masalha, *Bible & Zionism*, 137–59.

further by their *de facto* annexation of over six hundred ten additional acres in the Raya valley, the heart of Nabi Saleh's historic agricultural land.[10] To say that this colony of squatters has prospered on their free, government-requisitioned real estate would be an understatement. Over the years it has grown into a comfortable gated-community of Tel-Aviv commuters. Halamish settlers have a nicely paved highway linking them directly to the coastal city. These settler families enjoy a developed community with multiple playgrounds, an indoor pool, community center, amphitheater, medical clinic, library, school, and several synagogues.[11] Altogether it has grown to more than twice the size of its Palestinian neighbor across the valley and with many luxuries completely denied to the original inhabitants.

Halamish also ensures that the Ein Al-Qaws spring is no longer accessible to the people of Nabi Saleh. Initially, the village leaders filed a legal complaint against the army's confiscation of their land. Surprisingly, in 1978 the Israeli High Court ruled that the confiscation was illegal and ordered that the land be returned to its rightful, Palestinian owners.[12] As happens regularly, however, the High Court's ruling was never enforced, and the Halamish settlers never complied. The ruling was merely a judicial fig leaf issued to paper over Israel's ongoing exploitation. Over the years, villagers have submitted numerous additional complaints about trespass, property damages, and even physical assault—all of them dismissed for lack of evidence.[13] In the meantime, Halamish continues to expand, transforming the valley by turning the spring into an enclosed bathing-picnic area for the exclusive use of Halamish residents and their (non-Palestinian) guests.[14]

Israel's Jewish Colonization Association (ICA) issued another military order in February 2010 declaring that the spring and the surrounding area were now a protected archaeological site.[15] Any physical alteration of the spring area was banned—in theory. Apparently, archaeological sites in the West Bank are similar to closed military zones; the prohibitions apply only to Palestinians. Halamish settlers continued their development activities while the military government did nothing but turn a blind eye whenever Nabi Saleh residents were harassed or attacked while attempting to access their spring and nearby farmland.

10. United Nations, "How Dispossession Happens," 15.

11. Ehrenreich, "Is This Where the Third Intifada Will Start?," 3.

12. HCJ 32/78, *Tamimi v. Defense Minister* (unpublished); cited in Tabar and Bari, *Repression of Non-violent Protest*, 10n5.

13. United Nations, "How Dispossession Happens," 17.

14. See the Halamish settlement website, which includes a photo of the spring encircled by concrete and complimented by a picnic table at https://binyamin.org.il/565/.

15. Baumgarten-Sharon, *Show of Force*, 8.

Nabi Saleh villagers begin their weekly march. Photo by the author.

Still, the residents of Nabi Saleh have not given up. Since December of 2009, the villagers have hosted a weekly protest march. On this particular Friday morning in 2014, Terry and I mingled with the crowd of persistent villagers, waving Palestinian flags and holding homemade banners. All the women linked arms as they stretched across the narrow dirt road and marched ahead, loudly singing their protest songs beneath the brilliant, blue Palestinian sky. The children, all enthusiastic veterans in their own right, held up handwritten Arabic signs and waved colorful Palestinian flags as their voices joined in with their mothers', aunts', and sisters'. More silently, a few men and a handful of teenage boys marched along with their families. I wondered if most of the village men were off at work, or had they become disillusioned with this weekly exercise? I discovered later that they normally remained back in the village to protect their homes and elderly family members from possible attack by soldiers, as often happens. I wondered if any of these intrepid people still truly hoped that they might yet be allowed to walk all the way to their spring, its cold water bubbling out of a large, grey stone protruding from the valley floor.

We would soon find out.

The army was obviously expecting us.

In anticipation of the march, the local commander issued his weekly military order under Emergency Defense Regulation 101, declaring the entire village a closed military zone. By the stroke of an Israeli officer's pen, Nabi Saleh becomes a regular no-man's land where any group of ten or more people entering or leaving the village becomes subject to assault, arrest, and imprisonment.[16] Over the years, well over one hundred villagers have been shot and injured by live ammunition and tear gas shells. Many have been handcuffed, beaten, gassed, fined, interrogated, and jailed for violating the weekly order.

Israeli soldiers strategizing as they approach Nabi Saleh. Photo by the author.

A half-dozen gray-green Jeeps and armored vehicles sped into the intersection at the end of the village road, all skidding to a sideways, dusty stop about one hundred yards away from us. Several dozen soldiers, all heavily armed, quickly poured out and fanned out across the rocky ground

16. Taber and Bari, *Repression of Non-violent Protest*, 11; Baumgarten-Sharon, *Show of Force*, 14–16. Emergency Military Regulation Order No. 101, "Order Regarding Prohibition of Incitement and Hostile Propaganda Actions," prohibits more than ten people from gathering together for political activities without prior approval from the area's military commander—approval which would never be granted. Israeli soldiers possess sweeping powers to suppress such gatherings in any way they see fit and to imprison participants for up to ten years.

into a large pincer movement directed at the village. Staring at the villagers loomed a large, gray sniper tower crowned with an enclosed turret, rising as a steel and concrete monument to never-ending Zionist domination.

Sniper towers are common in the West Bank. This one overlooks the village of Nabi Saleh. Photo by the author.

Our goal was simple and peaceful: walk to the Ein Al-Qaws spring located about one quarter mile away in the bottom of the valley. That was all.

It was not going to happen today.

We had only travelled about fifteen yards when tear gas shells and canisters[17] began falling from the sky, pelting the ground, skipping and jumping around us. Nearby explosions brought clouds of tear gas wafting through the air like low-lying, noxious fog.

---

17. Tear gas can be delivered in various containers. Some are bulbous canisters with a narrow end fired from the muzzle of a gun. Others are metal cylinders approximately three inches long and three eighths inches in diameter. The cylinders, which I am calling shells, are fired like bullets through the barrel of a gun.

Israel soldier takes aim before firing at the villagers. Photo by the author.

Yes, in the Occupied Territories, even something as simple as walking to a nearby pool of water becomes a revolutionary, terrorist act in the eyes of a government enforcing an ethnic nationalist, military occupation.

The villagers began shouting at the soldiers to stop shooting, while the international visitors all coped as best they could. Most were well prepared with a cloth they could douse in water to cover their face. Others brought out a sliced onion as inhaling onion vapors fools the brain in a positive way as it denies the gas's chemical effect by muting its suffocating sensation. The villagers were expert at evading the gas or dealing with its effects, and it did not dampen the children's enthusiasm one bit. The flags continued to fly.

Soon the teenage boys moved up front and pulled out their sling shots to return fire—like modern-day Davids challenging the Zionist Goliath.[18] Rocks propelled by slender sixteen-year-old arms retaliated against high-powered rifles, rubber bullets, gas, sound grenades, armored vehicles, and soldiers in flak jackets wearing helmets with protective visors. A few boys

18. Israeli news outlets always justify the army's violent methods of "crowd control" by describing them as acts of self-defense when confronted by violent protesters. Over the years, I have witnessed a number of these confrontations. In my experience, Israeli soldiers have *always* been the aggressors in very *asymmetrical* confrontations where they clearly held the upper hand.

set tires on fire to obscure the soldiers' vision so that, hopefully, fewer gas canisters or bullets hit their target.

Teenagers throw rocks against Israeli munitions. Photo by the author.

It was not much of a contest.

Few of the rocks came close to touching a soldier, while demonstrators were forced to back off in order to keep out of range of Israeli fire.

I moved forward, downhill off the roadside to take pictures and talk to the soldiers. I was grateful that one of the village organizers, Bassem Ta-mimi, led my wife Terry away from the gas clouds and falling canisters.

As I continued to walk toward the soldiers, well to the right of the road, the village teenagers would shout out my name and say, "Look out" as they continued to throw their stones. Rocks, tear gas, and sound grenades all continued to fly unhindered.

When I got close enough, I shouted out to several of the nearest soldiers, "Why? Why are you doing this? They only want to walk to their spring."

Initially, they shouted at me to go back. Eventually, they simply ignored me.

I was certainly not the only Westerner who came to protest the grotesque inhumanity they perpetuated against the occupied Palestinians. This was not the first or the last time I witnessed the considerable inequities in these sorts of clashes, confrontations that pro-Israel advocates typically describe as violent, offensive riots that force nonviolent Israeli soldiers to defend themselves against unprovoked, vicious attack.[19]

I later discovered that we had gotten off easy this particular Friday.

Over the years, many villagers and visitors, all unarmed, have been seriously injured and a good number were also killed by the Israeli guardians. Protesters have been hit directly by tear gas canisters and shells, sound grenades, rubber bullets, and even live ammunition, causing bodily harm and death.[20]

As the morning slid into late afternoon, a mutual cease-fire emerged with members of both sides trickling back to where they had come from. The soldiers climbed into their vehicles and the villagers shifted their attention to village chores.

---

19. In a 2016 interview with the Jewish online journal *Forward*, journalist Ben Ehrenreich, who has spent considerable time covering the West Bank and Nabi Saleh, stated that he contacted the Israeli military which confirmed that "*they have no records at all of any soldiers ever being killed in a stone-throwing incident*"; see Avni, "Ben Ehrenreich." Ehrenreich also points out the absurdity of drawing a false equivalency between Palestinian rock-throwers and well-armed Israeli soldiers, "I don't think it's an exaggeration to say that there have been millions of stones thrown at Israeli soldiers since the first intifada. Yet not a single Israeli soldier has been killed by one. Many hundreds of Palestinians have been killed at demonstrations by Israeli bullets, but it never occurs to us to ask if the Israeli cause wouldn't be better served if Israel disowned all forms of violence." For Ehrenreich's own story of living in the West Bank, including Nabi Saleh, and witnessing Israel's military occupation, see his fine book *The Way to the Spring*.

20. For a litany of the many injuries suffered by both villagers and visitors, see "Military Steps"; Baumgarten-Sharon, *Show of Force*, 18–21; Ehrenreich, "Is This Where the Third Intifada Will Start?"; Goldman, "Nabi Saleh," 6–8; Taber and Bari, *Repression of Non-Violent Protest*, 12–14. There are many stories of people being killed and injured by direct hits with tear gas shells. The Israelis always insist that such "accidents" are inevitable. However, I know from personal experience that Israeli soldiers will aim these shells directly at protesters. At another protest elsewhere, I watched two soldiers aim a rifle directly at me from atop the Annexation Wall and fire two tear gas shells, with the obvious intent of hitting me directly. Fortunately, the soldiers were far enough away, and because tear gas shells are larger than actual bullets, I was able to watch the shells' trajectories and dodge out of the way in time.

After everyone else had gone home Terry and I remained, waiting for our bus. It did not take long for Mr. Bassem Tamimi—the same gentleman who had helped Terry earlier—to invite us into his home for coffee while we waited. I asked Bassem about his life, his wife and children, his village, and his commitment to continuing this campaign of peaceful resistance against Israel's occupation.

Mr. Tamimi is a soft-spoken, articulate man (in English as well as Arabic) with penetrating blue eyes and an easy smile. As we sat on his long living room couch, he pulled out a photo album to show us pictures of past marches and confrontations, many of them more violent than what we had experienced. Together we viewed a Belgian documentary about Nabi Saleh and Halamish, entitled "Thank God It's Friday," that had been broadcast throughout Europe.[21] We also learned about the Nabi Saleh Facebook page and website.[22]

His wife, Nariman, appeared with our coffee—coal black Arabic coffee which I have grown to love. Nariman is a perfect complement to her husband. She is a strong, protective woman who is not afraid to defend her home, her village, and her extended family. As she sat with us, her dark blue hijab wrapped tightly around her oval face, her dark eyes flashed with anger as she told her own stories about the repeated destruction of her home by recklessly aggressive Israeli soldiers. She described the constant worry she feels for her children who are continually at risk of being awoken by a flashlight in their eyes, yanked out of bed in the middle of the night, and hauled off for interrogation at the local army barracks.

What parent would not worry?

Our bus finally arrived after a lengthy and pleasant visit. Terry and I both hugged Mr. and Mrs. Tamimi as we said our goodbyes. As we took our seats on the bus, I looked over at the red-roofed buildings of Halamish. I wondered if any Halamish residents kept a pair of binoculars near a window in order to watch Nabi Saleh's weekly efforts to visit their spring. I suspect that the struggles of Nabi Saleh make for curious viewing by these

---

21. I recommend watching *Thank God It's Friday*, directed by Jan Beddegenoodts, produced by Jan Beddegenoodts and Niel Iwens with Cameltown Productions. The filmmakers spent two years filming in both Nabi Saleh and Halamish. They document numerous village protests and IDF incursions into the Palestinian village, including the murder of two village men by IDF gunfire. Personally, I find the interviews with Halamish residents most distressing because of their overt combination of Jewish privilege with callous indifference to the suffering of others.

22. See the Nabi Saleh Solidarity website at https://nabisalehsolidarity.wordpress.com/about/ and on Facebook at https://www.facebook.com/Nabi-Saleh-Solidarity-177013109017209.

right-wing, religious settlers.[23] They undoubtedly believe that they have already won the contest.

Do they root for the soldiers shooting at us?

Do they applaud when someone is injured?

Do they ever stop to ask themselves, what right do we have to take away their water?

Does anyone's conscience prick them enough to see their Palestinian neighbors as fellow human beings, no different than themselves?

We left Nabi Saleh having enjoyed a friendly conversation with a generous man and his hospitable wife. They were not bitter, but rather were hopeful. Their primary concern is ensuring that their children, grandchildren, and great-grandchildren will have a safe, peaceful, and sustainable future in the family village.

Why should the Tamimi family and their neighbors be seen as criminals in their own homeland by Zionists, or by anyone else?

23. At a different village protest a few years prior to this, I watched young men from the neighboring, religious settlement climb a large gravel hill in order to have a better view of the protesters dodging the tear gas and rubber bullets fired at them by IDF soldiers. Their finger-pointing and periodic laughter told me that we were providing their afternoon entertainment.

Chapter 10

A Day in the South Hebron Hills

As I MENTIONED IN the first chapter, my first trip to Israel occurred in 2009 through an academic exchange program between the college where I taught and a school in Jerusalem. I had planned to extend my stay after the coursework was finished in order to visit a few out-of-the-way places not typically listed on the standard tours—something I strongly recommend every visitor to Israel do for themselves.[1] I had discovered a number of Israeli humanitarian organizations that provided tours for visitors explaining their work on behalf of the Palestinian people. I booked two: one with *ICAHD* (the Israeli Committee Against House Demolitions), the other with *Breaking the Silence*.[2] As BtS explains in their publication, "Why I Broke the Silence":[3]

> For all of us, breaking the silence was the result of a direct and painful encounter with the occupation. It is the result of realizing that we cannot remain silent in the face of the blatant injustice

1. Several Israeli and Palestinian organizations offer tours in the West Bank. The group *Youth Against Settlements* offers regular tours of the Hebron city center explaining the reasons for the tension and open conflict occurring between the different communities living there; see https://kuminow.com/yas/, https://www.facebook.com/media.yas/, and https://twitter.com/YASHebron."

2. To learn about the work of *ICAHD*, see the organization's website at https://icahd.org/; for *Breaking the Silence* see https://www.breakingthesilence.org.il/.

3. Breaking the Silence, "Why I Broke the Silence," 3.

we saw through the window of the military jeep, or ignore the plight of those whose homes we forcefully raided in the middle of the night. The act of breaking the silence is our resolution to rise up against injustice, against the repression of freedom, and against the callous hardening of the heart, ever present in the occupation itself, and in all of us who served it.

These former soldiers become storytellers, collecting and publishing the personal accounts of other soldiers like themselves. It is no surprise, then, that Israel's government, led by Prime Minister Benjamin Netanyahu, has worked to shut the organization down.[4] After all, freedom of speech and the defense of universal civil liberties are not the core values of an ethnocratic Zionist state like Israel. Nevertheless, in order to cleanse their own guilty consciences members of *Breaking the Silence* confess their sins to the Israeli public; a public deeply entrenched in denial over what it means to be an occupying, military power, brutally controlling the lives of over four-and-a-half million Palestinians. I once asked a woman who worked with *B'Tselem*, a civilian, anti-occupation group, how such widespread, uniform denial was possible. She paused, shook her head and replied, "I don't understand it myself. I can only explain it as a form of mass psychosis."[5]

I had signed up for a tour of Hebron, a city south of Jerusalem with a growing community of Jewish settlers who, with government and military support, have unilaterally annexed a large part of the city center, expelling Palestinian families and businesses in order to take over their buildings.[6] Years ago, Israeli soldiers walked through the once-thriving Palestinian neighborhood on Yehuda street, welding doors and windows shut from the outside, often with families still inside, permanently closing down shopkeepers and family homes. During my subsequent visits to the West Bank, I have visited Hebron, been searched at the checkpoint guarding Yehuda street, and photographed the welds that unilaterally banished families and businesses from the properties that had been passed down for generations. Jewish settlers walk about freely, while Palestinians hurry along hugging the walls.

4. See "Defending Breaking the Silence"; "Government Advancing Bill to Ban Breaking the Silence"; Sales, "Israeli Officials Condemn Breaking the Silence"; Shaul, "Netanyahu Wants to Repress My Group."

5. For more about *B'Tselem: The Information Center for Human Rights in the Occupied Territories*, see https://www.btselem.org/.

6. For detailed information about the hostility of Jewish settlers and Israeli soldiers toward the Palestinian residents of Hebron, see the list of *B'Tselem's* published reports at https://www.btselem.org/publications/117/all; for *B'Tselem* articles, see https://www.btselem.org/search?gs=hebron as well as https://www.btselem.org/topic/hebron; for *B'Tselem* videos of settler violence in the south Hebron hills, see https://www.btselem.org/settler_violence_updates/during-corona-crisis.

**Palestinian doors welded shut from the outside by Israeli soldiers.
Photo by the author.**

When I arrived at the early morning rendezvous site, our veteran guides told us that there had been a change of plans. A recent outburst of settler violence had prompted our tour's rerouting into the hill country south of the city. After loading up, the old yellow school bus was nearly full of Western visitors like me, mainly from Germany and Sweden but with a sprinkling of Americans and Australians. We were traveling from Jerusalem to the West Bank, initially on the well-maintained Israeli highway before transitioning onto the roughshod roads of the Occupied Territory.[7]

It was my first experience of passing through an Israeli checkpoint. Soldiers entered the bus and scrutinized our passports as they scanned everyone's face, looking for Arabs or anyone else traveling to or from an Arab country. We all passed the test this time, but in subsequent years I have taken many more bus rides where Palestinian passengers fell victim to this obvious racial profiling. Sometimes a soldier singles them out immediately

7. The West Bank is traversed by two separate and very unequal road systems. One is for Jews, which is multi-laned, direct, and well maintained. The other road complex for Palestinians is typically narrow, circuitous and filled with holes. There are sections where Jewish and Palestinian cars can share the road, but the cars are marked by different color license plates. I have heard several stories from friends about Palestinian drivers being harassed and forced off the road by Jewish drivers.

and quickly escorts them off the bus while those of us with less Arab-like features are allowed to continue. Over the years, I have become familiar with, but no less disturbed by, these public acts profiling and segregation. Only Palestinians are forced to stand in line at checkpoints, waiting to be searched at the leisure of their sentries, travel permits scrutinized as they answer the questions of suspicious, gruff young men and women in military uniform roughing them up.

At this first stop one of our guides explained the deception behind this particular checkpoint. While it created the appearance that we were just now passing over the Green Line (Israel's internationally recognized eastern border)[8] and entering into the West Bank,[9] in fact, we had been driving through Occupied Territory, well east of the Green Line, long before we left Jerusalem. A great deal of Jerusalem's municipal boundary, including all of east Jerusalem and the Old City—with its high walls surrounding the temple mount, the Dome of the Rock, and numerous Christian holy sites—are located *in the West Bank*. I suspect that few tourists realize that the money they spend visiting Israel's main tourist attraction contributes to the financial exploitation of illegally held Palestinian land.[10] Sadly, even if they did realize it, a good many of them would approve.

As our journey turned south, the pockmarked road soon dwindled into a narrow dirt track cutting through expansive rolling hills covered in

8. The Green Line is the Armistice border that Israel agreed to with the Arab countries that had attacked it in 1948. Until the Six Day War in 1967, it served as part of Israel's eastern border.

9. Before the 1967 war, the "West Bank" was controlled by Jordan which is located on the east side of the Jordan River. From a Jordanian perspective, the territory conquered by Israel was on the west bank of the Jordan. Thus, an Israeli going into the Occupied Territory must travel *east* in order to enter the *West* Bank.

10. After Israel's victory in the 1967 war, it immediately "unified" west Jerusalem with the predominantly Palestinian east Jerusalem. Israel also expanded the unified city's municipal boundary by annexing twenty-seven square miles from the West Bank. The boundaries of pre-war east Jerusalem had encompassed a mere two-and-a-half square miles. This immediate expansion of Jerusalem's municipal boundary from two-and-a-half to twenty-seven square miles not only engulfed thousands of acres of Palestinian farm land, but included twenty-eight Palestinian villages and neighborhoods. Jerusalem's "city limits" have continued to expand into West Bank territory over the decades. Currently, a plan for "Greater Jerusalem" will eventually encompass one hundred ninety-three square miles of the West Bank stretching almost to Jericho. For maps of this ever-expanding boundary, see Imseis, "Facts on the Ground," 1067–68; Cheshin, Hutman and Melamed, *Separate and Unequal*, 263, 265. For details on the annexation of Palestinian land by expanding the city's municipal boundary, see *B'Tselem*, "East Jerusalem," https://www.btselem.org/jerusalem; and the Israel Ministry of Foreign Affairs paper, "Jerusalem," https://mfa.gov.il/ MFA/AboutIsrael/State/Jerusalem/Pages/Jerusalem%20The%20Citys%20Development%20from%20a%20Historica.aspx.

rocks, sprouting gray boulders with the occasional bush or tuft of grass. I could tell that we were on the northern end of the Negev desert. The bus came to a stop and released us into the middle of nowhere. We had two young men as our guides, both of medium height and lanky build. The leader doing most of the talking was a young man in his mid-twenties crowned with a resplendent mane of bright red hair matted into dreadlocks hanging below his waist. He had obviously left his military service far behind. Both men explained that they had served their three years with the IDF in Hebron and the surrounding countryside. They were intimately familiar with the region's recent history because they were part of it.

Palestinian man talks about the destruction of his village with members of Breaking the Silence on either side. Photo by the author.

Drawing our attention to the left, our guides pointed out the remains of what used to be a Palestinian village. Every home had been bulldozed, flattened to the ground after the area had been declared a "closed military zone." Our guides had assisted in demolishing the village and removing its inhabitants. Israel was planning to erect another Jewish settlement nearby. Our guides then pointed us to the right. On the far side of a small valley was the Jewish settlement, its red-tile roofing glistening in the bright sunshine. It had plenty of room to grow and no racial integration to contend with. In the language of political Zionism, the rocky ground had been "redeemed" because it was now "Judaized."

In the valley bottom was a modest olive grove. Between us and the trees were several huts blending perfectly into the hillside. A handful of villagers had refused to abandon their orchard. Sneaking back home after their deportation, three determined families had cobbled together new homes from the fractured rubble the bulldozers left behind. Carefully placed pieces of broken concrete were raised up into oval walls just over four feet high with an opening left for an entrance. The ceilings consisted of long tarps fastened together, stretched across the ovals and held up by poles, the edges kept in place by a final layer of rubble.

In the background, a new, illegal Jewish-only settlement built after the area was designated a "closed, military zone." In the foreground, the rubble-huts built by Palestinians who returned for their olive grove after their village was destroyed by the Israeli government. Photo by the author.

Makeshift Palestinian home built of rubble and tarps. Photo by the author.

A man with huge, calloused hands greeted us with a warm smile and invited us into his makeshift house. He and our dreadlocked, dissident leader hugged each other and spoke in Arabic as the rest of us crouched down to pass through the doorway. It took a few seconds for my eyes to adjust in the dim light. The dirt floor was covered with colorful, dust-suppressing rugs. Several small children played together while keeping well away from us visitors. Their smiling mother quickly invited us to have a seat on the floor as her husband and our guides set up a large easel and clip board with several maps in front of us.

Our tour leader then told us a story.

Every eighteen-year-old Jewish citizen of Israel, both male and female, is expected to serve a three-year tour of duty with the IDF. Our guide described the first gathering of his graduating class with the uniformed orientation officer sent to introduce the transition ahead of them from civilian life to military training. The officer dimmed the lights and began a slide show. His program consisted of picture after gruesome picture of dead Palestinians. Nothing else. Only the relentless repetition of mangled, lifeless, bloodied Palestinian bodies, men, women, and children splayed out awkwardly on the bare ground.

Leaving his roomful of coed teenage eyes to linger on the final grue-some imagine, the soldier announced, "Soon you too will learn that the hap-piest day of your life is the day you kill your first terrorist."

Our guide paused. I was stunned.

I imagine that every other high-school graduate sitting with my guide in that darkened room can also recall the lessons driven home by the fe-tishized, trophy images of human corpses. In fact, before leaving I asked our guide for clarification. Was there no nuance? Did the orientation officer clarify his meaning? Are you sure you're not forgetting something?

My red-headed guide repeated one word, No. No. No.

The IDF officer said what he meant. He believed what he said and intended to confront these fresh recruits with his convictions about the central purpose of their IDF service.

Lesson #1—all Palestinians, regardless of age or gender, are terrorists (or the breeders of future terrorists).

Lesson #2—it is every Israeli's responsibility, since every Israeli is obli-gated to serve in the IDF, to eliminate Palestinians.

Chapter 11

A Family Reunion Spoiled by Party-Crashers

THE AL-AZZEH FAMILY WAS excited about their upcoming reunion. The party had been in the planning stages ever since they all learned that the brother living in America was bringing his family back to Aida camp for a lengthy visit. It had been a long time since the widowed, family matriarch, now suffering from Alzheimer's disease, had seen all of her children, their wives and husbands, and all her grandchildren gathered together in one place. This brother had left the West Bank years before and emigrated to America where he became a citizen and a successful business man. He now wanted his children to spend time with their grandmother while they still had the chance. Mohammed Al-Azzeh, my photojournalist friend whose shooting is described in chapter 5, was also a happy member of the noisy, rambunctious celebration, embracing his uncle from America and the numerous cousins who all spoke with an American accent.

The elderly mother's home is relatively large compared to other dwellings in the Aida refugee camp. Once it became clear in the early 1950s that Israel would not welcome returning refugees anytime soon, the United Nations decided that they must be moved out of tents and into more permanent homes. UN officials (who were supplying the refugees with tents, food, and clothing) met with family leaders to determine how large each family's plot of ground should be. They began with a head count. How many children in the family? Even then, the Al-Azzeh family was a large household. So, they were allowed to build their new home of concrete cinder blocks on a sizeable piece of dirt. Over the decades, it evolved into a comfortable home with a small garden, a few fruit trees, and a courtyard with grape vines hanging from a trellis, all surrounded by a protective six-foot wall, as is common in that part of the world.

It was late afternoon and the clan was enjoying their time together. The adults were sitting on chairs in the courtyard while the army of children ran pell-mell through grandma's house and garden. The widowed head of the family was basking in the delightful presence of all those she loved, sons and their wives, daughters and their husbands, grandchildren, cousins, nieces, nephews and infants all together for the first time in many years.

Suddenly, the family's celebration was interrupted by a loud crack as the front door was smashed open. Several dozen soldiers, with automatic weapons pointed at the stunned family, announced that they wanted Mohammed. Everyone, including the frail grandmother, was pushed to the floor and made to lay on their stomachs. Women were yanked out of their chairs, heavy boots pressed against their backs to keep them down. The visiting uncle descended the stairs from his second-floor bedroom. Holding up his US passport, he asked what was happening and explained that he was an American citizen. A soldier ripped the passport out of his hand. Two others grabbed his arms and pushed him down the flight of stairs. As soon as he hit the floor, several more began kicking him in the chest and sides, breaking several of his ribs.[1]

The soldiers searched the home, making a mess of everything. When they finally found Mohammed in another upstairs bedroom, he was savagely kicked and beaten before being thrown into the back of a waiting truck. Several months earlier, Mohammed, who works as a photojournalist, was shot in the face at close range by an Israeli soldier as he stood on the veranda of his apartment taking pictures (see chapter 5). His attackers focused their punches on the parts of his face most damaged by the rubber bullet. The fragile areas were not hard to miss as Mohammed still bore the stitches and bandaging received at the hospital following his recent surgeries. Leaving shock, chaos, broken bones, children's screams, and a desperate family behind them, the soldiers climbed back into their trucks and sped off with Mohammed into the darkness.

---

1. I have copies of the photos taken by his daughter with her cell phone documenting his beating.

After harsh interrogation and time in a jail cell, Mohammed returned home to inform his family that the IDF was angry over the lawsuit he had filed against them. Mohammed had found a lawyer and was bravely suing the Israeli army, demanding that they admit his recent shooting was unjustified. He also sued for compensation over the physical and psychological damage created by the Israeli bullet fired at close range into his face. He also wanted the soldier responsible to be punished for his dangerous abuse of power. All of these would be reasonable demands in a democratic society with an equitable justice system, but that is not where Mohammed lives. He lives in the West Bank under military rule.

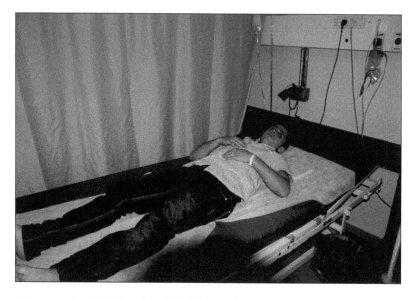

Young man in a Bethlehem hospital after being beaten by Israeli soldiers because he would not agree to work as their informant. Photo by the author.

In the Occupied Territories, a late-night house raid with a few physical beatings is a central component of IDF legal strategy. Here is the logic: If you think you can beat us in court, we will first beat you senseless in your home. It is a lesson in "Military Occupation 101"—when a Palestinian does something the Israelis do not like, they beat him (or her) into submission. I saw it once in a boy's face lying in a hospital bed. He had refused a soldier's demand that he become an IDF informer in the Dheisheh refugee camp. I observed the same occupation lesson at Nabi Saleh. I witnessed its effects in the south Hebron hills. Now I saw them vividly in Mohammed's broken, battered face. His arrest was another threat. The message was, stay down and keep quiet or we will do even worse things to you. His crime was "rebelliousness," for Mohammed was refusing to live in fear. While the armed forces of Zionist domination screamed, "Stay down!" Mohammed chose peacefully to stand up and to challenge them within their own system. He was pushing back against the oppression of a military regime that imagined it had the whimsical right to wield the power of life and death over him. Every oppressor demands that those they subjugate remain on their knees while quietly waiting for the benevolent scraps tossed from the master's table. Mohammed, however, was refusing to follow the oppressor's script. He was not planning terrorist attacks or planting car bombs. He was simply demanding justice, however unlikely that would be (unsurprisingly, Israel's military courts rule 90 to 97 percent of the time in their own favor).[2]

Working to ensure that the Al-Azzehs never forget their place in the world of political Zionism, Mohammed's case has repeatedly been delayed. It has never gone to trial. He has yet to receive an apology or compensation. His family struggled to pay his medical expenses, while the anonymous soldier who had aimed to kill an unarmed man returned home in Israel where he was undoubtedly applauded for his heroic service at keeping Israel safe.

TORTURING AN ENTIRE POPULATION

Over the years I have come to marvel at the general climate of peaceability that has spread throughout the vast majority of West Bank Palestinians since the end of the Second Intifada in 2005. Unfortunately, most of the Western world naively accepts Israel's version of their "conflict," where Palestinians are cast as the villains in Israel's heroic (even miraculous) story of democratic nation-building. Palestinians are regularly caricatured as malicious antisemites, another in a long line of people who hate Jews simply because they are Jews, ignoring the fact that Palestinian Jews lived harmoniously beside their Muslim neighbors long before the birth of Zionism.[3] Many Israeli leaders repeat the refrain that Palestinians are always the aggressors working to destroy an innocent Jewish nation—"to drive them into the sea" is their favorite phrase. The IDF, on the other hand, only responds reluctantly

---

2. Tilly, *Beyond Occupation*, 75; Haffar, *Courting Conflict*, 218–19. Ninety-seven percent of the cases brought before Israel's military courts conclude with a plea bargain. This itself is not unusual, but the extreme sentences laid down by military law, combined with the prejudice inherent within the system, causes the accused to plead guilty in order to secure a lighter sentence rather than go to trial where they will almost certainly lose.

3. See Jacobson and Naor, *Oriental Neighbors*.

in self-defense.[4] Sadly, Christian Zionists are inclined naively to consume Israel's nationalistic propaganda without question.

Yet, as my wife and I visit Israel and live in the West Bank, we consistently witness the exact opposite. I never cease to be amazed at the *incredible powers of restraint* exercised by an entire people enduring massive brutalization on a daily basis. Yes, some openly resist their oppression. But their efforts at resistance, which is a universal human right long recognized under international law, are generally meek and mild (even seemingly ineffective) in comparison to the shocking dehumanization imposed on them by Israel's military regime. Resistance is the inevitable flip-side of occupation. As long as there is an occupation, there will be resistance in one form or another. As long as Israel remains the occupier, it will always be the aggressor. Westerners who lionize the courageous resistance movements that fought against their German occupiers in World War II, should be the last to condemn Palestinian resistance today. The obvious double standard is the fruit of a debilitating moral blindness that refuses to acknowledge the actual facts on the ground in Occupied Palestine.

My mind often returns to the stories I heard from the red-headed veteran who first introduced me to the occupation. Years later I discovered that his graduating class was not the only crop of recruits being indoctrinated (brainwashed) into imagining that all Palestinians are terrorists. Many IDF veterans who share their stories with *Breaking the Silence* testify to the widespread racial prejudice that infests the Israeli military. In the organization's largest collection of veteran confessions, entitled *Our Harsh Logic: Israeli Soldiers' Testimonies from the Occupied Territories 2000–2010*, the editors explain:[5]

> Almost every use of military force in the Territories is considered preventive. Behind this sweeping interpretation of the term lies the assumption that every Palestinian, man and woman, is suspect, constituting a threat to Israeli citizens and soldiers.

The assumption that *every* Palestinian poses a threat to Israel exposes the ideology of political Zionism dressed up in a military uniform. Israel's racial animus toward Palestinians is *not* a defensive attitude reluctantly adopted in the face of unwarranted Palestinian aggression. This prejudice existed long before 1948 as a central tenet of political-revisionist Zionist thinking. It has always served as a primary source of fuel for the Zionist

---

4. Recall former Israeli Prime Minister Golda Meir's famous lament that "we can forgive the Arabs for killing our children, but we can never forgive them for forcing us to kill their children"; for several sources, see https://en.wikiquote.org/wiki/Golda_Meir.

5. Breaking the Silence, *Our Harsh Logic*, 2.

engine driving Israel's heartless, land-hungry program of Judaization—that is, the removal of as many Palestinians as possible from as much Palestinian land as possible to be replaced with as many Jewish settlers as possible. The approved method for systematically cowing Israel's victims into accepting their fate is simple: non-stop intimidation and violence. The official IDF term for its strategy is the *searing of consciousness*. In other words, Israel holds the red-hot branding iron while Palestinian consciousness suffers the searing. As former IDF soldiers have explained:[6]

> The term "prevention of terror" gives the stamp of approval to any action in the Territories. . . . In this way, the IDF is able to justify methods that serve to intimidate and oppress the population overall . . . the IDF established the principle behind its methods, calling it a "searing of consciousness." The assumption is that resistance will fade once Palestinians as a whole see that opposition is useless. In practice, as the testimonies show, "searing of consciousness" translates into intimidation and indiscriminate punishment.

There is a gruesome, inhumane parallel between Israel's interest in searing Palestinian consciousness and the goal of America's CIA torture program implemented after 9/11. Several US investigations have uncovered the thinking that lay behind the methods used by CIA interrogators. By torturing their detainees (a fact they hoped to obscure with the euphemism "enhanced interrogation techniques"), the interrogators hoped to create a state of "learned helplessness" in their victims.[7] Psychologists had discovered the condition described as "learned helpless" in laboratory experiments with dogs confined in cages wired to transmit electrical current. The dogs were shocked with random jolts of electricity in all sections of the cage for no apparent reason. Eventually, after discerning that there was no pattern to their pain, the dogs abandoned their efforts to escape the electric shocks. Instead, they curled up in a ball on the floor and refused to move, shivering with anxiety and whimpering as they endured the unpredictable jolts of electricity.

The poor dogs finally learned that they were helpless. They stopped searching for an escape, abandoned all resistance, and surrendered, exhausted, to their abuse.

Israel is applying the same CIA method of torture collectively to the native inhabitants of the Occupied Territories as were applied to so-called

---

6. Breaking the Silence, *Our Harsh Logic*, 8–9.

7. See Feinstein, *Senate Report 113–288*, xx, xxviiin32, 21, 26, 32, 464; Aceves, "Interrogation or Experimentation?," 75–102.

"enemy combatants" at Guantanamo Bay, Abu Ghraib, and other US black sites. They have been shut up in a large cage and treated like experimental dogs, continually shocked with indiscriminate acts of violence. All day every day, the IDF tortures innocent human beings, working to burn this lesson into Palestinian consciousness: they are helpless. There is nothing they can do for themselves but to stop resisting, lay down, curl up in a ball, whimper like a defeated animal, and surrender all hope.

I have the deepest admiration and respect for all those who refuse to cooperate with Israel's torture program, who refuse to whimper quietly in a corner by surrendering themselves to the cruelty of a seared consciousness. No one has the right to abuse another human being in this way. No one should ever be expected (much less required) to roll over and accept another's blasphemous abuse of God's image within them. Neither can the Christian church, for *whatever* reasons, be relieved of its responsibility for passing by on the opposite side of the road, eyes averted, ignoring the bloodied neighbor lying in the ditch (Luke 10:25–37). All Palestinians (as well as all Jews and gentiles around the world) display the identical image of God which expresses an aspect of what it means to be human every time they peacefully rise up before those who would beat them down. It is God's own image that resists and insists, "No more. Our Creator does not intend us for this. We want equality. We want justice."

Chapter 12

Christian Zionism Surrenders to Ethnocracy

THROUGH ITS UNCRITICAL ACCEPTANCE of the official Zionist/Israeli version of Jewish history, contemporary Christian Zionism has readily assimilated the blood-and-soil story line of ethnic nationalism created by men like Ben Zion Dinur (chapter 3). The results starkly appear in Christian Zionism's deeper allegiance to the fantasies of Dinur's historiography and its Romantic origins than to the biblical story line and the diversity of Jewish tradition. For example, Barry Leventhal, professor at Southern Evangelical Seminary in North Carolina, echoes political Zionism's intoxication with Dinur's mystical, blood-and-soil nationalism when he writes:[1]

> God has implanted a Zionist component into the Jewish DNA
> ... God has so worked in the collective soul of the Jewish people
> that we experience moments of recall built into the psychic
> memory of the nation Israel.

Professor Dinur could not have said it better himself. A collective, psychic memory of ethnic nationalist identity, divinely encoded into every Jew's DNA, has continually been wooing the Jewish people—at least, those who give sufficient attention to their true nature—back to the land of Palestine

1. Leventhal, "Israel in Light," 243.

like a school of seafaring salmon drawn irresistibly to their inland spawning grounds. Leventhal's words are a characteristic example of Christian Zionism's applause for the innate territorial "yearning" that supposedly tugs at the heart of every ethnic Jew (remember, it's in the DNA) now separated from her native soil.[2]

Exposing this close mapping of Christian Zionist apologetics on top of the standard, political Zionist historiography will set the agenda for this chapter and the next. Evaluating their shared paradigm in the light of Scripture will be an important theme running throughout the arguments that follow. I will also look at the complicated and highly discriminatory ways in which political Zionism fuses ethnicity with national sovereignty in order to create a Jewish, ethnocratic state. The next chapter will then focus on Zionist claims to unilateral ownership over all the land between the Jordan River and the Mediterranean Sea. In this way, I will establish the foundation for my own critique of Christian Zionism's intellectually shallow and morally bankrupt support for Israel's ethnocratic status quo.

ETHNOCRACY AND THE JEWISH NATION-STATE

Oren Yiftachel, a professor at Ben-Gurion University, has produced an important political and social analysis of Israeli society entitled *Ethnocracy:*

2. For additional examples, see Bailey, "Should Christians," 195; Goldberg, "Historical and Political," 115; Larsen, "Celebration," 307; Vanlaningham, "Jewish People," 120. McDermott, "Introduction," 15–18, tries to break this connection by insisting that Zionism is "not merely nationalism," hoping to distance nineteenth-century Zionism from the concurrent rise of nationalist movements in Central and Eastern Europe. He first points out that, with the exception of Greece and Italy, no European cultures or languages were as ancient as the Jewish connection to Israel. Secondly, he cites Hastings, *Construction of Nationhood* (without including relevant page numbers), to establish that European nationalism did not emerge with Romanticism but through the influence of Protestantism and the Hebrew Bible. Although McDermott creates a number of problems for himself, I will only mention two. First, the relative age of an ethnic group's claim to a supposed homeland has no bearing on that claim's historical legitimacy, something that must be adjudicated by other means. McDermott's argument here is based on a *non sequitur*: the fact that Germany and others were relative newcomers to the nationalist scene is irrelevant to demonstrating the veracity of Zionism's assertion that it (supposedly) represents an ancient, unbroken claim of Jewish nationalism to the land of Israel. McDermott's second argument falls into the trap of category confusion, since he fails to distinguish between different types of nationalism and their respective influences. Suggesting that a vague "European nationalism" was influenced by Protestant Bible reading fails to address the specific characteristics of the Romantic, blood-and-soil nationalism (as opposed to civic, citizenship nationalism) embraced by political Zionism. This confusion allows McDermott to ignore the obvious ideological symmetry between Romanticism and political Zionism.

Land and Identity Politics in Israel/Palestine (2006).[3] He is not the only Jewish scholar to describe his country as an ethnocracy, but he does offer the most detailed vivisection exposing the inner workings of Israel's ethnocratic machinery, the legal as well as the human architecture of Jewish ethnic nationalism in twenty-first-century Israel.[4]

Political Zionism, especially when combined with the emphasis on ethnic exclusivism of revisionist Zionism (see chapter 4), was destined eventually to construct an ethnocratic state. In describing Israel as an ethnocracy, Professor Yiftachel lays bare the state-sanctioned racism deeply woven into the fabric of Israeli society. He explains that *ethnocracy is a state apparatus (consisting of laws, government, military force, etc.) constructed by a dominant ethnic group. Its purpose is to secure and to expand the ethnic majority's control over contested, multiethnic territory, its remnant minorities, and the state's social-political operations.* Yiftachel's description of Israeli ethnocracy coincides perfectly with Australian anthropologist, Patrick Wolfe's studies into the characteristic, formal structures that emerge from settler colonial societies over time.

The primary objective of every settler colonial enterprise is *expanding settler control over territory.* As Wolfe explains, "the primary object of settler-colonization is the land itself."[5] Maintaining control and exploiting the land's resources requires the settler society to construct a system, a structure, for ensuring permanent settler dominance. Thus, noting that a society has its origins in settler colonialism is more than a historical observation, a comment on the past. It is actually a description of the "society's primary structural characteristic"; it is an essential insight into the present. Professor Wolfe puts it succinctly when he writes, "invasion [by settlers] is *a structure not an event*" (emphasis mine). The "logic" of this settler colonial structure creates "a sustained institutional tendency to eliminate the Indigenous population."[6] Because the settlers come to stay, the native peoples are obliged to go, willingly or unwillingly, alive or dead. Eliminating the native is a nonnegotiable corollary to territorial control. Native land must become settler property. Eventually, colonial rhetoric evolves to find ways of reversing the peoples' original relationship to the land. As in Australia, the settlers and their descendants are eventually declared to be the only true Australians, while the native Aborigines (Australia's original inhabitants) were

3. See also Yiftachel, "'Ethnocracy,'" 725–56.
4. Also see Kimmerling, *Invention and Decline*, 180–86.
5. Wolfe, *Settler Colonialism*, 163.
6. Wolfe, *Settler Colonialism*, 163; also 2–3.

legally segregated and denied equality by the nation's constitution.[7] They become aliens in their own land. Justification for this pernicious reversal of fortunes occurs by denigrating the native culture (as barbaric, wasteful, inefficient, illiterate, uneducated, and unproductive) while applauding the many benefits and improvements brought to the land by settlers (modern medicine, advanced technology, higher education, and making the desert bloom).[8] Settler rationalizations for ethnic cleansing know no bounds until finally the formation of a new, collective, national memory erases every trace of the new state's "criminal legacy of genocidal theft."[9]

Professor Wolfe's description of Australian history and its treatment of the land's Aboriginal peoples tells the story of every nation that arises from the foundations of settler colonialism, including the state of Israel and its ethnic cleansing of the Palestinians. Israeli ethnocracy is the poisonous fruit of political Zionist, settler colonialism.[10] Forgetting its true history and disguising its discriminatory, ethnic majority rule is a crucial step in the development of any ethnocratic society, particularly in today's postcolonial world. In our times, an ethnocratic state must craft a democratic façade if it hopes to cultivate hospitable diplomatic relationships on the international stage. Yiftachel explains how Israel cleverly distinguishes its regime *features* (how it appears to outsiders) from its *structures* (how it actually operates) in order to maintain this façade.[11] For instance, Israel's acceptance into the United Nations demanded that the nascent nation-state wear a veil of "formal democratic appearance" to deflect attention away from the "centralizing, coercive, and authoritarian"[12] reality of Israel's discriminatory, internal operations. Like the Wizard of Oz, Israel does not want outsiders to catch a glimpse of the madman pulling levers behind the curtain.

Keeping in mind that a modern ethnocracy needs to project a *faux* democratic image, we can better understand one of the mantras of many an Israeli politician: that Israel is *both* a Jewish *and* a democratic state. Even a little thought reveals the innate contradiction at the heart of that mantra. *Democracy for whom?* Yiftachel hits the nail on the head when he explains

---

7. Wolfe, *Settler Colonialism*, 30.

8. Wolfe, *Settler Colonialism*, 26–27.

9. Wolfe, *Settler Colonialism*, 33.

10. On political Zionism as settler colonialism, see Dana and Jarbawi, "Century"; Erakat, *Justice for Some*, 28, 54–55, 60; Kattan, *From Coexistence to Conquest*, 21–26; Pappé, *Ethnic Cleansing*, 7–13; Pappé, "Zionism as Colonialism"; Robinson, *Citizen Strangers*, 4–10; 19–21; Rodinson, *Israel*, 12–19, 35–96; Yiftachel, *Ethnocracy*, 12–13, 55–57.

11. Yiftachel, *Ethnocracy*, 35–37, 100.

12. Yiftachel, *Ethnocracy*, 3–20, especially 19.

that the "focus on regime features, and silence over structure appear to have blinded most scholars" who write about Israel's democratic values.[13] Incurious observers mesmerized by the ephemeral *features* of Israeli ethnocracy remain blind to its entrenched, undemocratic *structures*. Christian Zionism tops the list of Israel's blinded, uninformed devotees. This is why they consistently repeat superficial, propagandistic accounts of Israel and its governance over the Occupied Territories while apparently lacking any awareness of Israel's widespread structural abuses.[14]

Furthermore, Israel's story of perpetual victimhood as a beleaguered nation under continual attack from antisemitic Arabs also helps to convince the world that its mythical, tribal story line is, indeed, an accurate account of Jewish history. David Larsen's shameful chapter on Islam in his book, *Jews, Gentiles & the Church*, illustrates how Christian Zionism has swallowed this line of fictionalized Zionist history, hook, line, and sinker. Larson repeatedly claims that Palestinian/Arab/Muslim (he uses the terms interchangeably) resistance to the state of Israel is evidence of "the implacable and irrational nature of this [Muslim] hatred for everything Jewish" that has existed "from time immemorial."[15] Professor Dinur would be pleased, for he and his ideological comrades supplied the fodder for Israel's highly successful public relations campaign disseminating this myth of "ancient Jewish nationalism" inevitably opposed by ancient, antisemitic enemies.

By uncritically repeating Israeli propaganda, writers like Larsen are merely polishing their ethnocratic credentials. The popularity of such writings in the evangelical church is a spiritual travesty, for the well-attested facts tell a very different story. Christians have not always served as enthusiastic mouth pieces for a secular Israeli government. In fact, many of the earliest and most vocal opponents of political Zionism in Palestine were not Muslims but, in fact, Christians.[16] Furthermore, the early anti-Zionist opposition mounted by Arab Christians, Muslims, and Jews had nothing to do with antisemitism, despite early Zionist claims to the contrary. Instead, Palestinian anti-Zionism had everything to do with the growth of Palestinian nationalism, which was a thoroughly ecumenical endeavor. This pro-Palestinian, *nationalistic* hostility toward Zionism was an *anti-colonial* response that began to organize during the British Mandate and its efforts

13. Yiftachel, *Ethnocracy*, 100.

14. Examples of Christian Zionism's superficial approach to issues arising from Yiftachel's distinction between features and structure appear in Nicholson, "Theology and Law," and Khalloul, "Theology and Morality."

15. Larsen, *Jews, Gentiles*, 164, 159; also see 153, 161, 163, 165. Larsen is a retired professor at Trinity Evangelical Divinity School.

16. O'Mahony, "Palestinian Christians," 44–48; Porath, *Emergence*, 295–98, 303.

to assist in the creation of the state of Israel. Misreading Arab nationalism and anti-colonialism as new expressions of an "eternal antisemitism" was the egregious mistake of white, European, Ashkenazi (see chapter 4 note 25) Jewish immigrants projecting their own racial sensitivities, constructed during centuries of *European* antisemitism, onto the Arab residents of their new, foreign land, a land that they knew very little about.[17]

Palestinian Christians, Muslims, and Sephardi/Mizrahi (see chapter 4 note 25) Jews had worked cooperatively and lived together harmoniously for centuries.[18] Yet, their collective fears were raised by the growing influx of white, European (Ashkenazi) immigrants and the multiplication of their Jewish-only colonies built on Palestinian farmland, purchases that displaced indigenous farmers from their homes. *Political Zionism was the new face of European colonialism sponsored by the British government.* This is what disturbed Arab Palestinians, binding Muslims, Christians, and Jews alike in their hostility toward the Zionist threat.[19] It is not surprising, then, that Palestinian opposition to Zionist immigration and settlement intensified after Great Britain's announcement in the Balfour Declaration that His Majesty's government was actively supporting "the establishment in Palestine of a national home for the Jewish people."

Unfortunately, to tweak an old saying, state-sponsored deception can travel twice around the world before the truth can pull its boots on. Sadly, the Christian Zionist enthusiasm for Israeli ethnocracy, with its historic demonization of Muslims and the Palestinian people, is testament to deception's lasting power as well as the mind-numbing effects of theological wishful thinking, ideological blindness, academic ignorance, and public naiveté.[20]

17. Jacobson, *Oriental Neighbors*, 4.

18. Jacobson, *Oriental Neighbors*, 2, 19, 20, 22, 25, 49–50, 72. Jacobson provides evidence of (1) the distinction Arab leaders made between Jews and Zionists, as well as (2) the Sephardi/Mizrahi identification of white, European, Ashkenazi Jewish immigrants as "foreigners" and "occupiers" working to upend the harmony of Palestine's "indigenous people, Jews and Arabs alike" in their shared homeland. For further evidence see Flapan, *Zionism and the Palestinians*, 123–24, 150; Porath, *Emergence*, 25–32, 53, 59–61, 226, 304; Segev, *One Palestine*, 29, 70–71, 106, 325; Segev notes that the majority of indigenous Jews were orthodox and thus strongly anti-Zionist (16–17), and in the 1920s eight out of ten immigrants to Palestine were Ashkenazi (237).

19. O'Mahony, "Palestinian Christians," 45. Najib Azouri, a Syrian Christian in the Greek Catholic church, wrote a book in 1905 where he warned about the impending threat of Zionist colonialism in Palestine. O'Mahony says, "Najib Azouri was perhaps the first Arab who mentions the problems which would be created by the ambitions of Jews returning to Palestine, foreseeing the growth of a Jewish national movement aiming at the revival of the old monarchy of Israel."

20. A similar example lives on in the repeated claim that Iranian leaders have

WHAT DOES IT MEAN TO BE A JEW?

A foundational task for Israeli ethnocracy was establishing a formal distinction between the ruling ethnic majority and everyone else. Who are the insiders, and who are the outsiders? How was the young nation-state going to define Jewishness? Who exactly qualified for Jewish citizenship?[21]

It is no accident that Christian Zionism, with its own theological commitments to the resurrection of a Jewish national territory, has wholeheartedly embraced political Zionism's modern, nationalistic redefinition of what it means to be a Jew. To the evangelical mind, Israel's current ethnocratic state is the centerpiece for their apocalyptic hopes and dreams. Consequently, Christian Zionism marches in lockstep with Israel's insistence on defining Jewishness exclusively in terms of ethnicity/nationality.[22] Tuvya Zaretsky, a leader with the organization *Jews for Jesus*, is representative when he asserts that many people[23]

> wrongly assume that the religion of Judaism defines the Jewish
> people. . . . The source of birthright is found in the genes. . . .
> Only a Jew could make more Jews. Throughout the millennia

---

publicly declared Iran's desire to wipe Israel off the map. The former president of Iran, Mahmoud Ahmadinejad, supposedly made this threat in 2005 at a World without Zionism conference held in Tehran. However, numerous experts on Iran who speak fluent Persian were quick to point out that the publicly released translation of Ahmadinejad's speech was incorrect. When his words are properly translated, the Iranian president did not make a threat but expressed a wish in poetic language that "this regime occupying Jerusalem [i.e., political Zionism] must vanish from the page of time"; see Cole, "Ahmadinejad"; Cole, "Ahmadinejad We Are Not"; Cole, "Hitchens Hacker"; Dosa, "Explanation"; Weisbrot and Naiman, "Arash Norouzi Explains." In 2012 even Israel's Minister of Intelligence and Atomic Energy, Dan Meridor, admitted that no Iranian leader had never threatened Israel; see Mackey, "Israeli Minister Agrees." Nevertheless, Christian Zionists, as well as the Western press, continue maliciously to accuse Iran, together with other Muslim states, of plotting to destroy Israel.

21. See Orr's detailed analysis of this historical, political debate in *The UnJewish State*. It did not take long for the nascent state to learn that an exclusively secular answer to the question "who is a Jew" could not work.

22. Yes, religion plays a role in defining Jewishness for the purposes of Israel's citizenship laws, but it is a political expedient that has nothing to do with religious practice or devotion. It also is the basis for Israel's two different types of citizenship, one for Jews and one for non-Jews. Israel's success at using the *feature* of citizenship to disguise its discriminatory *structure* will be examined in chapter 14.

23. Zaretsky, "Israel the People," 39, 44. For further examples of Christian Zionism's commitment to a hereditary Jewish ethnicity, see Blaising, "Biblical Hermeneutics," 98; Blaising, "Theology," 85; Larsen, "Celebration," 307; McDermott, *Israel Matters*, 4; Merrill, "Israel According to Torah," 28–37; Saucy, *Progressive Dispensationalism*, 206–7; Vlach, *Has the Church?*, 154.

there was an unbroken chain of generations from Abraham to modern Jewish people.

Zaretsky illustrates how successfully political Zionism's historical invention of an ancient, unchanging, ethnic identity has established itself in public opinion (in both Jewish and Christian circles) as the determining feature for Jewishness. The Zionist fascination with genetic testing to determine a person's Jewishness is not surprising, then, given that political Zionism prioritizes ethnic connection to the land in a way that simply had not been true for millennia. It is not surprising that the search for a "Jewish blood theory" was quick to take root in the realm of Zionist biology.[24] Professor Shlomo Sand, author of the important book, *The Invention of the Jewish People*, and professor of history at the University of Tel-Aviv, provides a chilling overview of the early Zionist enthusiasm, not only for Jewish genetics but for *eugenics*, as well.[25] Yaacov Zess, a Zionist physician, was not far from the mainstream when he published an essay in 1929 declaring that racial hygiene was more important to the Jewish people than physical hygiene: "we, more than other nations, need racial hygiene. . . . For us, eugenics in general . . . is of even greater value than for other nations!"[26]

It is not surprising to hear critics of this quest for a "Jewish gene" point out the obvious parallels with Nazi Germany's Nuremberg laws which meticulously traced Jewish genetic heritage.[27] Avraham Burg, former speaker in the Israeli Knesset and author of the book, *The Holocaust Is Over: We Must Rise From Its Ashes*, has insisted that "after the Shoah, genetic Judaism has to end."[28] In a similar vein, Shlomo Sand notes that "it is a bitter irony to see the descendants of Holocaust survivors set out to find a biological Jewish identity: Hitler would certainly have been very pleased!"[29] To top

24. See Sand, *Jewish People*, 266–68, 272–80.

25. The eugenics movement believed it could improve the genetic composition of the human race by regulating human reproduction; at times, it included forced sterilization.

26. Quoted in Sand, *Jewish People*, 267.

27. Burg, *Holocaust*, 236–37; Kimmerling, *Invention and Decline*, 183.

28. Burg, *Holocaust*, 234.

29. Sand, *Jewish People*, 319; Sand surveys (270–80) the modern history of Jewish genetic testing. He summarizes the results by saying, "Yet so far, no research had found unique and unifying characteristics of Jewish heredity based on a random sampling of genetic material whose ethnic origin is not known in advance. . . . The bottom line is that, after all the costly 'scientific' endeavors, a Jewish individual cannot be defined by any biological criteria whatsoever." Also see Corcos, *Myth of the Jewish Race*; Kirsh, "Population Genetics in Israel"; Patai and Wing, *Myth of the Jewish Race*; Rabinowitz, "DNA Testing to Prove Judaism"; Rabinowitz, "Israel's Rabbinical Courts"; Shapiro, *Jewish People*; Slepkov, "Israel's Rabbis." Qumsiyeh, *Sharing the Land*, 18–30, also offers

things off, the search to discover Jewish genes has yet to produce results able to withstand peer review. This is largely because Zionist prejudices shape the researchers' conclusions according to their usefulness in supporting a desired political outcome. Dr. Sand quotes Israeli geneticist Raphael Falk's description of Jewish genetics as the art of "first shooting the arrows and then drawing the target around them."[30] From this perspective, it appears that current Zionist genetic research also has a great deal in common with Ben Zion Dinur's approach to Zionist historiography.

THE OLD TESTAMENT BACKGROUND

Actually, the roots of Judaism's intra-community debate over ethnicity vs. religion begins in the earliest stories of the Old Testament. The biblical account of ancient Israel describes two equally legitimate paths to community membership. On the one hand, the tribes of Israel all claimed descent from the patriarchs, Abraham, Isaac, and Jacob. Physical lineage was the initial route to Israelite identity.[31] At first, Israelite inheritance was traced through the father, as one would expect in a patriarchal society. However, for reasons that remain unclear, Jewish heredity was switched to the mother's line sometime in the second century AD.[32]

On the other hand, Israel was never a closed community. Interested outsiders, non-Israelites, were always welcome to ally themselves with Abraham's descendants provided they were willing to shoulder the obligations of the Sinai covenant, to be circumcised, to worship Abraham's God alone, and to share in Israel's fortunes, whether they be good or bad.[33] These "outsiders" who became "insiders" were converts, sometimes called proselytes, to Israelite religion and its resulting lifestyle. Proselytes became genuine children of Abraham, and some such as Philo insisted that they acquired an equal status to the native born.[34] Anthropologists refer to this

---

a helpful discussion; Qumsiyeh is a professor of genetics at Yale University.

30. Sand, *Jewish People*, 274.

31. On the difficulty, however, of positing a distinctive "ethnicity" to ancient Israel, see Dever, "Archaeology," 553.

32. Cohen, "Crossing the Boundary," 25–26. The bipolar nature of the question appears in this redefinition where *religious* authorities determine *physical* lineage.

33. Christensen, "Nations," 1047: "ancient Israel was open to non-Israelites from the start, according to Deuteronomy."

34. Philo, *Spec.* 1.51–53; 4.178; *Virt.* 102–4, 219; also see *Somn.* 2.273; *Spec.* 1.308. Stuehrenberg, "Proselyte," 504, points out that Roman catacomb inscriptions identifying proselytes buried with the Jews indicates that "they were accepted as full members of the community." Ezekiel 47:22–23 says proselytes have a share with the tribes of

acquired status as "fictive kinship"—a term describing the convert's new *fictional* lineage enabling them to take on *"the normative legal status* of someone who was Jewish by birth (Lev. 18:26; 19:33; Num. 15:14–16).["][35] Against this background, Zionists such as Zaretsky are guilty of serving as Zionist propagandists when they utter such falsehoods as "only a Jew could make more Jews."

While the short-lived rule of David and Solomon over a United Kingdom created breathing space for the emergence of an Israelite nation-state, the divisive rebellion that erupted after Solomon's death put Israel's national fortunes into a slow but steady decline.[36] In short, Assyria's destruction of northern Israel/Samaria in 722 BC, followed by the Babylonian conquest and exile of Judah's southern kingdom in 587/6 BC, set the religious wheels in motion for the genesis of a new understanding of what it meant to be a child of Abraham. Obviously, physical descent remained an important factor, but three historical interlopers gave increasing significance to the role of *religion* and *fictive kinship* in turning outsiders into children of Abraham.

The first interloper was the Assyrian empire. The Assyrian conquest of Samaria and Galilee virtually eliminated the northern ten tribes in approximately 722 BC. The majority of Israelites had their tribal identities erased as they were intermingled and resettled throughout a vast Assyrian empire. The second interloper was the Babylonian conquest of Judea in 587/6 BC. Even though the Babylonian exile removed only the upper echelons of Judean society, the majority of the exiles chose not to return to their homeland when they were eventually given the chance in 538/7 BC.[37] This body of contented exiles would lay the foundations for Babylon's future reputation as an important seat of Jewish, rabbinical learning.

Israel in the "promised inheritance"; also see Judith 14:10 and the story of Aseneth's conversion in *Joseph and Aseneth*; Steuhrenberg, "Proselyte," 503.

35. Burns, "Conversion and Proselytism," 484 (emphasis mine). Ancient rabbis and modern scholars both debate whether a proselyte was acceptable as "a Jew" or as someone "like a Jew." All agree, however, that the proselyte's *legal status* was identical to that of the native born, and his descendants were thoroughly Jewish. See Cohen, "Crossing the Boundary"; Dunn, *Jesus, Paul*, 143; Feldman, "Conversion to Judaism"; Katzoff, "'God of Our Fathers'"; Schiffman, *Who Was a Jew?*; Sanders, *Paul*, 206, notes that "the formal definition of a true proselyte and a faithful native-born Israelite is the same."

36. For a review of ancient evidence regarding Israel's status as a "nation," see Liverani, "Nationality and Political Identity," 1031–36.

37. Consequently, there may well be Arab, Mizrahi Jews in Palestine today who could theoretically trace their lineage (if it were possible) back to the ancient Judeans left in place by the Babylonians. The problem for Jewish genetics, however, is that: first, this particular community forms a small subset of Jews in Israel today; and second, the Arab/ Mizrahi are distinct from the Ashkenazi Jews who immigrated to Palestine from Europe.

These two events of scattering and exile marked the beginning of what is called the Jewish Dispersion or Diaspora. Forever after more Jews lived outside their original homeland than lived within it. Jewish communities sprung up all throughout the known world where the exiles faced new challenges at adapting to life in foreign lands. The only thing these dispersed exiles had left was obedience to the covenant, the Torah, and faith in Abraham's God—in other words, *they had religion*. Even though a Jewish remnant returned to Judea from Babylon to construct a second temple with a priesthood and sacrifices (see the books of Ezra and Nehemiah), and there would eventually be new rulers over a short-lived independent state (the period in between the Maccabean Revolt and the Roman conquest), the Diaspora had already created an international Judaism.

The third interloper appeared in the form of foreigners, the new people-groups surrounding the displaced exiles. As Jewish communities established themselves, synagogue services attracted interested visitors who often grew increasingly sympathetic to the Jewish faith. We can assume that these religious transactions were hospitable because of the sizeable increase in the Jewish community all throughout the Diaspora. More than a few historians are convinced that the great numerical growth of the Jewish people in Diaspora can only be accounted for by mass conversions.[38] For instance, Uriel Rappaport, professor of Jewish history at the University of Haifa, insists that:[39]

> Given its great scale, the expansion of Judaism in the ancient world cannot be accounted for by natural increase, by migration from the homeland, or any other explanation that does not include outsiders joining it.

Those outsiders brought their outsider genes along with them. The "great scale" of sympathetic outsiders created a great scale of genetic mixing. It is not hard to see why the search for an identifiable Jewish genetic code continues to fail. No, there is *not* an unbroken ethnic lineage running from Abraham through ancient Israel culminating in all Jewish people today. That has always been a myth. The reality of the Diaspora, with Jews marrying converts and others over a very long period of time, is explanation enough for why Arab Jews look like Arabs; why European Jews look European; and

---

38. For an extensive account of Judaism's expansion around the world through mass conversions, see Sand, *Jewish People*, 150–249; for a discussion of the biblical, second temple, and Rabbinic literature on Jewish proselytes, see McKnight, *Light*, 11–19, 25–43, 49–89.

39. Sand, *Jewish People*, 154, quoting from Rappaport's unpublished doctoral dissertation completed in 1965; also see Patai and Wing, *Myth*, 51–118.

why Ethiopian Jews look Ethiopian. It's because they are.[40] The universal Jewish distinctive is religion, not genetics, not ethnicity, and not nationality. Unfortunately, the long-term dominance of state-controlled educational curricula has produced an Israeli populous that firmly believes the myth. "Zionist pedagogy produced generations of students who believed wholeheartedly in the ethnic uniqueness of their nation" such that by the end of the twentieth century "the average Israeli knew that he or she belonged to a definite genetic group of fairly homogeneous ancient origin.[41] It is easy for ethnocentric falsehoods like these to persist when they are shielded beneath the protective bubble of an all-encompassing, nationalistic mythology.

Keeping this complex historical background in mind, it is not surprising to learn that Zionist historiography ignores the crucial developments in Jewish life that occurred in the Dispersion. The realities of an ancient Diaspora create too many challenges to the hegemony of political Zionist historiography. The exiled Judeans who chose to remain in Babylon were not the only Jewish group existing abroad. Diaspora Jews settled contentedly in their various new homelands, and this dispersion continued unabated through the centuries. *There is no historical evidence* of a Diaspora-wide "longing to return" to the fatherland as political Zionists like Ben Zion Dinur have repeatedly asserted. In summarizing the ethos of Jewish literature composed throughout the Diaspora, Eric Gruen concludes that "a sense of displacement did not dominate Jewish consciousness in communities strewn around the Mediterranean. It is noteworthy that Jews seem to have felt no need to fashion a theory of Diaspora."[42] This fact also fills out the explanation as to why, from its inception, political Zionism ridiculed and demeaned Diaspora Jews. Political Zionism wanted to erase the Diaspora's formative role in shaping world Judaism as we know it today. This Diaspora piece—the largest piece—of Jewish history explains why there has never been any such thing as a unifying, Jewish ethnicity nor a single Jewish nation ceaselessly longing to return to its native soil. Ever since the Assyrian slave-drivers forced Jews into permanent exile; and ever since the Babylonians pillaged Judean villages and destroyed the temple in Jerusalem, the only consistent, identifying feature of the Jewish people has been their religion.

---

40. Patai and Wing, *Myth*, 241, conclude their study of Jewish genetics by saying, "Jewish groups from different parts of the world are very different genetically . . . [while] Jews of a certain area tend to resemble the surrounding non-Jews more than they resemble Jews from other parts of the world"; also see 32–33, 37–39, 49–50, 90, 116, 189, 193, 261.

41. Sand, *Jewish People*, 273, 275.

42. Gruen, "Judaism in the Diaspora," 98; see his entire chapter on pp. 95–120.

Chapter 13

Ethnocracy, Galatians 3:6–9, and the Redefinition of God's Covenant People

MEGACHURCH PASTOR JERRY FALWELL stumped his way across the nation in 1976 holding a series of "I Love America" rallies. His goal was to rejuvenate the conservative, Republican political principles he believed essential to the country's future. Out of those rallies arose Falwell's influential political organization, the Moral Majority. Fusing his Southern Baptist principles (in the 1950s and 1960s Falwell opposed civil rights and racial desegregation) to the conservative, Cold War policies of the Republican party, Falwell became one of America's most vocal advocates for Christian Zionism. In his mind, loving America went hand in hand with loving Israel. In fact, he once told an ABC TV reporter, "You can't belong to Moral Majority without being a Zionist."[1] Ensuring that both nations remain militarily unassailable was the only moral thing to do, in his mind. Christian love requires supplying your closest allies with whatever weapons they want. Combatting "leftist" criticisms of either American or Israeli government policies was as essential to Falwell's view of morality as was fighting abortion. America and Israel, standing together in mutual military might, were the world's two shining beacons of morality, freedom, and democracy. Churchmen like

---

1. Kaplan, *Our American Israel*, 221.

Jerry Falwell and John Hagee illustrate how inseparable political Zionism and Christianity can become in American, conservative circles.

How can we explain Christian Zionism's deliberate conformation to political Zionism's invented traditions of blood-and-soil nationalism, a nationalism in constant need of larger military budgets and more American armaments? This question is especially pressing in light of Christian Zionism's blind indifference to Israel's long-standing crimes against the Palestinian people.[2] By baptizing Israeli ethnocracy into the muddy waters of Christian Zionism, the evangelical church has raised up a syncretistic idol bent on hammering the square peg of Zionist ethnocentrism into the round hole of gospel equality.

One of the syncretistic distortions created by Christian Zionism's acceptance of Israel's ethnocentric story line appears in the repeated refrain that "the church is never called Israel," "the church is not spiritual Israel," "the church does not replace Israel," "the church is not true Israel."[3] This mantra is restated again and again in Christian Zionist literature. For political Zionist ethnocracy, Jewish Israel must remain ethnically distinct. Christian Zionism shouts, "Amen!" but then adds its own twist. Not only must Israel remain ethnically distinct, it must also remain distinct from the Christian church since Israel has its own unique and glorious role to play in God's apocalyptic plans for this world (see chapters 7 and 8).[4]

Paul's surprising Letter to the Galatian church, however, has a very different story to tell. Here the apostle and former pharisee firmly addresses any and all forms of Christian faith that would require believers in Jesus to take on Jewish identity markers or to espouse any form of ethnic supremacy. Paul's unprecedented message to this nascent community of Jesus followers in Asia Minor will help to clarify why the Christian church must not fall in line with an ethnocratic ideology where Israel's blood-and-soil nationalism becomes an ingredient of God's plan for a people bearing his name.

---

2. This alone cannot explain evangelicalism's coldheartedness toward Palestinian suffering and Israeli abuse, but exploring that particular corner of evangelical immorality is beyond the scope of this book.

3. See various iterations of this point in Blaising, "Israel and Hermeneutics," 162; Blaising, "Theology of Israel," 87, 98, 100; Burns, "Future of Ethnic Israel," 228; Hoch, "New Man," 108, 113, 118–19, 126; Glenny, "Israelite Imagery," 179, 183, 185–87; Horner, *Future Israel*, 272–73; McDermott, "History of Supersessionism," 43; McDermott, *Israel Matters*, xii, xvi, 19–31, 70; Vlach, *Church*, 149–50, 151, 154, 164, 179, 181–82, 183, 201; Vlach, *Has the Church?*, 149, 151–55.

4. Some like Gerald McDermott do acknowledge a covenantal connection between Israel and the Christian church, but the two remain segregated as Christians are only allowed the (fictitious) status of "associate" membership; see *Israel Matters*, 27.

JESUS RECONFIGURES ISRAEL'S COVENANT

Richard Longenecker points out that in Galatians 3:6–9 "Paul's exegesis of Scripture in these verses (and throughout the rest of chapters 3 and 4) goes far beyond the rules of historico-grammatical exegesis as followed by biblical scholars today."[5] Longenecker's accurate observation is telling. Most evangelical interpreters and scholars assert that the literal results of grammatical-historical interpretation is the gold standard for an accurate reading of the Bible. But Paul never got that memo. Instead, as we will see, the apostle interpreted Hebrew Scripture in ways similar to his Jewish contemporaries, none of whom concerned themselves with the niceties of historico-grammatical literalism.[6] Although this is certainly the starting point for good biblical interpretation, it is only the beginning. We have seen how New Testament authors regularly "transgress" these rules of literalism. Now Paul's message from Galatians will stretch those acceptable boundaries even further as he interprets the Old Testament in ways that had "no precedent in early Judaism."[7]

By the time Paul the former pharisee wrote his Letter to the Galatians he had been working as a missionary among Jews and gentiles for well over a decade. Paul had been investing his life into persuading members of the synagogue, as well as pagans in the open market, that a crucified Jew named Jesus was, in fact, the resurrected, ascended Lord and Savior of the world. After developing his apostolic ministry in his hometown of Tarsus (Acts 9:30; 11:25–26), Paul did not undertake his new missionary work (Acts 13:1–3) with a blank slate. He well knew the long-standing expectations for gentile proselytes joining the Jewish community. Proselytes received a new paternity by way of fictive kinship to father Abraham. In this way, former outsiders became insiders, legitimate children of Abraham with a new lineage. Proselytes entered into the Abrahamic covenant as full-fledged members of God's covenant people.[8]

Paul's Jewish-Christian, Galatian opponents—he calls them the circumcision group in Galatians 2:12—infuriated the apostle by seeking to make Jesus' followers into heirs of the line and tradition of Abraham in

---

5. Longenecker, *Galatians*, 110.

6. See Longenecker's classic book, *Biblical Exegesis in the Apostolic Period*.

7. Harlow, "Early Judaism," 405.

8. See Hahn's insightful discussion in *Kinship by Covenant*, 37–48. He explains how ancient covenants formed and confirmed kinship ties (including fictive kinship) in the cultures of the southern Mediterranean, Asia Minor, and the Middle East; see his discussion of kinship and covenant in Second Temple Judaism and the book of Galatians, 238–77.

the manner of the old covenant. Drawing from Jewish proselyte traditions, Paul's opponents applied the same requirements of circumcision and Torah observance to gentile members of the Galatian church. Receiving salvation and the gift of the Spirit was not enough for this circumcision group. They required gentile disciples to become converts to Judaism after they had come to faith in Christ. For this circumcision party, gentile believers in Jesus needed to become *proper* proselytes, to both Judaism and the Jesus community.

Paul would have none of it.

Christ's community, composed of Jews and gentiles, was something entirely new, creating One New Man/Person, a New Humanity, as explained in Ephesians 2:15 as we saw in chapter 8. The old Jewish paradigm for gentile proselytes was irrelevant to the followers of Jesus. More startling than this, Paul insisted that Jewish children of Abraham also had their relationship to God radically transformed by the salvation accomplished by Jesus' death, resurrection, and the gift of the Spirit. For Paul, the first priority for both Jews and gentiles had nothing to do with circumcision or Torah. Since the advent of Christ, salvation for everyone was dependent on faith in Jesus and his gospel, full stop. Paul had no interest in teaching gentiles how to become Jews, and he did not want anyone else in his churches undermining that message. Instead, Paul was teaching both gentiles and Jews about the redefining power of walking *in the faith* of Abraham. To this end, Paul reminded his readers that Abraham was blessed for his faith (Gen 15) long before he was told to be circumcised (Gen 17).[9] Drawing from Genesis 15:6, Paul writes:

> Consider Abraham: "He believed God and it was credited to him as righteousness." Understand, then, that those who believe are children of Abraham. (Gal 3:6–7 NIV)

The death and resurrection of Jesus had radically transformed how all God's people were defined or formed. From now on entering into a covenant relationship with Abraham's God—a status Paul denotes with the word "justify" or "make righteous" (Gal 3:8)—was established through trust in, or allegiance to, the resurrected Jesus alone (Gal 2:15; 3:2–5, 14, 22–25;

---

9. Second Temple Judaism had closely tied Abraham's faith in Genesis 15 to his obedience, either to the command to be circumcised in Genesis 17, or his willingness to sacrifice Isaac in Genesis 22. Different groups forged the connection between Abraham's faith and his obedience, more or less extensively, in various ways. Paul is distinctive in cutting that tie and insisting that Abraham's faith stands on its own; see Longenecker, *Galatians*, 110–13; Silva, "Galatians," 795.

6:6).[10] Allegiance to Christ forges the new kinship bond that gentiles need in order to become members of the Abrahamic covenant and the family of God. Furthermore, that same faith commitment is also required of Jews. For Paul, covenant relationship with Abraham's God is now defined through the resurrected Jesus, not through birth into the Jewish community nor by becoming a Jewish proselyte. *Circumcision and Torah observance are no longer the defining signs of covenant membership.* Paul applies Genesis 15:6 universally, without distinction to all of humanity, Jew and gentile alike.[11] Faith in Christ is the definition of being a part of God's people, this is true for everyone, gentiles *and* Jews (Gal 5:6; 6:15). E. P. Sanders makes the crucial observation in his classic work, *Paul and Palestinian Judaism*: "It is most striking that Paul thought that everyone—whether Jew or Gentile—must *transfer* from the group of those who are perishing to the group of those who are being saved."[12] Gentiles who believe in Jesus are not folded into physical Israel any more than physical Israel can be folded into Paul's Galatian church by circumcision and Torah.

Having first established the universal necessity of faith alone in verses 6 and 7, Paul continues his unprecedented line of argument in verses 8 and 9:

> Scripture foresaw that God would justify the Gentiles by faith, and announced the gospel in advance to Abraham: "All nations will be blessed through you." So those who rely on faith are blessed along with Abraham, the man of faith. (Gal 3:8–9 NIV)

God had declared Abraham righteous (justified), while he was still an uncircumcised gentile, simply because he trusted God to remain faithful. At this point, Paul abruptly pulls the rug out from under his opponents once and for all by interpreting God's covenantal blessing to Abraham—"all nations will be blessed through you"—as an Old Testament announcement of the New Testament gospel. In other words, Abraham's justifying faith in God

---

10. See the two very useful and important books by Matthew Bates, *Salvation by Allegiance Alone* and *Gospel Alliance*.

11. Hardin, "Equality in the Church," 227, attempts to defend the continuing significance of circumcision for Jewish believers in Jesus, in part, by arguing that Galatians is addressed only to gentile members of the Galatian church. This position is similar to Zionist efforts at arguing that 1 Peter is addressed only to Jewish members of the church (see chapter 7). In both instances, I find the arguments equally unconvincing. Hardin's claims remain vague since he does not elaborate in what respects circumcision (and Torah observance) would remain valuable for Jewish Christians, in Paul's view.

12. Sanders, *Paul and Palestinian*, 548. Sanders goes on to point out that the only possible parallel to Paul's view appears in the Qumran community who insisted that all other Jews must repent and join their "new covenant" if they hoped to be saved; also see Sanders, *Paul, the Law*, 68–70, 172–78; Westerholm, *Perspectives*, 374.

was of the same sort as the Christian's justifying allegiance to Christ[13]—a claim certain to knock the socks off of Paul's opponents. Accordingly, God foreknew that a day would come when faith in Jesus Christ was all *anyone* would need to be in right relationship with Abraham's God, and that is, *in effect*, what Abraham was told in Genesis 15. Therefore, "all nations will be blessed," just as Abraham was blessed. The nations are blessed as Abraham was, through faith, even as Abraham was justified through faith while he was still uncircumcised. By shifting his focus from "those who believe" in verses 6 and 7 to "the Gentiles by faith" in verses 8 and 9, Paul sharpens his point. The Jewish proselyte paradigm in Paul's reasoning simply did not apply to gentile members of the Galatian church, regardless of the arguments of the circumcision group.

In short, Paul insists that anyone, whether Jew or gentile, who trusts in Jesus and his gospel is considered righteous before God, in the same way that Abraham was "reckoned" to be righteous on the basis of his faith. Consequently, *trust in the resurrected Jesus has become the exclusive avenue to kinship with Abraham.* This applies to everyone equally. Physical descent from Abraham is no longer relevant in this regard. Only through faith in Christ does anyone become a child of Abraham and thus a member of the Abrahamic covenant that has been fulfilled in Christ's new covenant. We see a similar thought pattern in Paul's Letter to the Romans when he states that "not all who are descended from Israel are Israel. Nor because they are his descendants are they all Abraham's children" (9:6–7; also see 4:16). Here Paul insists that only those Jews who pledge their allegiance to Jesus as Messiah can now claim the title Israel. They alone are true Israel. Yet, even this redefinition stops short of explicitly applying the title Israel to believing gentiles who are also, clearly, children of Abraham through faith (Rom 4:16–17; 9:8, 24, 30–32; also Gal 3:14, 26–29). The golden thread running through all of this is Paul's theological reading of Genesis 15:6 which has significant theological payoff regarding Zionism.

First, while Christian Zionists are correct in insisting that the New Testament never refers to the Christian church as the "new" or "true" or "spiritual" Israel, they fail to grasp why this is so. Rather than protecting physical Israel's distinct identity apart from the church, it actually serves to distinguish the Jewish-gentile community of Jesus followers as a new type of human community or people of God (chapter 8). The Jesus movement constitutes a "third race," as it were, with respect to both physical Israel and the gentile world. The Christian community is the New Humanity described in

---

13. I realize that using the term Christian in this context is a bit anachronistic, but it helps with clarity.

Ephesians 2. Abstruse objections against the idea of people being stripped of their ethnic identities are more rhetorical misdirection than substantive critique.

It is the church's unique identity that explains why Paul does not declare the Jesus movement to be the new Israel. Even though his arguments lean conceptually in that direction and have led some to use such language, Paul never does.[14] While anti-Jewish prejudice played a part in the way that many interpreters throughout the centuries have seen fit to do what Paul does not—designate the Christian church as the true, spiritual Israel—part of why they did so is due to the shape of Paul's argument. This too betrays a fundamental point of Paul's language, that a new covenant humanity is created in Christ, not just that Israel is transposed to the Christian church. Paul well knows that actual Israelites exist. He is one. He never denies that Jews should bear the title Israel, since Israel has served a singular role in salvation history (Rom 9–11). On that basis, the ancient moniker remains theirs even though their many blessings have been transposed into another key and rewritten for a new community by the Jewish maestro, Jesus Christ.[15]

Second, the Apostle Paul's interpretation was not bound to the plain sense meaning of texts as understood by the grammatical-historical method.[16] Had New Testament writers like Paul been bound to modern rules of Bible reading, they could never have produced the interpretations we find all over the New Testament and certainly in Galatians. Rather, Paul, along with his Jewish contemporaries, had several other reading strategies, and they were not limited to literalist readings of Scripture. While Paul uses some of his contemporaries' intuitive methods, his conclusions are deeply formed by his experience and the revelation he received regarding salvation through Christ. Jews who did not follow Jesus did not follow or emulate Paul's unprecedented rereading of the Abrahamic covenant in light of his faith in the resurrected Jesus. Paul clearly reinterpreted the Old Testament promises while reading backward, looking at the story of Abraham through a gospel lens. New Testament scholar, Bruce Longenecker, insightfully remarks on Paul's apostolic penchant for finding "scripture to say Pauline things."[17] Since the coming of Christ, the Christian significance of Scripture is no longer

---

14. The possible exception appears in the hotly contested verse, Galatians 6:16. Though I incline toward the view that Paul is referring to the mixed Jewish-gentile community as Israel, I also recognize the troublesome ambiguity of Paul's words.

15. Sanders, *Paul, the Law*, 171–79, offers a helpful explanation of these complicated issues, admitting that "the terminology is confusing."

16. Fortunately for him, he had no such rules to contend with.

17. Longenecker, *Triumph*, 163; see his helpful discussion of Paul's way of reading Scripture and why he is disinterested in a rigid historical literalism, 162–71.

anchored or limited to its original, historical setting. It is now anchored in its fulfilment—Jesus Christ. With the coming of the new age, Paul wants to hear the voice of Scripture cultivating and strengthening his apprehension of the gospel. Insofar as Paul's explicitly gospel-focused method of interpretation violates the literalistic confines of historical-grammatical interpretation, it also explains why Christian Zionism has difficulty acknowledging Paul's argument in Galatians 3—which brings me to my final point.

Christian Zionism's overweening defense of Israel's past, present, and future ethnic uniqueness blinds them to the *universal* importance of texts like Galatians 3:6–9. For example, Robert Saucy, formerly a professor of systematic theology at Talbot School of Theology, attempts to exegete Galatians 3 and concludes that:[18]

> Paul sees the inclusion of Gentiles in the new covenant *only* in fulfillment of the provision of blessing for "all peoples," which in the Abrahamic covenant are manifestly *not Israel* . . . [Gentile inclusion] does *not* entail the identification of Gentiles with Israel.

However, Saucy's account leaves us with troubling questions. Since Israel is defined through the Abrahamic covenant, and Paul believes that covenant membership is now determined by faith alone, how is it that believing gentiles and believing Jews are still kept apart? Although it is true that Paul does not identify Christian-gentiles with Israel, it is equally true that Christian-Jews are associated with Christian-gentiles as fellow members of the new covenant, a status they do not share with non-Christian Jews. Paul's understanding of the Abrahamic covenant is clearly loosed from its historical setting, yet Saucy insists upon interpreting Paul through the framework of Genesis 12 rather than reading Genesis 12 through the eyes of Paul. Saucy can only reach his odd reconfiguration of Paul's argument by ignoring the apostle's description of "those who believe" as *children of Abraham*, the gold ring of Israelite identity. That Saucy's exegesis (and he is hardly alone in doing this) so misrepresents Paul's logic testifies to the power of Christian Zionist ideology to reshape the New Testament in ways unrecognizable to its authors.

Saucy's distorted exegesis represents *the interpretive crux that blinds Christian Zionists to the truth of Israeli ethnocracy*. It is the tip of a colossal, ideological iceberg sinking the church's gospel witness before a watching world. Christian Zionism's exegetical mistakes illustrate how our theological paradigms, once they are firmly fixed in our brains, can control the way

18. Saucy, *Progressive Dispensationalism*, 132 (emphasis mine).

we see, evaluate, and respond to the world around us.[19] Christian Zionism puts secular Israel in a unique, elevated position set apart from the rest of humanity, and it fights hard to keep it there. Modern Israel is the apple of God's eye and the Christian Zionist loadstone to world history and cosmic salvation, since the modern nation-state exists in direct continuity with Old Testament Israel. Consequently, the Christian Zionist commitment to secular Israel, based on their misreading of Scripture, allows them to give carte-blanche endorsement to an often-abusive government. The church condones (or at least turns its back to ignore) not only the bloody history of political Zionist aggression but also its continuing exploitation of the land's native residents. Such evangelicals are more profoundly shaped by ethnocratic Zionist propaganda than they are by Scripture and thus find themselves justifying Israel's continuing criminality.

For example, each week since March 2018 Israeli soldiers have gunned down unarmed demonstrators, men, women, and children, at the Gaza prison fence (190 people, including 55 minors, were killed in 2018 alone, with over 28,000 wounded).[20] Yet, "pro-life" evangelicals have nothing original to say in the face of Israel's state-sponsored terrorism against a people they confine and persecute in the world's largest open-air prison.[21] Imagine the Christian (and global) outcry if the circumstances were reversed and Palestinian guns were killing imprisoned Jews on a weekly basis. Israel's outlandish human rights abuses are allowed to slide because two arrogant, ethnocentric belief systems (one Jewish, the other Christian) elevate "ethnic Israel." Thus, a secular state is seated in a higher realm far above the inconvenient fray of morality, human rights law, and the Christian love ethic. Christian Zionism's mental, moral, and spiritual captivity to the debased, ethnocentric creed of political Zionism is a far cry from what Paul had in mind when he admonished the Roman church "not to conform any longer to the pattern of this world, but [to] be transformed by the renewing of your mind. [For] then you will be able to test and approve what God's will is—his good, pleasing, and perfect will" (Rom. 12:2 NIV).

19. I highly recommend George Lackoff's books, *Don't Think of an Elephant!*, *The Political Mind*, and *Moral Politics*, to understand the power of mental "framing" and the way it controls the things we see and don't see, including how we respond to life's situations. Lakoff is a professor of cognitive science and linguistics who applies his work to political discourse. His writing style is highly accessible, and his insights are equally applicable to understanding the way theological commitments determine a person's social, political, and cultural attitudes.

20. Figures gathered by *B'Tselem* and the United Nations; "Israeli Security Forces"; Holmes and Holder, "Gaza Border Protests."

21. Pappé, *Biggest Prison on Earth*.

When explaining Paul's idiosyncratic approach to biblical interpretation, Bruce Longenecker suggests that "Paul seems to assume that a valid reading of scripture presupposes a cruciform, Christlike character embodied within the reader (or community of readers)."[22] I agree. Christlike character is essential if we are to understand Paul, Scripture, the gospel, and the path of godly living in this fallen world. Only by denying ourselves and picking up our cross on a daily basis will Christians acquire the spiritual sensitivity and insight needed to understand and apply Scripture in ways that accord with our Father's holiness, grace, mercy, and lack of favoritism (Jas 2:1–13).

Conversely, when a Christlike, cruciform character is absent—or is suppressed and distorted beneath the ideological weight of ungodly, human objectives—Bible reading is easily transformed into magical incantation, calling forth the bewitching voice of approval for whatever ungodly beliefs and behaviors our ideological taskmasters demand of us. If those ideological demands happen to include justifying the unjustifiable and ignoring the oppression of other human beings, so be it. After all, we are told, physical Israel is special, a nation set apart by God.

I honestly do not know how else to explain Christian Zionism's consistent disregard for the plain sense of New Testament teaching. I don't understand how Christian Zionists fail to see the effect of Christ's grace as creating one new people, equalizing Jew and gentile in God's peaceable kingdom. I simply cannot understand the excuses employed that whitewash Israel's century long, settler colonial program of ethnic cleansing in Palestine. The type of cruciform life seen at the heart of Paul's way of Bible reading would never condone Israel's persistent, inhumane criminality toward the Palestinian people nor would it pretend not to notice. The evangelical compulsion to provide biblical proof texts to rationalize Zionist ways of thinking and behaving has overwhelmed too much of the church and demolished too much of its witness.

---

22. Longenecker, *Triumph of Abraham's God*, 169.

Chapter 14

Territory, Part 1

How to Disguise an Ethnocracy

MRS. EREKAT SAT WITH me at her daughter's kitchen table holding the family's youngest grandson on her lap. She had agreed to tell me the story of how she became a young, Palestinian refugee in 1948. Mrs. Erakat knows English well, but her daughter, Ghada, was sitting with us to translate if necessary and to ease her mother's nervousness.

She was a child growing up in a small, Palestinian village just a few miles south of Jerusalem. Everyone in the region had heard the news about the bloody massacres committed by Jewish soldiers in the village of Deir Yassin, also near Jerusalem, and elsewhere.[1] When Mrs. Erakat's father learned that Jewish soldiers were headed toward their village he quickly gathered up his wife and children, grabbed a handful of belongings for them to carry, and ran to join in the stream of terrified people hoping to put as much distance as possible between themselves and the advancing soldiers.

---

1. For details on the Deir Yassin massacre, see Pappé, *Ethnic Cleansing*, 90–92; Suárez, *State of Terror*, 256–58. Jacques de Reynier, head of the International Red Cross delegation in Palestine, was an early eyewitness on the scene. Suárez quotes excerpts, filled with grisly details, from Reynier's report describing the things he saw and heard while searching the remains of Deir Yassin soon after its destruction. News of the slaughter spread quickly by word of mouth. The rumors created panic among Palestinian villagers throughout the region, causing many to abandon their homes and flee at the news of approaching Jewish troops.

That unplanned escape happened more than seventy years ago. Mrs. Erekat has never returned to the home she was forced to abandon in 1948. She couldn't if she wanted to, for the entire village was demolished by those soldiers. Earlier that day I had the opportunity to watch a multimedia production complete with maps and photographs of that same village, both before and after its evacuation. The program was made to fulfil a young woman's class assignment at Bethlehem University. The post-1948 photos showed scattered village ruins poking up here and there like crumbling tombstones through the wild greenery that long ago had overtaken Mrs. Erakat's childhood home.

Those ruins, like the remnants of hundreds of other destroyed villages, are now a part of Israel. Israeli law (see below) prevents Mrs. Erakat from ever returning to the place where she was born. In saving themselves and their children from an advancing army eager to sweep away unwanted Palestinians, Mrs. Erakat's parents had no idea that their youngest child would still be living as a refugee in the year 2020. But the creation of three quarters of a million Palestinian refugees is a central part of Israel's story and how it managed to acquire 78 percent of the land of Palestine.

Jewish sovereignty over a national territory is the third component in Christian Zionism's three-part definition of biblical Israel. Chapters 12 and 13 addressed the issues of Jewish ethnicity and nationhood, the first two elements comprising the Zionist trifecta of Israel's ethnic identity, nationhood, and territory. We are now in a position to examine this third issue and how Israel's ethnocratic focus on territorial control builds racial discrimination into the nation's daily affairs. Understanding political Zionism's attitude to the land is key to unlocking the heart of Israel's ethnocratic rule.

Like any other country, modern Israel's national identity has always been conditioned by the acquisition of territory. Political Zionism's secular roots appear in the openness its early leaders had toward establishing their Jewish homeland in whatever available territory an imperial sponsor would be willing to offer them. Initially, regions of Argentina, Azerbaijan, and Uganda (among others) were suggested as possibilities.[2] But, in the end, none of these offerings for colonial settlement were considered suitable. Early Zionist leaders were nothing if not politically astute. As a minority movement with little backing in the Jewish community, they quickly grasped the symbolic value of founding a new Jewish state in the land of Palestine. A great deal of planning, lobbying, political arm-twisting, fundraising, and recruitment were required before any nationalist dream could become reality. They knew that it would be far easier to raise money for a

2. Pappé, "Zionism as Colonialism," 624.

Jewish state in Palestine than it would be to sell the vision of a Jewish state in Uganda or Azerbaijan.

As the passions of political Zionism were primarily stirred by the Romantic, blood-and-soil rhetoric of ethnic nationalism, the biblical "holy land" finally took center stage in the Zionist imagination. Not only would it provide greater symbolic leverage for Zionist leaders working to promote their new vision, it also adhered more closely to Romantic, nationalist ideology. The shift to Palestine was a natural development for an embryonic movement intoxicated with the mystical air of "ancient people returning to their ancient homelands." Although Zionist leaders did not originally use the Bible as an authoritative source for their territorial mandate—the irreligious David Ben-Gurion would change that forever—they quickly learned how to tug at Jewish heartstrings by appealing to those Old Testament references that painted exalted images of territorial restoration, references that the New Testament either neglects or reinterprets (see this chapter and the next). As fate (or providence) would have it, Great Britain had a long tradition of Christian Zionism, predisposing key British government officials to seize the moment for turning Zionist dreams into reality (see chapter 3).[3]

Great Britain also had a long, successful history of extending its colonial rule around the world. Standing among the victors after World War I, Great Britain was perfectly positioned to advance its own geopolitical interests in the Middle East while shepherding the settler colonial dreams of European Zionism.[4] For their part, Zionist leaders saw Great Britain as a pliable partner, strong enough to protect Jewish settlements against any resistance offered by recalcitrant natives, but sympathetic enough to Zionist goals to allow them free reign in pursuing their own agenda.[5] The com-

3. On the development of English, Christian Zionism and its contribution to political Zionism, see Sand, *Invention of the Land*, 141–56.

4. Sand, *Invention of the Land*, 156–75. As Sand concludes, the British were "convinced that the restoration of the Jews to Palestine would earn the British a safe imperial foothold there until the end of days and possibly even later" (173).

5. Contrary to the standard Zionist story line, Great Britain did *not* use its Mandate to sabotage Zionist aspirations in Palestine. Mandatory authorities did, periodically, try to balance the scales of the Zionist/Palestinian power dynamics, but they *never* worked to subvert the goal of the Balfour Declaration—much to the chagrin of Palestine's anti-Zionists. Segev, *One Palestine*, 95, 190, 192, 335, documents the propensity of Zionists to lobby for the removal of British officials who treated the Palestinians even-handedly. While some British officials were certainly antisemites, Segev quotes one British, colonial administrator as saying, "He was not surprised that many British officials came to Palestine with pro-Jewish sympathies and left with pro-Arab inclinations" (*One Palestine*, 333n, also 341, 480–82). Although apologists for political Zionism continue to ignore the historical evidence, this piece of Zionism's mythical historiography has been thoroughly debunked; see Khalidi, *Iron Cage*, and Segev, *One Palestine*.

mon interest uniting these political crosscurrents was the task of taking and controlling Arab land.

In this respect, political Zionism was doubly unique. First, its colonial aspirations were unique in that there was no Jewish mother country providing resources and commissioning its citizens to conquer new territories under the motherland's national flag. Second, political Zionism was a unique expression of European, blood-and-soil nationalism. Whereas other expressions of Romantic nationalism, as appeared in Germany, Italy, Poland, Norway, the Baltic states, and elsewhere, looked to reclaim nearby territories already inhabited by their own nationalist activists, political Zionism was forced to look elsewhere outside of Europe. So, Jewish, settler colonialism arrived in Palestine with a new enthusiasm and determination marching in lock step with the post-war, military might of the British Empire. This Romantic dream was further enabled by British rule in Palestine from 1917 to 1948.[6] As Israeli historian, Ilan Pappé, observes, "Above all, it was British military might that enabled the 'return' of the Jews to Palestine."[7] British control paved the way for an influx of European, Ashkenazi immigrants determined to wring an Arab-free, Jewish homeland from a region long populated with generations of indigenous Arabs.[8]

I will not rehearse here the profusely documented history of how Zionist military forces, both official and unofficial, cleansed Palestine of its indigenous people during the war of 1947–49, or how that cleansing process was continued into the 1950s, 1960s, and 1970s up through today.[9] The only point of continuing debate, especially among Zionist apologists, is the question of intentions. Was the Nakba the result of a comprehensive, deliberate plan? The evidence convinces me that it was. But, however one answers that question, the fact remains that a thorough, ethnic cleansing occurred, leaving three quarters of a million people homeless refugees.[10] The fact that

6. Although the authorization of Britain's Mandate over Palestine was not implemented by the League of Nations until 1922, the British general Edmund Allenby captured Jerusalem and several other key population centers in 1917, effectively beginning Britain's military control over Palestine.

7. Pappé, "Zionism as Colonialism," 628.

8. I use this term loosely. Remember that the "Arab" influence in the native population was only one among many ancestral people groups, including Israelites and Jews, to merge into the people we call Palestinians.

9. Readers who wish to educate themselves can begin by reading: Abdo and Masalha, *Oral History*; Flapan, *Birth*; Khalidi, *All That Remains*; Khalidi, "Plan Dalet"; Masalha, *Expulsion*; Masalha, *Politics*; Morris, *Birth*; Morris, *Righteous Victims*; Pappé, *Ethnic Cleansing*; Pappé, *Making*; Pappé, *Ten Myths*; Shlaim, *Iron Wall*.

10. Piterberg, *Returns*, 56, gets it right when he concludes that the argument over intentions is a distraction from the horrible fact that it happened under Zionist supervision.

Christian Zionists continues to ignore or to explain away this troubling part of Israel's history simply illustrates the extent to which Christian Zionism requires a latently colonialist, anti-intellectual, protective bubble in order to thrive.

CREATING SECOND CLASS CITIZENS: THE LAW OF RETURN

As a Jewish nation-state, Israel has always prioritized Jewish nationality above others. Zionist leaders are not afraid to state this fact publicly. The Israeli actress, Rotem Sela, discovered this when she naively sent out an Instagram message insisting that Israel "is a nation of all its citizens." Israel's Prime Minister, Benjamin Netanyahu, provided a quick, public rebuke when he replied, "Israel is not a country of all its citizens . . . Israel is the nation-state of the Jewish nation—and it's alone."[11]

Netanyahu's message to Ms. Sela may seem baffling to western readers who live in countries where citizenship and nationality are synonymous. To our minds, a French national is someone who lives in France, possessing French citizenship. Nationality and citizenship are the same thing. But not in Israel. Decoding Netanyahu's statement uncovers the duplicity of Israel's ethnocracy and the verbal gymnastics the Israeli government uses to hide its deeply rooted, racist structure.[12]

In the absence of an official constitution,[13] Israel has established a series of "Basic Laws" which function as an evolving quasi-constitution defining Israeli government organization and civil rights in an extemporaneous fashion. Most recently, in 2018, the Israeli Knesset passed this legislation: "Basic Law: Israeli—The Nation-State of the Jewish People."[14] Paragraph 1(c) states explicitly what many people have always understood: "The exercise of the right to national self-determination in the State of Israel is *unique to the Jewish People*" (emphasis mine). In other words, among all the different citizens living in Israel, Jewish citizens enjoy a unique status. That privileged status affords them many benefits not enjoyed by others, including

11. Spiro, "Netanyahu to Rotem Sela."

12. The long history of duplicitous misrepresentations made by leaders of political Zionism is well-attested; see Flapan, *Zionism and the Palestinians*, 57, 74, 132, 144, 147, 240–43, 265, 294; Lustick and Berkman, "Zionist Theories"; Segev, *One Palestine*, 109–10; Morris, *Birth*, 62n24, 25.

13. Despite the fact that this was a prerequisite for United Nations membership.

14. See Ben-Youssef and Tamari, "Enshrining Discrimination"; "Jewish Nation-State Law"; Yiftachel, "Nation-state Law's Present Absentees"; read the entire English text at https://knesset.gov.il/laws/special/eng/BasicLawNationState.pdf.

exclusive, Jewish access to land and its resources, as well as preferential treatment in receiving social benefits. In essence, Israel's Nation-State law placed an explicit, official stamp of approval onto the ever-present Zionist regime of ethnocratic dominance that has always discriminated against Israel's Palestinian citizens.[15]

The first legislative step in codifying Israel's ethnocracy came with the passing of Israel's *Law of Return* in 1950.[16] The Law of Return grants immediate citizenship to any Jewish person (and family members) who wants to make *aliya*, that is exercise his "right of return" to Israel. There is no naturalization process for Jews moving to Israel, in contrast to the state's treatment of non-Jewish immigrants. The Law of Return embedded a fundamental, Zionist principle into Israel's legal code—that Israel does not, because it cannot, grant citizenship to Jewish immigrants. Rather, the state can only *recognize* every Jew's intrinsic, natural citizenship within the Jewish, tribal nation-state. In effect, Jewish nationality is deemed to be a preexisting, global reality that merely finds concrete, territorial expression in the state of Israel, which naturally belongs to all Jews throughout the world. To my knowledge, no other country does this.[17] Israel imagines itself as the territorial instantiation of a worldwide, ethnically distinct community which

15. For instance, see "Mossawa Center's Briefing Paper on Human Rights." Israeli discrimination occurs on many levels. Following the colonial tactic of "divide and conquer," Israel segregates the Druze and Aramean populations into their own categories, despite the fact that both groups were identified as Palestinian prior to Israel's establishment. Although Druze and Aramean citizens enjoy somewhat better treatment than Palestinian citizens, neither group is granted a nationality status equivalent to Jewish nationality. Thus, they are still excluded from many of the exclusive benefits enjoyed by Jewish citizens of Israel. The non-Ashkenazi, non-white Jews in Israel also experience discrimination; see Yiftachel, *Ethnocracy*, 211–56, for details on Israel's discriminatory practices against Sephardi, Mizrahi, Oriental Jews. Dark-skinned Jewish immigrants from places like Yemen and Ethiopia also experience racist discrimination from large sectors of white, Israeli society; see Marlowe, "Israel's Mizrahi Activists"; Sayegh, "Racism." The history of Israeli racism includes the kidnapping of Yemeni newborns during the 1950s in order to put them out for adoption by white, Ashkenazi families; see Fezehai, "Disappeared Children."

16. Orr, *UnJewish State*, offers an extensive treatment of this law's origins and evolution up to the early 1980s, complete with extensive excerpts from Knesset debates and Supreme Court rulings. It offers helpful insight into the way Israeli legislators and judges have wrestled to articulate a universally acceptable definition of who qualifies as a Jew in Israel. Orr shows how legislative compromises, made in order to resolve this debate, led to the inclusion of Jewish religious law (halakah) with Israeli secular law. For a briefer presentation, see Kraines, *Impossible Dilemma*. An English translation of the law can be found at https://knesset.gov.il/laws/special/eng/return.htm.

17. Alam, *Israeli Exceptionalism*, 15.

already possesses collective rights of citizenship—even if at a distance—in its geopolitical nation-state.

In 1965 Israel established a National Population Registry that was given the responsibility of maintaining a complete list of all Israeli residents, cataloguing their personal information. On the basis of this registry, all residents are issued identification cards that they must carry whenever they go out in public. Residents are categorized according to their nationality and citizenship, although increased public attention on this distinction has caused the nationality label to be erased from newer citizen ID cards.[18] All Jews are registered as "Jewish nationals." Whereas, all Palestinians, both Muslim and Christian, are registered as "Arab nationals." There is no such thing as an all-inclusive "Israeli nationality," despite several unsuccessful lawsuits over the years that have tried to change this fact.[19] Even after the nationality line was omitted from the new ID cards, the document retains features that allow an experienced eye easily to distinguish Jewish from Arab nationals. Although Israeli passports identify their Jewish holders as "Israeli nationals," this is another dissimulation, an ethnocratic *feature* deployed by Israel outside the country in order to disguise the Israeli government's discriminatory domestic policies.

Israel's Nation-State law merely codifies what the Law of Return has always enforced. This also explains why Prime Minister Netanyahu can correct an ill-informed citizen by stating that Israel is "*not* a nation for all its citizens." The Israeli nation is composed only of Jewish nationals (most of whom live outside the country!). After answering a few questions, or providing relevant documentation if necessary to establish one's Jewishness, an immigrant to Israel automatically becomes both a Jewish national and Israeli citizen. As new citizens, these Jewish immigrants are now able to enjoy Israeli democracy in the Jewish nation-state. Consequently, an "ethnic democracy" like Israel can never be truly democratic.[20] This is the lie found

18. For a more detailed discussion of Israel's Population Registry and the institutionalized distinction between nationality and citizenship with its practical significance, see Cook, *Blood and Religion*, 14–18; Davis, *Apartheid Israel*, 82–108; Holzman-Gazit, *Land Expropriation*, 79–82; Ofir, "Understanding Israel's deception"; White, *Israeli Apartheid*, 44–49; White, *Palestinians in Israel*, 10–14. Yiftachel, *Ethnocracy*, 126–29, argues that Israel has created at least ten different *functional* (not legal) levels of citizenship, providing "a different citizenship package for each group" covering voting rights, residency rights, physical mobility, tax levels, and access to services and housing.

19. Gross, "Court rejection of Israeli nationality"; Orr, *The unJewish State*, 99–132; Rouhana, "Ethnic Privileges," 16–17; Sand, *How I Stopped*, 3; Sultany, "The Legal Structures," 208–209; Yiftachel, *Ethnocracy*, 93.

20. See Yiftachel's section on "Debating Israeli Democracy," in *Ethnocracy*, 84–100. He concludes that "a credible analysis of the Israeli regime . . . cannot conclude that

at the heart of the Israeli government's oxymoronic claim that it is "a Jewish and democratic state." Democratic citizenship rights for Palestinians are analogous to the democratic citizenship rights of African-Americans in the Jim Crow south. How many other democratic nations allow ethnically uniform communities to apply court-approved "suitability tests" to prospective residents that are administered by "admission committees" functioning as racial sieves to filter out people of unwanted ethnicities?[21] Yet, such overt discrimination is common practice for Israel's Jewish-only housing projects.

Israel's leaders have devised numerous schemes for stifling the liberties and the voices of their Arab national, Palestinian citizens, thereby safeguarding the Zionist prerogatives of the Jewish national majority. To mention only one additional example, pro-Zionist authors commonly defend Israeli democracy by pointing out that Palestinian citizens have the right to vote and that the Israeli Parliament (called the Knesset) has a number of Palestinian members.[22] These facts are held up as infallible proof of Israel's functioning democracy for all its citizens. What these authors never mention, however, are the obstructionist items in Israeli law that deny Palestinians any genuine political influence or representation. For instance, an Amendment 44 was added to Israel's Basic Law for the Knesset in 2016. Amendment 44 allows that body to expel duly-elected members if the majority believe they have criticized or questioned Israel's right to exist as an exclusively Jewish state.[23] Moreover, amendment 44 supplements Section 7(A) of that same Basic Law (added in 1985) by prohibiting candidates from running for the Knesset if they object (or are believed by the majority to object) to Israel's existence as an exclusively Jewish state. In other words, no one can run for political office if they believe that the Jewish state should change and become a genuine democracy, that is, a state for *all* of its citizens.[24] Thus, Israel imposes a pro-Zionist litmus test for all political candidates. Palestinians who dare object to living under a political Zionist ethnocracy quickly have their invitations to Israel's democratic dance rescinded. It's a bit like a slave being offered his freedom on condition that he first agrees to reject it. The fact is, Israel is *not* a democratic state no matter how often its defenders say otherwise.

Israel is a democracy, let alone a liberal democracy" (84).

21. Sultany, "Legal Structures," 216; Yiftachel, *Ethnocracy*, 114.

22. Khalloul, "Theology and Morality," 288–293; McDermott, "Introduction," 23–25.

23. For the text of amendment 44 with analysis, see https://www.adalah.org/en/law/view/599. On the many ways Israel limits the role of elected, Palestinian officials, see Amnesty International's report, "Elected but Restricted."

24. For the text of amendment 7(A) with analysis see https://www.adalah.org/en/law/view/530.

These ongoing constitutional tweaks merely perpetuate the Knesset's original intentions. From Israel's earliest days, its lawmakers connived at excluding Palestinians while disguising their efforts, making the "exclusion of the Arabs from full membership in the state less overt."[25] Meir Argov, one of the original architects of this system, was elected to the first Knesset in 1949. He was very candid at the time in discussing the various political tricks devised for denying Palestinians any real political influence or representation while maintaining Israel's appearance as a democracy:[26]

> [Arab citizens] sit in the Knesset, and they do not have all the rights. They do not enter all the committees. We do not let them get into all the committees . . . because we outsmarted them. . . . They do not enter the administration in the state, and that is an open secret.

Israel never intended to offer democracy to all its citizens. It is, after all, *an ethnocracy.*

Beyond its numerous strictures against democracy, the Law of Return further underscores Israel's antagonism toward Palestinian refugees. The seven hundred fifty thousand Palestinians (and their descendants) who were made refugees by the war of 1947–49 are categorically denied any right of return to the land they once called home. Israel maintains this position today, in direct violation of United Nations Resolution 194 passed in December of 1948. Thus, Jews around the world, even those with no historical family connections to the land of Israel, possess an inalienable right to citizenship in the state, whereas Palestinians, many of whom still possess the front-door keys to their abandoned homes, have no right of return, ever. As historian, Shira Robinson explains:[27]

> In its explicit privileging of the rights of all Jews in the world at the expense of native non-Jews, the Law of Return became Israel's first legal nail in the coffin against the homecoming of Palestinian refugees, and the cornerstone of racial segregation between Israeli citizens.

25. Shelef, *Evolving Nationalism*, 158.

26. Argov was a member of Israel's Mapai political party, an important center-left party during Israel's early years. The quote is taken from "Meeting Protocol of the Committee of Foreign Affairs," LPA, 2–7—1958-67 (January 1, 1959) cited in Shelef, *Evolving Nationalism*, 248n44.

27. Robinson, *Citizen Strangers*, 99.

ISRAEL'S OTHER CITIZENSHIP LAW

The second pillar of Israel's ethnocracy is the *Citizenship Law* of 1952.[28] Although English translations of the law typically refer to it as Israel's Nationality Law, that is a mistranslation intended to mislead the English reader into imagining that there is, indeed, a single category of Israeli nationality (or citizenship) encompassing all of its people equally.[29] However, the modern Hebrew word used throughout the legal text is citizenship (*ezrahut*) not nationality (*le'um*). The fact that Israel has established two different citizenship laws (while attempting to disguise this fact), segregating its population into two distinct types of citizens, each defined by its own peculiar, legal mechanisms, is profoundly suspicious, especially given Israel's atrocious track record when it comes to Palestinian human rights. The law "constitutionalizes" the distinction between Jewish nationality and Arab citizenship, providing the touchstone for Israel's ethnocratic subjugation of Palestinians as permanent, second-class citizens. In fact, all of Israel's non-Jewish citizens—anyone who does not qualify for citizenship/nationality as an *oleh* (a Jewish immigrant to Israel) under the Law of Return—possess an inferior legal status due to their lack of Jewish nationality. As a result, Jewish national-citizens enjoy far greater privileges and benefits that are forever denied to non-Jewish citizens only.[30]

Israel's 1952 Citizenship Law also contains a second strike against Palestinian refugees, creating additional obstacles intended to prevent them from ever returning to their homes, repossessing their property, or acquiring Israeli citizenship. The law stipulates in sections 2(c) and 3 that Israeli citizenship is only available to resident Palestinians (and their descendants) who can prove that they were living within Israel's borders from the day of Israel's establishment in 1948 to the implementation of the Citizenship Law in 1952. This stipulation eliminates from consideration the seven hundred and fifty thousand refugees who were expelled or fled to seek safety in areas outside of Israel's eventual borders. However, it also created a class of permanent Israeli residents who are denied citizenship. After the mayhem

28. For an English translation, see https://www.adalah.org/uploads/oldfiles/Public/files/Discriminatory-Laws-Database/English/37-Citizenship-Law-1952.pdf. Remember to replace the words "nationality" with "citizenship" and "national" with "citizen."

29. "Nationality Law" was the officially authorized English translation issued "in order to denote the broadest legal meaning of the term as it is understood in English," Robinson, *Citizen Strangers*, 108, 115.

30. Erekat, *Justice for Some*, 58–60. Bishara, "Zionism and Equal Citizenship," 137, describes it as the distinction between "essential" citizenship and "incidental" citizenship; also see Jabareen, "Hobbesian Citizenship"; Molavi, *Stateless Citizenship*; Rouhana and Sultany, "Redrawing the Boundaries"; Tatour, "Citizenship as Domination."

of war, many Palestinians could not produce the type of documentation required to prove that they had, in fact, maintained their residence within the country—at least, to the standards set up by Zionist officials with an interest in keeping Palestinians out. These people became residents without citizenship, unilaterally made stateless by the Citizenship Law. By the late 1960s, sixty thousand Palestinians living in Israel remained stateless because they were denied citizenship.[31] Of course, today the growing population of stateless Palestinians—whose lives are nevertheless controlled by the Israeli government—also includes the four and a half million people living in the Occupied Territories of the West Bank, east Jerusalem, and Gaza.

Those who do possess Israeli citizenship but are not Jewish nationals still confront far-reaching, discriminatory consequences. To offer just one example, many of Israel's state-sponsored, social benefits are only provided to military veterans. The government does not draft Palestinians into military service as it does Jews because it views them with deep suspicion as a "fifth column" of potentially traitorous agitators. Since few Palestinians sign up to serve in the occupying army currently subjugating their people, Palestinian citizens are denied the sorts of educational opportunities, bank loans, start-up grants, tuition assistance, medical care, employment opportunities, and new housing units that are readily available to Israel's Jewish nationals.[32] Thus, the combination of Israel's Law of Return along with its Citizenship Law securely ensure that Israel remain an ethnocratic state. The continuation of internal colonialism, displacement, and systemic discrimination that ensue from these laws are aptly described by Oren Yiftachel as Israel's "creeping apartheid."[33]

31. Robinson, *Citizen Strangers*, 111.

32. Kanaaneh, *Surrounded*, 4–8, 27–34. Less than 1 percent of Palestinian Israeli men (a few thousand) volunteer for Israeli military service, largely for economic reasons. They are kept in segregated units.

33. Yiftachel, *Ethnocracy*, 102, 113, 115, 121, 125–28, 276. President Jimmy Carter received immense opposition for entitling his 2006 book about the Israel-Palestinian peace process *Palestine: Peace Not Apartheid*. Yet, it is not unusual to find Israeli writers, speakers, and journalists using the word apartheid without overblown public reactions. There is also a significant difference between the way professor Yiftachel uses the word in comparison to President Carter's reference. Carter's book warned about the imminent dangers of apartheid rule in the Occupied Territories. Yiftachel, on the other hand, is describing the current state of affairs within both Israel and the Occupied Territories. Furthermore, whereas Carter was warning about something he believed was a possible development, Yiftachel is describing what he believes is Israel's current reality.

HOW SECOND-CLASS CITIZENS ARE
DENIED THEIR OWN LAND

Israel's discriminatory laws of citizenship and nationality were layered on top of a preexisting system of military law that was already suffocating Israel's Palestinian population: The Defense (Emergency) Regulations of 1945.[34] The state's military rule had exploited Palestinians for years, driving them from their homes, commandeering their property, and confiscating their land. For instance, military governors regularly annexed Palestinian land by first declaring it a closed military zone and then rezoning it at a later date for Jewish-only purposes (such as housing or new agricultural projects).[35] Over the years, Israel's ethnocratic bureaucracy devised a myriad of interlocking dispossession laws intended to secure political Zionist goals. Some laws barred the return of refugees, others displaced the minority of Palestinians who remained within the state (one hundred sixty thousand of an original eight hundred thousand people), and so on. Over time this has thoroughly Judaized the countryside, expanding the demographic dominance of the Jewish majority, and defending against the demographic "security threat" posed by Palestinian existence within the state.[36]

Below I have listed and briefly described a few of Israel's draconian laws and regulations that construct its iron-clad, ethnocratic territorial control:

- *Wartime confiscation*: At the beginning of the Arab-Israeli war, between 6 to 8 percent of the land in mandatory Palestine was legally owned by Jewish Zionists.[37] By the end of the war, Zionist forces occupied 78 percent of Palestine—a substantial increase over the 55 percent originally allocated to an Israeli state in the UN Partition Plan.[38] In the process, Jewish forces had confiscated between 1.2 and 1.4 million acres of abandoned land.[39] Over four hundred Palestinian villages had been vacated, i.e., cleansed of inhabitants and destroyed

34. Recall that these regulations are still in effect despite the supposed annulment of Military Law in 1966. Their enforcement was merely handed over to Israel's civilian police force.

35. Holzman-Gazit, *Land Expropriation in Israel*, 107.

36. Holzman-Gazit, *Land Expropriation in Israel*, 102, observes that "the issue of security acquired early on the status *a cultural master-symbol* in the Israeli system of societal beliefs" (emphasis mine).

37. Said, *Question of Palestine*, 23, says 6 percent; Yiftachel, *Ethnocracy*, 58, 109, says 8 percent.

38. Khalidi, *Iron Cage*, 1; Sultany, "Legal Structures," 201; Yiftachel, *Ethnocracy*, 58.

39. Holzman-Gazit, *Land Expropriation in Israel*, 104–5.

during the war, villages like Mrs. Erakat's.[40] Zionist leaders dubbed it "the Arab miracle."[41] Thousands of abandoned homes (still standing in villages that were not destroyed) were quickly taken over by Jewish immigrants. In the words of Tom Segev, "One group lost all they had, while the other found everything they needed."[42] Within five years, three hundred seventy new agricultural settlements were established with three hundred fifty of them built on confiscated, Palestinian land.[43] By 1954, one third of Israel's new Jewish immigrants were settled into abandoned Palestinian homes. And all of these ethnocratic developments inside the embryonic state were normalized by Israel's brutal application of the Defense (Emergency) Regulations. In effect, the Arab-Israeli war had succeeded as a vast, militarized land grab.

• *The Abandoned Property Ordinance, 1948*: Israel's first law overseeing the seizure of Palestinian property granted the Custodian of Abandoned Areas unilateral authority to transfer abandoned land to Jewish farmers. No considerations were made for refugees who might want to return to their homes after the conflict. They left home, so Israel took everything. Finders keepers, losers' weepers was the Zionist law of the land. The Ordinance also provided Israel with convenient legal cover as it had retroactive force, legalizing Israel's war-time illegalities, since such property seizures clearly violated International Law.

40. The numbers vary according to differing definitions of villages vs. urban communities and who is doing the counting. Khalidi, *All That Remains*, offers an encyclopedic accounting of four hundred eighteen destroyed villages/communities, see xxxi–xxxiv, 585–94, and 595–604 (listing the locations taken over by Jewish settlers); Morris, *Birth*, xvi–xx lists three hundred sixty-nine abandoned/destroyed villages together with the causes of their abandonment; xx–xxii list the names of Jewish settlements built on former Palestinian sites; Pappé, *Ethnic Cleansing*, xiii describes five hundred thirty-one villages and eleven urban neighborhoods that were ethnically cleansed, using the details collected by Abu-Sitta, *Palestinian Nakba*; also Yiftachel, *Ethnocracy*, 136.

41. Segev, *Seventh Million*, 161.

42. Segev, *Seventh Million*, 162. Segev elaborates: "Entire cities and hundreds of villages left empty were repopulated in short order with new immigrants. In April 1949 they numbered 100,000, most of them Holocaust survivors. . . . Free people—Arabs— had gone into exile and become destitute refugees; destitute refugees—Jews—took the exiles' places. . . . Most of the immigrants broke into the abandoned Arab houses without direction, without order, without permission. For several months the country was caught up in a frenzy of take-what-you-can, first-come, first-served. . . . Immigrants also took possession of Arab stores and workshops, and some Arab neighborhoods soon looked like Jewish towns in prewar Europe."

43. Holzman-Gazit, *Land Expropriation in Israel*, 104–5; Yiftachel, *Ethnocracy*, 136.

Furthermore, the Custodian had broad power to act at his own discretion without the right of appeal.[44]

- *The Waste Lands Regulations, 1948*: This Regulation allowed the Minister of Agriculture to zone as "waste land" any area that appeared to lie fallow. As waste land it automatically became state property. Defense Emergency Regulation, Section 125 was commonly used in tandem with the Waste Lands Regulations. Military commanders used Section 125 to close off Palestinian property for "security reasons," thereby preventing landowners from reaching their property. As the land remained uncultivated, it was soon declared "waste land" and confiscated by the state for distribution into Jewish hands.[45]

- *Absentee Property Regulations, 1948*, and *The Absentee Property Law, 1950*: A new Custodian of Absentee Property was appointed with the same unilateral powers as the old. Like previous Custodians, the new appointments also "could expropriate any property at their personal discretion."[46] The important difference appeared in a new classification procedure that shifted the labeling process from the land to the landowners. These laws (which remain in effect to this day) now classified land as abandoned if the owners were declared "absentees." Absentees are defined as Palestinians who fled their homes during the war. But the new term was expanded to include Palestinian-Israelis who were living in territory *outside of* Israel's designated borders, as defined by the UN Partition Plan; land that was eventually annexed to Israel *after* the war.[47] Thus, Palestinians *who had never left their homes* were suddenly labelled absentees because Zionist forces had invaded their territory—territory the UN Partition Plan had allocated for an Arab state! These people became "present absentees," an absurd (yet bizarrely iconic) ethnocratic label for other human beings if there ever was one. In other words, the people had not fled, so they were "present," but Israel wanted their property, so they were called "absentees" and made into internal refugees. Furthermore, because the status is

---

44. Holzman-Gazit, *Land Expropriation in Israel*, 106–7.

45. Sultany, "Legal Structures," 202–3.

46. Holzman-Gazit, *Land Expropriation in Israel*, 109. The Absentee Property Law remains in effect today (111n24).

47. Holzman-Gazit, *Land Expropriation in Israel*, 108–9; Masalha, *Politics of Denial*, 134, 142–45, 156. These confiscations occurred primarily in the area now known as the Little (or Arab) Triangle, which hugs a northern portion of the official Green Line.

hereditary, 25 percent of the Palestinians living in Israel today remain present absentees.[48]

- *The Development Authority Law, 1950*: The Development Authority was created in connection with the Absentee Property Law to facilitate further the "legal" transfer of absentee lands into Jewish hands. The Custodian of Absentee Property is empowered to transfer confiscated land to the Development Authority which in turn sells, mortgages, or leases that property to the state. In the words of Israeli professor Holzmann-Gazit, the Development Authority acts as "a land laundering agency" for the Israeli government, distancing elected officials from direct contact with the government's rampant land theft.[49]

- *The Land Acquisition Law, 1953*: As mentioned above, vast quantities of Palestinian land were seized during and after the war without any pretense of legal justification. As increasing numbers of Palestinian residents, who were not absentees, began submitting court claims for the return of their confiscated land, the government once again enacted "retroactive legalization that would legitimize all past seizures of land" through the Land Acquisition Law.[50] In one year alone, between March 1953 and March 1954, over three hundred thousand acres of Palestinian land was retroactively declared state property with no possibility of appeal. Oren Yiftachel likens this entire "legal" mechanism of permanently Judaizing Palestinian land "to a black hole into which Arab land enters but can never be retrieved."[51]

- *The Basic Law: Israel Lands, 1960*: This Basic Law is similar to the Nation-State Law in that it "constitutionalized" an already entrenched principle of political Zionism: permanent Jewish ownership of as much nationalized land as possible.[52] The law states that land, with all of its permanently attached structures, controlled by the government or its related agencies "shall not be transferred either by sale or in any other manner." In other words, Israel's public land will forever remain public land, remembering of course that Israel's public is defined by its Jewish nationality. To help protect this principle, Israel has several quasi-governmental agencies that are not accountable to Israeli citizens, such as the Jewish National Fund, the Jewish Agency, and the Israel Lands

48. Davis, *Apartheid Israel*, 100.
49. Holzman-Gazit, *Land Expropriation in Israel*, 110.
50. Holzman-Gazit, *Land Expropriation in Israel*, 112.
51. Yiftachel, *Ethnocracy*, 110.
52. An English translation is available at "Basic Law—Israel Lands."

Authority, which control large amounts of land in conjunction with the state. In fact, the Jewish National Fund is Israel's largest owner of agricultural land. Each agency is governed by charters and restrictive covenants that limit their services exclusively to the Jewish nation. Not only can public land never be sold or leased to non-Jews but even employing non-Jews to work on the land is strictly prohibited.[53] In effect, these agencies are "powerful tools in legalized discrimination against Arabs."[54] They also function as additional avenues for land laundering, securing blatantly discriminatory, ethnocratic objectives in direct contradiction to Israel's public-relations image as a nation "for all its citizens." No one can point to an Israeli law that *explicitly* prohibits Palestinian land ownership, since that piece of the governmental land theft apparatus is buried within the internal, restrictive covenants of non-governmental agencies like the Jewish National Fund. Nevertheless, Palestinian Israelis are systematically excluded from owning property in the ethnocratic nation-state. Today, 93 percent of Israel's land mass is "publicly" owned by the Zionist state and its related agencies, meaning that 93 percent of Israeli real estate is sequestered behind a tall Jewish national fence. One-third of that land is confiscated refugee property; the remaining two-thirds were confiscated from Palestinians who never left Israel.[55] Although Palestinians constitute 20 percent of Israel's population (with a small percentage living in mixed communities), they overwhelmingly reside in segregated towns within three localities (Galilee, The Little Triangle, and the Negev). All told, Palestinians currently own a mere 2.5 percent of Israel's land.[56]

This brief description of Israel's land laws accounts for only some of the ethnocratic mechanisms used to control public space, the balance of ethnic populations, and the Judaization process that is occurring within Israel's recognized borders. In earlier chapters, I described the extension of Israel's ethnocratic Zionism beyond those borders into the West Bank, but we have still only scratched the surface of this issue.

---

53. Holzman-Gazit, *Land Expropriation in Israel*, 64, 71.

54. Yiftachel, *Ethnocracy*, 146.

55. Yiftachel, *Ethnocracy*, 109.

56. In contrast to Christian Zionist assertions (made without corroborating evidence) that "Arabs own portions of land all over Israel proper," McDermott, *Israel Matters*, 117; also McDermott, "Implications and Propositions," 326. See Jabareen, "Controlling Land," 251, who cites the common figure of 2.5 percent, while Yiftachel, *Ethnocracy*, 109, 143, says 3 percent.

I do not have space here to explore all the details of Israel's continuing internal colonization of its Palestinian residents. Suffice it to say that the rampant demolition of Palestinian homes and the confiscation of Palestinian property in order to replace long-time residents with Jewish settlers continues unabated. This is especially the case in east Jerusalem, as well as in the Occupied Territory.[57]

THE SHAMELESS HEART OF ISRAELI ETHNOCRACY

During an interview with *Haaretz* newspaper, Israeli lawyer and Knesset member, Miki Zohar, bluntly summarized the blood-and-soil foundation that undergirds Israel's impregnable iron cage of ethnocratic dominance. He said:[58]

> We [Jews] must always maintain control over the mechanisms of the state, as the Jewish people have received this country by right.... [A Palestinian] doesn't have the right to national identity because he does not own the land of this country.... I am sorry to say this, but they have one conspicuous liability: they weren't born Jews.

Pause, and let those words sink in. Replace the words Jew and Palestinian with white and black, or Afrikaans and negro. How does it sound? It is racism, pure and simple. Zohar's words plainly reveal Zionist ethnocracy as the racist ideology it is.

Mr. Zohar is not a fanatic or an outlier. He is not an extremist within Israel's body politic. He represents the mainstream of Israeli political Zionism, the same people who intentionally constructed an ethnocratic regime. As an elected member of Israel's parliament, Zohar blithely summarizes

---

57. To learn more about this issue of home demolitions, I recommend books such as *An Israeli in Palestine: Resisting Dispossession, Redeeming Israel* by Jeff Halper. Halper is an Israeli professor of anthropology and one of the founders of ICHAD—the *Israeli Committee Against House Demolitions*. In this book, one of several he has written, Halper explains in brutal detail how extensively and cavalierly the Israeli government continues to exercise its powers of ethnocratic privilege by demolishing Palestinian homes and businesses in order to make way for more Jewish settlement. I also recommend the book *Separate and Unequal: The Inside Story of Israeli Rule in East Jerusalem*, written by three Jewish residents of the city (Amir Cheshin, Bill Hutman, and Avi Melamed). It makes for equally compelling reading. The authors—all leading figures in Jerusalem's political affairs—draw from their firsthand knowledge of government decisions aimed at eliminating Palestinian residents from east Jerusalem and discriminating against those who remain, all in its pursuit of Israel's demographic goals to further Judaize the West Bank.

58. Hecht, "The Lawmaker."

the overt, intentional racism that animates the Israeli nation-state. He articulates the heart of political Zionism—that might makes right, and Jewish might makes Zionist land theft right. He also highlights the centrality of land ownership in determining who's who in Israel's two-tiered citizenship program. In turn, his statement illustrates how thoroughly the Israeli public has internalized the state's mythical blood-and-soil historiography (see chapters 3 and 12). As a result, too many Israeli citizens, like Zohar, remain blind to historical reality, unaware that their so-called "right to the land" is neither a divine right, as we will discuss further in the next chapter, nor an historic, national right. Rather, it began as the imposition of a *British imperial right*, a holdover from a bygone and good riddance era when colonial empires defined what was right through their military might. *This* was the "conspicuous liability" that originally crippled the Palestinian people as non-Jews, for the power of the British Empire was backing political Zionism's quest for national autonomy while simultaneously ignoring Palestinian rights to self-determination in their own backyard.[59] The Zionist armies and militias did not occupy, confiscate, and steal Palestinian property in a noble enterprise sanctioned by a trans-historical, tribal right. Israel's origins are far more mundane. Zionist success depended on the same squalid brand of racism and brute force that has always declared victory in grossly asymmetrical warfare waged by settler colonial forces bent upon exploitation, ethnic cleansing, and racial domination.[60]

59. A right they were promised by the British government during World War I and were also guaranteed in the League of Nations charter under which Britain was (theoretically) to govern Palestine. Even though the Balfour Declaration was folded into Britain's Class A Mandate for Palestine, the League of Nations charter endorsed the Wilsonian principle of post-colonial, national self-determination for all Class A Mandates. Due to the Balfour Declaration, Palestine was the lone exception that violated the League's basic principles; see Erekat, *Justice for Some*, 16–17, 34–41; Khalidi, *Iron Cage*, 33–34, 39–43, 233n6.

60. Examples of Zeʾev Jabotinsky's, Chaim Weitzmann's, and David Ben-Gurion's racist, colonial attitudes toward Palestinians can be found in Flapan, *Zionism and the Palestinians*, 28, 56–57, 62, 70–71, 78, 86, 115–17, 129, 132–34, 168, 170, 176. Many Zionist immigrants shared the same racial biases as other white, European colonialists working to displace the dark-skinned natives of foreign lands. In this respect, they were men and women of their age. The tragedy, however, is their creation of a modern nation-state that perpetuates colonial attitudes of ethnic superiority in the twenty-first century.

Chapter 15

Territory, Part 2

Using the Bible to Excuse Ethnocracy

LIKE THE MAJORITY OF Christian Zionists, American pastor John Hagee has always defended Israel's right to ignore historical realities by turning a blind eye to the Palestinians who have lived in Israel-Palestine for centuries. During a speech in 2005 Hagee explained that "the Palestinians have never owned the land. . . . The land of Israel was given to Abraham, Isaac and Jacob, and their seed in an eternal covenant. . . . [It] belongs to the Jewish people today, tomorrow and forever."[1] Robert Benne, emeritus professor at Roanoke College, agrees with Hagee when it comes to unilaterally displacing today's Palestinians. He writes, "God has a continuing covenant with Israel that includes land and the promise of return. These combined special claims override even the 'natural rights' of the Palestinians to their land."[2] According to these comfortable, privileged westerners, whose living conditions are not under threat, Zionist ideology, supported by idiosyncratic Bible reading, effortlessly overrules human rights.

There is nothing new about using religion to excuse the crimes of settler colonialism. Colonial powers have always dismissed the existence of native peoples standing in their way, obstructing their divinely sanctioned plans for territorial conquest. Indigenous populations are messily inconvenient.

1. Nowlin, "Apocalypse Now."
2. Benne, "Theology and Politics," 245–46.

Zionist colonialism has been no different. Only two years after Britain's publication of the Balfour Declaration, Lord Balfour composed a memorandum
(August 1919) clarifying Britain's intentions for Palestine:[3]

> For in Palestine we do not propose even to go through the form
> of consulting the wishes of the present inhabitants of the coun-
> try. . . . The four great powers [notably, all colonial powers] are
> committed to Zionism and Zionism, be it right or wrong, good
> or bad . . . is of far profounder import than the desire and preju-
> dices of the 700,000 Arabs who now inhabit that ancient land.

Little has changed since 1919. Palestinians still do not matter. Contemporary Christian Zionists continue to work at constructing "biblical" arguments in support of Israel's unjust military and administrative conquest of
Palestine as described in the last chapter. In this chapter we will see that their
territorial arguments rely on the same dubious interpretive assumptions and
rhetorical strategies we exposed in chapters 6 and 7. There they argued—
with a rigid literalism contrary to the New Testament readings of the Old
Testament—that Jewish ethnicity and Jewish ethnic-nationalism (chapter
3) essentially made the occupation of Palestine by secular Israel a biblical
mandate. Therefore, my critique of Christian Zionism's territorial doctrine
will cover a bit of familiar ground (even if that is an unfortunate pun).[4]

THE ZIONIST STRAWMEN OF
BIBLICAL INTERPRETATION

A straw man argument is a diversionary tactic often used in debate. Straw
man arguments accuse the opponent of believing something that the person
does not actually believe, setting up a weak, specious form of argument easily knocked down, like a straw man. Focusing attention on the straw man
allows its creator to ignore the more substantive issues waiting to be addressed. It is a game of rhetorical shadowboxing that allows the supposed
victor to imagine that he has defeated a dangerous opponent when, in fact,
he has merely bested a bunch of his own homegrown hay.

For example, Christian Zionists often accuse those (like myself) who
do not agree with their claims that scripture condones Israel's displacement
of long-settled Palestinian communities of embracing an exclusionary,

3. Quoted in Said, *Question*, 16.

4. For readers unfamiliar with the alternative ways of reading Scripture that are
endorsed by non-Zionists, I recommend the books listed in the bibliography by Burge,
Chapman, Davies, Martin, Robertson, Sizer, and Wright.

replacement theology. Once again, this is the belief that God has rejected all of Israel for all time because Israel, in the New Testament era and subsequently, rejected Christ. I first addressed this straw man in chapter 6. But, as we saw earlier, arguing that the Jewish people do not have a biblically based claim to the land of Palestine today has nothing to do with believing that God has rejected all of Israel, or all Jewish people, in favor of a gentile church. The two assertions are logically distinct, like a Venn diagram with no overlapping center. Christian Zionists betray their own tunnel vision through their stubborn refusal to engage the conversation that serious non-Zionist biblical interpreters are offering them.

A second straw man argument that fails to take biblically sound opposition to Christian Zionist views seriously is the argument that non-Zionists are guilty of some variety of anti-materialism in how they read Scripture.[5] In other words, Zionists assume that Christians who deny modern Israel's right to the land are simultaneously denying the materiality of Christian salvation. For example, Barry Horner claims that non-Zionists demonstrate "a more Gnostic form of spirituality that so abhors the inclusion of materiality and the alleged inferiority of carnal territory."[6] Similarly, Nicholas Brown asserts that non-Zionists who deny the importance of Israel's reclaiming the land "move Jesus towards Platonic idealism."[7] But in making such claims Zionists are committing another logical error called a *hasty generalization*. They mistakenly imagine that if something is true for a part, it must also be true for the whole. In other words, if non-Zionists do not believe that modern Israel's occupation of Palestine is the necessary, literal fulfillment of a literal, territorial promise, then non-Zionists must also reject the literal fulfilment of other physical aspects of Christian salvation. But this accusation is patently absurd. If I tell my granddaughter that she cannot eat a particular piece of cake (perhaps, I am saving it for someone else), does that necessarily mean that I have forbidden her from ever eating any cake at all for all time?

Endorsing the modern, territorial state of Israel as the only possible fulfilment of biblical prophecy is hardly the only way of affirming the physical, fleshly fulfilment of God's redemptive work. I find myself affirming with most, if not all, evangelical non-Zionists the future physical reality of the new heavens and the new earth described in the book of Revelation, as well as the current redemption of our physical bodies, eventually to be

5. Horner, *Future Israel*, 45; Kaiser, "Land of Israel," 224, citing Berkhof's warning against "docetism and spiritualism"; McDermott, "Implications and Propositions," 325.

6. Horner, *Future Israel*, 45.

7. Brown, *For the Nation*, 91.

consummated at the resurrection based on the very real, very fleshly resurrection of the Lord Jesus. For Christian Zionists like Craig Blaising to insist
that rejecting the modern state of Israel as the fulfilment of biblical prophecy is somehow incoherent or logically inconsistent, simply reveals a lack of
imagination.[8] Learning to step outside the constraints of one's cultural and
theological conditioning in order to view Scripture sympathetically from
different angles and to imagine alternative possibilities and where those
may lead is an important skill required of anyone doing theology.

Gerald McDermott presents an extreme version of this hasty generalization. He warns his readers to "beware the geographical-docetic temptation that anti-Zionism proffers . . . [suggesting] that land, earth and territory
do not matter to embodied human existence."[9] Elsewhere he claims that
non-Zionists anticipate an homogenized eternity, a coming "world of undifferentiated souls" and "undifferentiated individuals" with no ethnic or
cultural distinctives.[10] Others agree, accusing non-Zionists of believing that
every ethnicity will be erased and melded together into an eternal, human
uniformity where all people are alike.[11] None of these accusations are true,
however. Such alarmist claims stretch the possibility of constructive argument well beyond the breaking point. Each and every one of these charges is
another straw man fallacy of exaggeration. The book of Revelation describes
the eternal gathering of all God's people "from every nation, tribe, people
and language, standing before the throne" (Rev 7:9). Our human distinctives will obviously be retained. Denying Israel's need to reoccupy the land,
therefore, has nothing to do with denying individual distinctives.

ASSIMILATION TO MYTHICAL, ZIONIST HISTORIOGRAPHY

As I argued in chapters 12 and 13, Christian Zionism's ardent defense of
Israel's territoriality reveals its wholesale assimilation to the mythical historiography of Israeli political Zionism. The language Christian Zionists
use to defend modern Israel goes well beyond explicit scriptural teaching.
Their myth-making subversion of the Bible and history reveals itself in their
claim that Jews in the Dispersion always longed to return to their homeland,
as well as in their repetition of the Romantic language of blood-and-soil

8. Blaising, "Israel and Hermeneutics," 163–64.

9. McDermott, "Introduction," 29.

10. McDermott, *Israel Matters*, 116.

11. Blaising, "Theology of Israel," 86, 96–97; Horner, *Future Israel*, 186, 246, 269–70, 315, 318.

nationalism, adding emotive weight to their flawed reasoning.[12] While it is true that Jewish liturgies and prayers interceded for God's blessings on Jerusalem as well as a future national return, these prayers always anticipated that this return would be preceded by God acting to bring about a spiritual renewal at the coming of the Messiah.[13] The Talmudic scholar Daniel Boyarin has convincingly demonstrated that the Jewish people were quite comfortable with their worldwide Dispersion, stretching back for centuries. New Testament scholar, Gary Burge, documents this fact as well from ancient Jewish sources.[14]

The Jewish Diaspora began in the Old Testament era, long before the Roman invasion of Palestine. Another oddity of political Zionist historiography is the invention of a "second Exile" performed by the Romans in response to the First and Second Jewish Revolts. The actual, "first" exile described in the Old Testament is generally ignored altogether by both political and Christian Zionists.[15] Jerusalem was sacked twice by the Romans: first in 70 AD when they destroyed the Herodian Temple, and second, in 135 AD when Rome crushed the Bar Kochba Revolt and banned Jews from entering Jerusalem's old boundaries. In stylizing these events as heroic, ethnic nationalist revolts (in fact, there was nothing nationalistic about either of them) that sparked a (Second) Exile under Rome, political Zionism falsifies Jewish history in order to create an artificial impetus behind their "heroic," nationalistic call for a Jewish return to the Land today—in other words, the earlier ethnic-national revolts were squashed, but we Zionists are the new Maccabees, defenders of the new Masada, the new Bar Kochbas.

The problem with this piece of the Zionist narrative, however, is the fact that the Romans did not exile conquered people as did the Assyrians and the Babylonians. The Romans eventually banned all Jews from entering Jerusalem, which was renamed Aelia Capitolina, and many rebels were sold into slavery or taken to Rome as trophies, but no attempts were made to empty the countryside of its Jewish population. The fact that Christian Zionists follows suit in repeating this unhistorical notion of a second exile is further evidence of its cooption by political Zionist mythology.

In his books, *Powers of Diaspora*[16] and *A Traveling Homeland*, Boyarin explains in detail how the Talmud eventually came to be seen as "the

12. Bailey, "Should Christians Support," 195; Goldberg, "Historical and Political," 115; McDermott, "Introduction," 16.

13. Sand, *Invention of the Land*, 18–20, 132.

14. Burge, *Jesus and the Land*, 15–24.

15. For example, see Ellisen, *Who Owns the Land*, 17; Jelinek, "Dispersion and Restoration," 243; Kinzer, "Zionism in Luke-Acts," 153, 161.

16. Written by Daniel and his brother Jonathan.

portable homeland of the Jewish people."[17] The Dispersion was understood as God's alternative to Israel's territorial-state, for he intended the Babylonian exile and its subsequent worldwide expansion to accomplish the nation's "regeneration through statelessness."[18] The Dispersion was actually a return to Israel's original homeland, since Abraham was first called to leave Babylon before he was sent into the land of Canaan, a territory where he always remained a stranger. Once relocated to its original homeland in Babylon, Israel was in a better position to fulfil God's plan for his people to become missionaries to the world.[19] Whether or not evangelical Christians agree with Rabbinic Judaism and the self-understanding of the Jewish people in Diaspora is beside the point. The fact is that the Boyarin brothers are describing the traditional attitudes held by the vast majority of Jewish people prior to the invention of political Zionism.

The Israeli historian, Shlomo Sand, author of the book, *The Invention of the Jewish People*, has written another important historical work entitled *The Invention of the Land of Israel* in which he documents Judaism's long-standing *disinterest* in returning to the land.[20] In fact, along with the Boyarins, he demonstrates how this pervasive disinterest in the land grew into an explicit, Rabbinic warning *against* anyone setting his sights on reestablishing Jewish life in Zion. Returning to the land was a sin. The Babylonian Talmud expresses three reasons why Jews are never to consider any such thing, which certainly helps to explain the vehement rabbinic opposition against political Zionism when the movement first arose.[21] On the basis of carefully considered historical evidence, Sand concludes:[22]

> In contrast to the mythos so skillfully woven into the State of Israel's Declaration of Independence, such a longing to settle in the Land *never truly existed* . . . the degree to which the Land of Israel *did not* attract the "original children of Israel" is nonetheless astounding.

Yet, Christian Zionists continue to repeat the political Zionist mythology about Diaspora Jews yearning, longing, pining to return *en masse* to Zion—a yearning which pulled at their hearts like a magnet—as if encoded into their very DNA. This supposed longing, it is argued, is what called

17. Boyarin, *Traveling Homeland*, 5.

18. Boyarin and Boyarin, *Powers of Diaspora*, vii–viii, 10.

19. For each of these points, see Boyarin, *Traveling Homeland*, 5–6, 39, 43–44.

20. Sand, *Invention of the Land*, 102–32, 177–96.

21. Ketub. 13.111.

22. Sand, *Invention of the Land*, 117, 126 (emphasis mine); also see Boyarin, *Traveling Homeland*, 83.

them to fulfil their political destiny in Zion.[23] Such overwrought pathos may warm the blood of a certain class of ideologues, but the problem remains: at no point does this modern reconstruction come into contact with either Jewish history or the biblical record.

Another important study entitled *Civil Religion in Israel*, written by two Israeli professors of political studies, goes a long way in explaining the ideological bridge connecting Zionist mythology to this particular emphasis in Christian Zionist argument. Professors Liebman and Don-Yehiya provide many examples of how the leaders in Israel's early *kibbutzim* and *moshavim* movements (two different sorts of communal, agricultural communities) replaced the traditional language of Jewish religious liturgies with emotional, ideological expressions of blood-and-soil, ethnic nationalism— often, quite literally.[24] They conclude that "the reverence Zionist-socialism manifested toward the land, nature, and physical communion between man and nature is far more evocative of paganism than of Judaism." One widely used, rewritten Passover liturgy was transformed into a Zionist love song, praising the early settlers' devotion to Israel's beloved soil: "And we shall cross the stormy seas until we reach you and cling to you. In our blood and toil we shall redeem you until you are entirely ours."[25] David Ben-Gurion, the leader of Labor Zionism, took every opportunity to drive this point home as he often slandered Jews remaining in the Diaspora and insisted that no Jew could live "a fully Jewish life" outside of the land of Israel.[26] Zionism invented a new covenant with nature and the soil that replaced the nation's old covenant with God.[27] In fact, both God and divine redemption were eliminated from the nationalist equation altogether.

This secular hijacking of Jewish religious language is the point of origin for Christian Zionism's regular descriptions of the mysterious union connecting the Jewish people to their homeland. Barry Horner illustrates this assimilation when he claims that the land "*epitomizes an indivisible union* between territory and people."[28] John Jelinek echoes David Ben-Gu-

---

23. It is also remarkable to observe how Christian Zionism's addiction to Zionist propaganda causes its proponents to ignore important, anti-Zionist critics like Sand.

24. Liebman and Don-Yehiya, *Civil Religion*, 30–58. They explain the numerous ways in which Labor Zionism in particular harnessed religious forms to sacralize and extoll the value of agricultural labor in "redeeming" both the nation and the homeland when Jews get their hands dirty working in their native soil.

25. Liebman and Don-Yehiya, *Civil Religion*, 33. This book is drawing from Reich, *Changes and Developments*; I have been unable to obtain a copy of Reich's work.

26. Liebman and Don-Yehiya, *Civil Religion*, 88.

27. Liebman and Don-Yehiya, *Civil Religion*, 39.

28. Horner, *Future Israel*, 223.

rion when he exclaims that "in Israel's perception, life without the land was *scarcely life as God's people.*"[29] Gerald McDermott parrots Zionism's pagan covenant with nature when he insists that the people and the land are "as integral to each other *as soul and body*" (all emphases mine).[30]

All of this language used by Christian Zionists is lifted wholesale from this mythic, ethnic nationalist playbook crafted by early Israeli Zionists. Christian Zionism's infatuation with the essentialist connection supposedly tying the holy land to the Jewish people unwittingly mimics the bastardized liturgies of Israel's early irreligious community leaders. Rather than being rooted in Scripture or history, this ideology is a thoroughly ahistorical doctrine waiting to ensnare the next Zionist protégé. The Old Testament account of Israel's Deuteronomistic history[31] does explain how God would use the promised land as an earthly venue for enacting his covenantal promises of distributive justice—blessings for obedience and curses for disobedience—as described in the book of Deuteronomy (Deut 4:39–40; 5:28–33; 6:1–25; 7:12–16; 8:1, 6–20; 11:8–32; 28:1–14, 15–68; 30:1–20). God promised that Israel would be blessed for its obedience to the covenant with prosperity in the land but cursed for its disobedience with hardship and suffering in the land. For the biblical authors, whatever "spiritual" connection existed between the people and the land was *a covenantally defined, juridical connection* far removed from the mystical, organic, blood-and-soil superstition promoted by both Christian and political Zionism today.

GIVING VOICE TO NEW TESTAMENT SILENCE

Michael Vlach is a theology professor at The Master's Seminary, founded by John MacArthur in Los Angeles. In his 2009 dissertation defending Christian Zionism, Vlach makes an important confession. He says, "Granted, there is no undisputed New Testament verse that explicitly states 'Israel will be restored to its land and have a special service to the nations.'"[32] Vlach's honesty is refreshing, except that he then goes on to account for this silence by resorting to Christian Zionism's favorite argument from silence.

29. Jelinek, "Dispersion and Restoration," 235. Zionist advocates may respond by saying that this disinterest in returning to the land is symptomatic of Judean sinfulness (though scripture never condemns their decision) or a deficiency in their Jewish identity (as if arrogance, bullying, paternalism, and self-righteousness made for reasonable argument).

30. McDermott, *Israel Matters*, 15–16.

31. A description of the pattern of historical development that unfolds through the books of Deuteronomy, Joshua, Judges, Samuel, and Kings.

32. Vlach, *Church*, 203.

He insists that the lack of any explicit New Testament teaching about Israel's repossession of the land testifies to the writers' convictions that the Old Testament promises, understood literally, remained in effect.[33] Thus, there was no need for the New Testament to repeat what the Old had already explained.

I want to address Vlach's argument about the importance of New Testament silence by exploring the way Zionist interpreters understand the book of Acts, specifically the disciples' question put to Jesus in Acts 1:6, and Peter's speech in Acts 3:18–21. These verses are frequently used to lay the foundation for Christian Zionism's belief that apostolic silence demonstrates apostolic endorsement of Old Testament, antecedent theology.

Darrell Bock, a leading scholar of Luke-Acts who teaches at Dallas Theological Seminary, has been the most consistent and influential advocate for this position.[34] The argument goes like this: The resurrected Jesus spent forty days with his disciples, during which time he "spoke about the kingdom of God" (Acts 1:3 NIV). After Jesus tells them to wait in Jerusalem for the gift of the Holy Spirit, the disciples ask a question: "Are you at this time going to restore (apokathistaneis) the kingdom to Israel?" (v. 6 NIV). Jesus replies, "It is not for you to know the times or dates the Father has set by his own authority" (v. 7 NIV). Bock and others draw several conclusions from this brief exchange.

First, the disciples' uncomplicated query appears to presume a traditional understanding of national Israel's future restoration to the land. Otherwise, we are told, the question would have contained additional details about the things they still did not understand. The question's simplicity, therefore, suggests that the Old Testament's perspective on the land must have been the content of Jesus' post-resurrection teaching about the kingdom of God, reinforcing the disciples' traditional expectations of a literal fulfilment of the Old Testament promises.

Second, since Jesus did not chide the disciples or offer any corrections to their question, we may further assume that Jesus accepted the question's premise, giving his tacit approval to their traditional expectations. After all, Jesus only says that they cannot know the timing of Israel's restoration, again implying that the prophetic vision of literal, territorial reclamation is allowed to stand.

33. Vlach, *Church*, 125; Vlach, *Has the Church?*, 162–64.

34. See Bock's expositions of Acts 1 and 3 in "Biblical Reconciliation," 174–77; "Israel in Luke-Acts," 111–12; *Progressive Dispensationalism*, 180, 237, 268; and "The Reign," 45–47, 58–62; also see Kinzer, "Zionism in Luke-Acts," 150–53, 160–64; Saucy, *Case*, 268–71; Vlach, *Has the Church?*, 163, 190–92; Vlach, "Israel and the Land," 120.

Third, Peter's sermon in Acts 3 expands on the question of Israel's restoration when Peter tells the crowd to "repent and turn to God, so that your sins may be wiped out, that times of refreshing may come from the Lord, and that he may send the Christ . . . even Jesus. He must remain in heaven until the time comes for God to restore (apokatastaseōs) everything, as he promised long ago through his holy prophets" (Acts 3:19–21 NIV). Several points are drawn from these verses:

1. This segment of Peter's speech is an elaboration of the earlier exchange in Acts 1:6–7. Now Peter explicitly connects God's "restoration of everything" to the fulfilment of God's promises "made through prophets" (v. 21), the same prophets who had "foretold that his Christ would suffer" (v. 17). Assuming the literal fulfilment of the prophetic promises, and the acceptance of antecedent theology, the restoration of all things (3:21) becomes synonymous with restoring the kingdom to Israel (1:6).

2. Although Bock does not follow this next line of argument, other Zionist interpreters take up Albrecht Oepke's (1881–1955) intemperate statement in his *Theological Dictionary of the New Testament* article where he asserts that the Greek word for restoration (apokathistēmi), used in both Acts 1:6 and 3:21, is a "technical term" for "the restoration of Israel to its own land."[35] With this the Zionist case is made. The pieces fit together like this:

The resurrected Jesus taught the disciples (over forty days) to anticipate national Israel's literal kingdom reign in the promised land just as it was foretold by the prophets. Peter's temple speech in Acts 3 confirms the implications drawn from Acts 1. Since this was already the traditional, Jewish expectation, the New Testament writers felt no need to dwell on the subject further. The result is the New Testament's silence on this matter.

But I do not think this argument by implication works. Here is why.

I begin, first, with Oepke's error. The Greek word for restore/restoration is *not* a technical term signifying Israel's future reign in its own land. It is simply the word for "restore." What exactly is being restored and how that restoration occurs depends on the context and the other words used in the sentence. Yes, Jeremiah 16:15 and Josephus's history, *The Antiquities of the Jews* (11.2), both use this word when reminding their readers of

---

35. Oepke, "apokathistēmi, apokatastasis," 388. Later in his article, Oepke notes that the word's "technical meaning is weakly developed" (391), which is something of an understatement ignored by the Christian Zionists who cite him; see Saucy, *Case*, 268, and Kinzer, "Zionism in Luke-Acts," 151.

God's promise "to restore" Israel to the land. But the big picture of "Israel's future return to rule with God in the promised land" is not evoked by this word alone. Rather, in each case, that bigger picture is conveyed through the broader context of what is being discussed in each passage. Elsewhere, this word denotes the restoration of Jeremiah's relationship with God (Jer 15:19); the restoration of family ties (Mal 3:24); and Jesus' restoration (healing) of the physically impaired (Mark 3:5; 8:25; Matt 12:13; Luke 6:10). The word itself is not a technical term carrying a load of interpretive freight for Zionist territoriality.

Second, we should remember that Luke offers no details about the specific content of Jesus' kingdom teaching during his forty days on earth. I think that it is safe to assume that whatever Jesus said was consistent with his kingdom teaching in the synoptic Gospels. The suggestions offered by Christian Zionists are merely hypotheses that happen to support their preferred conclusions. But arguing that Jesus must have reiterated a literal reading of the prophetic promises; that Jesus certainly would have corrected the disciples' question had they been off the mark; that Jesus' failure to correct the disciples must mean that he approved of their thinking; that the disciples would certainly have acquired a clear understanding of the kingdom after forty days with the resurrected, master teacher; all of these suggestions are merely additional arguments from silence. We simply do not know what Jesus taught during those forty days, and the book of Acts does not fill in the blanks.

Third, it may be worth remembering that the conversation in Acts 1—in fact, the entire forty days of prior instruction—occurred before the disciples received the gift of the Holy Spirit, an important event occurring between the stories in Acts 1 and Acts 3. With that fact in mind, I could suggest it is more reasonable to posit that the Spirit-deficient disciples continued their typical struggle with understanding Jesus' forty days of kingdom teaching, just as they had struggled during his pre-crucifixion ministry. Recall that they often failed to understand what Jesus was saying to them (Mark 7:17–18; 9:17–19; 10:24–26; Matt 16:7–9; Luke 2:50; 9:45; 18:34), even after several repetitions (Mark 8:31–33; 9:9–10, 31–32; 10:32–34; 16:8; Matt 16:21–22; Luke 24:12). Sometimes Jesus rebuked them for being hard-hearted or dull (Mark 8:14–21; Matt 15:16), but at other times he said nothing at all to correct their lack of understanding (at least, in our written versions of the events). Occasionally, a Gospel writer explains that the disciples simply had "hardened hearts" (Mark 6:52; 8:16–21).

Perhaps we should also recall that Jesus had already given a lengthy answer to the disciples' question about timing during his earthly ministry (Mark 13:24–37 and parallels). I might just as easily posit that Jesus'

noncontroversial acceptance of the disciple's question could be read as patient tolerance for their continued dull-wittedness, especially since Jesus anticipates the dramatic transformation soon to occur on the day of Pentecost.
I am not suggesting that we can know any of these things. But I am pointing
out that there are other ways to speculate about the unknown background
to Acts 1:6.

Fourth, as we ponder what the content of Jesus' post-resurrection
teaching referred to in Acts 1 might have been, I suggest that we not forget
Luke's previous, far more detailed account of Jesus' post-resurrection teaching in Luke 24. The fact that both the Gospel of Luke and the book of Acts
were written by the same author as two volumes to a single work provides
good reason to understand Acts 1 in light of Luke 24.

Luke 24:13–35 contains an earlier conversation between the resurrected Jesus and two disciples walking down the road to Emmaus before the
Spirit is poured out. They too had believed that Jesus would bring the redemption of Israel (vv. 19–21). They had also heard the women's story about
Jesus' empty tomb (vv. 1–12). Yet, they were confused and despondent in
the aftermath of everything that had recently happened, not associating
any of these tragic events with Jesus' earlier, predictive instruction. As they
express the reasons for their despair, Jesus (in his own inimitable way) calls
them "fools" who are "slow to believe" (v. 25). He tells them, probably quite
emphatically, what all the prophets had already explained, that "the Christ
had to suffer these things and then enter his glory" (v. 26). Recall that prior
to his crucifixion Jesus had already explained the necessity of his suffering
and death several times. He had also referred to his eventual resurrection,
yet the disciples had never understood his meaning. Not then. Not now.
They remained obtuse.

As I have pointed out several times, if this Old Testament plotline of
messianic, redemptive suffering and resurrection were as literal, uniform,
and self-evident as Jesus seems to indicate (and as Christian Zionists insist),
then why have these two pious Jews, together with the rest of Jesus' disciples,
never recognized it before? Why were they not rejoicing over the multiple,
literal, obvious ways in which Jesus' death and resurrection had fulfilled
Old Testament expectations? Why had the disciples never grasped Jesus'
multiple predictions about his sufferings in Jerusalem?

The answer to these rather obvious questions begins to unfold in verse
27. "Beginning with Moses and all the prophets, Jesus explained to them
what was said in all the scriptures concerning himself." It is important to
notice that Jesus' explanation is not dependent on prophetic foresight, in
which case the disciples might have already seen it for themselves. Instead,
it depends entirely on Jesus' own messianic hindsight. The contextual

elements surrounding this verse are as important as the sentence itself. The teacher is the scarred and resurrected Jesus. The background is the actual, historical fulfilment of "all that the prophets have spoken." The resurrected Teacher now offers these forlorn followers a final tutorial in *how to read the prophets backward*, in retrospect. Jesus demonstrates that prior to Calvary, reading the prophets literally was obviously insufficient. Jonah, Isaiah, and Zechariah were not predictably predictive. No one but Jesus had anticipated what his fulfilment of prophecy would actually involve. But now that God's plan has been realized, Jesus is able retrospectively to connect the prophetic dots with his own nail-pierced hands, showing these men, "This prophecy was fulfilled here. That prophecy was fulfilled there."

The story's framing also establishes the need for spiritual illumination in order to apprehend Jesus' teaching. Verse 16 inexplicably notes that initially the two men "were kept from recognizing him." Verses 30–32 then describe a sudden eye-opening as Jesus prayed, causing the two men to reflect on the personal transformation that occurred as Jesus "opened the scriptures" to them.[36] The picture is fairly clear. Grasping the "literal" significance of Old Testament promises and predictions requires (a) divine illumination as the resurrected Jesus instructs us in (b) how to reread the Scriptures from back to front, reenvisioning God's promises in light of their actual fulfilment in the life, death, resurrection, ascension, and continuing activity of the Lord Jesus. This walk down Emmaus Road thoroughly undermines those evangelicals who are obsessed with prophetic literalism.[37]

Now we have established the proper context for hypothesizing about the conversation in Acts 1. No, we still do not know the content of Jesus' instruction. But what we do know is that: (a) the disciples' comprehension of Jesus' teaching could have been limited, as in the Gospels, because they had not received the Holy Spirit; (b) they had frequently struggled to understand Jesus' teaching, even after he had walked with them for years and explained it to them several times; (c) Jesus did not always bother to correct

36. For a detailed examination of this dynamic connecting spiritual illumination to prayer and the work of the Holy Spirit, see my book *Jesus the Intercessor*, especially 98–108.

37. David Larsen's claim that "the very literally fulfilled prophecies of Christ's first advent would incline us to expect a similar literality in connection with the prophecies of His second advent" is the very opposite of what the New Testament evidence leads me (and others) to conclude. Larsen's claim illustrates how difficult it can be to step outside of our traditional, religious frameworks (in his case, evangelical, evidentialist apologetics and "common sense" interpretation) when we read Scripture, even when that framework is distorting or concealing "the plain sense" meaning we are seeking to understand. Often our frameworks can blind us to our own blind spots; see Larsen's essay, "Celebration," 312.

the disciples' misunderstandings and inappropriate outbursts. Reading Acts as the second volume to Luke's Gospel suggests to me that the popular Christian Zionist attempts at supplying the mysterious content to the New Testament's persistent silence about Israel's return to the land produce *the most unlikely* suggestions. If the Gospel record counts for anything, then we need to accept the unexpected surprise that comes with the vision of the kingdom of God as taught by Jesus and captured throughout the New Testament.

When Peter associates Israel's restoration with the fulfilment of prophecy in Acts 3:18, his emphasis on *the predictions of messianic suffering* draws a much closer connection to Jesus' words in Luke 24:25–27 than it does to Acts 1. In fact, the vocabulary in each passage describing how "all the prophets had spoken about the sufferings of the Christ" is nearly identical. The now Spirit-filled apostle speaking in Acts 3 demonstrates that he has finally assimilated the retrospective method of reinterpretation after the fact that Jesus used in Luke 24. An emphasis on "literal" or "traditional" modes of fulfilment is not a priority for Peter's method of reading the prophets. Insisting that Peter's vision for "the restoration of everything/Israel" must include national Israel's territorial reign imputes to Peter what he is not saying.

Furthermore, the sum total of these observations leads me to agree with one of Bruce Waltke's closing, critical comments in the book, *Dispensationalism, Israel and the Church*. Waltke notes that Bock's argument, based as it is on the "verbal linkage of 'restore' in Acts 3:21 and Acts 1:6," manages to ignore "Peter's own mature reflections on what the prophets promised about the restoration of everything in 2 Peter 3:13."[38] In that letter Peter reassuringly tells his readers, "In keeping with his [God's] promise we are looking forward to *a new heaven and a new earth*, the home of righteousness" (NIV). Notice that national Israel's return to the land is not included in Peter's future hope. Once again, the New Testament silence is deafening with respect to national Israel's territorial restoration.

Peter's complete abandonment of territoriality for God's people is also evidenced in 1 Peter. His identification of Jesus' disciples as "elect strangers in the world, scattered" across the earth (1 Pet 1:1 NIV) takes up the language of Israel's Dispersion and applies it to the new, multiethnic Jesus community. Peter makes the new Christian Diaspora the theological framework for his letter's ethical teaching. The church's physical Dispersion becomes a metaphor for the believers' spiritual alienation from the corrupted world around them. Christians are told to fully embrace their alien status

38. Waltke, "Response," 355.

in contemporary society and to "live their lives here as strangers in reverent fear" (1:17). The church must purify itself as a holy people, "abstaining from evil desires as aliens and strangers in the world" (2:11).

Peter's moral logic is the undoing of the old covenant connection between land, people, and morality. There Israel's responsibility to be a holy people had a direct bearing on their continued possession of the promised land. But Peter has abandoned that way of thinking. His repeated description of the Christian life (for *both* believing Jews *and* gentiles) conceives of the people of God and their future in ways diametrically opposed to Zionism's prioritizing the reestablishment of Israel in the Judean landscape. Peter expresses himself absolutely, without nuance or proviso. He does not add any caveats, clarifying how he is *really* only speaking to *some* of God's people, but for others there *is still a place* for expecting a dirt and mortar homeland in the here and now. No. Only when Christ returns will the entire planet (2 Pet 3:13) become a holy land suitable for God's holy people. Until then, there is no place in this world where the Lord's disciples are not to know themselves as strangers and aliens.

A NEW REPLACEMENT THEOLOGY?

Undisciplined enthusiasts can easily get themselves into trouble. Christian enthusiasts are no exception. For certain Christian Zionists, an obsession with the glorious exaltation of a future territorial Israel can lead to an almost idolatrous adoration of the nation's supposed role in world history. At times, this adulation comes close to overshadowing the work of Christ, as if God's eventual accomplishments on Israel's behalf will somehow supplement Christ's otherwise deficient work of redemption. In effect, national Israel becomes Christ's co-captain leading Team Redemption to global victory. I am tempted to call this unsettling tendency *Israelolatry*: that is, the inappropriate exaltation of the nation Israel to a near Christlike status.

Traditional dispensational theology has always toyed with this idolatrous temptation in its rhetoric of anticipation. Dispensationalists are not simply anticipating Christ's return to earth; they are anticipating Israel's return to the land where the nation will finally be exalted (sometimes, it seems, with greater enthusiasm than they confer on the hope for the returned Messiah). Only then can Israel fulfil its "mission" as God's agent of "worldwide peace as nations come under Messiah's rule" in Jerusalem.[39] In the words of Robert Thomas, New Testament professor at The Master's Seminary, "His [Christ's] restoration of Israel furnishes the channel for

39. Saucy, "Israel as a Necessary Theme," 178.

bringing salvation to the nations."[40] Dispensationalism's salvific vision of Israel's essential role in mediating global salvation offers an uncomfortable vision of Israel's mission so closely identified to the work of Christ, as if they were dual mediators. This has always struck me as a diminution (whether intentional or not) of Christ's work and glory.

More recently, representatives of the New Christian Zionism have taken this discomfiting rhetoric to new levels. Chief offender in this trend is Gerald McDermott, whose several contributions to the book, *The New Christian Zionism*, make this painfully clear. Below is a list of his theological claims about the centrality of national Israel to Christ's redemptive work in the world. I have tried not to take any of them out of context.

- "Not only is Israel a witness to the nations (Is 43:10) but God deals with the nations *through* Israel [*sic*]. In their relationship to Israel, the nations in some mysterious way come into contact with the God of Israel. They respond to God and are judged by God in this secret relationship."[41]

- "Israel shows us who we are and who God is. . . . She shows us who we are before God."[42]

- "'Salvation is from the Jews' (Jn 4:22). Therefore we need Israel to know God. Israel shows us that we live by grace . . . only if the church learns from the judgment Israel has suffered will she be able to know God's mercy."[43]

- "God is still lovingly confronting the nations through Israel and . . . Israel is still God's servant for the redemption of the world in some mysterious way."[44]

The New Christian Zionism maintains that Christ is the only Savior but believes that the world is eventually attracted to Christ's salvation by *the radiance of Israel*. It is the eschatological awesomeness of *Israel*; the superiority of *Israel's* culture; the exemplary nature of *Israel's* peace-loving society; these are the things that will finally draw the world irresistibly to Jesus' throne. McDermott writes in the present tense, indicating that contemporary Israel is in the process of accomplishing this mission. The irony of his claims is astounding.

40. Thomas, "Mission of Israel," 270.
41. McDermott, "Implications and Propositions," 328.
42. McDermott, "Implications and Propositions," 329.
43. McDermott, "Implications and Propositions," 330.
44. McDermott, "Implications and Propositions," 330.

To say that "God is still lovingly confronting the nations" through an ethnocratic state rooted in the blood-soaked soil of military aggression, ethnic cleansing, systematic racial discrimination, and the Jewish minority's unrelieved oppression of the Palestinian majority is, in fact, a remarkable example of the antiquated, colonial, imperial-mindedness we saw in chapters 3 and 12. It is the type of thing Roman emperors said about their expanding domain after the latest bloody conquest. Those shocked or offended by my response here reveal how little they understand the inhumane accomplishments of political Zionism in Israel's modern and bloody history.

Claiming that "in some mysterious way the nations of the world come into contact with God" as they relate to Zionist Israel invites the world to know an elitist, partisan, oppressive God who acts only in his own selfish interests. When I read these kinds of Zionist claims, I am continually reminded of Paul's words in 1 Timothy 2:5 (NIV), "For there is one God and one mediator between God and humanity, the man Christ Jesus, who gave himself as a ransom for all."

Jesus sacrificed himself as both Israel's corporate representative, as well as the representative of all human kind. His death was a sufficient ransom for all of us. No other national instantiation of the human collective is required. Jesus fills that role perfectly well all by himself. On that basis, Jesus alone qualifies as the sole mediator between this world and our Creator. The New Testament never offers the slightest indication that the resurrected, ascended Christ will one day share his mediatory work with anyone else. It is the good news about a crucified redeemer nailed to a wooden cross, resurrected from the tomb, now applying grace to every conscience by the work of the Holy Spirit which creates the irresistible attraction to Christ's throne, not the superior cultural attainments of anyone's nation-state.

The nations of the world do not meet the Holy One through a relationship with national, territorial, ethnocratic Israel. Believers meet God and learn the truth about themselves, their identity as sinners redeemed, by looking to the nail-pierced Jesus of Nazareth, the last Adam who gave his life to undo the curse of human rebellion (Rom 5:12–21). Jesus' own pain and suffering reveal the depth of human wickedness. Ethnocratic Israel's ongoing crimes against humanity are a resounding testament, not only to the sins of political Zionism, but to the total depravity of every humanly designed kingdom in this fallen world. It is only the life and ministry of Jesus, the ultimate Suffering Servant, which shows me how to live as a saved sinner, redeemed by God's grace and mercy. Zionist Israel has no role to play.

Appealing to Israel's divine ministry working itself out today in an inexplicably "mysterious way," is evidence of how terribly misguided unconstrained, ideological obsessions can become. Christian Zionism's *a priori* attachment to a principle of antecedent theology, which is then hyper-inflated with the pagan mysticism of Zionist, blood-and-soil, ethnic nationalism, has created a strange brand of ideologically driven theology completely out of touch with the New Testament. When taken together, it makes for a noxious mixture giving rise to Israelolatry, an ideological captivity utterly foreign to the mind of Christ.

Chapter 16

Why Anti-Zionism Is Not a Form of Antisemitism

It is increasingly difficult to offer any critical comment on Israeli government policies, no matter how illegal and inhumane they may be, without being labeled an antisemite by one Zionist organization or another. As I write this, Roger Waters (Pink Floyd's former bass player) is being lambasted as an antisemite in the international press for his involvement with and promotion of the documentary "The Occupation of the American Mind." This documentary is an excellent exposé on the effectiveness of Israel's national propaganda machine—the work of the Israeli Foreign Ministry—which misleads the public about Israel's action toward the Palestinians and intimidates Israel's critics.[1] The US Secretary of State under President Trump, Mike Pompeo, has also recently announced that he "is considering labeling some of the most prominent humanitarian organizations in the world, including Amnesty International, Human Rights Watch and Oxfam, as 'anti-Semitic'" because they have the audacity to condemn Israel's long history of human rights abuses.[2]

Christian Zionists like Mike Pompeo and President Trump's evangelical supporters extend the reach of Israel's propaganda machine, regularly

1. Watch the film on Youtube at https://www.youtube.com/watch?v=dPo-YohJR-g.

2. Hudson, "Trump Administration."

repeating as fact Israeli public relation ploys, intimidations, and *ad hominem* attacks. As the Jewish philosopher, Judith Butler, explains, "The charge of antisemitism has become an act of war."[3] Neither are Christian Zionists above slanderous misrepresentation as we see in the recent book, *The New Christian Zionism*. This volume brings a group of scholars together with the purpose of producing, as the publisher notes, "an integrated biblical vision." However, a good number of the contributors unfairly dismiss Israel's critics within the church, labeling them as religious liberals, universalists, spiritualizers, gnostics, and Docetists, epithets clearly deployed with derogatory intent.[4] Non-Zionists are also tarred with the scurrilous brush of exclusionist supercessionism.[5] All of this language is intended to suggest that non-Zionist Christians are also antisemites.[6]

The American-Jewish historian, Norman Finkelstein, is correct when he laments that "the worst enemies in the struggle against real anti-Semitism are the philo-Semites," that is people who claim to love Israel.[7] Christian Zionists certainly lead the philo-Semitic entourage as they tout evangelicalism's devotion to both Israel and the Jewish people. However, Christian Zionists cherish Israel, first and foremost, because they believe the modern nation-state is the key piece of their end-times puzzle. Israel becomes an adjunct to Christian Zionist hopes for the second coming of Jesus Christ. Evangelical adulation effectively "Christianizes" the Zionist nation-state, making it sacrosanct, immune to criticism, which effectively props the door open for Israel's own eventual demise by means of endless ethnic conflict, growing militarization, and the relentless oppression of others. "By turning a blind eye to Israeli crimes in the name of sensitivity to past Jewish suffering, they [Israel-lovers] enable Israel to continue on a murderous path that foments anti-Semitism and, for that matter, the self-destruction of Israelis."[8]

The very serious charge of antisemitism hurled by Christian Zionists at their opponents requires a measured and substantive rebuttal. But before we can untangle the popular conflation of antisemitism with anti-Zionism, so effectively propagated by both Israeli public relations and evangelical philo-Semites, we need to pause and consider the theological issue of original sin and how it affects the way Christians think about these issues. Then we

---

3. Butler, *On Anti-Semitism*, xii.

4. Benne, "Theology," 224, 245–48, Blaising, "Biblical Hermeneutics," 85, 97; McDermott, "Implications," 324–25; Tooley, "Theology," 203–4, 217–19;

5. McDermott, "Implications," 322–23.

6. Benne, "Theology," 235, 245; Bock, "How Should," 314.

7. Finkelstein, *Beyond Chutzpah*, 85.

8. Finkelstein, *Beyond Chutzpah*, 85.

will use all of this to offer clearer definitions that fair-minded interlocuters should be able to embrace.

THE PROBLEM OF ORIGINAL SIN

Because I am an evangelical Christian, I approach the subjects of antisemitism and anti-Zionism as someone who believes in the historic doctrine of original sin. Due to our first parents' act of disobedience against their Creator (Gen 3), all people, regardless of race or ethnicity, are born into this world with an innate propensity to rebel against God—a propensity that we all act out from the day we are born. The biblical doctrine of the fall into sin provides explanation for why every human endeavor falls short of what God intends. The doctrine allows the Christian soberly to evaluate actions (personal or corporate) for how they also fall short. That humans always manage to fall short of God's expectations is not because God is impossible to please, but because every human activity is infected by sin. Every human aspiration, in the hands of fallen human beings, eventually falls prey to the sinful effects of ego, self-interest, greed, selfish ambition, prejudice, hostility toward outsiders, and a myriad of other deeply ingrained, wicked tendencies characteristic of the human species. While the personal and collective expressions of original sin will vary with time, location, and historical context, there are no exceptions to this tragic component in human history. If the doctrine of original sin is true, it is true for gentiles and Jews; it is true for Americans and Israelis. No one is exempt.

The only way to counter the corrupting influence of our innate human sinfulness is a journey that begins with the self-awareness this doctrine can elicit. Practicing self-examination with a view to confession and repentance is critical. Individuals must recognize this fault in their nature, their need for a Savior, and the moral transformation demanded by God's call to live righteously. While repentance in this sense is an individual process, if a society hopes to shed the hold of corporate or systemic sin, then governments, businesses, and other embodiments of power must likewise strive to become transparent. Governments too in this sense must repent, confess their collective guilt, take responsibility for the suffering caused by governmental (and other societal) injustice, and work to remedy the damage caused by coercive, discriminatory, or violent state policies. The primary social responsibility of the Christian church is both to exemplify and to proclaim God's expectations for a redeemed and righteous humanity. This means identifying sin as sin, wherever and however it appears. God's calling, then, requires the church to speak and to behave prophetically.

The words of the Old Testament prophets demonstrate God's concern for state practices and government actions as well as individual behaviors.[9] The prophet Amos is a good example. Speaking to the northern kingdom of Israel, he first announced God's impending judgment on Israel's neighbors, the Syrians, Philistines, Edomites, and others who are condemned for their savagery in warfare (Amos 1:3—2:3). Then Amos turns to the northern kingdom of Israel and condemned its neglect of the poor, the corruption and inequities of its judicial system, and the failed leadership of the wealthy upper-class who luxuriate in their riches and deepen the economic divide separating the rich from the poor. He proclaims:

> They trample on the heads of the poor
>> as upon the dust of the ground
>> and deny justice to the oppressed. (2:7)
> You oppress the righteous and take bribes
>> and you deprive the poor of justice in the courts. (5:12b)
> Woe to you who are complacent in Zion. . .
> You notable men of the foremost nation, to whom the people of Israel come!
> You lie on beds inlaid with ivory
>> And lounge on your couches.
> You dine on choice lambs
>> And fattened calves. (6:1–4)

Amos condemns the social expressions of sin at all levels, including corrupt officials, economic elites bent on exploitation, a deformed judicial system, and the needless bloodshed caused by wars of conquest.

Fortunately, there are modern examples of how a prophetic Christianity may continue to walk in Amos' shoes by bringing God's call for confession and repentance to secular states today. After three hundred years of colonial, apartheid rule in South Africa, establishing the domination of white settlers over native, black Africans, the newly elected government of President F. W. de Klerk began the process of dismantling the country's all-pervasive apartheid regime. A key component of this liberation process was

---

9. In drawing from the ministry of the Old Testament prophets, we cannot forget that they were operating within the framework of God's covenant with Israel which was constituted as a theocratic state. Consequently, there is no one-to-one correlation between the prophetic message spoken to ancient Israel and the universal application of those words to secular nations today. However, the prophetic critique of Israel's covenant breaking is rooted in God's judgment on individual and systemic wickedness (as violations of the covenant). As heirs to the Spirit of prophecy which animated the prophets, the Christian church must continue to apply God's judgments against national sin as a part of its gospel proclamation, calling sinners to confession and repentance so that they might enter into God's new covenant in Christ.

the *South African Commission on Truth and Reconciliation*, established in 1995. The Commission's main goal was to uncover the long-buried truth about the country's history of state sponsored repression, discrimination, police brutality, extra-judicial killings, and torture. Public hearings were established where people could hear the stories of both victims and perpetrators. The objective was not to prosecute past crimes, but to publicize the nitty gritty details about the nation's racist history in order to facilitate national healing and personal reconciliation.[10]

As we have seen in previous chapters of this book, Israel, too, has many reasons to confess, repent, and make amends for its history of crimes against the native people of Palestine. It is long past time for an Israeli-Palestinian Truth and Reconciliation Committee. People of conscience, including both Jews and Christians, need to serve as their nation's conscience, identifying national sins and agitating for public ownership, confession, and repentance. This is the only path that can begin the transformation necessary for undoing the systemic violence and ongoing criminality perpetuated in the name of national security.

William Stringfellow was a Christian social and political critic who understood better than most how dreadfully the perverse effects of humanity's fall into sin penetrated the heart of every nation, including America. Stringfellow's 1973 book, *An Ethic for Christians & Other Aliens in a Strange Land*, begins with a compelling thesis statement: "This book is about the political significance of the fall. The fall is where the nation is. The fall is the locus of America."[11] But America is not alone. Stringfellow is clear—the fall is the locus of every nation-state because sin has burrowed into the heart of all God's creation.

The Christian's duty is to see this fallen world afresh and to speak and act accordingly. The world must be viewed from the perspective of Jesus Christ and his kingdom, knowing that the ethics of God's kingdom will always prove subversive to the national, cultural, social, political, and economic status quo of every nation-state. The great irony for Christian Zionists appears in their false consciousness, for they mistakenly imagine that by supporting Israel's ethnocratic, territorial, militaristic identity *they are* viewing Israel through the lens of God's kingdom. Nothing could be further from the truth, however. In fact, this Zionist devotion to an earthly, secular state is merely another example of cultural captivity within the church. One that severely cripples the church's gospel witness.

10. See the South African Truth and Reconciliation Commission website at https://www.justice.gov.za/trc/.

11. Stringfellow, *Ethic*, 19.

The Old Testament prophets raised a uniform, collective dissent against such misguided, nationalistic thinking. If criticizing Israel is antisemitic, then the Old Testament prophets were the original antisemites. For the multiethnic, global Christian community, not only is the church's critique of modern Israel's glaring examples of systemic sin *not* a form of antisemitism, it is a biblical—certainly an Old Testament—imperative. All Christians around the world have the same responsibility to speak truth to power in their own countries, as well as to their neighbors and allies, as best they can.[12] Jewish Christians are called to provide the same gospel witness in holding Israel to account and demanding justice, peace, and equality for all. So also must the Palestinian Christian church speak out against the corruption and injustices committed by the Palestinian leadership, just as every American Christian is obligated to condemn the manifold abuses of American empire. Theologian Stanley Hauerwas puts it well when he explains that "the presence of the church will or should be culturally disruptive wherever it finds itself."[13] Such disruption is one of the signs of the true church living out its vocation in this world.

THE PROBLEM OF DEFINITION

If ever Christian Zionists and non-Zionists are going to be able to talk, not only will they need to wrestle with the meaning of the biblical witness that repentance is key if "justice is to roll on like a river" (Amos 5:24 NIV), but they are going to have to choose their words carefully. Meaningful conversations always depend upon mutually acceptable definitions of the key terms in a debate. Speaking the same language does not guarantee that we are using words in the same way. Take the term "antifa" and what it connotes in a given debate. Is the word referring to an organized far left political faction (for which there is little evidence)? Or is it referring to an ideology loosely adopted by many protesters who are concerned that the far right is edging steadily toward overt fascism—thus, antifa as in anti-fascist. In any conversation of importance, we always need to ask ourselves if everyone in the conversation agrees on what they are talking about and the meaning of the words they are using. Do they share the same definitions of common

---

12. Of course, many nations do not provide their citizens with either the rights or the opportunities for political dissent, at least not in public. Each national church must find its own path in living out the civic dimension of its faithfulness to the kingdom of God in its own national context.

13. Hauerwas, *War*, 170.

terminology critical to the discussion? This is often the point where problems arise, as is often the case when it comes to the subject of antisemitism.

I first gave my definition of non- or anti-Zionism in the book's Introduction. When I use these terms, I have two separate but related issues in mind: non-Zionism is a *theological position* that contains a specific *political application*. The theological issues engage Christian Zionists in particular. The questions of political application engage Zionists of all stripes, Christian and non-Christian alike.

Unfortunately, my use of words like anti- or non-Zionism, almost guarantees that many Christian Zionists, as well as Jewish defenders of Zionist Israel, will accuse me of being an antisemite. Making that accusation, however, begs an important question which frequently remains unexamined. Does criticizing a political ideology and the consequences of its national implementation constitute evidence of prejudice or discrimination against an entire group of people, some of whom live in that nation-state? Logically, the answer to this question must be no. Perhaps a comparison will help to clarify the issue. If I criticize white segregationists in the American south because they want to bar African American children from white-only schools, am I also necessarily criticizing all white people? Or am I criticizing all of white America? Of course not. The same logic applies to the popular confusion of anti-Zionism with antisemitism. Criticizing the policies and behavior of a political Zionist nation-state should not be confused with antisemitism. Another reality that makes this clear is that there are many Jews who are critical of political Zionism as well.

Yet, this very confusion pops up regularly in Christian Zionist discussions. Why? In order to answer that question, I must address one more critical issue. We first must articulate a broadly acceptable definition of what antisemitism is. Searching for that definition takes us to the heart of the modern problem.

Historically, antisemitism has been defined as acts and attitudes expressing anti-Jewishness or anti-Judaism, whether Jewish identity is defined by religion or by race/ethnicity. The Jewish editors of the book *On Anti-Semitism: Jewish Voice for Peace, Solidarity and the Struggle for Justice* provide a clear, succinct definition when they say, "we understand antisemitism as discrimination against, violence towards, or stereotypes of Jews for being Jewish."[14] Until recently, this was the generally accepted definition: slander, hostility, and discrimination aimed at the Jewish people.

More recently, however, a new twist has been added to the definition, which in effect, dramatically redefines the term. Not long after Israel's 1967

14. See "Appendix I," 213, from Jewish Voice for Peace, *On Anti-Semitism*.

victory in the Six-Day War, pro-Israel apologists began to warn the world about "the *new* antisemitism."[15] These warnings were intensified after Israel's victory in the October 1973 Yom Kippur War with Egypt and Syria.[16] Not so coincidentally, the "newness" of this new antisemitism appeared in the criticism of the modern state of Israel and the Zionist vision that drives it. Zionist Israel was now described as "the Jew among the nations," isolated and selectively criticized simply because it was a Jewish state.[17] Those who were sounding this new alarm insisted that the ancient, gentile hatred of all things Jewish was now expressing itself through political commentary, United Nations resolutions, and human rights organizations critical of Israel's behavior in the Middle East. Zionist Israel became the new, collective target of the world's antisemitic animus.

One of the first books to describe this alleged new antisemitism appeared in 1974 and was published by the Anti-Defamation League of B'Nai B'rith. It was simply entitled *The New Anti-Semitism.*[18] The book's authors argued that criticism of Israel's wartime behavior parroted the old antisemitic paradigm in which "Jews are tolerable, acceptable in their particularity, *only* as victims," but once the Jewish collective, i.e., Israel, demonstrated its power and independence (as it had in 1967 and 1973), "the non-Jewish world finds this so hard to take that the effort is begun to render them victims anew."[19] Christian Zionists have not lagged behind in adopting this new line of argument. For instance, Robert Benne repeats the new antisemitism's assertions when he writes, "for too many Christians the very fact that they [Israel] can defend themselves changes their status as the oppressed to that of the oppressor, even though Israeli actions are always defensive."[20] Benne's ideological blindness is apparent.

15. On the connection to the Six Day War, see Finkelstein, *Holocaust Industry*, 31–32, 37–38.

16. Finkelstein, *Beyond Chutzpah*, 24.

17. Chesler, *New Anti-Semitism*, 4, 180; Dershowitz, *Chutzpah*, 121, 210; Foxman, *Never Again?*, 39; Perlmutter and Perlmutter, *Real Anti-Semitism in America*, 162–63; Schoenfeld, *Return of Anti-Semitism*, 147. For a wide-ranging discussion of this development, see Finkelstein, *Beyond Chutzpah*, 32–65.

18. Forster and Epstein, *New Anti-Semitism*; also see Perlmutter and Perlmutter, *The Real Anti-Semitism in America*. For a critical analysis of the new antisemitism, see Finkelstein, *The Holocaust Industry*, 32–38; Finkelstein, *Beyond Chutzpah*, 21–85; Khalidi, "Chilling and Censoring"; Lerman, "Antisemitism Redefined"; Magid, "On Antisemitism and Its Uses."

19. Forster and Epstein, *New Anti-Semitism*, 16; on p. 152 Jewish critics of Israel are called "anti-Jewish Jews" and "house Jews" (referring to the Soviet use of Jewish spokesmen). For further discussion, see Finkelstein, *Beyond Chutzpah*, 24.

20. Benne, "Theology," 245.

What this argument fails to contend with are the legitimate critiques of the modern state of Israel. If anti-Zionist critiques are muted, then no matter how illegal or contemptible the behavior of Israel's officials, military, or other Zionist actors, the Jewish state becomes immunized against criticism—even that of other Jews—because the Jewish state cannot be criticized without such criticism amounting to antisemitic prejudice. Jewish historian Norman Finkelstein hits the nail on the head when he concludes that "the consequences of the calculated hysteria of a new anti-Semitism haven't been just to immunize Israel from legitimate criticism. Its overarching purpose . . . has been to deflect criticism of an unprecedented assault on international law."[21]

The political campaigns spearheaded by advocates of the new perspective on antisemitism have proven themselves extremely successful in both the United States and western Europe. Drawing from the work of the International Holocaust Remembrance Alliance (IHRA), the US State Department's definition of antisemitism now includes several items prohibiting criticisms of Israel. These include the following three sentences:[22]

"Denying the Jewish people their right to self-determination, e.g., by claiming that the existence of a State of Israel is a racist endeavor."

"Applying double standards by requiring of it a behavior not expected or demanded of any other democratic nation."

"Drawing comparisons of contemporary Israeli policy to that of the Nazis."

Granted, the State Department's definition begins with a disclaimer admitting that "criticism of Israel similar to that leveled against any other country cannot be regarded as antisemitic." But finding agreement on which statements qualify as unacceptable "criticism of Israel," on the one hand, and which are merely "criticism similar to that leveled against any other country," on the other hand, is nearly impossible given the subjective, ideologically driven evaluations made by pro-Israel, pro-Zionist advocacy groups.[23]

21. Finkelstein, *Beyond Chutzpah*, 45. For more on Israel's many violations of international law, see Erakat, *Justice for Some*; Kattan, *From Coexistence*; Quigley, *Case*.

22. The IHRA definition of antisemitism is available online at https://www.holocaustremembrance.com/sites/default/files/press_release_document_antisemitism.pdf. The State Department definition can be found at https://www.state.gov/defining-anti-semitism/.

23. Naturally, my critics will reply by saying that Israel's anti-Zionist critics engage in their own ideological bias, an antisemitic bias. My answer to this charge, insofar as it is aimed at me, appears in the evidence provided in this book. I am not offering naked accusations. I am making a rational argument based on empirical and historical evidence.

These three sentences contain very problematic assumptions. Why is there an assumption that world powers will demand that Israel behave in a way never required "of any other democratic nation"? It is exactly because Israel claims to be a democracy that the entrenched, systemic injustices of Israeli ethnocracy—the state's pervasive, continuing land theft; its two-tiered system of citizenship; systemic discrimination against Palestinian Israelis; the expansion of illegal, Jewish-only settlements in the West Bank; the imprisonment, persecution, and flagrant military attacks against the people living in Gaza—are highlighted and criticized. Furthermore, there is a great difference between denying a state's right to exist, and criticizing the fact that it currently exists *as an ethnocratic state* that privileges one ethnicity above others. This study has also shown that the earliest critics to compare the policies of political Zionism to German Nazism were Israeli Zionists themselves (chapter 5).[24] Given the shared ideological heritage of these two movements, rooted as they both are in blood-and-soil, Romantic nationalism, Israel's continuing insistence on ethnic identity as the nation's *raison d'être* makes ignoring these similarities an exercise in anti-intellectualism and denial.

Those three statements by the State Department function as rhetorical gatekeepers handing organizations like the Anti-Defamation League all the leverage they need to police public discourse about Zionism, including the power to suppress legitimate disagreements with Israel's actions and policies. In short, these statements provide the firepower to ensure that *no* mere criticism of acts of injustice perpetrated by Israel is *ever* heard as a criticism "similar to that leveled against another country." The US State Department is now peddling an extremely problematic definition that can circumscribe free speech. If legitimate critique of Zionist ideologically motivated abuses cannot be fairly aired and considered, then the global community winds up with its head firmly in the sand whenever questions are raised about Israel's conduct. Political Zionist's mistreatment of the Palestinians and their belligerency toward neighboring nations are areas where calls for collective confession and repentance will never even be allowed on the agenda, much less be heard.[25]

24. Also see the examples in Ofir, "Weaponizing."

25. Of course, if a state, organization, or individual denies Israel's right to exist simply because it is a state for Jews, insisting that no state in any shape, form, system, polity, or configuration should ever exist for Jews simply because the Jewish people can never deserve a land to call their own, then we would have a clear case of antisemitism. I am not denying that some may hold that position and, therefore, deserve condemnation. However, the historical background to the anti-Israel resistance in much of the Arab world demonstrates that the roots of this resistance were actually an anti-colonial, anti-imperialism movement. To the extent that this may have evolved into a simple

ANTISEMITISM BY PROXY?

Of course, an antisemite may criticize Israel as a backhanded way of expressing prejudice against Jews. We could call this antisemitism by proxy. If someone is prejudiced against Jews, knowing that Israel is a Jewish nation-state governed by Jews, that person may well channel his antisemitic prejudice through criticisms of the Jewish state—possibly hoping to disguise his underlying antisemitism in the process.

The problem, however, with judging critics of Israeli policies in this way is that it transforms the pro-Zionist defender into an armchair psychologist who deftly uncovers the hidden, antisemitic motives of all Israel's critics. The amateur psychoanalyst's conclusions *might* be true, but such a verdict, if based only on speculation, is hardly compelling. For a charge of antisemitism to be cogent and convincing, motives and facts need to be carefully weighed. The important question becomes: is the charge valid?

If a critic of Israeli policies also demonstrates a general disdain for Jewish people as Jews, that is one thing. If it can be shown that Israel's critic is intentionally attacking Israel's behavior only as a proxy argument for expressing his hatred of world Jewry, such critics can then be dismissed as antisemites. At the same time, however, the fact that an antisemite may make a charge against Israel does not automatically invalidate the charge. At the end of the day, defending Israel from a specific accusation must be based on the question of the truth or falsity of a given charge. After all, it is possible, even for an antisemite, to raise legitimate objections to Israel's abusive actions. If Israel is to be judged by the same standards required of any other democratic nation, then the defense cannot be to push back in each and every case with a charge of antisemitism; that is a red herring (even if the Israel critic is an antisemite). Unless the facts are taken into account, such a charge can only serve to deflect attention away from Israel's wrongdoing.

My own sense is that cases of antisemitism by proxy are relatively rare. In my survey of anti-Zionist literature and studies critical of Israel and its policies toward the Palestinians, I have yet to find an author with an apparent antisemitic motivation. It is possible, of course, that some critics hide their true motivation, but guessing at that is the red herring we ought to avoid. Anti-Zionist literature typically goes to great lengths to ground its accusations in verifiable facts, statistics, personal accounts, and historical documents. Naturally, pro-Zionist apologists may contest the ways in which anti-Zionist writers use their sources. That is a legitimate conversation and

---

animosity for all things Jewish, it must be condemned, but making this distinction also calls for careful scrutiny.

not one that begins with unfounded accusations of antisemitism lobbed as a preemptive strike.

A large percentage of the most trenchant and insightful critics of Israel's love affair with political Zionism are Jews, many of them Israeli Jews who write from their own experience. Authors and organizations like *B'Tselem*, Max Blumenthal,[26] Mark Braverman,[27] *Breaking the Silence*,[28] Avraham Burg,[29] Judith Butler,[30] Noam Chomsky,[31] Uri Davis,[32] Norman Finkelstein,[33] Simha Flapan,[34] Neve Gordon,[35] the *Israeli Committee Against House Demolitions*,[36] Jeff Halper,[37] *Jewish Voice for Peace*,[38] Carolyn L. Karcher,[39] Baruch Kimmerling,[40] Antony Lerman,[41] Gideon Levy,[42] Michael Neumann,[43] Ilan Pappé,[44] Miko Peled,[45] Gabriel Piterberg,[46] Maxime Rodinson,[47] Shlomo Sand,[48] Avi Shlaim,[49] Tom Segev,[50] Israel Shahak,[51] and

26. Blumenthal, *Goliath*, and *51 Day War*.

27. Braverman, *Fatal Embrace*.

28. *Our Harsh Logic*, and see https://www.breakingthesilence.org.il/.

29. Burg, *Holocaust Is Over*.

30. Butler, *Parting Ways*.

31. Chomsky, *Fateful Triangle*; Chomsky and Pappé, *Gaza in Crisis*.

32. Davis, *Apartheid Israel*.

33. Finkelstein, *Beyond Chutzpah*; *Gaza*; *Holocaust Industry*; *Image and Reality*; and *Method and Madness*.

34. Flapan, *Birth of Israel*, and *Zionism and the Palestinians*.

35. Gordon, *Israel's Occupation*.

36. https://icahd.org/.

37. Halper, *Israeli in Palestine*.

38. Jewish Voice for Peace, *On Anti-Semitism*.

39. Karcher, *Reclaiming Judaism from Zionism*.

40. Kimmerling, *Invention*; *Israeli State*; and *Zionism and Territory*.

41. Lerman, *Making and Unmaking of a Zionist*.

42. Levy, *Punishment of Gaza*; Mr. Levy writes a regular column for the Israeli daily newspaper *Haaretz*, https://www.haaretz.com/.

43. Neumann, *Case Against Israel*.

44. Pappé, *Biggest Prison*; *Ethnic Cleansing*; *Forgotten*; *Idea of Israel*; *Making*; and *Ten Myths*.

45. Peled, *General's Son*.

46. Piterberg, *Returns of Zionism*.

47. Rodinson, *Israel: A Colonial-Settler State?*

48. Sand, *How I Stopped*; *Invention of the Jewish People*; and *Invention of the Land*.

49. Shlaim, *Collusion*; *Iron Wall*; *Israel and Palestine*; and *War*.

50. Segev, *1949*; *1967*; *One Palestine, Complete*; and *Seventh Million*.

51. Shahak, *Jewish History*.

Oren Yiftachel[52] make up only a small sampling of the many Jewish voices speaking out against the inhumane exploits of political Zionism. All of these authors and more base their accounts on hard evidence documenting Israel's consistent acts of cruelty and discrimination. The pro-Zionist practice of attacking Zionist Israel's Jewish critics as "self-hating Jews" is nothing more than an atrocious *ad hominem* slander that contains its own form of ironic antisemitism. As Judith Butler pointedly asks, "So under what conditions does a passion for justice become renamed as antisemitism," or (I would add) self-loathing?[53] Christian Zionists need to answer an additional question: Under what conditions does a humanly devised nation-state become immune to criticism for its immoral failings?

Israel's Zionist defenders commonly launch the accusations of antisemitism and "self-loathing Jew" as rhetorical hand grenades intended to silence, intimidate, and even to destroy their ideological opponents. It is not hard to imagine that being publicly tarred as an antisemite in Israel is emotionally devastating. Such accusations, and the fear of them, prevent many people from ever speaking out in public in the first place. This Zionist bullying tactic silences debate and shuts down the free exchange of information. It also helps to create an illusion of righteous indignation while encouraging uninformed listeners to take close-minded comfort in vicariously sharing the misplaced outrage of Israel's pro-Zionist defenders.

Fortunately, organizations such as *Jewish Voice for Peace* and a number of American Jewish authors are taking the lead in pushing back against the American establishment's promotion of this new antisemitism canard. Whatever one thinks of those who criticize Zionist Israel, all should recognize that it takes a great deal of courage for Jewish activists to point out Israel's crimes against humanity while advocating for Palestinian human rights.[54]

POLITICAL ZIONISM HAS ALWAYS BEEN IN FAVOR OF ANTISEMITISM

One of the real ironies about the new antisemitism concerns the pivotal role that antisemitism has played in propping up the goals of political Zionism. The father of political Zionism, Theodor Herzl, together with other

---

52. Yiftachel, *Ethnocracy.*

53. Butler, "Foreword," x.

54. I highly recommend the writings (and the activism) of people like Max Blumenthal, Mark Braverman, Judith Butler, Noam Chomsky, and Rebecca Vilkomerson. They are doing God's work.

key Zionist leaders, believed that all non-Jews are inherently antisemitic. This essentialist belief asserted by Hertzl and others goes hand-in-hand with political Zionism's insistence that all Jews are bound together by race. For Herzl, Max Nordau (1849–1923), Leon Pinsker (1821–91), and other key leaders in the movement's early days, gentile hostility was inevitable wherever Jews and gentiles are forced to live in proximity. Herzl would also say that all Jews carry the seeds of antisemitism within them wherever they go. Gentiles could not help but react negatively. The very presence of Jews sowed the antisemitic seeds that would spread like weeds, and gentiles could not help but react negatively to the presence of Jews.[55] The only feasible solution to this "Jewish problem," as it was called, was to gather Europe's Jews together in their own national homeland where they could live segregated lives, unable to spark gentile offense.

Herzl's pessimistic view of Jewish/gentile relations explains why the Jewish philosopher Hannah Arendt described political Zionism as "Zionism with a bad conscience."[56] The fact that Herzl's views on antisemitism were every bit as subjective, dogmatic, and ahistorical as the typical antisemite's accusations against Jews did not diminish their popularity. Establishing a Jewish homeland was never a cure but always an amelioration for the distress Jews experienced by living in a world marked by antisemitism. From this historical vantage point, political Zionism appears as a fatalistic, sectarian movement working to isolate the Jewish people from the perpetual dangers of irrational, gentile hostility. Herzl's original, essentialist, ethnically based formulation of political Zionism has never been displaced among political Zionists. It shapes the ethos of Zionist thinking to this day. It continues to direct (whether explicitly or implicitly) the Zionist policies of Israel's government, and it animates the defensive cries of Israel's contemporary defenders who automatically assume that Israel's critics can *only* be motivated by antisemitism or, if Jewish critics, then self-loathing.[57]

Building on Herzl's assumption about the true nature of antisemitism, he and his disciples were also convinced that they could use gentile hatred to their advantage. In fact, it hardly overstates the case to say that they welcomed it with open arms. Herzl wrote that "it is the anti-Semites who will

55. Herzl, *Jewish State*, 39–49. Also see Arendt's analysis in "Herzl and Lazare," 339; "Zionism Reconsidered," 347, 353, 358; "Jewish State," 380, 384–85; "Answers to Questions," 479.

56. Arendt, "Antisemitism," 47.

57. Once again, Arendt, "To Save the Jewish Homeland," 393, makes the essential deduction: "Obviously this attitude is plain racist chauvinism and it is equally obvious that this division between Jews and all other peoples—who are to be classed as enemies—does not differ from other master-race theories."

be our staunchest friends, the anti-Semitic countries our allies."[58] Zionists could count on this, he said, because they of all people would be especially eager to assist Zionism in removing the Jews from Europe.[59] Once political Zionists found it expedient to embrace the synergy that their goals for a Jewish state could have with the antisemitic desire to eliminate Jewry from their midst, strange bedfellows provided impetus to the Zionist cause for an Israeli homeland. Fusing an appreciation for the synergy achieved in accepting the inevitability of antisemitism with the political Zionist redefinition of Jewishness as a racial-ethnic category, it was a very short step to embracing the racially configured theories of ethnic nationalism steadily infecting nineteenth-century Europe.[60]

Max Nordau, Herzl's cofounder of the Zionist Organization in 1897 (later renamed the World Zionist Organization), highlighted the pivotal role played by Jewish ethnic identity in his 1902 publication, *Zionism and Anti-Semitism*. Nordau contended that their new movement grew "out of the awakened consciousness of their [the Jews'] racial qualities, out of their ambition to save the ancient blood."[61] Riding the European wave of race-based, blood-and-soil nationalism, now infused with the self-serving instincts valorized by the increasingly popular teachings of social Darwinism,[62] Herzl, Nordau, and other advocates of political Zionism urged their fellow Jews to embrace their "national destiny" by working for a Jewish state that would be forged by Jews for Jews alone. According to historian Helmut Smith, something new had been introduced to the world stage: an ethnic

58. From *The Complete Diaries of Theodor Herzl*, 1:83–84; quoted in Arendt, "Herzl and Lazare," 341n10.

59. Arendt, "Answer to Questions," 479, describes political Zionism's self-serving exploitation of antisemitism as its "original sin." This component of Herzl's thought paved the way for multiple Zionist leaders collaborating with the Nazis—a collaboration that included significant violations of the allies' trade blockade against Germany during World War II; see the abundant evidence in Brenner, *51 Documents*.

60. See the helpful discussion in Smith, *Continuities of German History*, explaining the historical cross-currents between racial typologies, racism, ethnic nationalism, colonialism, and social Darwinism in nineteenth-century, European social and political movements. Arendt synthesizes the final effects of these influences when she describes political Zionism as "the ideology of most Central European national movements. It is nothing else than the uncritical acceptance of German-inspired nationalism," upholding "the nation" as "an eternal organic body with [its own] inherent qualities"; see Arendt, "Zionism Reconsidered," 366.

61. Nordau and Gottheil, *Zionism and Anti-Semitism*, 16–17. Recall that the new categorization of the Jews, all Jews everywhere, as a distinct racial group was "a novelty" that arose in Europe in the 1870s; see Smith, *Continuities of German History*, 173.

62. Smith, *Continuities of German History*, 190, says that "it would be hard to overstate the general influence of social Darwinism."

nationalism based on the principle of *exclusion*.[63] In effect, political Zionism takes on some of the self-same dark impulses of the German, racial nationalism that eventually gave birth to National Socialism, the Nuremberg Laws, nationwide euthanasia, and Jewish concentration camps. In Israel, this will lead to forced displacement, violent military reprisals, military occupation, disinheritance, and apartheid toward the Palestinian people.

Ideas of population transfer, expulsion, ethnically purified territory, the need for *Lebensraum* (the purified land a nation thinks it needs for natural expansion), and setting aside contained reservations to house alien ethnic groups, all became acceptable ways of thinking about nationalism at the same moment a handful of urbane, pioneering political Zionists started to imagine a new Jewish, ethnically pure nation-state.[64] Much of the rest of the world would serve as the Zionist's unwitting handmaiden, for Herzl was convinced that his Zionist utopia would always be bound together by the outside forces of never-ending, gentile hostility.

We are now in a better position to understand how and why the new antisemitism has come to dominate the debate about Israel. I am not suggesting that every Zionist defense of Israel is self-consciously drawing breath from Herzl's ghost. Still, ghosts can linger whether or not anyone is looking for them. The beginnings of a political or social movement can shape its development far beyond its foreseeable future. Like an oil tanker that takes miles to slowly change course, social movements tend to remain set in their ways, following the course set by their founders unless something intervenes. Firsthand contact with either the founders or their writings is not necessary to carry on their legacy. Tradition, inertia, familiarity, the *status quo*, the new normal, personal convenience, or mission all provide ongoing impetus once the course has been set.

Akiva Orr (1931–2013) was an Israeli teacher and political activist who had the vision and moral clarity to see beyond his comfort zone. His parents fled Germany in 1934 and settled in Palestine. Akiva grew to embrace Zionism wholeheartedly. But he was endowed with the rare ability to think critically about himself, his environment, and the society around him. Even though he was not religious, he understood the personal and

---

63. Smith, *Continuities of German History*, 214–17, 223.

64. Smith, *Continuities of German History*, 223–25. Arendt, "Antisemitism," 55, cuts to the heart of the matter when she criticizes political Zionism's emphasis of "racial essentialism" as an irrational position "conform[ing] perfectly to the National Socialists who crystalized their world view of a *Volksgemeinschaft* [ethnic community] in antisemitism . . . The Zionist substance theory appeared to be a perfect match for conditions in Germany . . . [but] since Zionism is based in an utterly unhistorical theory [of race], it proves incapable of any real analysis."

collective importance of confession and repentance. By the time Akiva reached middle age he was an outspoken critic of political Zionism and its stultifying dominance over all the people of Palestine. He came to the conclusion that Israel must exorcise itself of Herzl's ghost once and for all. In his book, *The UnJewish State* (published in 1983), he offers a profound meditation on Zionism's moral failings, and the utter bankruptcy of believing that political Zionism's warnings about the Jews' perpetual victimhood contains the essence of Jewish identity. He observed:[65]

> This [belief that Jews are destined to suffer] is satisfactory [as effective propaganda] *as long as discrimination and persecution exist.* When they cease, *they have to be imagined,* even secretly longed for, and when even this phobia becomes insufficient for sustaining the sense of Jewish identity, *there is a genuine existential problem.*

With these words, Akiva Orr unmasks the existential vacuum found at the heart of political Zionism. He also explains why the new antisemitism is really political Zionism's white-flag-signaling ethnocratic Israel's existential crisis. If national identity is a function of antisemitic hatred, then maintaining that identity demands the never-ending discovery of new sources of antisemitism, even where it does not exist.

In the movie *The Village*, written and directed by M. Night Shyamalan, the story unfolds of an eighteenth-century village constructed behind a tall, wooden barricade. The village is in the middle of a dense forest, and the barricade protects the villagers from deadly monsters that live in the woods. Except, we eventually learn that none of this is real. A few villagers discover that there are no dangerous creatures stalking through the forest. Generations of villagers have been duped by a founding conspiracy concocted by the village elders who wanted to isolate their village from the world outside. The question now becomes: who will choose to remain inside the village walls after learning that there are no monsters in the forest?

Of course, historical antisemitism is *not* fictional; tragically, it continues to exist, and in places appears to be growing. To suggest otherwise would be ignorant and dangerous. Every person of conscience must oppose genuine antisemitism whenever and wherever they find it, whether that requires personal intervention or structural transformation. But the "new antisemitism" is a different thing altogether. It was conceived in the racist dogmatism of nineteenth-century ethnic nationalism. It was then manipulated to serve the interests of a peculiar Zionist view of the world. It is now being used to manipulate anyone who criticizes Israel, to brand people of

65. Orr, *UnJewish State*, 183 (emphasis mine).

conscience as antisemites, and to silence those who challenge Israel's ethnocratic system of repression.

If criticizing Israel is all it takes to reveal a person's antisemitic underbelly, then the Old Testament prophets were the original antisemites, the first self-loathing Jews. If the prophets' overpowering moral vision for justice, truth, and mercy is to have any relevance for the church in our day, which is something I presume Christian Zionists will care about, then Zionist Israel must be held to the same prophetic standards as any other nation that institutionalizes discrimination, oppression, war, and militarism. Threats of slander and physical attack did not silence the prophet Amos. Neither should they silence conscientious men and women today who care about justice for the oppressed.

Chapter 17

State-Sponsored Terrorism
Up Close and Personal

ACT ONE

THE SPRING AND SUMMER of 2014 was an eventful, bloody period for Palestinian-Israeli relations. My wife Terry and I were once again living with our Palestinian family in the Aida Refugee Camp. I was busy conducting interviews with people who had been attacked by Israeli soldiers, listening to their stories, looking at their scars, stitches, bandages, and even casts for their broken bones. Several times I was offered a tour through their homes where I was shown the wanton damage left behind by soldiers who seemed to enjoy destroying Palestinian property.

One night, suddenly, the atmosphere in the refugee camp plunged into stomach churning anxiety and fear. On June 12 at 10:15 pm, three Jewish teenagers hitchhiking in the West Bank were kidnapped near the illegal settlement of Alon Shvut. The teens, Naftali Frenkel (sixteen), Gilad Shaer (sixteen), and Eyal Yifrah (nineteen) climbed into a car with two Palestinian men only to be shot dead shortly thereafter.

The public eventually learned that at 10:25 pm Gilad Shaer called the police while still sitting in the backseat of the car. The emergency call was automatically recorded. In a hushed tone, Gilad whispered, "They kidnapped me."[1] Almost immediately, another voice was heard yelling, "Put your heads down!" As Hebrew music played on the car radio in the background, a volley of semiautomatic gunfire rang out followed by singing in Arabic.

Gilad's call lasted for two minutes and nine seconds. At first it was ignored. Police thought it was a prank call. Several hours later, they listened again and realized that the call was real. This mistake led to a number of officers being fired. An Israeli judge immediately put the call and its contents under a gag order. No officials were allowed to talk about it or to hint at its existence. By the time it was leaked to the press on July 1, eighteen days later when the victims' dead bodies were finally discovered, the situation in the West Bank had changed dramatically.

The morning after the kidnapping, government officials announced a search and rescue operation called "Operation Brother's Keeper." The entire West Bank was quickly smothered beneath a new military campaign. Before it was over, four hundred people would be arrested, most of them due to alleged associations with Hamas, and held in military detention. This meant that they were kept without charges and locked away indefinitely in a military prison without trial.[2] Reports indicated that some of them were "being toughly interrogated" (in Israeli reporting, this is often a euphemism for torture) to procure "quick information."[3] Between five to twelve Palestinians would be killed by Israeli soldiers, including four unarmed teenagers, one elderly man who died of a heart attack when soldiers burst into his home, and a thirty-year-old man suffering from mental health problems who could not understand the orders shouted at him in Hebrew.[4] Only Palestinians objected to these casualties at the time.

The Israeli prime minister Benjamin Netanyahu immediately announced that the Hamas organization was responsible, despite the fact (as would later be revealed) that the government had no evidence to support that charge. The Hamas leadership in Gaza denied any knowledge of

1. Eldar, "Was Israeli Public Misled?"; Hartman et al., "Listen."

2. Hasan, "Debunking Israel's 11 Main Myths"; Rudoren and Kershner, "Israel's Search."

3. Harel, "Israeli Campaign." For more on the history of Israel's use of torture, see Dayif et al., *On Torture.*

4. "Reporting Contradictions" by *The Guardian* reported seven Palestinians killed. Levs et al., "Israel's Netanyahu Says," reported that the Palestinian Cabinet claimed twelve people were killed. Rudoren and Kershner, "Israel's Search," reported five.

the kidnapping.[5] The president of the Palestinian Authority in the West Bank, Mahmoud Abbas, also insisted that Hamas was innocent. Even Israel's national police spokesman, Mickey Rosenfeld, confessed to a BBC correspondent that the government did not have any incriminating evidence against Hamas, suggesting instead that the kidnapping was a rogue operation—which is exactly what it turned out to be.[6] Both kidnappers (identified early in the investigation) were members of a rebel faction that had repeatedly committed suicide attacks in the past to sabotage cease fire agreements with Israel as well as unification talks between Hamas and the Palestinian Authority.[7] Yet, for more than two weeks Israeli authorities actively encouraged hopes of an eventual rescue (while hiding Gilad's emergency phone call) and actively fomented anti-Palestinian sentiment across the country. The Israeli government even sent the mothers of the three victims to speak before the United Nations Human Rights Council to plead for their sons' safe return.[8]

The fact that Hamas and the Palestinian Authority had recently completed a series of unity talks that produced a shared government agreement for both Gaza and the West Bank certainly suggested that Hamas leaders were telling the truth. This was a very bad time to torpedo their new, long-debated agreement by committing such a poorly planned kidnapping. Hamas leaders are reputed to be nothing if not strategic. But the last thing the Israeli government wanted to see was unified leadership over all Palestinians living adjacent to their borders. In fact, Israel's Prime Minister, Benjamin Netanyahu, had publicly condemned the Hamas-PA unification agreement, insisting that it be nullified by Abbas.[9] Israel had always adhered to the old, colonial strategy of divide and conquer, working to keep the Palestinian people, both inside and outside of Israel, fragmented into various, uncoordinated contingents. The Israeli government would fight tooth and nail against any form of Palestinian political unity.

Unfortunately, none of these Palestinian denials nor any contrary information that came to light prevented Netanyahu from making bellicose public statements accusing Hamas and calling for revenge.

---

5. Hamas is the democratically elected political party that rules over the people of Gaza. The West Bank is governed by the Palestinian Authority. Since the Oslo Accords, the PA's Security Services has functioned as the West Bank arm of the Israeli Security Forces.

6. "Hamas Not Complicit"; Zavadsky, "It Turns Out."

7. Eldar, "Accused Kidnappers."

8. Al-Gharbi, "Israel, Not Hamas." The speech by Naftali Frankel's mother may be seen on Youtube at https://www.youtube.com/watch?v=rswuKg32mqg.

9. Al-Gharbi, "Israel, Not Hamas"; Rudoren and Kershner, "Israel's Search."

In the West Bank, Operation Brother's Keeper was turning everything and everyone upside down. Soldiers were searching the Occupied Territory with a fine-tooth comb. Like always, Israel maintained complete control everywhere. In the course of two weeks and four days over thirteen hundred locations were raided by Israeli soldiers; be they residential, commercial, or religious. These raids inevitably destroyed much of the property being searched as my discussion below will illustrate. These searches made shambles of homes, businesses, community centers, and college campuses, with food stuffs, belongings, equipment, and inventory destroyed. Soldiers undertaking these operations also managed to pillage over three million dollars in cash and personal property.[10] One irony in this was revealed in a piece journalist Amos Harel wrote for the daily newspaper *Haaretz*. He noted, "The complete absence of armed resistance in the West Bank so far makes Israelis believe this is a low-cost operation."[11]

The Israeli army invaded the Aida Camp on a daily basis—sometimes multiple times per day. There is no reason to believe that they were not doing the same thing in every other refugee camp as well. Thousands of tear gas canisters were shot into streets, alleyways, balconies, and open windows and doors. Anyone seen in public became a potential target. It was impossible for children to play outside. No one could go about their daily business without putting themselves at risk. Night raids became the norm. People awoke in the middle of the night to sounds of yelling and screaming as neighbors were whisked away under cover of darkness. The daily morning gossip included the latest information about who had been arrested and taken away in the night. Often, the affected families had no idea what the charges were or where their father, brother, or cousins had been taken.

Our host family has three young daughters who were rarely allowed outside. A child could easily be in the wrong place at the wrong time as the entire West Bank had become the wrong place. Our family's middle daughter, Selma, a beautiful brown-eyed girl with an infectious laugh, developed a stutter. Apparently, it was her body's way of coping with the extreme anxiety created by perpetual, unpredictable chaos and violence.

I will never forget the look on Selma's face the day I hurried past her with my camera in hand hoping to photograph yet another military intrusion. As I ran toward the soldiers, I heard a tortured cry behind me, "No, David! Don't go!" Looking back, I saw the tear-stained face of a terrified

10. Al-Gharbi, "Israel, Not Hamas."
11. Harel, "Israeli Campaign."

little girl, the face of someone who knew that people who confront Israeli soldiers often never come home.

Sadly, on July first, Naftali, Gilad, and Eyal's dead bodies were discovered a few miles north of the West Bank city of Hebron. All three lay together in a shallow grave covered with a small mound of rocks. The tragic story of their kidnapping had come to an end.

At the boys' funeral, Netanyahu gave a speech describing the three Jewish teenagers as "gifted, pure, honest and decent" young men whose murders "at the hands of evil men" illustrated the "broad moral gulf (that) separates us from our enemies. They sanctify death, we sanctify life. They sanctify cruelty, and we mercy and compassion. That is the secret of our strength."[12] He went on to quote the Jewish poet Haim Bialik: "Vengeance for the blood of a small child."[13]

That evening, before an emergency cabinet meeting in Jerusalem, Netanyahu confirmed that the teenagers were "murdered by animals. . . . Those who perpetrated the abduction of our youths were members of Hamas—the same Hamas that Abu Mazen [another name for Mahmoud Abbas] made a unity government with. This has severe repercussions . . . Hamas is responsible. Hamas will pay, and Hamas will continue to pay."[14]

In referring to Hamas Netanyahu actually meant all the people of the Occupied Territories would "continue to pay." Following the cabinet meeting, Israel began another massive bombing campaign against the people of Gaza.[15] It was called "Operation Protective Edge." Every evening, Ayed and I watched the evening news in horror as various networks broadcast the day's bombing attacks and the slaughtering of innocent people. Israel was now showing the world just how deeply they chose to sanctify life, mercy, and compassion in Palestine.[16]

12. Levs et al., "Israel's Netanyahu Says."

13. Shabi, "Israel's Dominant Media."

14. Ellis and Schwarz, "Mom Speaks Out"; "Live Updates"; Levs et al., "Israel's Netanyahu Says."

15. "Live Updates."

16. For details about the extreme levels of carnage created by Operation Protective Edge, see Blumenthal, *51 Day War*; Finkelstein, *Gaza*, 211–356; Finkelstein, *Method and Madness*, 135–265.

The nation's wrath was on full display. Fighter jets, missiles, and bombs sent fireballs into the air day after day, each explosion marking the collapse of more homes, schools, hospitals, and utility plants. Palestinian civilians were dying *en masse.*[17]

Knesset member Aryeh Deri, chairman of the ultra-orthodox Shas political party, made an announcement calling for "God to avenge their blood."[18] On the other hand, Zahava Gal-On, a member of Israel's Knesset and chairwoman of the liberal Meretz political party, called on Netanyahu "to show restraint and avoid escalation" by "refusing to get dragged down by the voices . . . who seek revenge and . . . collective punishment."[19] She went on to say, "There should be a distinction between the perpetrators, who should be punished to the full extent of the law, and the moderate forces in the PA (Palestinian Authority) . . . who have condemned the kidnapping."[20] But hers was the rare voice of sanity. Very few of her colleagues were so balanced.

Gangs of "right-wing Jewish racists," to quote the Israeli journalist Chemi Shalev, began to rampage through the streets of Jerusalem and other mixed communities, in broad daylight as well as after dark, looking for people to lynch chanting "death to leftists, death to the Arabs."[21] Shalev lamented that "the gangs of Jewish ruffians man-hunting for Arabs are no aberration . . . it is an ongoing presence . . . encompassing ever larger segments of Israeli society nurtured in a public environment of resentment, insularity and victimhood."

In Jerusalem a Palestinian taxi driver was attacked with tear gas by a seventeen-year-old boy.[22] Teenagers approached likely looking strangers

17. Finkelstein analyzes and critiques the UN Report that followed Israel's 2014 attack on Gaza; see *Gaza*, 305–56. Below is a list of comparative statistics from that report. It clearly documents the results of Israel's Dahiya doctrine:

	Gaza	Israel
Civilians killed	1,600	6
Children killed	550	1
Homes severely damaged/destroyed	18,000	1
Places of worship damaged/destroyed	203	2
Kindergartens damaged/destroyed	285	1
Medical facilities damaged/destroyed	73	0

18. "Live Updates."

19. "Live Updates."

20. "Live Updates."

21. Leuenberger, "Hopelessness as Luxury"; Shalev, "Berlin, 1933 and Jerusalem, 2014."

22. "Live Updates."

with curious questions, then listened for the person's accent in order to identify their targets. Palestinians were chased through the streets in broad daylight, verbally and physically attacked on streets, buses, and in cafés.[23] Two Palestinian children barely escaped kidnapping attempts by Jewish mobs.[24]

On the morning of July 2, three yeshiva students from an illegal settlement kidnapped a Palestinian teenager named Mohammed Abu Khdeir. He was forced into a car on the streets of east Jerusalem. Hours later his dead body was found in the Jerusalem Forest. He had been beaten, stabbed, and burned alive.[25] A few days later Mohammed's cousin, Tariq Khdeir, age fifteen, was visiting from America when he was severely beaten near the Khdeir family home by two members of the Israeli Border Police.[26] The beating was caught on video by two different neighbors living nearby. Thankfully, by this time more enlightened, humane Israelis were speaking out publicly, calling for peace and condemning the spreading violence and accusing Netanyahu of incitement.

Sadly, there seemed no way to turn back the momentum of violence once this extreme Zionism of mob rule had been unleashed. The political Zionist genie of anti-Palestinian hostility had been incited to escape its bottle.

A Facebook page called "The People of Israel Demand Revenge" appeared, gathering thirty-five thousand likes and hundreds of messages calling for death to all Arabs.[27]

Large pro-vengeance rallies appeared in the streets of Jerusalem and Tel Aviv. One of the more commonly held signs read, "Hating Arabs isn't racism; it's values!"[28]

The Foreign Minister, Avigdor Lieberman, said that it was time to give Israel's Palestinian citizens "a clear message" that "the place for these people is not Israel."[29]

In a similar vein, a former Knesset member, Michael Ben Ari, posted an online video calling for "death to the enemy."[30] Every listener knew who

---

23. Leuenberger, "Hopelessness as Luxury."

24. Leuenberger, "Hopelessness as Luxury"; Shabi, "Israel's Dominant Media."

25. Ma'an News Agency, "Official: Autopsy."

26. Hasson, "Beaten Palestinian Youth." Israeli television created a good mini-series about these events entitled "Our Boys," coproduced by HBO and Keshet Studios.

27. Shabi, "Israel's Dominant Media."

28. Shabi, "Israel's Dominant Media." I also saw this sign myself in a newspaper photo at the time.

29. Shabi, "Israel's Dominant Media."

30. Shabi, "Israel's Dominant Media."

the enemy was: it was not just the two Palestinian murderers in the West Bank but all Palestinians.

British Prime Minister David Cameron and President Barack Obama each condemned the murders as "appalling, inexcusable" and a "senseless act of terror."[31] Only Palestinians were condemning the terrorist carnage unleashed against Gaza.

On June 1 an American friend who worked as an independent photo-journalist came knocking at our family's door late in the evening. Through her network of local contacts, Karen had learned that following the discovery of the victim's dead bodies, the Jewish settler community in Hebron had taken to the streets, rioting, destroying Palestinian shops, and attacking Palestinian cars, sometimes pulling drivers and passengers out to be beaten. Karen was looking for someone who would take her to Hebron, but all her contacts had refused. Now she was asking Ayed for help.

I immediately asked if I could accompany her as we double-teamed Ayed, working to overcome his reluctance to help. He eventually called a number of friends and family but none would agree. The buses had stopped, and no taxis were willing to take the risk. We eventually called it a night and agreed to catch the first bus to Hebron in the morning.

Shortly after dawn, Karen and I met and walked to the nearest bus stop. Karen speaks Arabic (my Arabic was worse than rudimentary). After climbing onto the public bus, she talked to the driver about where we wanted to go and where he might be willing to drop us off. In the middle of the night, Karen had received additional news. Israeli Security Forces believed they knew the kidnappers' identities, although they had not yet been caught. Her contacts informed her that two large homes near Hebron, each housing the multi-generational families of the two suspects, had been destroyed the previous evening in the riots.

Israel has a long history of punishing Palestinians by destroying family homes. The rationale for doing so in criminal cases is to create a deterrent. This is a twisted logic that defies international law's prohibition against collective punishment. The message Israel seeks to convey with such acts is that doing something bad will be met with the demolition of the homes of family members. This response represents a holdover from the brutal legacy left behind by the British army during the Mandate period following World War I. During the occasional Arab revolts mounted against Zionist settlement and mandatory rule, British commanders armed and trained members of Zionist militias to collaborate with them in suppressing Palestinian dissent. Together the British army and Zionist forces blew up many Palestinian

---

31. Levs et al., "Israel's Netanyahu Says."

houses believing this would deter rebellion.[32] Such is the blinding power and illogic of colonialism. But this British-Zionist collaboration also proved extremely helpful to Zionist colonialism, since these British-led military operations gave the Zionist forces a significant advantage in training, weaponry, and experience when the time came to fight the 1947–49 war. Israel's commitment to home demolitions has never ended.

Karen and I hopped off the bus and began walking the rubble strewn streets near Hebron. We were on our way to photograph two demolished homes and interview the families.

Nothing prepared me for what I saw.

Both houses were spacious, two-story buildings made to accommodate large, extended families with grandparents, in-laws, cousins, and nieces, as well as parents, brothers, and sisters. In each house, everything that was breakable had been broken. Everything that could be smashed lay in pieces. Nothing remained upright. All the furniture was broken, with cushions and upholstery ripped apart. Toilets, sinks, windows, doors, mirrors, all smashed and useless.

Bathroom mirrors, shelves, mirrors, and sink destroyed. Photo by the author.

32. Golani, *Palestine between*, 201. During the 1936–39 Arab revolt some two thousand Arab homes were demolished by British and Zionist military forces.

Foodstuffs were strewn across the kitchen floor, every bag slit open, every storage jar smashed, every appliance ruined. The tilting refrigerator looked as if it had been attacked by a rabid bayonet in a feeding frenzy. It was covered from top to bottom on all sides with deep punctures, the insides ripped out.

The remains of two kitchens. Cabinets torn off the walls; foodstuffs strewn across the floor. Photo by the author.

Boot heels had crushed family photos on the floor, frames broken, pictures ripped out of their albums and torn into pieces. Every mirror lay on the floor broken into a thousand little fragments. All clothing had been torn from every closet, thrown from every drawer, then ripped and sliced as the drawers were smashed.

This used to be a living room. Photo by the author.

At times, I had to stop and marvel at the profound level of industry and determination, not to mention the remarkable attention to detail, required to accomplish such overwhelming devastation. It wreaked of hatred while testifying to a meticulous expertise. Were it not so ruthlessly savage the results might have been admirable.

Walking upstairs to the second floor was difficult because the stairway no longer existed. Someone had taken a jackhammer to every stone step, pulverizing it into dust. When I finally managed to climb up through the rubble, I found that the second floor had been sacked by the same barbarism that had demolished the ground floor, but with one crucial difference in tactics—explosives were used. Both families told us that they were forced to remain seated at the dinner table in order to better appreciate the work of the Israeli wrecking crew. Then they were taken outside to watch the fireworks created by the bomb planted on the second floor.

What was left of the second floor after the Israelis detonated their bomb inside the home. Photo by the author.

Fissures running through the homes supporting walls. Photo by the author.

The explosions left both homes structurally damaged. Large fissures ran through the walls from top to bottom, suggesting the houses would have to be rebuilt. When I first peered at the second floor, it looked and smelled like the inside of an oven. The bomb created a fireball that burned everything in its reach. The walls were scorched black, covered in soot, clothing and furniture charred like the remnants of an old bonfire. In each home, large sections of the roof and second-story walls were gone, leaving the insides exposed to the elements. At the second home, a large section of cinder block wall had flown through the air and landed on the roof of a car parked across the street, smashing it flat.

Large sections of the second-story wall were blown out by the Israeli bomb.
Photo by the author.

As Karen and I took pictures of the ruins, several adults picked through the mess, looking for anything they might be able to salvage. Outside, mothers and grandmothers sat on flimsy, white plastic chairs, holding distressed infants and small children on their laps while receiving consolation from their neighbors. One of the children was injured by one of the explosions.[33] I wondered to myself how any of these people would be able to begin again. I wondered how I would feel if the police appeared in the night to destroy my home in retribution for some terrible crime allegedly committed by my brother or cousin.

33. "Live Updates."

Fire-scorched walls and concrete rubble left behind by IDF soldiers.
Photo by the author.

As I was photographing the second-floor rubble of the second house, I noticed that I was being followed by a boy who looked about twelve or thirteen years old. He never said a word. He only walked close behind me like a forlorn shadow as I meandered through the ruins of what used to be his home. I had no idea if he spoke English, he wouldn't say. I told him how sorry I was for what had been done to him, and that I would show my pictures and tell his story to as many people as I could. I pantomimed a request, asking if I could take his picture. He nodded while standing atop a pile of concrete fragments with the twisted ends of iron rebar protruding. The wall behind him was black with soot. Light cut across his face from an open window, blown out by Israeli explosives. I will never forget his face. In fact, I keep his picture in my office. He is a boy in shock, his expression hovering somewhere between confusion, despair, and anger. I have no doubt that, unless the grace of God somehow intervenes, he too will grow up to hate Israel. And why wouldn't he?

What must this Palestinian boy think of Israel now? Photo by the author.

ACT TWO

I have told only half of my story about Israeli-Palestinian violence in the summer of 2014. The second half is actually where this particular story begins because this part of the tragedy occurred on May 15, a full month before the three young hitchhikers were kidnapped and murdered.

In the midst of Operation Brother's Keeper, Ayed casually told me that his distant nephew had been shot and nearly killed by Israeli soldiers on Nakba Day the previous month. Nakba Day is May 15, proximate to the day (which shifts from year to year) Israel celebrates its independence. While Jewish Israelis commemorate the declaration of independence which initiated the war in 1948, Palestinians, especially the descendants of refugees living in the Occupied Territories, memorialize the tragedy of their displacement by ethnic cleansing. Palestinians retell the stories handed down from generation to generation of how they were driven from their homes, rounded up, and expelled, losing everything they had—a loss that often included relatives and friends who did not survive. I have been honored to hear a few of these personal histories from elderly residents in the Aida camp.

In its continuing efforts to suppress memories of the Nakba, the Israeli government passed a law in May 2011 banning commemorations of Nakba Day, particularly if an event intended to use public space, buildings, or finances.[34] But the law was written so broadly that even privately sponsored events such as marches, parades, film festivals, public lectures, or other commemorative activities are regularly ruled illegal and shut down by force.[35] The law is one more way in which Israel denies the right of free speech to all its citizens.[36] In the Occupied Territories, however, Nakba Day remains popular and an opportunity for collective remembrance frequently including public protests held outside of Israeli military facilities.

The notorious Ofer prison, also known as Incarceration Facility 385, is one of these facilities located near the West Bank village of Beitunia. Surrounded by high concrete walls and a tall barbed-wire fence, the Ofer military prison holds some thirteen hundred Palestinian prisoners, a large percentage of them minors (between the ages of twelve to seventeen) detained in violation of the UN Convention on the Rights of the Child, which Israel ratified in 1991.[37] A British parliamentarian, visiting the prison with a group of his peers in 2010, reported his shock at seeing young children ushered into a courtroom as if they were members of a chain gang. As he tells the story, he "heard a jangle of chains outside the [courtroom] door. . . . Army officers led child detainees into the military courtroom. The children's legs were shackled, they were handcuffed."[38] He marveled at the brazenness, not to mention the cruelty, of Israeli behavior. They hadn't bothered to change their normal routine with minor prisoners even for a group of

34. Since the Nakba is commemorated on or near Israel's Independence Day, and Palestinians view those events as a reason for mourning, not celebration, the government decided to prohibit anyone from publicly marking their Independence Day as a day of mourning. For a survey of the legal contest over this law, see https://www.adalah.org/en/law/view/496. An English copy of the law may be found at https://www.adalah.org/uploads/oldfiles/Public/files/Discriminatory-Laws-Database/English/33-Budget-Foundations-Law-Amendment40-Nakba-Law.pdf.

35. To read the law, see previous footnote. Also see Kadari-Ovadia, "Israeli University Cancels"; Strickland, "Israel Continues to Criminalize."

36. See Schocken, "Chilling Effect."

37. See https://web.archive.org/web/20130429231541/http://www.machsomwatch.org/en/ofer_mon_221110_morning for a report of children in chains brought before a military court.

38. Hass, "Otherwise Occupied."

visiting foreign officials. Keeping in mind that under military detention not only can a prisoner be held indefinitely without charge or trial, but when a trial finally occurs over 95 percent of the accused are found guilty. The most common charge against children is stone-throwing, which can lead to a minimum sentence of three years (or more) in prison. According to the Israeli Knesset, the state hands down one thousand indictments each year for throwing rocks.[39]

Little wonder that Ofer prison is a favorite place for protests and demonstrations on Nakba Day.

May 15, 2014, would prove especially memorable for three Palestinian families because it was the day their teenage sons were shot with live ammunition by Israeli soldiers. All three had a rifle bullet pass through his chest with a sniper's pinpoint accuracy. Nadim Nawareh (seventeen) and Mohammed Salameh (sixteen) fell to the ground like marionettes after someone cut their strings. Mohammed al-Azzeh (fifteen) miraculously survived only because of an interfering rib and a fortuitous angle of fire.

In the morning hours, a predictable confrontation unfolded between unarmed demonstrators carrying signs and Israeli soldiers blocking the streets of Beitunia. A crowd of protesters gathered on one of the roads leading toward the prison chanting anti-occupation slogans and calling for the release of certain prisoners held in Ofer.

Using standard Israeli methods of crowd dispersal, a line of soldiers blocked their way and began to shoot rubber bullets and tear gas into the crowd. Teenage boys responded by throwing rocks at the soldiers, all of whom were well protected by shields, helmets, visors, and body armor.

Fakher Zayed owns and operates a carpentry shop along the very street where the demonstration took place. He was watching the day's activities from his second-floor apartment balcony directly above his store. For security purposes, he had installed more than half a dozen CCTV cameras along the street as well as on both corners of his building.[40] The video cameras ran twenty-four hours each day. Not only did Mr. Zayed witness the pivotal events that unfolded that day, there were multiple angles of the shootings caught on video tape.

The morning confrontation between protesters and soldiers had begun to subside by the time Mohammed al-Azzeh arrived around noon. He left school early that day in order to meet with friends at the rally, but he was late and arrived shortly after the large demonstration had dwindled. Several teenage stragglers continued to throw rocks, and soldiers were returning

---

39. Hasson, "High Court"; Reuters, "Israel Ramps Up."
40. Watson et al., "Father Blames."

fire with rubber bullets. Mohammed had not thrown anything, neither was he holding anything in his hands. The video recording shows Mohammed standing among several friends near the far corner of Mr. Zayed's workshop when an Israeli bullet passed through the left side of his chest.[41] Bending over at the waist, he turned and walked away from the street when a man noticed that he was bleeding from his chest. Mohammed later told reporters that he did not feel anything, but he did see blood dripping onto the ground. As he wondered to himself where the blood was coming from, friends noticed blood seeping from his chest. A group of boys picked him up and carried him to a nearby ambulance as he started to collapse.

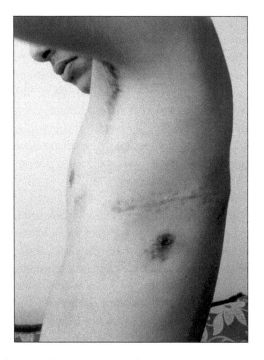

Mohammed shows me the scars he carries from being shot in the chest by an Israeli soldier. Photo by the author.

According to the surgeons who saved Mohammed's life, the bullet had been deflected by one of his left ribs, causing it to barely miss his heart.[42] It then passed through his left lung and exited out his back. Not long after Mohammed was released from the hospital, I was able to interview him and

41. For Mohammed's interview with Defense for Children International and the video footage of his shooting, see https://www.youtube.com/watch?v=G5pZoUudCNE.

42. Al-Haq, "Evidence of Wilful Killing."

photograph his wounds. He had three bright red scars to remind him that he was a subject of Israeli occupation: one scar on his chest and two on his back; two circular scars marking the bullet's pathway, and one oblong scar to remind him of the drainage tube that had prevented fluid from accumulating in his lung and chest cavity.

Approximately one hour and fifteen minutes after Mohammed left the scene in an ambulance, Nadim Nawareh was walking across the same street where earlier in the morning he had thrown a few stones at soldiers. He had posed no real danger to the soldiers as they were uphill from the street, over sixty yards away standing behind a cinderblock wall. As Nadim passed along the road at 1:45 pm, all he carried was his school backpack, straps slung over both shoulders. He held nothing in his hands. Mr. Zayed heard another blast of live fire—easily distinguished from the sounds of tear gas or rubber bullets—and saw Nadim fall to the ground.[43] The bullet passed through Nadim's chest and into his backpack where his father would later find it with bloody school papers and a compilation of plays by the Russian playwright, Anton Chekhov.

As a group of schoolboys grabbed Nadim's body to carry him to an ambulance, they were peppered by a continuous volley of rubber bullets. A Palestinian medic, wearing a bright orange medic's vest, was knocked to the ground as he helped carry Nadim to the ambulance. He had been hit in the back of the head by a rubber bullet.[44] One hour later, Nadim was pronounced dead at the Palestine Medical Complex in nearby Ramallah.[45]

Thirteen minutes after Nadim died in a Ramallah hospital, Mohammed Salameh was shot in the right side of his back as he was walking away from the same group of Israeli soldiers, down the same section of street in front of the same video cameras. The doctor's report stated that the bullet exited Mohammed's chest "from his left parasternal area."[46] He was driven to the hospital where he immediately received a thoracotomy (a procedure to open his ribcage). The doctors determined that the bullet had apparently

43. See the CNN report about the shootings of Nadim Narwarah and Mohammed Salameh, as well as an interview with Nadim's father, here https://edition.cnn.com/videos/world/2014/05/22/pkg-watson-4a-west-bank-teens-shot.cnn. Also, clips of the raw video footage capturing both shootings are posted on the *B'Tselem* website: https://www.btselem.org/releases/20140520_bitunya_killings_on_nakba_day. To see a forensic video analysis of Nadim's shooting, conducted by the organization Defense for Children Palestine, watch https://www.youtube.com/watch?v=uonG5Q9ZuE8. For an interview with Mr. Zayed discussing the shootings, see https://www.972mag.com/watch-footage-shows-israeli-armys-killing-of-two-palestinian-teens/91084/.

44. "Israel: Killing of Children."

45. Al-Haq, "Evidence of Wilful Killing."

46. Al-Haq, "Evidence of Wilful Killing."

damaged his heart. He was pronounced dead at 3:15 pm after resuscitation attempts failed.

In three short hours, three unarmed Palestinian teenagers had all been shot through the torso at the same location by live fire from Israeli soldiers.

The Palestinian and Israeli press immediately picked up the story about the three Nakba Day shootings. The government's response was entirely predictable—lie and deny.

Defense Minister, Moshe Ya'alon, announced (before ever seeing the video) that the soldiers' actions were "appropriate" given that "they were in a situation where their lives were in danger."[47]

Roni Daniel, military correspondent for Israel's channel 2 news, suggested that the video footage had been staged or faked.[48] This charge was repeated during a CNN interview with Michael Oron, Israel's former ambassador to the United States, who suggested that the boys were alive in hiding somewhere.[49]

Army spokesman, Arye Shalicar, told reporters "that the film was edited and does not reflect the reality of the day in question."[50] Yet, "the reality of the day in question" involved an early demonstration where rocks were thrown and no one was shot with live ammunition, which was then followed by three boys being shot with live ammunition after the demonstrations had ended. No one provided any evidence that the film was edited.

The Israeli hasbara-propaganda campaign was in full swing, with numerous tall tales circulating on air and in print deriding another "Pallywood production" (Israeli media's disparaging term for Palestinian videos showing people being shot by Israeli soldiers) of supposedly fake footage depicting fake shootings and fake deaths staged with bad actors.[51] Other official spokespeople insisted that since no live ammunition had been fired that day, the bullets could only have come from Palestinians who were shooting their own people.[52]

The Israeli military was also busy trying to bury the evidence and prevent any further recordings of similarly incriminating events in the future. Mr. Zayed felt the wrath of Israeli security soon after he handed his video footage over to Human Rights Watch and Defense for Children

---

47. "Ya'alon Says."

48. "Ya'alon says."

49. A transcript of this interview appears at http://transcripts.cnn.com/TRAN-SCRIPTS/1405/22/wolf.02.html.

50. "Ya'alon Says."

51. Derfner, "Day of Catastrophe."

52. Khoury and Levinson, "IDF Says Forgery."

International—Palestine for their examination. On May 22, Israeli soldiers searched his carpentry shop and confiscated all of his DVR recording equipment.[53] When Zayed requested a receipt for his property, the officer in charge refused.

On June 13 the soldiers returned to confiscate his equipment again. When he reminded them that they had already taken it all, they searched all of his neighbors and took everyone else's recording equipment. "They left nothing," he said to Human Rights Watch. "I can't record anything and neither can the others."

On June 17, two dozen Israeli soldiers reappeared at Zayed's carpentry shop, but this time they drove him to Ofer prison for interrogation.

Mr. Zayed was taken into a small room by several captains. They accused him of fabricating the video footage. He was told that he had made the IDF (Israeli Defense Forces) look bad which caused them lots of problems. He was ordered to take down all his cameras within twenty hours. Numerous threats were peppered throughout the interview. The officers told him that they would use the law "to crush him." "We will squish you like a bug," he was told. "You are nothing." Of course, they threatened his family, saying that they "will unleash dogs" on his children.

He was then driven back to his business.

I don't know if Mr. Zayed has replaced his cameras and recording equipment. I hope to visit him someday and find out.

Eventually, the coordinated efforts at disinformation evaporated when the Israeli army finally admitted its guilt and arrested the shooter. A ballistics test conducted on the bullet found in Nadir's backpack identified both the rifle that was used and the shooter who pulled the trigger.[54] Nadir's family had asked that his body be exhumed for a post-mortem examination. It was performed in coordination with an IDF representative. Not only did X-rays track the bullet's path through Nadir's body, but the examiners discovered metal shavings from the bullet as well.[55]

When Nadir's father was interviewed by a reporter from the British daily, *The Guardian*, he confessed that he often thought about the soldier who shot his son. "I imagine that he may not be able to sleep or comprehend what he has done," he said. "I want to believe that he wants to pay his respects and offer his condolences and ask forgiveness for what he'd done."

---

53. Read the entire account at "Israel: Stop Threatening Witness."

54. Levinson and Kubovitch, "Policeman Faces Murder Charge"; Zonszein, "Border Cop Arrested."

55. Remember that the bullet had collided with a rib; see "Israel: Autopsy."

He suggested that he wanted to forgive the "boy soldier" who murdered his boy.[56]

Nearly four years later, after accepting a plea bargain, officer Ben Deri was sentenced to nine months in prison on one count of "causing death by negligence." Deri admitted that he had "accidentally" used live ammunition at Betunia.[57] The normal, minimal sentence for negligent homicide is seven years.[58]

None of the Palestinian mothers grieving for their teenage sons were ever invited to speak at the United Nations.

Following the well-worn path of most American presidents before him, with the notable exception of Jimmy Carter, President Obama never offered his public condolences to the Palestinian families, nor did he condemn these murders as "senseless acts of terror."

None of the leaders in the Palestinian Authority gave a single speech demonizing the Jews, calling for revenge, or demanding the blood of those Jewish "animals" who murdered their children.

No Palestinian leader stood to publicly pontificate on the way Israel "sanctifies death, while we sanctify life."

The West Bank did not erupt with violent gangs of Palestinian youth rampaging through the countryside hunting down Jewish settlers to lynch. No one was set on fire.

But Operation Brother's Keeper was only a few weeks away. And the asymmetrical cycle of violence continued.

56. Beaumont, "Ramallah Father."
57. Gross, "Israeli Cop Sentenced."
58. Patel, "Nine-Month Sentence."

Chapter 18

Restoring an Evangelical Conscience

I DECIDED TO APPROACH the soldier standing apart from his fellows. He looked like he was taking a break. His comrades were shooting rubber bullets, tear gas, and percussion grenades at a chaotic crowd of children at the end of the street. A dozen or so boys between the ages of ten to fourteen had gathered opposite the soldiers at the first sound of tear gas being fired into their neighborhood.

I try to talk with Israeli soldiers whenever possible, though it's usually difficult. They are typically too busy shooting at people. This particular soldier looked hot and uncomfortable wearing his oversized military outfit in the summer sun. He had stepped aside, lifted his gas mask, and pushed his helmet back from his forehead. He looked about twelve years old with a flushed face and reddish hair. I doubt if he had ever shaved.

I stood next to him but still had to shout in order to be heard above the noise of gun fire and explosive grenades. I asked him, "Why are you doing this?"

He shook his head, signaling that he hadn't heard me.

"Why are you shooting at those boys?" I yelled again.

This time he heard me. "What would you do if they threw rocks at your friends?" he answered.

I was struck by his response. He surely noticed my shocked expression as I processed the logic of his answer. In this young soldier's mind, firing toxic, potentially lethal munitions with high-powered assault rifles at Palestinian children was a perfectly normal thing to do when they threw a few rocks at you—even though you were decked out in heavy fatigues, boots, helmet, gas mask, and body armor.

I thought to myself, in what moral universe does his answer make any sense?

I raised my voice again to respond, "Well, they wouldn't be throwing rocks if you weren't here shooting at them!"

At this, the boy soldier waved me away as if I were a lost cause. He turned his back and rejoined his comrades, adding more rubber bullets to the barrage.

As I watched him pull the gas mask down over his face again, my mind was still swimming at the insane logic of his reply. An extremely bizarre sentence had rolled off this young man's tongue as if it were the most obvious answer in the world. Doesn't everyone know that twelve-year-olds who throw rocks at soldiers—the same soldiers who terrorize their neighborhoods and shoot their unarmed relatives in the streets—deserve to be shot? Isn't it obvious that their homes should be trashed, tear-gassed, bombed, and demolished?

Is it?

No, it isn't, not to me, and I dearly hope that this rationalization is less than obvious to my readers.

This young soldier expressed the logic of revenge administered through overwhelming, disproportionate force. This way of thinking about interactions between Palestinians and the Israeli military is known as the Dahiya Doctrine.[1] Although the term itself originated during Israel's assault on southern Lebanon in 2006, it has always been a key ingredient in Israeli-Palestinian relations going as far back as 1947. Israel attacks (or responds; whether one or the other, doesn't really matter as to the force of their intervention) with overwhelming, disproportionate force. In the Occupied Territories, the Dahiya Doctrine is another component in Israel's strategy "to sear" Palestinian consciousness and traumatize the population into learned helplessness, convincing them that resistance in futile.

The Palestinians, however, resolutely refuse the lesson.

I suspect that the young soldier I had questioned had subtly (and not so subtly) been socialized into thinking this way about Palestinians while growing up as a privileged, Ashkenazi member of Israel's ethnocratic,

---

1. See the history and descriptions in Hedges, "Psychosis," 45–46; Khalidi, "Dahiya Doctrine."

segregated society.[2] Certainly, his recent military training had worked in a way similar to US military training, deliberately stifling individualism in order to create a conformist who will follow orders. Such military training entails twisting a person's moral sensibilities, especially by dehumanizing the enemy, until he (or she) finally embraced his/her assigned role as a willing participant in the military rituals of brutalizing children armed with nothing but rocks. I pray that he may one day join the ranks of *Breaking the Silence* that he may find healing through confession and repentance.[3]

I offer a similar prayer for fellow Christians who faithfully support the political Zionist enterprise in the land of Palestine. We all have the opportunity either to defend or to deface human dignity. Robert Seiple, former president of World Vision, gets it right when he says:[4]

> Human value, human choice, and human hope are derived from the fundamental beliefs of the Christian faith. Human rights, and the vigorous pursuit of these rights, are part of the inescapable tapestry of Christianity. The rationale for Christian involvement in the human rights arena is one of the most natural understandings to emerge from this religion.

I fail to understand how people who claim to follow Jesus Christ can simultaneously exist in the same moral, or should I say, immoral universe inhabited by that young Israeli soldier. However, many Christian Zionists endorse Israel's Dahiya Doctrine, either giving it tacit approval by their silence, or worse, explicit approval by their public defense of Israel, thereby adding to Israel's dehumanizing of the Palestinian people. For too many Zionist Christians, Israeli propaganda is accepted as gospel. They parrot Israeli responses to critics: "Israel is always under attack, always on the defensive. Its very existence continually hangs in the balance." Israeli leaders (and other Zionist spokespeople) constantly appeal to their perpetually dire circumstances to explain their belligerent militancy. Israeli leaders have consistently weaponized references to the Holocaust, suggesting that their state is perennially threatened with literal extermination, in order to stave off international critique (or anything they imagine might be a critique).[5] And Christian Zionists toe this propaganda line, as well.

2. Recall that Ashkenazi Jews are of European heritage.

3. *Breaking the Silence* is an organization of Israeli veterans who criticize Israel's occupation by telling their own stories of what they did, what orders they received, while serving in the West Bank.

4. Seiple, "Christianity, Human Rights," 334.

5. See the examples listed in Ofir, "Weaponizing"; Wagner and Davis, *Zionism*, 40–45.

Thus, the sole nuclear power in the Middle East which receives nearly four billion dollars each year from the United States and possesses a larger, more powerful military than any of its neighbors, is somehow justified in pummeling a stateless, fragmented people confined to small, impoverished ghettos. The truth is that this conflict is an asymmetrical, lopsided, and excruciatingly uneven match. Imagine the foolishness of a fictional newspaper story from the 1870s describing General Sherman's justification for his genocidal policy for Native American extermination by warning Americans that the Sioux and the Cheyenne Indians threatened to exterminate the entire population of the United States. Yet, Christian Zionists somehow manage to remain tone deaf to the absurdity of such dire warnings while keeping themselves numb to "one of the most natural understandings to emerge" from the Christian faith—the struggle for human rights.

As we have seen, within the Zionist universe bad Scripture reading is used to justify bad theology and thus support bad behavior. *How we read the Bible matters.* In the past, popular misreadings of Scripture contributed to grotesque, antisemitic campaigns that were a betrayal of faithfulness to Jesus Christ. The church's story of episodic antisemitism will always be a stain on the pages of Christian history. Today similarly misguided ways of reading scripture are providing equally inexcusable justifications for the evangelical church's overt or tacit endorsement of Israel's crimes against humanity. Consequently, Christian Zionism has become another black mark of prejudice and oppression in the sadly convoluted annals of church history.

The critical undressing of Christian Zionist biblical interpretation dovetails horrifically with the personal stories and eyewitness accounts offered in this book. The connection between the scriptural and the moral failings of Christian Zionist belief are blatant and demonstrable. Bible reading and real-world results interlink in ways none should ignore. How we construct our ethical justifications for our preferred politics must not depend on idiosyncratic, arbitrary, and ad hoc rules of interpretation so often championed by Zionist biblical scholars.

While no theology is totally immune to reading some of its preferences into the text, the full-on surrender to self-interested decisions has allowed Christian Zionists to slide slowly into the arms of moral callousness. How else can Christian Zionists' noticeable silence in the face of Israel's habitual criminality be understood? But to fully understand this hardening, several more ingredients must be accounted for.

TWO COLONIAL PEAS SHARING
AN EXCEPTIONALIST POD

Israel and the United States share two additional features that help explain Christian Zionism's disregard for the suffering of the Palestinian people at the hands of Israel. Both the United States and Israel share common origins in settler colonialism and both embrace their country's historic role as an exceptional nation.[6] When these two cultural realities are intertwined in the minds of American Christians, the combination creates extremely fertile potting soil for the growth of staunch Christian Zionism. After all, America's status as a special nation certainly has not directed it away from abuses of power around the globe.

Richard Crossman was a British Labour MP appointed to the Anglo-American Committee of Inquiry established in 1946 in Britain's final effort to maintain its mandatory control over Palestine. On his first official visit to America, Crossman quickly discerned the taproot of US affinity for Zionist settlement in the Middle East. He called it "the frontier mentality." Crossman insightfully observed that European Jews were replicating the efforts of American settlers in opening the West:[7]

> Zionism after all is merely the attempt by the European Jew to rebuild his national life on the soil of Palestine in much the same way as the American settler developed the West. So, the American will give the Jewish settler . . . the benefit of the doubt, and regard the Arab as the aboriginal who must go down before the march of progress. . . . America, other things being equal, will always give their sympathy to the pioneer.

The quintessential demonstration of Crossman's cultural observations occurred with the publication of Leon Uris's best-selling novel, *Exodus*, in 1958.[8] Uris was a brilliant storyteller whose novel spun a prototypically heroic tale of Western expansion complete with desperate settlers hoping to build new homes in a barren wilderness populated with hostile savages. *Exodus* was quickly transferred to the silver screen in 1960, becoming a highly successful motion picture directed by Otto Preminger and starring a

---

6. For a thorough discussion of this fusion of two, national ideologies, see Kaplan, *Our American Israel*.

7. Kaplan, *Our American Israel*, 20; see 13–39. Crossman's assessment summarized a long-standing Zionist analogy. The US Supreme Court justice, Louis Brandeis (1856–1941), was a committed Zionist who described the early Zionist settlers in Palestine as the "Jewish pilgrim fathers. . . . The descendants of the [American] Pilgrim fathers should not find it hard to understand and sympathize [with them]"; cited in Oren, *Power*, 354.

8. Published by Doubleday.

young, blue-eyed, blond-haired Paul Newman playing the Zionist, military hero, Ari Ben Canaan.

Exodus portrayed a version of Israel's story that grabbed Americans by the scruff of the neck and didn't let go, convincing many (if only subconsciously) that Israel is us and we are them. America's past is Israel's present. The Zionists were fighting for their survival against bloodthirsty Palestinians just as American pioneers had desperately confronted the "savage" Sioux, Cheyenne, and Comanche. Zionist militias are like the US cavalry, protecting innocent settlers from unprovoked, native attacks. America and Israel are kindred nations, carrying forward the noble heritage common to every settler colonial state. Both nations stand on the shoulders of European pioneers who bravely forged a new civilization in a previously untamed wilderness, relying on the grit, ingenuity, and optimism of men and women willing to lay down their lives for a dream. David Ben-Gurion (Israel's first Prime Minister) expressed his own excitement about the effectiveness of Uris's novel in capturing the American imagination when he candidly effused, "As a piece of propaganda, it's the greatest thing ever written about Israel."[9]

Although this story of unstoppable European conquest is an extremely narrow, one-sided version of both American and Israeli history (to put it kindly), it remains the popularized version that continues to animate patriots in both countries. As a result, those who choose to believe in a sanitized, nationalist version of their country's past give little if any attention to the lethal means used to establish and defend these budding nations. Facing up to the history of rampant land theft, broken treaties, unprovoked assaults, the disproportionate use of force, massacres, and ethnic cleansing is a relatively recent development in both countries. Many devotees of a nation's heroic past continue to resist giving these darker elements of their national story any meaningful attention.

Adhering to their belief in national exceptionalism, some insist that ethnic cleansing was a necessary evil to achieve the greater good. On the other hand, those clinging to their national mythology continue to live in denial, choosing to believe that such atrocities never really happened. As evidence of the first defense, recall the New Historian Benny Morris who knows Israeli history better than most. He is convinced, "There are circumstances in history where there is justification for ethnic cleansing. . . . There would not have been a Jewish state without the displacement of those 700,000 Palestinians."[10] In other words, ethnic cleansing is justified when it's done for a good colonial cause.

9. Quoted in Kaplan, *Our American Israel*, 90.

10. Professor Morris goes on to say, "Therefore, it was imperative to uproot them. . . .

Still others, like the historian Ephraim Karsh, remain stubborn denialists. For them, ethnic cleansing never happened. Karsh's book *Palestine Betrayed* labors to exonerate Jewish forces of *any* responsibility for the flight of three quarters of a million Palestinian refugees during the 1947–49 war. He places *full* responsibility on the Palestinians themselves and their inept leaders.[11] Authors like Karsh offer the brand of myth-confirming "history" strongly preferred by most Christian Zionists. So, it is not surprising to find authors like David Larsen and Gerald McDermott repeating specious Zionist arguments alleviating Israeli forces of all responsibility for the Nakba, claiming that the Palestinian masses left of their own accord largely at the instigation of their leaders.[12] For all his moral turpitude, at least a man like Benny Morris is honest.

Overshadowing these ongoing, settler colonial debates about ethnic cleansing and native genocide is each nation's belief in its own brand of manifest exceptionalism.[13] US patriots are constantly marinated in a pervasive, cultural ethos asserting America's God-given role as global peacemaker and advocate for democracy, freedom, and Christian civilization throughout the world. This particular mindset (generally, a conservative one) has little room for considering the abundance of contrary evidence indicting America as a wanton imperial power quick to unleash the dogs of war (both military and economic) wherever the nation's leaders imagine US national interests are at stake—and America's leaders have always had vivid imaginations in this regard.[14]

Even the great American democracy could not be realized without the extinction of the Native Americans. There are instances that the overall, final good justifies harsh and cruel acts"; see Comet, "Waiting"; Shavit, "Survival."

11. Karsh, *Palestine Betrayed*, 124–26, 182–86, 237–39.

12. Larsen, *Jews, Gentiles*, 202; McDermott, *Israel Matters*, 84. For good, critical reviews of Karsh's *Palestine Betrayed*, see Miles, "Book Review"; Smith, "Palestine Betrayed." Miles accurately notes that "Karsh cherry picks his arguments . . . without making any attempt to contradict or counter the arguments of the new historians, with no demonstration of where their arguments are wrong." These words serve equally well to summarize Karsh's failed effort at undermining the work of the New Historians in his book, *Fabricating Israeli History*.

13. On the propaganda required to maintain the public image of American exceptionalism, see Sirvent and Haiphong, *American Exceptionalism*; for a more moderate assessment, see Wilsey, *American Exceptionalism*; for my own perspective, see *I Pledge Allegiance*. For the history of genocide committed against Native Americans, see Ostler, *Surviving Genocide*.

14. For detailed descriptions of US imperialism throughout the world, typically in the form of military coups and economic sanctions intended to advance American corporate interests, see Kinzer, *Overthrow*; McCarty et al., *Business*.

Israel shares much the same exceptionalist mythology. The nation's founding was launched from a platform of Jewish-national exceptionalism which binds Israeli society together to this day.[15] The Zionist dream of a restored Israel was intended to solve the nagging problems of European antisemitism by providing the world's Jews with a homeland of their own. Beyond this, Israeli exceptionalism becomes the ultimate exceptionalism for anyone who also believes that Israel is God's chosen nation. The fact that Israel's irreligious founders appealed to the Hebrew Bible for their territorial charter allows their claim to divine right (no matter how hypocritical or utilitarian) to sink its hooks deeply into the hearts of American evangelicals.

The fact that Christian Zionists can habitually refer to the "biblical promises" as God's casual justification for modern Israel's brutal displacement of hundreds of thousands of resident human beings is an alarming example of how quickly thoughtless, ideological religion can degenerate into religion without conscience.[16] Daniel Juster is especially heartless when he explains that Palestinians suffering is due to their "refus[al] to recognize what God says about the Jewish people and their connection to the land of Israel."[17] Such Zionist assertions of territorial privilege are a naked defense of twentieth-century, settler colonialism; a colonialism sanctioned by an arcane, interpretive jujitsu that twists Scripture in an ideological death grip. I cannot imagine a more colonial act than to inform a native people that the foreigners who now control their lives had every right to drive them from their homeland and take over their property because the foreigners' sacred writings told them it was a good thing to do. Pious explanations cannot conceal the sociopathic mindset at work in this so-called theology.

The Zionist conflation of political conservatism, the ethos of national exceptionalism, a sanitized myth-history of settler colonialism, blended together with a biblical justification for imagining that the helm of Israel's history is steered by God's own hand, all connect with parallel elements in American Christianity. It comes as no surprise, then, that American Christian Zionists loyally support Israel's government while overtly (or tacitly) shutting their eyes to Israel's crimes. The pervasiveness of this steamy cultural concoction leaves Christian Zionists with a serious moral problem:

---

15. See Alam, *Israeli Exceptionalism*, 3–22.

16. For sad examples of how easily evangelical appeals to scripture will completely erase the Palestinian people, see Bailey, "Should Christians?," 188; Benne, "Theology and Politics," 245–46; Bock, "Biblical Reconciliation," 183; Bock, "How Should?," 308; Brown, "Is It Sinful?," 221–22; Glaser, "Dangers," 104, 110–12; Parshall, "Legal Issues," 209–210; Rydelnik, "Hermeneutics," 69n11.

17. Juster, "Messianic Jew," 68, also 69. He refers to decisions based on human empathy as products of "unbiblical, humanistic reasoning" (67–68).

disciples of Jesus Christ are supposed to speak truth to power, not roll over for the powerful.

A QUESTION OF TRUTH IN ACTION

Christians, of all people, must be committed to knowing, speaking, and standing up for the truth, regardless of the disappointment, ugliness, or difficulty involved. Archbishop Desmond Tutu, the architect of South Africa's Truth and Reconciliation committees, confronts every disciple of Jesus Christ with Christianity's unavoidable, humanitarian imperative when he declares:[18]

> We have been constrained by the imperatives of our biblical faith. Any person of faith has no real option. In the face of injustice and oppression it is to disobey God not to stand up in opposition to that injustice and that oppression. Any violation of the rights of God's stand-in [i.e., human beings who bear God's image] cries out to be condemned and to be redressed, and all people of good will must willy-nilly be engaged in upholding and preserving those rights as a religious duty.

Standing up for human rights by standing against human oppression is every Christian's solemn duty. Following Jesus requires an intellectual reckoning; one that demands difficult self-scrutiny, confronting the discriminatory presuppositions which blind us to the evidence we do not want to see. Honest self-criticism is a necessary spiritual discipline for every Christian. Without it we are unable to confess our sins and make a turn toward obedient living. Without it we remain blind to the truth.

Stark evidence of such blindness appears in the fact that inquisitive readers looking for a Christian or a biblical perspective on modern Israel would never discover the work of the New Historians by reading Christian Zionist literature. Christian Zionists habitually restate the pro-Zionist version of Israel's founding as if it were the only legitimate version of events. Alternatives do not exist, no matter how thoroughly documented or widely accepted by historians they may be. Christian Zionism thrives inside its own peculiar, nationalist bubble, betraying a narrow mindedness strangely content with a troubling lack of research. For, despite their claims to "scholarship," Christian Zionist writers seem content to document their assertions with little more than a visit to the brochure rack in the Jerusalem Chamber of Commerce.

18. Tutu, "First Word," 3.

As Israeli professor Oren Yiftachel (see chapters 12 and 13) warns outside observers, anyone who wants to understand the true nature of Israel's ethnocratic society must become sensitive to the differences between societal *features* and *structures*. The unfortunate fact is that all governments lie. Israel's government is no exception. Officially orchestrated features exist to be manipulated. That is their purpose, for public features serve the purposes of public relations. Israel's deeply ingrained structures of Jewish ethnocratic domination have remained constant and will not allow for a genuine, liberal democracy that represents all of its citizens. The reason for this is simple. In governing a multiethnic state, *political Zionism is and always will be inherently anti-democratic.* That is the rigid, structural reality lying beneath the deceptive, superficial features of Israeli public relations. That is also the central reality that Christian Zionists refuse to recognize.

Self-serving ideologies are always the enemy of honest, self-critical investigation, which often requires the honest investigator to change her mind, adopt a new perspective, and view the material at hand quite differently. Dogmatically held theological positions can have the same damaging effects as political ideology insofar as they encourage investigators to keep a closed mind, ignoring new or unconventional information that threatens to upset the time-honored apple cart.[19] Unfortunately, Christian Zionist literature falls prey to these dangers as their ideological priorities undermine their research and skew their historical accuracy. One example will suffice to demonstrate the problem. In naively repeating Israel's ongoing lament over the constant "existential threat" to Israel's existence posed by Palestinian resistance to their occupation, Christian Zionists keep themselves ignorant (or worse yet, cynical and unbelieving) about the acute imbalance in the accounting of Israeli vs. Palestinian deaths and injuries.

If Americans Knew is an organization that collects and publicizes—with publicly available supporting documentation—comparative statistics

---

19. In making these claims, I am not assuming a foundationalist view of historical reconstruction or "truthfulness" as if proper empirical investigation will always reveal the one, complete, unchanging truth for all to see. That attitude is actually a guiding principle behind Christian Zionist interpretation as it applies the grammatical-historical method to Biblical interpretation, looking for the plain sense meaning of a text that will be self-evident to everyone. I realize that the interpreter's own perspective always has an influence on the way reading and research occur. Every interpretation or conclusion is an *approximation* of the subject's "true" meaning, always open to future revision. But it is also true that not all interpretive approximations are equally compelling or competent. In fact, some interpretations are so uncompelling and incompetent that only those held captive to an ideology buttressed by a particular interpretation (or newcomers who know next to nothing about the subject) will find them satisfactory.

detailing the Israel-Palestinian conflict.[20] Their information (covering the period from September 29, 2000, to March 26, 2020) illustrates the extremely lopsided nature of Israeli-Palestinian suffering:

	Israelis	Palestinians
Killed by rocket attacks/airstrikes	30	4,000
Children killed	134	2,172
Total killed	1,270	10,001
Total injured	11,895	95,299

Family and community trauma, pain, suffering, and violent death can never be quantified. Every death is tragic and lamentable. However, the term "existential threat" certainly does not describe Israel's situation in this conflict. Israel's Zionist devotees in the Christian church need to awaken from their Zionist slumber and understand this.

20. See https://ifamericansknew.org/. For corroborating documentation confirming the lopsided nature of this conflict, see B'Tselem, "Fatalities"; Fisher, "This Chart"; Taylor, "Lopsided."

Conclusion

Life in God's Kingdom Is Not Complicated

OVER THE YEARS I have attended various presentations on "the problems" of Israel-Palestine where the speaker opened his talk by saying something to the effect that "the issues are very complicated."[1] Whenever I hear this remark, I find myself needing to suppress an instinct to interrupt and correct the speaker because the Israel-Palestine conflict is actually not complicated at all. Not for the secularist. Not for the Christian. Norman Finkelstein, a Jewish historian who has devoted his academic career to studying this conflict, writes, "Looking back after two decades of study and reflection, I am struck most by how *un*complicated the Israel-Palestinian conflict is."[2]

He's right.

Anyone interested in learning about this conflict for themselves will quickly discover that the documentary record is overwhelming once it is uncovered. I hope that my readers will broaden their horizons by investigating the well-researched, authoritative works (many of them included in this book's bibliography) available from writers like Uri Davis, Nora Erakat, Norman Finkelstein, Rashid Khalidi, Baruch Kimmerling, Ilan Pappé, Avi Shlaim, Tom Segev and others. I suggest beginning with the non-propagandistic work of an actual historian such as Ilan Pappé, a scholar who has also spent his entire academic career focusing on this subject. His book *Ten Myths About Israel* is as good a place as any to begin. Then move on to his thoroughly documented and emotionally overwhelming history, *The Ethnic Cleansing of Palestine*. Books like these will plant the reader's feet firmly in the genuine historical playing field.

---

1. For instance, see Ben-Shmuel, "Overview," 1: "Our conflict, the Israeli-Palestinian conflict, is complicated, and frustrating."

2. Finkelstein, *Beyond Chutzpah*, 2 (emphasis mine).

Granted, none of these critics of political Zionism and the role it has played in shaping Israel's development are biblical scholars. Nor are they theologians. None of them, to my knowledge, claim to be a Christian. But that should not matter. Truth is always true, no matter who does the telling. As certain Reformed theologians like to say, *all truth is God's truth*, regardless of where it is found or who makes the discovery. Anyone open to learning new information regarding Palestinian oppression must reach beyond the distorting constraints of evangelical, Zionist mantras so often repeated in church settings, school curricula, partisan politics, and other venues of religious/cultural conformity. One way to approach the task of correcting the historical record while simultaneously correcting one's spiritual vision would be to read Ilan Pappé while returning to a study of Jesus and his teaching about life in the kingdom of God. The Gospels remind us all that faithfulness to Jesus is more important than any political ideology, including Zionism.

Jesus defines Christian discipleship very simply: a disciple is someone who "obeys everything Jesus has commanded" (Matt 28:20). The Lord's definition is short and sweet, challenging but not complicated. When we immerse ourselves in the New Testament Gospels, learning again about the things that Jesus commands us to do; the type of people he requires us to become; we discover (or are reminded) that life in God's kingdom demands a reversal of conventional, human priorities.[3] His is an upside-down kingdom. The ways of this world are antithetical to the way of Jesus. In God's kingdom, the last will be first and the first will be last.[4] The rich and powerful are left behind while the poor and the suffering are loved and embraced.

Jesus' parable of the good Samaritan drives these kingdom priorities home. Kingdom righteousness shows itself by intervening and offering practical assistance to the person who lies abandoned and injured in the ditch, even if he is an enemy (Luke 10:25–37). Conventionally defined righteousness (demonstrated by the priest and Levite) ignores the beaten stranger, walking past on the opposite side of the road. But the citizens of God's kingdom prioritize sacrificial service to the underdog, offering mercy to the one who has been robbed and trampled underfoot by injustice.[5]

3. For the treatments of Jesus' reversal theme, see Crump, *I Pledge Allegiance*, 29–45; Kraybill, *Upside-Down Kingdom*; Verhey, *Great Reversal*. For central Gospel passages, see Mark 8:35 and parallels; Mark 9:35; 10:15, 25 and parallels; Mark 10:31, 44 and parallels; Matt 5:3–11; 18:4; 20:16; 23:11–12; Luke 6:20–22, 24–26; 14:11; 18:14.

4. Matt 19:30; 20:16, 27; Mark 9:35; 10:31; 10:44; Luke 13:30.

5. Naturally, Zionists will justify their loyalty to Israel by insisting that this sentence describes the historic plight of Jews who suffer from antisemitism. Of course, all

Loyalty to the kingdom of God supersedes every other allegiance for disciples of Christ. As the Lord tells us, "Seek the kingdom of God *first*, and everything else will take care of itself" (Matt. 6:33 my paraphrase). Confessing Jesus as Lord trumps every other loyalty, without exception. Every affection must submit to Christ's scrutiny, surrendering to his pruning. Since the kingdom of God is an international, global empire, individual nationalities are recognized and appreciated, but all segregating national*isms*, whether ethnic, religious, cultural, or territorial, are as foreign to life in God's kingdom as a cuckoo bird coopting a robin's nest. At several points in his ministry, Jesus was asked questions that opened the door for him publicly to endorse Jewish, territorial nationalism. The most obvious instances are when he was questioned about paying taxes to Caesar (Matt. 22:15–22; Luke 20:20–26), and when he is questioned by Pontius Pilate (Mark 15:1–15; Matt. 27:11–26; Luke 22:66–23:25). In each situation, Jesus has nothing to say about either ethnic or spiritual loyalty (of any sort) to Jewish nationalism, the land, Jerusalem, or the temple.

Jesus' silence is striking, for all species of nationalism are built upon an Us-Them mentality that inevitably fosters jealousy, possessiveness, and competition, which invariably leads to aggression, gives birth to hostility, and eventually erupts into conflict. As the old adage says, a nation is a group of people bound together by a common myth about their ancestry and shared hostility toward their neighbors.[6] The current situation in Israel-Palestine is a textbook example of what happens when powerful, ethnocentric nationalism is allowed to have its way. Similarly, Christian advocates for Zionist ethnic nationalism illustrate the theological distortions that can mislead anyone who forgets Jesus' priority of seeking God's kingdom first.

No right-thinking disciple of Jesus Christ can applaud an ethnocratic nation-state. When Jesus says that the greatest of his disciples must first become a servant to everyone (Mark 9:35; 10:43), he flatly excludes any possibility of exploiting ethnic advantage. We dare not limit Jesus' kingdom ethic solely to individual decision. That is the crippling American temptation plaguing American Christianity. The Christian church is a global collective called to obey Jesus collectively and so to provide a collective witness to the world of how Jesus wants all humanity to live peaceably together in him. Certainly, ethnic, racial, territorial, and national barriers will always exist in this temporal world, but they can never become sanctioned reifications for God's people.

---

antisemitism (when properly defined) must be combated everywhere. But neither the citizenry of Jewish nationals nor the Zionist state of Israel are the underdogs suffering systemic injustice and collective oppression at the hands of Palestinians.

6. Connor, *Ethnonationalism*, 114n10.

No disciple can ever say to another human being, I deserve better than you because of my race, ethnicity, territory, or religion. Furthermore, *no disciple has any business endorsing a political system or a culture that is founded on ethnic discrimination and segregation.* Loyalty to God's kingdom becomes especially urgent whenever a country, state, nation, or nation-state systematically oppresses segments of its population and violates their human dignity through violence, discrimination, or other state-sponsored forms of mistreatment. God's people can never condone such misbehavior. They must speak up and act out against it.

Even if I allow, for the sake of argument, that the modern state of Israel *is* God's chosen nation, and that its occupation of the land is essential to the eventual return of Christ; even then, nothing about the theological underpinnings of Christian Zionism can possibly justify Israel's overwhelmingly abusive, inhumane, and soul crushing mistreatment of the Palestinian people. There is no logical, spiritual, or theological reason preventing Christian Zionists from condemning Israel's immoral activities. However, rather than walking in the footsteps of the Old Testament prophets who criticized Israel vehemently, Christian Zionists leap to Israel's defense at every turn, even adding their voices to the unwarranted caricature of Israel's critics as antisemites.[7]

The Israeli nation-state, built in accordance with the principles of political Zionism, violates every piece of moral instruction Jesus commands his disciples to obey. In itself this is not surprising. After all, no nation-state should ever be confused with either the church or the kingdom of God. Neither patriotism nor nationalism have anything at all to do with the righteousness of God's kingdom. What is surprising, however, is the way that modern disciples of Jesus, who identify theologically and politically with Zionism, will enthusiastically contribute their money, political support, and energies to supporting ethnocratic Israel and shielding the nation-state as a perpetually embattled victim.

THE SIMPLICITY OF MORAL CHARACTER

I remain convinced that the central issues in this debate are not complicated at all. The crux of this supposed complexity is tied up with where the story of Palestine and Israel is thought to begin.[8] Israel's pro-Zionist propagandists have worked hard for over seventy years to hide from public scrutiny the details of the nation-state's beginnings. They have enjoyed overwhelming

---

7. For an entire book built on this premise, see Horner, *Future Israel.*

8. For example, see Guerrero, "When Does?"; Shabi, "Israel's Dominant."

success, and they have only increased their propaganda efforts over time.[9] Consumers of Western media never learn about Israel's flagrant history of hiding and destroying evidence because almost all Western reporting occurs inside a temporal bubble that I call APR time (meaning After Palestinians Respond). Palestinian violence is typically portrayed as unprovoked, irrational aggression devoid of any background or context. We are told, or left to infer, that Palestinians are congenitally prone to irrational violence leading to terrorism. Rarely do we hear about what was happening immediately prior to the latest Palestinian "attack." Most Western media will offer images of frightened Israelis hiding in their personal bomb shelters, waiting out the latest binge of irrational Arab volatility. What is rarely communicated are the Israeli actions against the Palestinians that preceded the Palestinian response. The message (implicit and sometimes explicit) is that Palestinians are senselessly bent upon killing innocent citizens of the Jewish state. Yet, that image, even if carried by established Western media, is typically a lie or a distortion that finds its way to newspapers, radio, and television as the result of the Israeli propaganda machine.

The point here is not to excuse, much less to endorse, anyone's acts of violence. I personally believe that to be a follower of Jesus I am called to be a pacifist. All violence is wrong and must be condemned. However, as Christians committed to all truth, we need to be honest about when and how this history of violence began. The violence playing out in Israel-Palestine is not an ancient antagonism going back to "time immemorial." That is another myth created by Zionist propaganda. This is actually a very modern antagonism that began at the tail-end of the Western colonial period when the first wave (in 1882 to be precise) of European, Zionist settlers began immigrating into Palestine. The collision of two embryonic national movements, one Palestinian, the other Jewish, was inevitable.[10] The fact that the Palestinians were natives to the land, while the European, Zionist settlers were foreigners arriving beneath the protective arm of the British Empire, set the stage for an intractable conflict and eventual Palestinian defeat. This is a yet another simple story of European colonialists taking land by force of arms from the native people. Woodrow Wilson's chief foreign policy advisor, Colonel Edward House, warned the president against endorsing the Balfour Declaration after a meeting with Lord Balfour in Washington, DC. He openly

9. See Hazkani, "Catastrophic Thinking"; Lisa Goldman, "Classified"; Aderet, "Activists"; Cook, "Why Is Israel Blocking."

10. See Khalidi, *Palestinian Identity*, especially his section on "peasant resistance to Zionist settlement," 89–117.

condemned the Declaration, saying, "It is all bad and I told Balfour so. They are making [the Middle East] a breeding place for future war."[11]

Colonel House's warning was prophetic. Only apologists for political Zionism will deny that the instigators of the Israel-Palestinian conflict have always been the European, Jewish colonizers. *The historical truth really is that simple.* It is impossible, therefore, to understand the problems of Israeli society without first acknowledging the nation's original sins of ethnic cleansing, the deliberate construction of a Jewish, ethnocratic state, or the wholesale land and property theft upon which the nation-state is built.

It is impossible to understand rocket fire from Gaza without first acknowledging the gross inhumanity of Israel's unilateral confinement of nearly two million people inside an open-air prison surrounded by a large, barbed-wire fence and the Israeli army. It is impossible to understand Palestinian anger inside Gaza apart from knowing how the Israeli armed forces have used this malnourished human population for target practice (with consciences mollified beneath the deceptively warm blanket of Zionist propaganda).

Israel's occupation of the West Bank must be seen for what it is: the inherently evil work of a secular state that uses its military to inculcate a conquered population with the lessons of learned helplessness and a seared consciousness (see chapter 10).

Yes, some Palestinians have responded to their oppressive circumstances by turning to violence. Frankly, why should anyone be surprised at such a development? I suspect that many Christian Zionists would have made similar choices had they been born and raised under similar military occupation.[12] But the fact is that the majority of Palestinians, both Christian and Muslim, openly reject violence and choose to resist Israeli oppression through nonviolent actions like sit-ins, marches, and protests—peaceful actions that are inevitably broken up by violent Israeli soldiers.[13] My friend

---

11. Quoted in Oren, *Power*, 360. Balfour hoped that the United States would take over the administration of Palestine and help to protect its Zionist settlers. House's opposition was rooted in both his understanding of the region as well as his anti-imperialist instincts.

12. Doyle, "21st-Century Palestinian Church," 151–64, writes condescendingly about the surprise he felt when he first met Palestinian Christians in Gaza who pray for their Jewish persecutors! Unfortunately, Doyle fails to recognize the tremendous irony of his essay since he remains blind to the ways in which these Palestinian Christians understand their Lord more deeply than he does.

13. On Palestinian nonviolence, see Alexander, *Christ at the Checkpoint*; Ateek, *Justice, and Only Justice*; Barghouti, *Boycott, Divestment, Sanctions*; Chacour, *Blood Brothers*; Chacour, *We Belong to the Land*; Katanacho, *Land of Christ*; Qumsiyeh, *Popular Resistance*; Zaru, *Occupied with Nonviolence*.

Munther Amira, a Palestinian social worker and well-known nonviolent activist, was arrested in 2018 and sent to prison for six months merely for standing on a sidewalk and holding up a cardboard sign objecting to Israel's habit of imprisoning Palestinian children.[14]

Israeli politicians often dismiss Israel's critics by accusing them of trying to "delegitimize the state" or of "denying Israel's right to exist." But aside from the fact that these empty rebuttals sidestep the substance of whatever criticisms are being made against Israel, they also beg a number of moral questions. First, by what right can any nation-state justify its existence? Christian Zionists, and some Jewish Zionists, insist that Israel exists in the land of Palestine by divine right, arguing that Palestinian claims of ancient occupancy must give way before the biblical promises of land for Israel. Given the realities for Palestinians on the ground, this appears as nothing more than a pious sounding whitewashing of a bloody, religious and secular Zionist imperialism. Furthermore, the query itself is a trick question.[15] The biblical claims of Christian and Jewish Zionists are only convincing to likeminded coreligionists. International relations cannot reasonably be conducted on the basis of such subjective, sectarian, religious, territorial claims. To think otherwise is a recipe for rampant chaos and bloodshed the world over.

Two recent examples clearly illustrate this point. The first appears in the rise of Hindu violence against the Muslim and Christian communities in India (attacks both in the streets and in the legislature) since the ascent of Prime Minister Modi and his Hindu nationalist party in 2014. In the words of a journalist for the British newspaper, *The Guardian*, religious nationalism is "tearing India apart."[16]

A similar dynamic is at work in the region of Nagorno-Karabakh, the centerpiece of a war between Armenia and Azerbaijan. This part of the world has a long history of territorial disputes rooted in traditional ethnic-religious tensions. The Turkish genocide of 1.5 million Armenians between 1914 and 1923 was the result of these hostilities boiling over and leaving slaughter in their wake.

14. More specifically, Munther was protesting Israel's arrest and imprisonment of sixteen-year-old Ahed Tamimi from the West Bank village of Nabi Saleh. Ahed was arrested after slapping an Israeli soldier on the face. The soldier was one of a group who had shot her young cousin in the head only moments before; see Marom, "Military Court Sends"; "Israeli Court Sentences." Munther's arrest is additional evidence testifying *against* Israel's claims to democracy. Genuine, liberal democracies allow for freedom of speech, whereas Israel prohibits free speech both within its borders and in the West Bank.

15. See the helpful discussion in Munayyer, "Does Israel?"

16. See Subramanian's ominously titled article, "How Hindu Nationalism Is Tearing India Apart."

It is irresponsible for leaders with influence to stand idly by while turning a blind eye to the long-term, destructive effects of violent, yet intoxicating, tribalism.

The only "right" that any nation-state ever has for its existence in this fallen world is the right it creates for itself through the exercise of power. The Balfour Declaration conferred no legal rights to political Zionism. Rather, it was merely one more imperial declaration from the world's largest colonial power which imagined it somehow had "the right" to take foreign land away from the people who lived on it and hand it over to another people who wanted it for themselves.[17] Unfortunately, might makes right on the international stage, which means that supposed "rights" are typically the actual wrongs committed by those who most successfully wield the greatest power. Does America have a right to exist? Or Australia? Does any settler colonial state have a right to exist? Regardless of anyone's preferred answer to that historical question, the fact is that these nations do exist, as does Israel.

The important question, then, is *how* these nations choose to exist. *How do they conduct themselves*? How do they treat their citizens and their neighbors? On this score, by any generally recognized, ethical, humanitarian standard, *Israel has no right to exist in its current expression*. No nation has any moral legitimacy—which is what the language of rights is grasping at—when it intentionally constructs an ethnocratic system that elevates one ethnic group above all others while systematically oppressing outsiders; when it hoards social benefits almost exclusively for (Jewish) military families; when it creates selection committees intent on excluding Palestinians from Jewish-only neighborhoods; when it requires its citizens to carry ethnic identity cards for the purposes of racial profiling. No one can possibly delegitimize Israel more than the Zionist state delegitimizes itself through its deeply entrenched, structural racism and brutal military occupation. For that reason alone, no person of conscience can ever affirm Israel's right to exist *as a Jewish ethnocracy*.

PEACE DEPENDS ON JUSTICE

Without true justice for everyone, peace programs merely rearrange the deck chairs on a sinking ship. Human beings have a stubborn knack for not allowing themselves to suffer oppression indefinitely. Resistance is inevitable. Thus, the only realistic, long-term strategy for positive peace is the

---

17. See the right-minded discussion of the Balfour Declaration and its effects in Said, *Question of Palestine*, 15–37.

creation of equity and justice for all parties.[18] As I write this conclusion, the US and Israeli governments are discussing the time frame for Israel's implementation of President Trump's so-called "Deal of the Century," the latest road map for "peace" between Israel and the Palestinians.[19] Yet, this new plan is really a very old plan with some tinkering. For example, the document's opening statement asserts that "Palestinian leaders must embrace peace by recognizing Israel as the Jewish state, rejecting terrorism in all its forms, allowing for special arrangements that address Israel's and the region's vital security needs."[20]

As usual, all the preconditions for peace are laid exclusively upon the Palestinians. Israel is not required to meet any prerequisites; it remains free to go about its military occupation as usual, without adjustment. Furthermore, despite the fact that no one ought to agree to recognize Israel "as the Jewish state" rather than "a state for Jews," it is well known that Yasir Arafat, former leader of the Palestinian Liberation Organization (PLO), publicly recognized Israel's existence as the Jewish state in 1988 when he announced, "We accept two states, the Palestine state and the Jewish state of Israel."[21] At that time, he also renounced terrorism, and the governing Palestinian Authority over the West Bank (the PA, of which the PLO is a member) continues to reject and guard against violence to this day. Finally, as always, the "special arrangements" prioritizing Israel's "vital security needs" in the region repeat Israel's preferred code language for its maintenance of military control over all Palestinian internal affairs. As always, no one requires Israel to renounce violence as a precondition to peace negotiations. The fact is that military occupation is itself a form of terrorism, yet the United States has never demanded that Israel end its occupation as a precondition for peace. Neither is Israel ordered to dismantle its illegal settlements or its discriminatory, ethnocratic regime. On such pathological inequities have all Israeli-Palestinian "peace agreements" been founded. But, then, Israel holds all the power.

By reaffirming the unjust *status quo*, President Trump's so-called Deal of the Century offers another great deal for Israel at the expense of disadvantaged Palestinians.[22] Israel will retain all of its illegal settlements,

18. There are important differences between negative and positive peace. Negative peace is the absence of violence achieved through means that keep enemies apart, such as cease-fires or barriers. Positive peace is achieved in harmonious relations that do not require military deterrence capabilities or enforced separation; see Galtung, "Peace."

19. The full text of the US proposal is available "Peace to Prosperity."

20. "Peace to Prosperity," 8.

21. Lohr, "Arafat Says."

22. See "Revealed."

complete with their six hundred thousand illegal residents, as well as all the land illegally annexed by the wildly serpentine route of Israel's Separation Wall. The truth is that Israel's continuing West Bank settlement program killed any possibility of a genuine two-state solution long ago. As a result, Israel has backed itself into a corner as it continues to deny these realities on the ground. Talk of a two-state solution nowadays only manages to distract attention away from Israel's nonstop land theft and creeping apartheid.

Fortunately, there are important alternative voices inside Israel who recognize these problems and have offered practical road maps to equitable solutions. Given the current circumstances, the only feasibly just and fair resolution to this conflict is the creation of a *one state, bi-national agreement, including Israel and the Occupied Territories, guaranteeing equal rights for all its citizens.*[23] For example, both Jeff Halper and Oren Yiftachel have drawn up practical proposals for navigating the transition from Israel's current state of affairs to a single, bi-national state that would both protect and serve the interests of all its citizens, Israelis and Palestinians alike.[24]

Naturally, political Zionists, who have invested themselves in maintaining the current power dynamics, will initially reject such bi-national proposals, which is why international pressure must be brought to bear against the Israeli government. The evangelical church needs to lead the way in pressuring the US government to withhold assistance to Israel until it begins to move toward the creation of real justice and equality for all Palestinians living under its control. The evangelical church is the largest pro-Israel lobbying bloc in the United States. It is long past time for the church to consolidate its political influence and apply it uniformly to the cause of real justice and lasting peace in the Middle East.

The church can take a number of important, practical steps to help this cause. First, informed disciples, who care about seeking God's kingdom *first* in this world, must become outspoken advocates for justice on behalf of the Palestinian people. Become an active member and financial supporter of organizations like Jewish Voice for Peace and the US Campaign for Palestinian Rights.[25] Talk to friends, pastors, church elders, and anyone else who will listen about the state sponsored abuse Israel inflicts upon Palestinians today.

Write to your elected officials demanding that all US aid to Israel must end until Israel begins to change its ways and becomes a liberal democracy

---

23. Outstanding questions about the refugees' right of return and compensation for lost property would need to be negotiated.

24. See Halper, *Israeli in Palestine*, 207–33, 273–300; Yiftachel, *Ethnocracy*, 259–94.

25. See their websites at https://jewishvoiceforpeace.org/, and https://uscpr.org/.

for all its citizens. Tell them that you do not appreciate your tax dollars being spent to prop up an anti-democratic, discriminatory, ethnocratic regime in the Middle East. The United States is Israel's #1 international enabler making its continuing injustice possible. Whenever I inspect a used tear gas canister in the West Bank, it always says Made in America. This inhumane collusion must end.

Write letters to the editors of your local newspaper or favorite online news sources whenever a new story appears about another Zionist assault against Palestinians in Israel, Gaza, or the West Bank. Of course, every nation has a right to defend itself. But no state has the right to abuse an entire group of people and then cry foul when the oppressed react because they have finally had enough. Remember that Israel is both the more powerful bully and the incessant instigator in this ridiculously uneven conflict. Political Zionism has victimized Palestinians for over seventy years with impunity. It is long past time for that to stop.

Second, support the BDS movement (Boycott, Divestment, Sanctions) by adhering to its guidelines about which companies and products to avoid due to their complicity in Israel's military occupation.[26] Urge family and friends to join the campaign as well. Send letters to your elected officials asking them to end government contracts with companies that collaborate with Israel's occupation. The BDS movement is particularly important because it is a Palestinian grassroots organization that advocates for change through peaceful, nonviolent ways of protest. I once interviewed two BDS organizers, both of whom were Christians, in their Bethlehem office. They both emphasized the movement's condemnation of violence and their own insistence on exclusively nonviolent actions whenever they organized groups or led events.

Third, if you have the chance to visit Israel, don't be a typical tourist. Jesus is not interested in watching his people walk where he walked, but he is extremely concerned about watching his people walk as he walked. This means breaking away from the standard, church tour itinerary. Instead, book a tour into the West Bank with *Breaking the Silence* or the *Israeli Committee Against House Demolitions*. Any trip to Bethlehem should include a tour of the Aida Refugee Camp.[27] See for yourself what the effects are of Israel's continuing occupation.[28] More than that, set aside time to volun-

26. See Barghouti, *Boycott*; also see the website at https://bdsmovement.net/. A country by country list of companies and organizations subject to BDS because of their involvement in supporting Israel's occupation can be found at https://bdsmovement.net/get-involved/join-a-bds-campaign.

27. Try Murad Tours at http://www.muradtours.com/tour-item/bethlehem-tour/.

28. For booking a tour see https://www.breakingthesilence.org.il/tours/1 and

teer with the *Israeli Committee Against House Demolitions* and help them to rebuild a Palestinian home that has been illegally demolished by Israeli authorities.

Visit Bethlehem University, Bethlehem Bible College or Nazareth Evangelical College to learn about the efforts the Palestinian church is making to raise up a new generation of Christian leaders.[29] Bethlehem Bible College hosts an international conference that they call *Christ at the Checkpoint*.[30] They invite both Zionist and non-Zionist Christian speakers to share their different perspectives, to worship together, and to see for themselves how Palestinian Christians are building faithful communities of faith while working for peace and justice in their land. The conference also has a YouTube channel—check it out; watch and learn. Or better yet, attend one of these conferences yourself.

Try to visit one of the numerous Palestinian churches in the West Bank and take the time to worship with the congregation on a Sunday morning. Stay afterwards for conversation and fellowship. Have a cup of coffee and talk with the people about their life experiences. Be open. Ask questions. You will probably receive a dinner invitation before you leave. The most important harbinger of lasting peace will be the growth of multiethnic congregations where Jewish and Palestinian Christians come together as one body, worshiping together, bearing one another's burdens, and meeting each other's needs on both sides of the Green Line.[31]

Only those voices demanding compassion and fair play for *everyone equally* will be the messengers of lasting, positive peace in The Land. American Christians must unite and lead the way in highlighting this embattled cause, demanding justice for oppressed and exploited people. The prophet Jeremiah speaks as clearly to us today as he did to the kingdom of Judah centuries ago:

---

https://icahd.org/extended-study-tours/.

29. Visit their websites at https://www.bethlehem.edu/, https://bethbc.edu/, and https://www.nazcol.org/.

30. See the website and registration information at https://christatthecheckpoint.bethbc.edu/.

31. Once again, the arbitrary nature of ethnic labels is a problem. There are many Palestinian Jews, although their ID cards label them as Jewish nationals. This identification separates them from their ethnic relatives who are labeled Arab nationals. All such labels ought to be irrelevant to the members of Christ's church who become brothers and sisters in one new family. Bethlehem Bible College is making concerted efforts through its *Christ at the Checkpoint* conference to bring Jewish and Palestinian Christians, Zionist and non-Zionist, together as brothers and sisters in Christ. Unfortunately, the college's leadership is regularly attacked and vilified for their efforts.

Do what is just and right. Rescue from the hand of his oppressor the one who has been robbed. Do no wrong or violence to the alien, the fatherless or the widow, and do not shed innocent blood in this place. (Jer 22:3 NIV)

Bibliography

Abdo, Nahla, and Nur Masalha, eds. *An Oral History of the Palestinian Nakba*. London: Zed, 2019.

Abu Hussein, Hussein, and Fiona McKay. *Access Denied: Palestinian Land Rights in Israel*. London: Zed, 2003.

Abu-Sitta, S. H., ed. *The Palestinian Nakba 1948: The Register of Depopulated Localities in Palestine*. London: Palestinians Return Center, 2000.

Aceves, William J. "Interrogation or Experimentation? Assessing Non-Consensual Human Experimentation during the War on Terror." *Duke Journal of Comparative & International Law* 29 (2018) 41–102. https://scholarship.law.duke.edu/cgi/viewcontent.cgi?article=1536&context=djcil.

Activestills. "Photos: Israeli Troops Shoot Palestinian Photographer in the Face." +972 magazine, April 9, 2013. https://www.972mag.com/photos-palestinian-photographer-shot-in-the-face-by-israeli-troops/.

Aderet, Ofer. "Activists: Israel State Archives Buries History to Save Government from Shame." *Haaretz*, May 22, 2016. https://www.haaretz.com/israel-news/.premium-activists-complain-that-in-state-archives-secrets-are-forever-1.5385437.

"Ahed Tamimi: Palestinian Slap Video Teen Gets Eight Months in Plea Deal." *BBC News*, March 21, 2018. www.bbc.com/news/world-middle-east-43487885.

Ahonen, Pertti, et al. *People on the Move: Forced Population Movements in Europe in the Second World War and Its Aftermath*. Oxford: Berg, 2008.

Alam, M. Shahid. *Israeli Exceptionalism: The Destabilizing Logic of Zionism*. New York: Palgrave Macmillan, 2009.

Alexander, Paul N., ed. *Christ at the Checkpoint: Theology in the Service of Justice & Peace*. Eugene, OR: Pickwick, 2012.

Al-Gharbi, Musa. "Israel, Not Hamas, Orchestrated the Latest Conflict in Gaza." *Aljazeera*, July 22, 2014. http://america.aljazeera.com/opinions/2014/7/israel-hamas-palestiniansconflictunitedstatesinternationallaw.html.

Al-Haq. "Evidence of Wilful Killing at Al-Nakba Day Protest." *Al-Haq*, May 24, 2014. http://www.alhaq.org/monitoring-documentation/6651.html.

Al-Ozza, Amaya, and Rachel Hallowell. *Forced Population Transfer: The Case of Palestine, Suppression of Resistance*. Bethlehem: BADIL, 2016.

Amnesty International. *Elected but Restricted: Shrinking Space for Palestinian Parliamentarians in Israel's Knesset*. London: Benenson, 2019.

"Appendix I: JVP Statements on Antisemitism." In *On Anti-Semitism, Solidarity and the Struggle for Justice*, edited by Jewish Voice for Peace, 213-16. Chicago: Haymarket, 2017.

Arendt, Hannah. "Answers to Questions Submitted by Samuel Grafton." In *The Jewish Writings: Hannah Arendt*, edited by Jerome Kohn and Ron H. Feldman, 472–84. New York: Schocken, 2007.

———. "Antisemitism." In *The Jewish Writings: Hannah Arendt*, edited by Jerome Kohn and Ron H. Feldman, 46–121. New York: Schocken, 2007.

———. "Herzl and Lazare." In *The Jewish Writings: Hannah Arendt*, edited by Jerome Kohn and Ron H. Feldman, 338–42. New York: Schocken, 2007.

———. "The Jewish State: Fifty Years After, Where Have Herzl's Politics Led?" In *The Jewish Writings: Hannah Arendt*, edited by Jerome Kohn and Ron H. Feldman, 375–87. New York: Schocken, 2007.

———. "To Save the Jewish Homeland." In *The Jewish Writings: Hannah Arendt*, edited by Jerome Kohn and Ron H. Feldman, 388–401. New York: Schocken, 2007.

———. "Zionism Reconsidered." In *The Jewish Writings: Hannah Arendt*, edited by Jerome Kohn and Ron H. Feldman, 343–74. New York: Schocken, 2007.

Ashly, Jaclynn. "Nabi Saleh: 'It's a Silent Ethnic Cleansing.'" *Al Jazeera*, September 4, 2017. www.aljazeera.com/indepth/features/2017/07/nabi-saleh-silentg-ethnic-cleansing-170702123734851.html.

Ateek, Naim Stifan. *Justice, and Only Justice: A Palestinian Theology of Liberation*. Maryknoll, NY: Orbis, 1990.

Avishai, Bernard. *The Tragedy of Zionism: Revolution and Democracy in the Land of Israel*. New York: Farrar, Straus and Giroux, 1985.

Avni, Sheerli. "Ben Ehrenreich Throws Stones at Conventional Wisdom About Israel." *Forward*, July 8, 2016. https://forward.com/culture/343816/ben-ehrenreich-throws-stones-at-conventional-wisdom-about-israel/.

Bailey, Mark L. "Should Christians Support the Modern State of Israel?" In *Israel, the Church, and the Modern Idle East: A Biblical Response to the Current Conflict*, edited by Darrell L. Bock and Mitch Glaser, 187–201. Grand Rapids: Kregel, 2018.

Barghouti, Omar. *Boycott, Divestment, Sanctions: The Global Struggle for Palestinian Rights*. Chicago: Haymarket, 2011.

Barth, Markus. *Ephesians 1–3*. Anchor Bible Commentary 34. Garden City, NY: Doubleday, 1974.

———. *Israel and the Church: Contribution to a Dialogue Vital for Peace*. Richmond, VA: John Knox, 1969.

"Basic Law—Israel Lands." https://mfa.gov.il/mfa/mfa-archive/1960-1969/pages/basic%20law-%20israel%20lands.aspx..

Bates, Matthew W. *Gospel Allegiance: What Faith in Jesus Misses for Salvation in Christ*. Grand Rapids: Brazos, 2019.

———. *Salvation by Allegiance Alone: Rethinking Faith, Works and the Gospel of Jesus the King*. Grand Rapids: Baker Academic, 2017.

Baumgarten-Sharon, Naama. *Show of Force: Israeli Military Conduct in Weekly Demonstrations in a-Nabi Saleh*. Translated by Zvi Shulman. Jerusalem: B'tselem, 2011. https://www.btselem.org/sites/default/files/sites/default/files2/201109_show_of_force_eng.pdf.

Bäuml, Yair. "Israel's Military Rule over Its Palestinian Citizens (1948–1967): Shaping the Israeli Segregation System." In *Israel and Its Palestinian Citizens: Ethnic Privileges in the Jewish State*, edited by Nadim N. Rouhana and Sahar S. Huneidi, 103–36. Cambridge: Cambridge University Press, 2017.

Beaumont, Peter. "Ramallah Father: I Want to Believe That the Boy Soldier Who Shot Dead My Son Seeks Forgiveness." *Guardian*, May 24, 2014. https://www.theguardian.com/world/2014/may/25/palestinian-territories-ramallah-nadeem-suwara.

Beiler, Ryan Rodrick. "Palestinians Mourn Woman Who Died after Inhaling Tear Gas." *+972 magazine*, April 15, 2014. http://972mag.com/photos-tear-gas-kills-woman-in-aida-refugee-camp/89713/.

Beit-Hallahmi, Benjamin. *Original Sins: Reflections of the History of Zionism and Israel.* New York: Olive Branch, 1993.

Benne, Robert. "Theology and Politics: Reinhold Niebuhr's Christian Zionism." In *The New Christian Zionism: Fresh Perspectives on Israel & the Land*, edited by Gerald R. McDermott, 221–48. Downers Grove: IVP Academic, 2016.

Ben-Gurion, David. *Like Stars and Dust: Essays from Israel's Government Year Book.* Beersheba, IL: Ben-Gurion University Press, 1997.

Ben-Shmuel, Ambreen Tour. "An Overview of the Israeli-Palestinian Conflict." In *The Land Cries Out: Theology of the Land in the Israeli-Palestinian Context*, edited by Salim J. Munayer and Lisa Loden, 1–39. Eugene, OR: Cascade, 2012.

Ben-Youssef, Nadia, and Sandra Samaan Tamari. "Enshrining Discrimination: Israel's Nation-State Law." *Journal of Palestine Studies* 48 (Autumn 2018) 73–87.

Berger, Yotam. "Israel Approves 1,450 New Homes in West Bank Settlements." *Haaretz*, December 26, 2018. https://www.haaretz.com/israel-news/israel-approves-1-450-new-homes-in-west-bank-settlements-1.6785734.

———. "Palestinian Teen Ahed Tamimi Reaches Plea Bargain, to Serve 8 Months in Israeli Prison." *Haaretz*, March 21, 2018. www.haaretz.com/misc/article-print-page/palestinian-teen-ahed-tamimi-reaches-plea-bargain-to-serve-8-months-i-1.5933423.

Berger, Yotam, and Jack Koury. "How Many Palestinians Live in Gaza and the West Bank? It's Complicated." *Haaretz*. March 28, 2018. https://www.haaretz.com/israel-news/how-many-palestinians-live-in-gaza-and-the-west-bank-it-s-complicated-1.5956630.

Bird, Michael F., ed. *Four Views on the Apostle Paul.* Grand Rapids: Zondervan Academic, 2012.

Bishara, Azmi. "Zionism and Equal Citizenship: Essential and Incidental Citizenship in the Jewish State." In *Israel and Its Palestinian Citizens: Ethnic Privileges in the Jewish State*, edited by Nadim N. Touhana and Sahar S. Huneidi, 137–55. Cambridge: Cambridge University Press, 2017.

Blaising, Craig A. "Biblical Hermeneutics: How Are We to Interpret the Relation between the Tanak and the New Testament on This Question?" In *The New Christian Zionism: Fresh Perspectives on Israel & the Land*, edited by Gerald R. McDermott, 79–105. Downers Grove: IVP Academic, 2016.

———. "Israel and Hermeneutics." In *The People, the Land, and the Future of Israel: Israel and the Jewish People in the Plan of God*, edited by Darrell L. Bock and Mitch Glaser, 151–65. Grand Rapids: Kregel, 2014.

———. "A Theology of Israel and the Church." In *Israel, the Church, and the Middle East: A Biblical Response to the Current Conflict*, edited by Darrell L. Bock and Mitch Glaser, 85–100. Grand Rapids: Kregel, 2018.

Blaising, Craig A., and Darrell L. Bock. *Progressive Dispensationalism*. Grand Rapids: Baker, 1993.

———, eds. *Dispensationalism, Israel and the Church: The Search for Definition*. Grand Rapids: Zondervan, 1992.

Blumenthal, Max. *The 51 Day War: Ruin and Resistance in Gaza*. New York: Nation Books, 2015.

———. *Goliath: Life and Loathing in Greater Israel*. New York: Nation Books, 2013.

———. "Israel Cranks Up the PR Machine." *Nation*, October 16, 2013. https://www.thenation.com/article/israel-cranks-pr-machine/.

Bock, Darrell L. "Biblical Reconciliation between Jews and Arabs." In *Israel, the Church and the Middle East: A Biblical Response to the Current Conflict*, edited by Darrell L. Bock and Mitch Glaser, 165–84. Grand Rapids: Kregel, 2018.

———. "How Should the New Christian Zionism Proceed?" In *The New Christian Zionism: Fresh Perspectives on Israel & the Land*, edited by Gerald R. McDermott, 305–17. Downers Grove: IVP Academic, 2016.

———. "Israel in Luke-Acts." In *The People, the Land, and the Future of Israel: Israel and the Jewish People in the Plan of God*, edited by Darrell L. Bock and Mitch Glaser, 103–15. Grand Rapids: Kregel, 2014.

———. "The Reign of the Lord Christ." In *Dispensationalism, Israel and the Church: The Search for Definition*, edited by Craig A. Blaising and Darrell L. Bock, 37–67. Grand Rapids: Zondervan, 1992.

Bock, Darrell L., and Mitch Glaser, eds. *Israel, the Church and the Middle East: A Biblical Response to the Current Conflict*. Grand Rapids: Kregel, 2018.

———. *The People, the Land, and the Future of Israel: Israel and the Jewish People in the Plan of God*. Grand Rapids: Kregel, 2014.

Borrell, Brendon. "The Truth Behind Tear Gas: Most of It Is Made in America." *Square*, February 26, 2014. http://www.takepart.com/feature/2014/02/26/how-us-sells-tear-gas-to-oppressive-regimes.

Braverman, Mark. *Fatal Embrace: Christians, Jews and the Search for Peace in the Holy Land*. Austin, TX: Synergy, 2010.

Breaking the Silence. *Our Harsh Logic: Israeli Soldiers' Testimonies from the Occupied Territories, 2000–2010*. New York: Metropolitan, 2012.

———. "Why I Broke the Silence." https://www.breakingthesilence.org.il/inside/wp-content/uploads/2018/02/Why_I_Broke_The_Silence_English.pdf.

Boyarin, Daniel. *A Traveling Homeland: The Babylonian Talmud as Diaspora*. Philadelphia: University of Pennsylvania Press, 2015.

Boyarin, Jonathan, and Daniel Boyarin. *Powers of Diaspora: Two Essays on the Relevance of Jewish Culture*. Minneapolis: University of Minnesota Press, 2002.

Brenner, Lenni, ed. *51 Documents: Zionist Collaboration with the Nazis*. Fort Lee, NJ: Barricade, 2002.

Brown, Michael L. "The People and the Land of Israel in Jewish Tradition." In *The People, the Land, and the Future of Israel: Israel and the Jewish People in the Plan of God*, edited by Darrell L. Bock and Mitch Glaser, 71–83. Grand Rapids: Kregel, 2014.

Brown, Mike. "Is It Sinful to Divide the Land of Israel?" In *Israel, the Church, and the Middle East: A Biblical Response to the Current Conflict*, edited by Darrell Bock and Mitch Glaser, 217–26. Grand Rapids: Kregel, 2018.

Brown, Nicholas R. *For the Nation: Jesus, the Restoration of Israel and Articulating a Christian Ethic of Territorial Governance.* Eugene, OR: Pickwick, 2016.

Brueggemann, Walter. *The Land: Place as Gift, Promise, and Challenge in Biblical Faith.* 2nd ed. Minneapolis: Fortress, 2002.

Burg, Avraham. *The Holocaust Is Over: We Must Rise from Its Ashes.* Translated by I. Amrani. New York: Palgrave MacMillan, 2008.

Burns, Joshua Ezra. "Conversion and Proselytism." In *The Eerdmans Dictionary of Early Judaism*, edited by John J. Collins and Daniel C. Harlow, 484–86. Grand Rapids: Eerdmans, 2010.

Burge, Gary M. *Jesus and the Land: The New Testament Challenge to "Holy Land" Theology.* Grand Rapids: Baker Academic, 2010.

———. *Who Are God's People in the Middle East? What Christians Are Not Being Told about Israel and the Palestinians.* Grand Rapids: Zondervan, 1993.

———. *Whose Land? Whose Promise? What Christians Are Not Being Told about Israel and the Palestinians.* Cleveland: Pilgrim, 2003.

Burns, J. Lanier. "The Future of Ethnic Israel in Romans 11." In *Dispensationalism, Israel and the Church: The Search for Definition*, edited by Craig A. Blaising and Darrell L. Bock, 188–229. Grand Rapids: Zondervan, 1992.

Butler, Judith. "Foreword." In *On Anti-Semitism, Solidarity and the Struggle for Justice*, edited by Jewish Voice for Peace, vii–xiii. Chicago: Haymarket, 2017.

———. *Parting Ways: Jewishness and the Critique of Zionism.* New York: Columbia University Press, 2012.

Carpenter, Joel. *Revive Us Again: The Reawakening of American Fundamentalism.* Oxford: Oxford University Press, 1997.

Carter, Jimmy. *Palestine: Peace Not Apartheid.* New York: Simon & Schuster, 2006.

Chacour, Elias. *Blood Brothers: The Unforgettable Story of a Palestinian Christian Working for Peace in Israel.* Grand Rapids: Chosen, 2003.

———. *We Belong to the Land: The Story of a Palestinian Israeli Who Lives for Peace and Reconciliation.* Notre Dame: Notre Dame University Press, 2001.

Chapman, Colin. *Whose Promised Land? The Continuing Crisis over Israel and Palestine.* Grand Rapids: Baker, 2002.

Cheshin, Amir S., et al. *Separate and Unequal: The Inside Story of Israeli Rule in East Jerusalem.* Cambridge, MA: Harvard University Press, 1999.

Chesler, Phyllis. *The New Anti-Semitism: The Current Crisis and What We Must Do about It.* Jerusalem: Geffen, 2015.

Chomsky, Noam. *The Fateful Triangle: The United States, Israel, and the Palestinians.* Chicago: Haymarket, 2015.

Chomsky, Noam, and Ilan Pappé. *Gaza in Crisis: Reflections on Israel's War Against the Palestinians.* Chicago: Haymarket, 2010.

Christensen, Duane L. "Nations." In *The Anchor Bible Dictionary*, edited by David Noel Freedman et al., 4:1037–49. New York: Doubleday, 1992.

Cohen, Gili, and Jack Khoury. "Palestinians to Exhume Body of Youth Killed in Nakba Day Protests." *Haaretz*, June 11, 2014. https://www.haaretz.com/body-of-palestinian-youth-to-be-exhumed-1.5251472.

———. "Palestinians: West Bank Woman Died After Inhaling Tear Gas." *Haaretz*, April 16, 2014. http://www.haaretz.com/israel-news/.premium-1.585727.

Cohen, J. D. "Crossing the Boundary and Becoming a Jew." *Harvard Theological Review* 82 (January 1989) 13–33.

Cole, Juan. "Ahmadinejad We Are Not Threat to Any." *Informed Consent*, August 27, 2006. https://www.juancole.com/2006/08/ahmadinejad-we-are-not-threat-to-any.html.

———. "Hitchens Hacker and Hitchens." *Informed Comment*, May 3, 2006. https://www.juancole.com/2006/05/hitchens-hacker-and-hitchens.html.

Collins, John J., and Daniel C. Harlow. *Early Judaism: A Comprehensive Overview*. Grand Rapids: Eerdmans, 2012.

Comet, Ari. "Waiting for Barbarians." *Haaretz*, January 9, 2004. https://www.haaretz.co.il/misc/1.936900.

Compton, Fared, and Andrew David Naselli, eds. *Three Views on Israel and the Church: Perspectives on Romans 9–11*. Grand Rapids: Kregel Academic, 2018.

Compton, John W. *The End of Empathy: Why White Protestants Stopped Loving Their Neighbor*. Oxford: Oxford University Press, 2020.

The Confession of Faith. Inverness: Eccles, 1981.

Connor, Walker. *Ethnonationalism: The Quest for Understanding*. Princeton: Princeton University Press, 1994.

Cook, Jonathan. *Blood and Religion: The Unmasking of the Jewish and Democratic State*. London: Pluto, 2006.

———. "Why Israel Is Blocking Access to Its Archives." *Aljazeera News*, June 10, 2016. https://www.aljazeera.com/news/2016/06/israel-blocking-access-archives-160609054341909.html.

Corcos, Alain F. *The Myth of the Jewish Race: A Biologist's Pont of View*. Bethlehem: Lehigh University, 2005.

Cossé, Eva. "The Alarming Rise of Anti-Semitism in Europe." *Human Rights Watch*, June 4, 2019. https://www.hrw.org/news/2019/06/04/alarming-rise-anti-semitism-europe.

Crites, Stephen. *In the Twilight of Christendom: Hegel vs. Kierkegaard on Faith and History*. Chambersburg, PA: American Academy of Religion, 1972.

Crump, David. *Encountering Jesus, Encountering Scripture: Reading the Bible Critically in Faith*. Grand Rapids: Eerdmans, 2013.

———. *I Pledge Allegiance: A Believer's Guide to Kingdom Citizenship in 21st-Century America*. Grand Rapids: Eerdmans, 2018.

———. *Jesus the Intercessor: Prayer and Christology in Luke-Acts*. Grand Rapids: Baker Academic, 1999.

Dajani, Souad R. *Ruling Palestine: A History of the Legally Sanctioned Jewish-Israeli Seizure of Land and Housing in Palestine*. Geneva: The Centre on Housing Rights and Evictions, 2005.

Dana, Tariq, and Ali Jarbawi. "A Century of Settler Colognialism in Palestine: Zionism's Entangled Project." *Brown Journal of World Affairs* 24 (Fall/Winter 2917) 1–23.

Davies, W. D. *The Gospel and the Land: Early Christianity and Jewish Territorial Doctrine*. Berkeley, CA: University of California Press, 1974.

———. *The Territorial Dimension of Judaism: With a Symposium and Further Reflections*. Minneapolis: Fortress, 1991.

Davis, Uri. *Apartheid Israel: Possibilities for the Struggle Within*. London: Zed, 2003.

Davis, Walter T., and Pauline Coffman. "Political Zionism from Herzl (1890s) to Ben-Gurion (1960s)." In *Zionism and the Quest for Justice in the Holy Land*, edited by Donald E. Wagner and Walter T. Davis, 3–27. Eugene, OR: Pickwick, 2014.

Dayif, Amany, et al., eds. *On Torture*. Jerusalem: Adalah, 2012.

"Defending Breaking the Silence." *Haaretz*, September 20, 2018. https://www.haaretz.com/opinion/editorial/defend-breaking-the-silence-1.6434494.

Derfner, Larry. "Day of Catastrophe for 'Pallywood' Conspiracy Theorists." +972 magazine, November 13, 2014. https://www.972mag.com/nakba-day-indeed-for-pallywood-conspiracy-freaks/98735/.

Dershowitz, Alan M. *Chutzpah*. Boston: Touchstone, 1992.

Dever, William G. "Israel, History of (Archaeology and the 'Conquest')." In *The Anchor Bible Dictionary*, edited by David Noel Freedman et al., 3:545–58. New York: Doubleday, 1992.

Dinur, Ben Zion. *Israel and the Diaspora*. Philadelphia: The Jewish Publication Society of America, 1969.

"Doctors Urge Rubber Bullet Ban." *BBC News*, n.d. http://news.bbc.co.uk/2/hi/health/2003999.stm.

Dodd, C. H. *The Epistle of Paul to the Romans*. London: Fontana, 1959.

Dosa, Shiraz. "The Explanation We Never Heard." *Literary Review of Canada* 15 (June 2007) 3–4. https://web.archive.org/web/20090202162938/http://lrc.reviewcanada.ca/index.php?page=the-explanation-we-never-heard.

Doyle, Tom. "The 21st-Century Palestinian Church within Israel." In *Israel, the Church, and the Middle East: A Biblical Response to the Current Conflict*, edited by Darrell L. Bock and Mitch Glaser. 151–64. Grand Rapids: Kregel, 2018.

Dunn, James D. G. *Jesus, Paul and the Law: Studies in Mark and Galatians*. Louisville: Westminster John Knox, 1990.

"East Jerusalem." *B'Tselem*, January 27, 2019. https://www.btselem.org/jerusalem.

Ehrenreich, Ben. "Is This Where the Third Intifada Will Start?" *New York Times Magazine*, March 15, 2013. https://www.nytimes.com/2013/03/17/magazine/is-this-where-the-third-intifada-will-start.html?auth=login-email&login=email.

————. *The Way to the Spring: Life and Death in Palestine*. New York: Penguin Random House, 2016.

Eldar, Schlomi. "Accused Kidnappers Are Rogue Hamas Branch." *Al-Monitor*, June 29, 2014. https://www.al-monitor.com/pulse/originals/2014/06/qawasmeh-clan-hebron-hamas-leadership-mahmoud-abbas.html.

————. "Was Israeli Public Misled on Abductions?" *Al-Monitor*, July 3, 2014. https://www.al-monitor.com/pulse/originals/2014/07/misleading-kidnapping-almoz-hamas-vengeance-hatred.html.

"Elected but Restricted." https://www.amnesty.org/en/documents/mde15/0882/2019/en/.

Elliott, John H. *1 Peter: A New Translation with Introduction and Commentary*. Anchor Bible 37B. New York: Doubleday, 2000.

Ellis, Earle E. *Paul's Use of the Old Testament*. Edinburgh: Oliver and Boyd, 1957.

Ellis, Ralph, and Michael Schwartz. "Mom Speaks Out on 3 Abducted Teens as Israeli PM Blames Hamas." *CNN*, July 15, 2014. https://www.cnn.com/2014/06/15/world/meast/west-bank-jewish-teens-missing/index.html.

Ellisen, Stanley. *Who Owns the Land?* Wheaton: Tyndale, 2003.

Emerson, Ralph Waldo. "Self-Reliance." https://math.dartmouth.edu/~doyle/docs/self/self.pdf.

Erakat, Noura. *Justice for Some: Law and the Question of Palestine*. Stanford: Stanford University Press, 2019.

"Evaluation of the Use of Force in Israel, Gaza and the West Bank: *Medical and Forensic Investigation*." http://www.orwatch.org/doc-en/PHR.pdf.

"Fatalities since Operation Cast Lead." *B'Tselem*, n.d. https://www.btselem.org/statistics/fatalities/after-cast-lead/by-date-of-death.

"Fatally Shot though Posing No Danger: Israeli Soldier Shot 'Iz a-Din Tamimi from Behind; He Was Fleeing after Throwing a Stone at the Soldier." *B'Tselem*, January 14, 2020. www.btselem.org/firearms/20180703_killing_of_iz_a_din_tamimi_in_a_nabi_saleh.

Feinberg, John S. "Systems of Discontinuity." In *Continuity and Discontinuity: Perspectives on the Relationship between the Old and New Testaments: Essays in Honor of S. Lewis Johnson Jr.*, edited by John S. Feinberg, 63–86. Westchester, IL: Crossway, 1988.

Feinberg, John S., ed. *Continuity and Discontinuity: Perspectives on the Relationship between the Old and New Testaments: Essays in Honor of S. Lewis Johnson Jr.* Westchester, IL: Crossway, 1988.

Feinberg, Paul D. "Hermeneuitics of Discontinuity." In *Continuity and Discontinuity: Perspectives on the Relationship between the Old and New Testaments: Essays in Honor of S. Lewis Johnson Jr.*, edited by John S. Feinberg, 109–28. Westchester, IL: Crossway, 1988.

Feinstein, Dianne. *Senate Report 113–288: Report of the Senate Select Committee on Intelligence Committee Study of the Central Intelligence Agency's Detention and Interrogation Program*. December 9, 2014. https://www.intelligence.senate.gov/sites/default/files/documents/CRPT-113srpt288.pdf.

Feldman, Louis H. "Conversion to Judaism in Classical Antiquity." *Hebrew Union College Annual* 74 (2003) 115–56.

Fezehai, Malin. "The Disappeared Children of Israel." *New York Times*, February 20, 2019. https://www.nytimes.com/2019/02/20/world/middleeast/israel-yemenite-children-affair.html.

Finkelstein, Norman G. *Beyond Chutzpah: On the Misuse of Anti-Semitism and the Abuse of History*. Berkeley: University of California, 2008.

———. *Gaza: An Inquest into Its Martyrdom*. Berkeley: University of California Press, 2018.

———. *The Holocaust Industry: Reflections on the Exploitation of Jewish Suffering*. London: Verso, 2000.

———. *Image and Reality of the Israel-Palestine Conflict*. London: Verso, 2001.

———. *Method and Madness: The Hidden Story of Israel's Assaults on Gaza*. New York: OR, 2014.

Flapan, Simha. *The Birth of Israel: Myths and Realities*. New York: Pantheon, 1987.

———. *Zionism and the Palestinians*. New York: Harper & Row, 1979.

Fisher, Max. "This Chart Shows Every Person Killed in the Israel-Palestine Conflict since 2000." *Vox*, July 14, 2014. https://www.vox.com/2014/7/14/5898581/chart-israel-palestine-conflict-deaths.

Forster, Arnold, and Benjamin R. Epstein. *The New Anti-Semitism*. New York: McGraw-Hill, 1974.

Fox, Tessa. "Shot in the Head and Arrested, Mohammed Tamimi Still in High Spirits." *Middle East Eye*, February, 28, 2018.

France, R. T. *The Gospel of Matthew*. Grand Rapids: Eerdmans, 2007.

Freedman, David Noel, et al., eds. *The Anchor Bible Dictionary*. 6 vols. New York: Doubleday, 1992.

Frisch, Hillel. "Knowing Your ABC: A Primer to Understand the Different Areas of Judea and Samaria." *Jerusalem Post*, April 23, 2016. https://www.jpost.com/magazine/knowing-your-abc-448963.

Galtung, Johan. "Peace, Negative and Positive." In *The Oxford International Encyclopedia of Peace*, edited by Nigel J. Young, 3:352–56. New York: Oxford University Press, 2010.

Gerdmar, Anders. *Roots of Theological Anti-Semitism: German Biblical Interpretation and the Jews, from Herder and Semler to Kittel and Bultmann*. Leiden: Brill, 2009.

Glaser, Mitch. "The Dangers of Supersessionism." In *Israel, the Church and the Middle East: A Biblical Response to the Current Conflict*, edited by Darrell Bock and Mitch Glaser, 101–18. Grand Rapids: Kregel, 2018.

Gleim, Sarah. "Skunk Water: A Weapon That Uses Stench to Control Crowds." *HowStuffWorks: Science*, November 12, 2015. https://science.howstuffworks.com/skunk-water-weapon-control-crowds.htm.

Glenny, W. Edward. "The Israelite Imagery of 1 Peter 2." In *Dispensationalism, Israel and the Church: The Search for Definition*, edited by Craig A. Blaising, and Darrell L. Bock, 156–87. Grand Rapids: Zondervan, 1992.

Golani, Motti. *Palestine between Politics & Terror, 1945–1947*. Waltham, MA: Brandeis University Press, 2013.

"Golda Meir Scorns Soviets: Israeli Premier Explains Stand on Big-4 Talks, Security." *Washington Post*, June 16, 1969.

Goldberg, Louis. "Historical and Political Factors in the Twentieth Century Affecting the Identity of Israel." *In Israel, the Land and the People: An Evangelical Affirmation of God's Promises*, edited by H. Wayne House, 113–41. Grand Rapids: Kregel, 1998.

Goldman, Eliezer, ed. *Yeshayahu Leibowitz: Judaism, Human Values, and the Jewish State*. Translated by Eliezer Goldman et al. Cambridge: Harvard University Press, 1995.

Goldman, Lisa. "Classified: Politicizing the Nakba in Israel's State Archives." *+972 magazine*, February 19, 2016. https://www.972mag.com/classified-politicizing-the-nakba-in-israels-state-archives/.

———. "Nabi Saleh Is Where I Lost My Zionism." *+972 magazine*, December 24, 2017. www.972mag.com/nabi-saleh-is-where-i-lost-my-zionism/131818/.

Gordon, Neve. *Israel's Occupation*. Berkeley: University of California, 2008.

Goren, Arthur A., ed. *Dissenter in Zion: From the Writings of Judah L. Magnes*. Cambridge: Harvard University Press, 1982.

"Government Advancing Bill to Ban Breaking the Silence." *Times of Israel*, October 16, 2017. https://www.timesofisrael.com/government-advancing-bill-to-ban-breaking-the-silence-report/.

Greenberg, Joel. "Fatal Shootings of Unarmed Palestinians Raise Concerns about Israeli Use of Force." *Washington Post*, January 28, 2013. https://www.washingtonpost.com/world/fatal-shootings-of-unarmed-palestinians-raise-concerns-about-israeli-use-of-force/2013/01/28/e08ffaaa-6988-11e2-95b3-272d604a10a3_story.html.

Gross, Aeyal. "Court Refection of Israeli Nationality Highlights Flaws of Jewish Democracy." *Haaretz*, October 3, 2013. https://www.haaretz.com/misc/article-print-page/.premium-is-israel-a-nationality-1.5344174.

Gross, Judah Ari. "Israeli Cop Sentenced to 9 Months for Killing Palestinian Teen." *Times of Israel*, April 25, 2018. https://www.timesofisrael.com/israeli-cop-sentenced-to-9-months-for-killing-palestinian-teen/.

———. "Two Palestinian Women in Court over Israeli Soldier Slap Video." *Times of Israel*, December 21, 2017. https://www.timesofisrael.com/two-palestinian-women-in-court-over-israeli-soldier-slap-video/.

Gruen, Erich S. "Judaism in the Diaspora." In *Early Judaism: A Comprehensive Overview*, edited by John J. Collins and Daniel C. Harlow, 95–120. Grand Rapids: Eerdmans, 2012.

Guerrero, Aldo. "When Does the 'Cycle of Violence' Start?" *Information Clearing House*, July 15, 2014. https://www.commondreams.org/views/2014/07/11/when-does-cycle-violence-start.

Haddad, Iyad. "IDF Soldiers Gather, Fingerprint Residents of a-Nabi Salah in Middle of the Night." *B'Tselem*, January 25, 2004. https://www.btselem.org/testimonies/20040125_soldiers_take_finger_prints_from_a_nebi_salah_residents.

Haffar, Lisa. *Courting Conflict: The Israeli Military Court System in the West Bank and Gaza*. Berkley: University of California, 2005.

"Hagee's Prosperity Gospel and Jews." *Talk to Action*, July, 27, 2009. www.talk2action.org/printpage/2009/7/27/142816/011.

Hagner, Donald A. *Matthew 1–13*. Word Biblical Commentary 33A. Dallas: Word, 1993.

Hahn, Scott W. *Kinship by Covenant: A Canonical Approach to the Fulfillment of God's Saving Promises*. Anchor Yale Bible Reference Library. New Haven: Yale University Press, 2009.

Halper, Jeff. *An Israeli in Palestine: Resisting Dispossession, Redeeming Israel*. London: Pluto, 2010.

"Hamas Not Complicit in Teens' Kidnap: Israeli Police." *Daily Star*, July 26, 2014. http://www.dailystar.com.lb/News/Middle-East/2014/Jul-26/265229-hamas-not-complicit-in-teens-kidnap-israeli-police.ashx.

Hardin, Justin K. "Equality in the Church." In *Introduction to Messianic Judaism: Its Ecclesial Context and Biblical Foundations*, edited by David Rudolf and Jowl Willitts, 224–34. Grand Rapids: Zondervan, 2013.

Harel, Amos. "Israeli Campaign Against Hamas Is Effort to Impose New Order in West Bank." *Haaretz*, June 19, 2014. https://www.haaretz.com/.premium-political-motives-drive-w-b-operation-1.5252468.

Hareuveni, Eyal. *By Hook and by Crook: Israeli Settlement Policy in the West Bank*. Translated by Zvi Shulman. Jerusalem: B'Tselem, 2010.

Harkov, Lahav. "B'Tselem Slams Israel at French Human Rights Award Ceremony." *Jerusalem Post*, December 10, 2018. https://www.jpost.com/israel-news/btselem-slams-israel-at-french-human-rights-award-ceremony-573965.

Harlow, Daniel C. "Early Judaism and Early Christian." In *Early Judaism: A Comprehensive Overview*, edited by John J. Collins and Daniel C. Harlow, 391–419. Grand Rapids: Eerdmans, 2012.

Halper, Jeff. *An Israeli in Palestine: Resisting Dispossession, Redeeming Israel*. London: Pluto, 2010.

Hartman, Ben, et al. "Listen: Recording of Kidnapped Teen's Distress Call to Police Released." *Jerusalem Post*, July 1, 2014. https://www.jpost.com/Operation-Brothers-Keeper/Recording-of-distress-call-to-police-by-kidnapped-teen-released-361169.

Harvey, Richard. "Towards a Messianic Jewish Theology of Reconciliation in Light of the Arab-Israeli Conflict: Neither Dispensationalist nor Supersessionist?" In *The Land Cries Out: Theology of the Land in the Israeli-Palestinian Context*, edited by Salim J. Munayer and Lisa Loden, 82–103. Eugene, OR: Cascade, 2012.

Hasan, Mehdi. "Debunking Israel's 11 Main Myths About Gaza, Hamas and War Crimes." *Huffington Post*, September 27, 2014. https://www.huffingtonpost.co.uk/mehdi-hasan/gaza-israel_b_5624401.html.

"The Hasbara Apparatus: Units, Tasks and Areas of Responsibility." http://molad.org/images/upload/files/37830581085043.pdf.

Hass, Amira. "Father of Palestinian Girl Slapping Israeli Soldier in Viral Video: She Was Upset Because Relative Was Shot in Head." *Haaretz*, December 21, 2017. https://www.haaretz.com/israel-news/.premium-palestinian-girl-slapped-soldier-because-relative-was-shot-father-says-1.5629212.

———. "In Nabi Saleh, the Palestinians Aren't Legally Blonde." *Haaretz*, December 25, 2017. www.haaretz.com/misc/article-print-page/.premium-in-nabi-saleh-the-palestinians-arent-legally-blonde-1.5629558.

———. "Otherwise Occupied / Labour Is Concerned." *Haaretz*, December 12, 2010. https://www.haaretz.com/1.5090677.

Hasson, Nir. "Beaten Palestinian Youth Is U.S. Citizen, Cousin of Murdered Kidnap Victim." *Haaretz*, July 5, 2014. https://www.haaretz.com/beaten-palestinian-youth-is-u-s-citizen-1.5254512.

———. "High Court: Israel Must Prove Stone-Throwing Law Doesn't Discriminate Arabs." *Haaretz*, January 28, 2017. https://www.haaretz.com/israel-news/.premium-high-court-israel-must-prove-stone-throwing-law-isnt-discriminatory-1.5491502.

Hastings, Adrian. *The Construction of Nationhood: Ethnicity, Religion and Nationalism*. Cambridge: Cambridge University Press, 1997.

Hauerwas, Stanley. *War and the American Difference: Theological Reflections on Violence and National Identity*. Grand Rapids: Baker Academic, 2011.

Hays, Richard B. *Echoes of Scripture in the Letters of Paul*. New Haven: Yale University Press, 1989.

———. *Reading Backwards: Figural Christology and the Fourfold Gospel Witness*. Waco, TX: Baylor, 2014.

Hazkani, Shay. "Catastrophic Thinking: Did Ben-Gurion Try to Rewrite History?" *Haaretz*, May 13, 2013. https://www.haaretz.com/.premium-ben-gurion-grasped-the-nakba-s-importance-1.5243033.

Hecht, Ravit. "The Lawmaker Who Thinks Israel Is Deceiving the Palestinians: 'No One Is Going to Give Them a State.'" *Haaretz*, October 28, 2017. https://www.haaretz.com/israel-news/.premium.MAGAZINE-the-lawmaker-who-thinks-israel-is-deceiving-the-palestinians-1.5460676.

Hedges, Chris. "The Psychosis of Permanent War." *Journal of Palestine Studies* 44 (November 2014) 42–51.

Herzl, Theodor. *The Jewish State*. San Bernadino, CA: n.p., 2014.

Hirst, David. *The Gun and the Olive Branch: The Roots of Violence in the Middle East.* New York: Faber & Faber, 1977.

Hobsbawm, Eric, and Terence Ranger, eds. *The Invention of Tradition.* Cambridge: Cambridge University Press, 1983.

Hoch, Carl B. "The New Man of Ephesians 2." In *Dispensationalism, Israel and the Church: The Search for Definition*, edited by Craig A. Blaising and Darrell L. Bock, 98–126. Grand Rapids: Zondervan, 1992.

Hoehner, Harold W. *Ephesians: An Exegetical Commentary.* Grand Rapids: Baker Academic, 2002.

———. "Israel in Romans 9–11." In *Israel, the Land and the People: An Evangelical Affirmation of God's Promises*, edited by H. Wayne House, 145–67. Grand Rapids: Kregel, 1988.

Holmes, Oliver, and Josh Holder. "Gaza Border Protests: 190 Killed and 28,000 Injured in a Year of Bloodshed." *Guardian*, March 29, 2019. https://www.theguardian.com/world/ng-interactive/2019/mar/29/a-year-of-bloodshed-at-gaza-border-protests.

Holzman-Gazit, Yifat. *Land Expropriation in Israel: Law, Culture and Society.* London: Routledge, 2017.

Horner, Barry E. *Future Israel: Why Christian Anti-Judaism Must Be Challenged.* Nashville: B&H Academic, 2007.

House, H. Wayne. "The Church's Appropriation of Israel's Blessings." In *Israel, the Land and the People: An Evangelical Affirmation of God's Promises*, edited by H. Wayne House, 77–110. Grand Rapids: Kregel, 1998.

House, H. Wayne, ed. *Israel, the Land and the People: An Evangelical Affirmation of God's Promises.* Grand Rapids: Kregel, 1998.

Hudson, John. "Trump Administration Considers Labeling to Humanitarian Groups 'Anti-Semitic.'" *Washington Post*, October 21, 2020. https://www.washingtonpost.com/national-security/human-rights-groups-state-department/2020/10/21/7554190c-13e8-11eb-82af-864652063d61_story.html.

Imseis, Ardi. "Facts on the Ground: An Examination of Israeli Municipal Policy in East Jerusalem." *American University International Law Review* 15 (2000) 1039–69. https://digitalcommons.wcl.american.edu/cgi/viewcontent.cgi?article=1280&context=auilr&httpsredir=1&referer=.

"Israel: Stop Threatening Witness to Killings." *Human Rights Watch*, June 19, 2014. https://www.hrw.org/news/2014/06/19/israel-stop-threatening-witness-killings.

"Israel Approves More than 4,000 New Settlement Units in Jerusalem." *Middle East Eye*, February 20, 2019. https://www.middleeasteye.net/news/israel-approves-more-4000-new-settlement-units-jerusalem.

"Israel: Autopsy Confirms Gunshot Killed Boy." *Human Rights Watch*, June 14, 2014. https://www.hrw.org/news/2014/06/14/israel-autopsy-confirms-gunshot-killed-boy.

"Israel: Killing of Children Apparent War Crime." *Human Rights Watch*, June 9, 2014. https://www.hrw.org/news/2014/06/09/israel-killing-children-apparent-war-crime.

"Israel: Stop Threatening Witness to Killings." *Human Rights Watch*, June 19, 2014. https://www.hrw.org/news/2014/06/19/israel-stop-threatening-witness-killings.

"Israeli Court Sentences Palestinian Activist Munther Amira to 6 Months after Ahed Tamimi Protest." *Telesur*, March 14, 2018. https://www.telesurenglish.net/news/

Israeli-Court-Sentences-Palestinian-Activist-Munther-Amira-to-6-Months-After-Ahed-Tamimi-Protest-20180314-0020.html.

"Israeli Security Forces Killed 290 Palestinians in 2018; Most Were Victims of a Reckless Free Fire Policy." *B'Tselem*, January 17, 2019. https://www.btselem.org/press_releases/20190117_2018_fatalities.

"Israeli Soldiers Assaulted Tamer Tamimi, 23, at Checkpoints Twice in One Day: He Was Abused and Beaten until He Lost Consciousness and Needed Hospital Care." *B'Tselem*, July 5, 2017. www.btselem.org/beating_and_abuse/20170705_soldiers_assault_tamer_tamimi.

"Israeli Tear Gas Kills Palestinian Woman in West Bank." *Middle East Monitor*, April 18, 2014. http://www.middleeastmonitor.com/20140418-israeli-tear-gas-kills-palestinian-woman-in-west-bank/.

Jabareen, Hassan. "Hobbesian Citizenship: How the Palestinians Became a Minority in Israel." In *Multiculturalism and Minority Rights in the Arab World*, edited by Will Kymlicka and Eva Pföstl, 189–218. Oxford: Oxford University Press, 2014.

Jabareen, Yosef. "Controlling Land and Demography in Israel: The Obsession with Territorial and Geographic Dominance." In *Israel and Its Palestinian Citizens: Ethnic Privileges in the Jewish State*, edited by Nadim N. Rouhana and Sahar S. Huneidi, 238–65. Cambridge: Cambridge University Press, 2017.

Jacobs, Alan. *How to Think: A Survival Guide for a World at Odds*. Redfern, AU: Currency, 2017.

———. *The Year of Our Lord 1943: Christian Humanism in an Age of Crisis*. Oxford: University Press, 2018.

Jacobson, Abigail, and Moshe Naor. *Oriental Neighbors: Middle Eastern Jews and Arabs in Mandatory Palestine*. Waltham, MA: Brandeis University Press, 2016.

Jelinek, John A. "The Dispersion and Restoration of Israel to the Land." In *Israel, the Land and the People: An Evangelical Affirmation of God's Promises*, edited by H. Wayne House, 231–58. Grand Rapids: Kregel, 1998.

"Jerusalem: The City's Development from a Historical Viewpoint." https://mfa.gov.il/mfa/mfa-archive/1998/pages/jerusalem-%20the%20city-s%20development%20from%20a%20historica.aspx.

"The Jewish Nation-State Law and Its Implications for Democracy, Human Rights, and the Middle East Peace Process." Mossawa Center: Haifa, 2019. http://www.mossawa.org/eng//Public/file/1Nation-State%20Position%20Paper%20-%2020%20March%202019.pdf.

Jewish Voice for Peace, ed. *On Anti-Semitism, Solidarity and the Struggle for Justice*. Chicago: Haymarket, 2017.

Jiryis, Sabri. *Democratic Freedoms in Israel*. Translated by Meric Dobson. Beirut: Institute for Palestine Studies, 1972.

Juel, Donald. *Messianic Exegesis: Christological Interpretation of the Old Testament in Early Christianity*. Philadelphia: Fortress, 1988.

Juster, Daniel C. "A Messianic Jew Looks at the Land Promises." In *The Land Cries Out: Theology of the Land in the Israeli-Palestinian Context*, edited by Salim J. Munayer and Lisa Loden, 63–81. Eugene, OR: Cascade, 2012.

Kadari-Ovadia, Shira. "Israeli University Cancels Event Marking Nakba Day, Citing Violation of Law." *Haaretz*, May 16, 2019.

"Kairos Palestine Document." https://www.kairospalestine.ps/index.php/about-kairos/kairos-palestine-document.

Kaiser, Walter C., Jr. "The Land of Israel and the Future Return (Zechariah 10:6–12)." In *Israel, the Land and the People: An Evangelical Affirmation of God's Promises*, edited by H. Wayne House, 209–27. Grand Rapids: Kregel, 1998.

Kanaaneh, Rhoda Ann. *Surrounded: Palestinian Soldiers in the Israeli Military*. Stanford: Stanford University Press, 2009.

Kaplan, Amy. *Our American Israel: The Story of an Entangled Alliance*. Cambridge: Harvard University Press, 2018.

Karcher, Carolyn L. ed. *Reclaiming Judaism from Zionism: Stories of Personal Transformation*. North Hampton, MA: Olive Branch, 2019.

Karsh, Efraim. *Fabricating Israeli History: The "New Historians."* London: Cass, 2000.

———. *Palestine Betrayed*. New Haven: Yale University Press, 2010.

Katanacho, Yohanna. *The Land of Christ: A Palestinian Cry*. Eugene, OR: Pickwick, 2013.

Kattan, Victor. *From Coexistence to Conquest: International Law and the Origins of the Arab-Israeli Conflict, 1891–1949*. London: Pluto, 2009.

Katzoff, Binyamin. "'God of Our Fathers': Rabbinic Liturgy and Jewish-Christian Engagement." *Jewish Quarterly Review* 99 (Summer 2009) 303–22.

Kelly, J. D. N. *A Commentary on the Epistles of Peter and Jude*. Reprint. Peabody, MA: Hendrickson, 1988.

Khalidi, Dima. "Chilling and Censoring of Palestine Advocacy in the United States." In *On Anti-Semitism, Solidarity and the Struggle for Justice*, edited by Jewish Voice for Peace, 181–92. Chicago: Haymarket, 2017.

Khalidi, Rashid. "The Dahiya Doctrine, Proportionality, and War Crimes." *Journal of Palestine Studies* 44 (November 2014) 5–13.

———. *The Iron Cage: The Story of the Palestinians Struggle for Statehood*. Boston: Beacon, 2006.

———. *Palestinian Identity: The Construction of Modern National Consciousness*. New York: Columbia University Press, 1997.

Khalidi, Walid, ed. *All That Remains: The Palestinian Villages Occupied and Depopulated by Israel in 1948*. Washington: Institute for Palestine Studies, 1992.

———. "Plan Dalet: Master Plan for the Conquest of Palestine." *Journal for Palestine Studies* 18 (October 1988) 4–33.

Khalloul, Shadi. "Theology and Morality: Is Modern Israel Faithful to the Moral Demands of the Covenant in Its Treatment of Minorities?" In *The New Christian Zionism: Fresh Perspectives on Israel & the Land*, edited by Gerald R. McDermott, 281–301. Downers Grove: IVP Academic, 2016.

Koury, Jack, and Chaim Levinson. "IDF Says Forgery Likely in Video Showing Palestinian Teens' Deaths." *Haaretz*, May 22, 2014. https://www.haaretz.com/. premium-idf-shooting-video-forged-1.5249101.

Kimmerling, Baruch. *The Invention and Decline of Israeliness: State, Society, and the Military*. Berkeley: University of California Press, 2001.

———. *The Israeli State and Society: Boundaries & Frontiers*. New York: State University of New York Press, 1989.

———. *Zionism and Territory: The Socio-Territorial Dimensions of Zionist Politics*. Berkeley, CA: University of California Press, 1983.

Kimmerling, Baruch, and Joel S. Migdal. *The Palestinian People: A History*. Cambridge: Harvard University Press, 2003.

Kinzer, Mark S. "Zionism in Luke-Acts: Do the People of Israel and the Land of Israel Persist as Abiding Concerns in Luke's Two Volumes?" In *The New Christian*

Zionism: Fresh Perspectives on Israel & the Land, edited by Gerald R. McDermott, 141–65. Downers Grove: IVP Academic, 2016.

Kinzer, Stephen. *Overthrow: America's Century of Regime Change from Hawaii to Iraq.* New York: Holt, 2006.

Kirsh, Nurit. "Population Genetics in Israel in the 1950s: The Unconscious Internalization of Ideology." *ISIS, Journal of the History of Science* 94 (2003) 631–55.

Kittel, Gerhard, and Gerhard Friedrich, eds. *Theological Dictionary of the New Testaement.* 10 vols. Grand Rapids: Eerdmans, 1964–76.

Kohn, Jerome, and Ron H. Feldman. *The Jewish Writings: Hannah Arendt.* New York: Schocken, 2007.

Kraines, Oscar. *The Impossible Dilemma: Who Is a Jew in the State of Israel?* New York: Bloch, 1976.

Kramer, Andrew E. "Armenia and Azerbaijan: What Sparked War and Will Peace Prevail?" *New York Times*, October 22, 2020. https://www.nytimes.com/article/armenian-azerbaijan-conflict.html.

Kraybill, Donald B. *The Upside-Down Kingdom.* Scottsdale, PA: Herald, 1978.

Kuhn, Thomas S. *The Structure of Scientific Revolutions: 50th Anniversary Edition.* Chicago: Chicago University Press, 2012.

Laqueur, Walter, and Barry Rubin, eds. *The Israeli-Arab Reader: A Documentary History of the Middle East Conflict.* 6th ed. New York: Penguin, 2001.

Laqueur, Walter. *A History of Zionism: From the French Revolution to the Establishment of the State of Israel.* New York: Schocken, 2003.

Larsen, David L. "A Celebration of the Lord Our God's Role in the Future of Israel." In *Israel, the Land and the People: An Evangelical Affirmation of God's Promises*, edited by H. Wayne House, 301–23. Grand Rapids: Kregel, 1998.

———. *Jews, Gentiles & the Church: A New Perspective on History and Prophecy.* Grand Rapids: Discovery House, 1995.

Leibowitz, Yeshayahu. "The Religious Significance of the State of Israel." In *Yeshayahu Leibowitz: Judaism, Human Values, and the Jewish State*, translated by Eliezer Goldman et al., 214–20. Cambridge: Harvard University Press, 1995.

Lerman, Antony. "Antisemitism Redefined: Israel's Imagined National Narrative of Endless External Threat." In *On Anti-Semitism, Solidarity and the Struggle for Justice*, edited by Jewish Voice for Peace, 7–20. Chicago: Haymarket, 2017.

———. *The Making and Unmaking of a Zionist: A Personal and Political Journey.* London: Pluto, 2012.

Lessing, Gotthold. "On the Proof of the Spirit and of Power." In *Lessing's Theological Writings*, translated by Henry Chadwick, 51–56. Stanford: Stanford University Press, 1957.

Leuenberger, Christine. "Hopelessness as Luxury: Perspectives from Contested Jerusalem." *Palestine-Israel Journal*, n.d. https://pij.org/blogs/305.

Leventhal, Barry R. "Israel in Light of the Holocaust." In *The People, the Land, and the Future of Israel: Israel and the Jewish People in the Plan of God*, edited by Darrell L. Bock and Mitch Glaser, 213–48. Grand Rapids: Kregel, 2014.

Levinson, Chaim, and Yaniv Kubovitch. "Policeman Faces Murder Charge in Nakba Day Shooting of Palestinian Teen." *Haaretz*, November 12, 2014. https://www.haaretz.com/cop-faces-murder-charge-in-shooting-of-palestinian-teen-1.5327631.

Levs, Josh, et al. "Israel's Netanyahu Says of Slain Teens: 'May God Avenge Their Blood.'" *CNN*, July 1, 2014. https://www.cnn.com/2014/07/01/world/meast/israel-teenagers-death/.

Levy, Gideon. "Netanyahu Didn't Even Call to Congratulate B'Tselem." *Haaretz*, December 8, 2018. https://www.haaretz.com/opinion/.premium-netanyahu-didn-t-even-call-to-say-congratulations-to-b-tselem-1.6725365.

———. *The Punishment of Gaza*. London: Verso, 2010.

———. "The Story behind Ahed Tamimi's Slap: Her Cousin's Head Shattered by Israeli Soldier's Bullet." *Haaretz*, January 5, 2018. www.haaretz.com/misc/article-print-page/.premium-behind-ahed-tamimi-s-slap-her-cousin-s-head-shattered-by-idf-bullet-1.5729500.

———. "The Threat of the 'Demographic Threat.'" *Ha'aretz*, July 22, 2007. https://www.haaretz.com/1.4954256.

Lewis, Donald. *The Origins of Christian Zionism: Lord Shaftesbury and Evangelical Support for a Jewish Homeland*. Cambridge: Cambridge University Press, 2010.

Liebman, Charles S., and Eliezer Don-Yehiya. *Civil Religion in Israel: Traditional Judaism and Political Culture in the Jewish State*. Berkeley: University of California Press, 1983.

Lincoln, Andrew T. *Ephesians*. Word Biblical Commentary 42. Dallas: Word, 1990.

"Live Updates, July: Teens' Bodies Found." *Haaretz*, July 1, 2014. https://www.haaretz.com/misc/article-print-page/live-updates-july-1-teens-bodies-found-1.5253971.

Liverani, Mario. "Nationality and Political Identity." In *The Anchor Bible Dictionary*, edited by David Noel Freedman et al., 4:1031–37. New York: Doubleday, 1992.

Loden, Lisa. "Where Do We Begin? The Hermeneutical Questions and Their Effect on the Theology of the Land." In *The Land Cries Out: Theology of the Land in the Israeli-Palestinian Context*, edited by Salim J. Munayer, and Lisa Loden, 40–62. Eugene, OR: Cascade, 2012.

Lohr, Steve. "Arafat Says P.L.O. Accepted Israel." *New York Times*, December 8, 1988. https://www.nytimes.com/1988/12/08/world/arafat-says-plo-accepted-israel.html.

Longenecker, Bruce W. *The Triumph of Abraham's God: The Transformation of Identity in Galatians*. Edinburgh: T. & T. Clark, 1998.

Longenecker, Richard N. *Galatians*. Word Biblical Commentary 41. Dallas: Word, 1990.

Lustick, Ian S., and Matthew Berkman. "Zionist Theories of Peace in the Pre-state Era: Legacies of Dissimulation and Israel's Arab Minority." In *Israel and Its Palestinian Citizens: Ethnic Privileges in the Jewish State*, edited by Nadim N Rouhana and Sahar S. Huneidi, 39–72. Cambridge: Cambridge University Press, 2017.

Ma'an News Agency. "Official: Autopsy Shows Palestinian Youth Burnt Alive." Ma'an News Agency, July 6, 2014. https://web.archive.org/web/20140708195202/http://www.maannews.net/eng/ViewDetails.aspx?ID=710089.

Mackey, Robert. "After Fatal Shooting of Palestinian, Israeli Soldiers Defend Use of Force Online." *New York Times*, December 11, 2011. https://thelede.blogs.nytimes.com/2011/12/11/after-fatal-shooting-of-palestinian-israeli-soldiers-defended-use-of-force-online/.

———. "Israeli Minister Agrees Ahmadinejad Never Said 'Israel Must Be Wiped Off the Map.'" *The Lede*, April 17, 2012. https://web.archive.org/web/20120421002922/https://thelede.blogs.nytimes.com/2012/04/17/israeli-minister-agrees-ahmadinejad-never-said-israel-must-be-wiped-off-the-map//.

Magid, Jacob. "Cousin Filmed Slapping Soldiers with Ahed Tamimi Indicted on Assault." *Times of Israel*, December 31, 2017. https://web.archive.org/web/20180101140102/ https://www.timesofisrael.com/cousin-filmed-slapping-soldiers-with-ahed-tamimi-indicted-on-assault/.

Magid, Shaul. "On Antisemitism and Its Uses." In *On Anti-Semitism, Solidarity and the Struggle for Justice*, edited by Jewish Voice for Peace, 59–69. Chicago: Haymarket, 2017.

Marlowe, Jen. "Israel's Mizrahi Activists Are Fighting the Racist Nation State Law." *Nation*, May 27, 2020. https://www.thenation.com/article/world/israel-racism-mizrahis-palestinians/.

Marom, Yael. "Military Court Sends Leading Palestinian Nonviolent Activist to Prison." +972 *magazine*, March 14, 2018. https://www.972mag.com/military-court-sends-leading-palestinian-activist-to-prison/.

Marsden, George M. *Fundamentalism and American Culture: The Shaping of Twentieth-Century Evangelicalism 1870–1925*. Oxford: Oxford University Press, 1980.

Martin, Oren R. *Bound for the Promised Land: The Land Promise in God's Redemptive Plan*. Downers Grove: InterVarsity, 2015.

Masalha, Nur. *The Bible & Zionism: Invented Traditions, Archeology and Post-Colonialism in Palestine-Israel*. London: Zed, 2007.

———. *Expulsion of the Palestinians: The Concept of 'Transfer' in Zionist Political Thought, 1882–1948*. Beirut: Institute for Palestine Studies, 1992.

———. "A Galilee without Christians? Yosef Weitz and 'Operation Yohanan' 1949–1954." In *Palestinian Christians: Religion, Politics and Society in the Holy Land*, edited by Anthony O'Mahony, 190–222. London: Melisende, 1999.

———. *The Politics of Denial: Israel and the Palestinian Refugee Problem*. London: Pluto, 2003.

McCarty, Matthew Tapie, and Justin Bronson Barringer, eds. *The Business of War: Theological and Ethical Reflections on the Military-Industrial Complex*. Eugene, OR: Cascade, 2020.

McDermott, Gerald R. "A History of Christian Zionism: Is Christian Zionism Rooted Primarily in Premillennial Dispensationalism?" In *The New Christian Zionism: Fresh Perspectives on Israel & the Land*, edited by Gerald R. McDermott, 45–75. Downers Grove: IVP Academic, 2016.

———. "A History of Supersessionism: Getting the Big Story Wrong." In *The New Christian Zionism: Fresh Perspectives on Israel & the Land*, edited by Gerald R. McDermott, 33–44. Downers Grove: IVP Academic, 2016.

———. "Implications and Propositions." In *The New Christian Zionism: Fresh Perspectives on Israel & the Land*, edited by Gerald R. McDermott, 319–34. Downers Grove: IVP Academic, 2016.

———. "Introduction: What Is the New Christian Zionism?" In *The New Christian Zionism: Fresh Perspectives on Israel & the Land*, edited by Gerald R. McDermott, 11–29. Downers Grove: IVP Academic, 2016.

———. *Israel Matters: Why Christians Must Think Differently about the People and the Land*. Grand Rapids: Brazos, 2017.

———. "What Is the New Christian Zionism?" In *The New Christian Zionism: Fresh Perspectives on Israel & the Land*, edited by Gerald R. McDermott, 11–29. Downers Grove: IVP Academic, 2016.

McDermott, Gerald R., ed. *The New Christian Zionism: Fresh Perspectives on Israel & the Land*. Downers Grove: IVP Academic, 2016.

McKnight, Scot. *A Light among the Gentiles: Jewish Missionary Activity in the Second Temple Period*. Minneapolis: Fortress, 1991.

———. *Reading Romans Backwards: A Gospel of Peace in the Midst of Empire*. Waco, TX: Baylor University Press, 2019.

Mearsheimer, John H., and Stephen M. Walt. *The Israel Lobby and U.S. Foreign Policy*. New York: Farrar, Straus & Giroux, 2007.

Mendes-Flohr, Paul R., ed. *A Land of Two Peoples: Martin Buber on Jews and Arabs*. New York: Oxford University Press, 1983.

Merkle, Benjamin L. "A Typological Non-Future-Mass-Conversion View." In *Three Views on Israel and the Church: Perspectives on Romans 9–11*, edited by Jared Compton and Andrew David Naselli, 161–208. Grand Rapids: Kregel Academic, 2018.

Merrill, Eugene H. "Israel according to the Torah." In *The People, the Land, and the Future of Israel: Israel and the Jewish People in the Plan of God*, edited by Darrell L. Bock and Mitch Glaser, 27–37. Grand Rapids: Kregel, 2014.

Michaels, J. Ramsey. *1 Peter*. Word Biblical Commentary 49. Waco, TX: Word, 1988.

"Military Steps Up Use of Live 0.22 Inch Bullets against Palestinian Stone-Throwers." *B'Tselem*, January 18, 2015. www.btselem.org/press_releases/20150118_use_of_live_ammunition_in_wb.

Miles, Jim. "Book Review: Palestine Betrayed by Ephraim Karsh." *Top Scoops*, August 29, 2010. https://www.scoop.co.nz/stories/HL1008/S00201/book-review-palestine-betrayed-by-efraim-karsh.htm#a.

Molavi, Shourideh C. *Stateless Citizenship: The Palestinian-Arab Citizens of Israel*. Chicago: Haymarket, 2014.

Morris, Benny. *1948 and After: Israel and the Palestinians*. Oxford: Oxford University Press, 1990.

———. *1948: The First Arab-Israeli War*. New Haven: Yale, 2008.

———. *The Birth of the Palestinian Refugee Problem Revisited*. Cambridge: Cambridge University Press, 2004.

———. "Israel's Concealing of Nakba Documents Is Totalitarian." *Haaretz*, July 15, 2019. https://www.haaretz.com/opinion/.premium-israel-s-concealing-of-documents-on-the-nakba-is-totalitarian-1.7495203.

———. "The New Historiography: Israel Confronts Its Past." In *Making Israel*, edited by Benny Morris, 11–28. Ann Arbor: University of Michigan Press, 2007.

———. *Righteous Victims: A History of the Zionist-Arab Conflict, 1881–2001*. New York: Vintage, 2001.

———. "Waiting for the Barbarians." *Haaretz*, January 9, 2004. https://www.haaretz.co.il/misc/1.936900.

"The Mossawa Center's Briefing Paper on Human Rights for Arab Citizens in Israel: Discrimination against the Arab Minority in Israel." The Mossawa Center: Haifa, 2018. http://din-online.info/pdf/ms7.pdf.

Mosse, George L. *The Crisis of German Ideology: Intellectual Origins of the Third Reich*. New York: Schocken, 1981.

Munayer, Salim J., and Lisa Loden, eds. *The Land Cries Out: Theology of the Land in the Israeli-Palestinian Context*. Eugene, OR: Cascade, 2012.

Munayyer, Yousef. "'Does Israel Have a Right to Exist' Is a Trick Question." *Forward*, January 22, 2019. https://forward.com/opinion/417930/does-israel-have-a-right-to-exist-is-a-trick-question/.

Neumann, Michael. *The Case Against Israel*. Petrolia, CA: Counterpunch, 2005.

Newman, Carey C., ed. *Jesus and the Restoration of Israel: A Critical Assessment of N. T. Wright's "Jesus and the Victory of God."* Downers Grove: InterVarsity, 1999.

Nicholson, Robert. "Theology and Law: Does the Modern State of Israel Violate Its Call to Justice in the Covenant by Its Relation to International Law?" In *The New Christian Zionism: Fresh Perspectives on Israel & the Land*, edited by Gerald R. McDermott, 249–80. Downers Grove: IVP Academic, 2016.

Nordau, Max, and Gustav Gottheil. *Zionism and Anti-Semitism*. New York: Fox, Duffield, 1905.

Norton, Ben. "US and Israel Rewrite History of UN Resolution That Declared Zionism Is Racism." *Mondoweiss*, November 13, 2015. https://mondoweiss.net/2015/11/resolution-declared-zionism/.

Nowlin, Sanford. "Apocalypse Now: Why Pastor John Hagee Has Never Been More Politically Powerful—and Terrifying." *San Antonio Current*, September, 19, 2019. https://www.sacurrent.com/the-daily/archives/2019/09/10/apocalypse-now-why-pastor-john-hagee-has-never-been-more-politically-powerful-or-terrifying.

Oepke, Albrecht. "apokathistēmi, apokatastasis." In *Theological Dictionary of the New Testament*, edited by Gerhard Kittel and Gerhard Friedrich, 1:388. 10 vols. Grand Rapids: Eerdmans, 1964–76.

Ofir, Jonathan. "Understanding Israel's Deception Regarding Citizenship vs. Jewish Nationality." *Mondoweiss*, March 14, 2019. https://mondoweiss.net/2019/03/understanding-citizenship-nationality/.

———. "Weaponizing the Holocaust against Palestinians." *Mondoweiss*, January 20, 2020. https://mondoweiss.net/2020/01/weaponizing-the-holocaust-against-palestinians/.

O'Mahony, Anthony. "Palestinian Christians: Religion, Politics and Society, c. 1800–1948." In *Palestinian Christians: Religion, Politics and Society in the Holy Land*, edited by Anthony O'Mahony, 9–55. London: Melisende, 1999.

O'Mahony, Anthony, ed. *Palestinian Christians: Religion, Politics and Society in the Holy Land*. London: Melisende, 1999.

Oren, Michael B. *Power, Faith, and Fantasy: America in the Middle East: 1776 to the Present*. New York: Norton, 2007.

Orr, Akiva. *The UnJewish State: The Politics of Jewish Identity in Israel*. London: Ithaca, 1983.

Ostler, Jeffrey. *Surviving Genocide: Native Nations and the United States from the American Revolution to Bleeding Kansas*. New Haven: Yale University Press, 2019.

"Palestinian Photographer Shot in Face with Rubber Bullet." *Committee to Protect Journalists*, April 12, 2013. https://cpj.org/2013/04/palestinian-photographer-shot-in-face-by-rubber-bu/.

Palumbo, Michael. "What Happened to Palestine? The Revisionists Revisited." *Americans for Middle East Understanding* 23 (September-October 1990) 2–12.

Pappé, Ilan. *The Biggest Prison on Earth: A History of the Occupied Territories*. London: Oneworld, 2017.

———. "Critique and Agenda: The Post-Zionist Scholars in Israel." *History and Memory* 7 (Spring-Summer 1995) 66–90.

———. *The Ethnic Cleansing of Palestine*. Oxford: Oneworld, 2006.

———. *The Forgotten Palestinians: A History of the Palestinians in Israel*. New Haven: Yale University Press, 2011.

———. *The Idea of Israel: A History of Power and Knowledge*. London: Verso, 2014.

———. *The Making of the Arab-Israeli Conflict 1947–1951*. London: Taurus, 2015.

———. *Ten Myths about Israel*. New York: Verso, 2017.

———. "The Vicissitudes of the 1948 Historiography of Israel." *Journal of Palestine Studies* 39 (Autumn 2009) 6–23.

———. "Zionism as Colonialism: A Comparative View of Diluted Colonialism in Asia and Africa." *South Atlantic Quarterly* 107 (Fall 2008) 611–33.

Parshall, Craig. "The Legal Challenges at the Nexus of the Conflict." In *Israel, the Church, and the Middle East: A Biblical Response to the Current Conflict*, edited by Darrell Bock and Mitch Glaser, 203–15. Grand Rapids: Kregel, 2018.

Patai, Raphael, and Jennifer P. Wing. *The Myth of the Jewish Race*. New York: Scribner, 1975.

Patel, Yumna. "Nine-Month Sentence Is Not Justice, Says Father of 17-year-old Palestinian Killed by Israeli Soldier." *Mondoweiss*, April 25, 2018. https://mondoweiss.net/2018/04/sentence-palestinian-soldier/.

"Peace to Prosperity: A Vision to Improve the Lives of the Palestinian and Israeli People." https://web.archive.org/web/20200128183013/https://www.whitehouse.gov/wp-content/uploads/2020/01/Peace-to-Prosperity-0120.pdf.

Peled, Miko. *The General's Son: Journey of an Israeli in Palestine*. Charlottesville, VA: Just World, 2016.

Perlmutter, Nathan, and Ruth Ann Perlmutter. *The Real Anti-Semitism in America*. New York: Arbor, 1982.

Piterberg, Gabriel. *The Returns of Zionism: Myths, Politics and Scholarship in Israel*. London: Verso, 2008.

Porath, Y. *The Emergence of the Palestinian-Arab National Movement, 1918–1929*. London: Cass, 1974.

Pritz, Ray A. "The Remnant of Israel and the Messiah." In *Israel: The Land and the People; An Evangelical Affirmation of God's Promises*, edited by H. Wayne House, 61–73. Grand Rapids: Kregel, 1998.

Purkiss, Jessica. "Journalist Shot whilst Filming Soldiers Needs Constructive Facial Surgery." *Palestine Monitor*, April 18, 2013. https://www.palestinemonitor.org/details.php?id=9rjx5ga3595yewt2hevws.

———. "Shot, Hunted, Jailed: One Journalist's Ordeal." *Aljazeera*, July 7, 2013. https://www.aljazeera.com/features/2013/7/7/shot-hunted-jailed-one-journalists-ordeal.

———. "Teenager Shot in His Head in Aida Refugee Camp." *Palestine Monitor*, January 20, 2013. https://palestinemonitor.org/details.php?id=43innva2191y4pzkhj465.

Quigley, John. *The Case for Palestine: An International Law Perspective*. Rev. ed. Durham: Duke University Press, 2005.

Qumsiyeh, Mazin B. *Popular Resistance in Palestine: A History of Hope and Empowerment*. London: Pluto, 2011.

———. *Sharing the Land of Canaan: Human Rights and the Israeli-Palestinian Struggle*. London: Pluto, 2004.

Rabinowitz, Aaron. "Israeli High Court Allows DNA Testing to Prove Judaism." *Haaretz*, January 24, 2020.

———. "Israel's Rabbinical Courts Begin to Recognize DNA Tests, Potentially Opening Gateway to Proving Jewishness." *Haaretz*, September 1, 2019.

Rabkin, Yakov M. *A Threat from Within: A Century of Jewish Opposition to Zionism.* Translated by Fred A. Reed with Yakov M. Rabkin. London: Zed, 2006.

Raheb, Mitri. *I Am a Palestinian Christian.* Minneapolis: Fortress, 1995.

Ram, Uri. "Zionist Historiography and the Invention of Modern Jewish Nationhood: The Case of Ben Zion Dinur." *History and Memory* 7 (1995) 91–124.

Ravitzky, Aviezer. "Ultra-Orthodox and Anti-Zionist." *My Jewish Learning,* n.d. https:// www.myjewishlearning.com/article/ultra-orthodox-anti-zionist/.

Reich, Avshalom. "Changes and Developments in the Passover Haggadot of the Kibbutz Movement." PhD diss., University of Texas, 1972.

"Reporting Contradictions on Israeli Deaths." *Guardian,* July 2, 2014. https://www. theguardian.com/world/2014/jul/02/reporting-contradictions-on-israeli-deaths.

Reuters. "Israel Ramps Up Punishments for Stone-Throwers, Palestinians Protest." *Reuters,* July 21, 2015. https://www.reuters.com/article/us-israel-palestinians-stonethrowing/israel-ramps-up-punishments-for-stone-throwers-palestinians-protest-idUSKCN0PV0WW20150721.

"Revealed: New 'Deal of the Century' Details Shows Minimal Israeli Concessions." *Middle East Eye,* May 13, 2019. https://www.middleeasteye.net/news/deal-of-the-century-revealed-israel-palestine-conflict-us-trump-kushner.

Roache, Madeline. "Surge in Anti-Semitic Attacks Has Caused a 'Sense of Emergency' among Jews Worldwide, New Report Says." *Time,* May 2, 2019. https://time. com/5580312/kantor-center-anti-semitism-report/.

Robbins, Annie. "Shooting the Messenger: Occupation Film-maker al-Azzah Is Arrested, 3 Months after Being Shot in Head." *Mondoweiss,* July 5, 2013. https:// mondoweiss.net/2013/07/ messenger-occupation-filmmaker/.

Robertson, O. Palmer. *The Israel of God: Yesterday, Today, and Tomorrow.* Phillipsburg, NJ: P&R, 2000.

Robinson, Shira. *Citizen Strangers: Palestinians and the Birth of Israel's Liberal Settler State.* Stanford: Stanford University Press, 2013.

Rodinson, Maxime. *Israel: A Colonial-Settler State?* Translated by David Thorstad. New York: Monad, 1973.

Rogan, Eugene L., and Avi Shlaim, eds. *The War for Palestine: Rewriting the History of 1948.* Cambridge: Cambridge University Press, 2007.

Rouhana, Nadim N. "The Psychopolitical Foundations of Ethnic Privileges in the Jewish State." In *Israel and Its Palestinian Citizens: Ethnic Privileges in the Jewish State,* edited by Nadim N. Rouhana and Sahar S. Huneidi, 3–35. Cambridge: Cambridge University Press, 2017.

Rouhana, Nadim N., and Nimer Sultany. "Redrawing the Boundaries of Citizenship: Israel's New Hegemony." *Journal of Palestine Studies* 33 (Autumn 2003) 5–22.

Rouhana, Nadim N., and Sahar S. Huneidi, eds. *Israel and Its Palestinian Citizens: Ethnic Privileges in the Jewish State.* Cambridge: Cambridge University Press, 2017.

Rudolf, David. "Zionism in Pauline Literature: Does Paul Eliminate Particularity for Israel and the Land in His Portrayal of Salvation Available for All the World?" In *The New Christian Zionism: Fresh Perspectives on Israel & the Land,* edited by Gerald R. McDermott, 167–94. Downers Grove: IVP Academic, 2016.

Rudolph, David, and Joel Willitts, eds. *Introduction to Messianic Judaism: Its Ecclesial Context and Biblical Foundations.* Grand Rapids: Zondervan, 2013.

Rudoren, Jodi, and Isabel Kershner. "Israel's Search for 3 Teenagers Ends in Grief." *New York Times*, June 30, 2014. https://www.nytimes.com/2014/07/01/world/middleeast/Israel-missing-teenagers.html.

Ruether, Rosemary Radford, and Herman J. Ruether. *The Wrath of Jonah: The Crisis of Religious Nationalism in the Israeli-Palestinian Conflict*. New York: Harper & Row, 1989.

Rydelnik, Michael. "The Hermeneutics of the Conflict." In *Israel, the Church and the Middle East*, edited by Darrell Bock and Mitch Glaser, 63–82. Grand Rapids: Kregel, 2018.

Rylie, Charles C. *Dispensationalism*. Chicago: Moody, 1995.

Said, Edward. *The Question of Palestine*. New York: Vintage, 1992.

Sales, Ben. "Israeli Officials Condemn Breaking the Silence, and Restrict Its Activities." *Jewish Telegraphic Agency*, December 17, 2015. https://www.jta.org/2015/12/17/culture/israeli-officials-condemn-breaking-the-silence-and-restrict-its-activities.

———. "Netanyahu's Promise to Annex the West Bank Aettlements, Explained." *Jerusalem Post*, April 9, 2019. https://www.jpost.com/israel-news/benjamin-netanyahu/netanyahus-promise-to-annex-the-west-bank-settlements-explained-586212.

Sand, Shlomo. *How I Stopped Being a Jew*. Translated by D. Fernbach. New York: Verso, 2014.

———. *The Invention of the Jewish People*. Translated by Yael Lotan. London: Verso, 2009.

———. *The Invention of the Land of Israel: From Holy Land to Homeland*. Translated by Geremy Forman. London: Verso, 2012.

Sandeen, Ernest R. *The Roots of Fundamentalism: British and American Millenarianism, 1800–1930*. Chicago: Chicago University Press, 1970.

Sanders, E. P. *Paul and Palestinian Judaism: A Comparison of Patterns of Religion*. Philadelphia: Fortress, 1977.

———. *Paul, the Law, and the Jewish People*. Minneapolis: Fortress, 1983.

Saucy, Mark R. "Israel as a Necessary Theme in Biblical Theology." In *The People, the Land, and the Future of Israel: Israel and the Jewish People in the Plan of God*, edited by Darrell L. Bock and Mitch Glaser, 169–80. Grand Rapids: Kregel, 2014.

Saucy, Robert L. *The Case for Progressive Dispensationalism: The Interface between Dispensational & Non-dispensational Theology*. Grand Rapids: Zondervan, 1993.

———. "The Church as the Mystery of God." In *Dispensationalism, Israel and the Church: The Search for Definition*, edited by Craig A. Blaising and Darrell L. Bock, 127–55. Grand Rapids: Zondervan, 1992.

———. "Israel and the Church: A Case for Discontinuity." In *Continuity and Discontinuity: Perspectives on the Relationship between the Old and New Testaments: Essays in Honor of S. Lewis Johnson Jr.*, edited by John S. Feinberg, 239–59. Westchester, IL: Crossway, 1988.

Sayegh, Nadine. "Racism: In Israel Some Jews Are More Equal than Others." *TRT World*, July 9, 2019. https://www.trtworld.com/opinion/racism-in-israel-some-jews-are-more-equal-than-others-28109.

Scheindlin, Dahlia. "Against 'Hasbara': Explaining Ourselves to Death." *+972 magazine*, June 9, 2015. https://www.972mag.com/against-hasbara-explaining-ourselves-to-death/.

Schiffman, Lawrence. *Who Was a Jew? Rabbinic and Halakhic Perspectives on the Jewish Christian Schism*. Hoboken: KTAV, 1985.

Shlaim, Avi. *Collusion across the Jordan: King Abdullah, the Zionist Movement, and the Partition of Palestine*. New York: Columbia University Press, 1988.

———. *The Iron Wall: Israel and the Arab World*. New York: Norton, 2001.

———. *Israel and Palestine: Reappraisals, Revisions, Refutations*. London: Verso, 2009.

Schneer, Jonathan. *The Balfour Declaration: The Origins of the Arab-Israeli Conflict*. New York: Random House, 2010.

Schocken, Roni. "Chilling Effect of the Nakba Law on Israel's Human Rights." *Haaretz*, May 16, 2012. https://www.haaretz.com/opinion/chilling-effect-of-the-nakba-law -1.5158148.

Schoenfeld, Gabriel. *The Return of Anti-Semitism*. San Francisco: Encounter, 2005.

Schoenman, Ralph. *The Hidden History of Zionism*. Santa Barbara, CA: Veritas, 1988.

Scholch, Alexander. "Britain in Palestine, 1838–1882: The Roots of the Balfour Policy." *Journal of Palestine Studies* 22 (Autumn 1992) 39–56.

Segev, Tom. *1949: The First Israelis*. Translated by Arlen Neal Weinstein. New York: Free Press, 1986.

———. *1967: Israel, the War, and the Year That Transformed the Middle East*. Translated by Jessica Cohen. New York: Holt, 2007.

———. *One Palestine, Complete: Jews and Arabs under the British Mandate*. Translated by Haim Watzman. New York: Metropolitan, 2000.

———. *The Seventh Million: The Israelis and the Holocaust*. Translated by Haim Watzman. New York: Holt, 1991.

Seiple, Robert A. "Christianity, Human Rights, and a Theology That Touches the Ground." In *Christianity and Human Rights: An Introduction*, edited by John Witte Jr. and Frank S. Alexander, 320–34. Cambridge: Cambridge University Press, 2010.

Selengut, Charles. *Our Promised Land: Faith and Militant Zionism in Israeli Settlements*. Lanham, MD: Rowman & Littlefield, 2015.

Shabi, Rachel. "Israel's Dominant Media Narrative." *Aljazeera*, July 6, 2014. https:// www.aljazeera.com/indepth/opinion/2014/07/israel-dominant-media-narrative-20147675736829395.html.

Shafir, Gershon. *Land, Labor and the Origins of the Israeli-Palestinian Conflict, 1882–1914*. Berkley, CA: University of California Press, 1996.

Shahak, Israel. *Jewish History, Jewish Religion: The Weight of Three Thousand Years*. London: Pluto, 1994.

Shalev, Chemi. "Berlin, 1933 and Jerusalem, 2014: When Racist Thugs Are on the Prowl." *Haaretz*, July 2, 2014. https://www.haaretz.com/misc/article-print-page/. premium-racist-thugs-are-on-the-prowl-1.5254252.

Shapiro, Harry L. *The Jewish People: A Biological History*. Paris: UNESCO, 1960.

Shatz, Adam, ed. *Prophets Outcast: A Century of Dissident Jewish Writing about Zionism and Israel*. New York: Nation, 2004.

Shaul, Yehuda. "Netanyahu Wants to Repress My Group, Breaking the Silence. May, Don't Help Him." *Guardian*, February 8, 2017. https://www.theguardian.com/commentisfree/2017/feb/08/netanyahu-breaking-the-silence-israel-theresa-may.

Shavit, Ari. "Survival of the Fittest." *Haaretz*, January 8, 2004. https://www.haaretz. com/1.5262454.

Shehadeh, Raja. *Occupier's Law: Israel and the West Bank*. Beirut: Institute of Palestinian Studies, 1990.

———. "Op-Ed: Israel's New Settlement Law Is an Affront to Democracy." *Los Angeles Times*, February 9, 2017. www.latimes.com/opinion/op-ed/la-oe-shehadeh-israel-settlements-law-20170209-story.html.

Shelef, Nadav G. *Evolving Nationalism: Homeland, Identity and Religion in Israel, 1925–2005*. Ithaca, NY: Cornell University Press, 2010.

Sherwood, Harriet. "Palestinian Deaths Raise Concerns over Israeli Army Use of Live Fire." *Guardian*, January 27, 2013. https://www.theguardian.com/world/2013/jan/28/palestinian-deaths-israel-army-live-fire.

Silberstein, Laurence J. *The Postzionism Debates: Knowledge and Power in Israeli Culture*. New York: Routledge, 1999.

Silva, Moisés. "Galatians." In *Commentary on the New Testament Use of the Old Testament*, edited by G. K. Beale and D. A. Carson, 785–812. Grand Rapids: Baker Academic, 2009.

Sirvent, Roberto, and Danny Haiphong. *American Exceptionalism and American Innocence: A People's History of Fake News—from the Revolutionary War to the War on Terror*. New York: Skyhorse, 2019.

Sizer, Stephen. *Christian Zionism: Road-Map to Armageddon?*. Leicester, UK: InterVarsity, 2004.

———. *Zion's Christian Soldiers? The Bible, Israel, and the Church*. Leicester, UK: InterVarsity, 2008.

Slepkov, Noah. "Israel's Rabbis Think Genetic Testing Can 'Prove' Jewishness. They're Wrong." *Haaretz*, April 29, 2019.

Smith, Charles D. "Palestine Betrayed: Review." *Middle East Journal* 65 (January 2011) 155–58. https://www.researchgate.net/publication/236785833_Palestine_Betrayed_review.

Smith, Helmut Walser. *The Continuities of German History: Nation, Religion, and Race across the Long Nineteenth Century*. Cambridge: Cambridge University Press, 2008.

Sofer, Sasson. *Zionism and the Foundations of Israeli Diplomacy*. Translated by D. Shefet-Vanson. Cambridge: Cambridge University Press, 1998.

"Soldier Kills Palestinian Demonstrator Mustafa Tamimi, 28, by Shooting Tear-Gas Canister at Him." *B'Tselem*, December 11, 2011. www.btselem.org/firearms/20111209_killing_of_mustafa_tamimi.

Soulen, R. Kendall. *The God of Israel and Christian Theology*. Minneapolis: Fortress, 1996.

Spiro, Amy. "Netanyahu to Rotem Sela: Israel Is Not a Country of All Its Citizens." *Jerusalem Post*, March 10, 2019. https://www.jpost.com/Israel-News/Benjamin-Netanyahu/Netanyahu-hits-back-at-Israeli-actress-after-she-criticizes-Miri-Regev-582959.

Sternhell, Zeev. *The Founding Myths of Israel: Nationalism, Socialism, and the Making of the Jewish State*. Translated by David Maisel. Princeton: Princeton University Press, 1998.

Strickland, Patrick. "Israel Continues to Criminalize Marking Nakba Day." *Aljazeera*, May 14, 2015. https://www.aljazeera.com/news/2015/05/israel-nakba-palestine-150514080431980.html.

Stringfellow, William. *An Ethic for Christian & Other Aliens in a Strange Land*. Waco, TX: Word, 1973.

Stuehrenberg, Paul F. "Proselyte." In *The Anchor Bible Dictionary*, edited by David Noel Freedman et al., 5:503–5. New York: Doubleday, 1992.

Suárez, Thomas. *State of Terror: How Terrorism Created Modern Israel*. Northampton, MA: Olive Branch, 2017.

Subramanian, Samanth. "How Hindu Supremacists Are Tearing India Apart." *Guardian*, February 20, 2020. https://www.theguardian.com/world/2020/feb/20/hindu-supremacists-nationalism-tearing-india-apart-modi-bjp-rss-jnu-attacks.

Sultany, Nimer. "The Legal Structures of Subordination: The Palestinian Minority and Israeli Law." In *Israel and Its Palestinian Citizens: Ethnic Privileges in the Jewish State*, edited by Nadim N. Touhana and Sahar S. Huneidi, 191–237. Cambridge: Cambridge University Press, 2017.

Sussman, Leonard R. "'Jew,' 'Jewish People,' and 'Zionism.'" *ETC: A Review of General Semantics* 20 (September 1963) 372–75.

Tabar, Natalie, and Lauren Bari. *Repression of Non-violent Protest in the Occupied Palestinian Territory: Case Study on the Village of Al-Nabi Saleh*. Ramallah: Al-Haq, 2011. https://www.alhaq.org/cached_uploads/download/alhaq_files/publications/Nabi-Saleh.pdf.

Tatour, Lana. "Citizenship as Domination: Settler Colonialism and the Making of Palestinian Citizenship in Israel." *Arab Studies Journal* 27 (Fall 2019) 8–39.

Taylor, Adam. "The Lopsided Death Tolls in Israel-Palestinian Conflicts." *Washington Post*, July 11, 2014. https://www.washingtonpost.com/news/worldviews/wp/2014/07/11/the-lopsided-death-tolls-in-israel-palestinian-conflicts/.

Teveth, Shabtai. *Ben-Gurion and the Palestinians Arabs: From Peace to War*. Oxford: Oxford University Press, 1985.

Thomas, Robert L. "The Mission of Israel and of the Messiah in the Plan of God." In *Israel, the Land and the People: An Evangelical Affirmation of God's Promises*, edited by H. Wayne House, 261–80. Grand Rapids: Kregel, 1998.

Tibawi, A. L. "Special Report: The Destruction of an Islamic Heritage in Jerusalem." *Arab Studies Quarterly* 2 (1980) 180–89.

Tilly, Virginia, ed. *Beyond Occupation: Apartheid, Colonialism & International Law in the Occupied Palestinian Territories*. London: Pluto, 2012.

Toogood, Callum. "Two Youths Shot in Aida Camp on Same Day." *Palestine Monitor*, March 2, 2013. https://palestinemonitor.org/details.php?id=940fhza2945yg1fi9xnum.

Tooley, Mark. "Theology and the Churches: Mainline Protestant Zionism and Anti-Zionism." In *The New Christian Zionism: Fresh Perspectives on Israel & the Land*, edited by Gerald R. McDermott, 197–219. Downers Grove: IVP Academic, 2016.

Tutu, Desmond M. "The First Word: To Be Human Is to Be Free." In *Christianity and Human Rights: An Introduction*, edited by John Witte Jr. and Frank S. Alexander, 1–7. Cambridge: Cambridge University Press, 2010.

United Nations. "How Dispossession Happens: The Humanitarian Impact of the Takeover of Palestinian Water Springs by Israeli Settlers." United Nations, Office for the Coordination of Humanitarian Affairs Occupied Palestinian Territory. https://www.ochaopt.org/sites/default/files/ocha_opt_springs_report_march_2012_english.pdf.

Vanlaningham, Michael G. "The Jewish People according to the Book of Romans." In *The People, the Land, and the Future of Israel: Israel and the Jewish People in the Plan of God*, edited by Darrell L. Bock and Mitch Glaser, 117–31. Grand Rapids: Kregel, 2014.

Verhey, Allen. *Remembering Jesus: Christian Community, Scripture, and the Moral Life*. Grand Rapids: Eerdmans, 2002.

Vital, David. *The Origins of Zionism*. Oxford: Oxford University Press, 1974.

Vlach, Michael J. *The Church as a Replacement of Israel: An Analysis of Supersessionism*. Frankfurt: Lang, 2009.

———. *Has the Church Replaced Israel? A Theological Evaluation*. Nashville: B&H Academic, 2010.

———. "Israel and the Land in the Writings of the Church." In *Israel, the Church and the Middle East: A Biblical Response to the Current Conflict*, edited by Darrell L. Bock and Mitch Glaser, 119–34. Grand Rapids: Kregel, 2018.

———. "A Non-typological Future-Mass-Conversion View." In *Three Views on Israel and the Church: Perspectives on Romans 9–11*, edited by Jared Compton and Andrew David Naselli, 21–73. Grand Rapids: Kregel Academic, 2018.

Wagner, Donald E., and Walter T. Davis, eds. *Zionism and the Quest for Justice in the Holy Land*. Eugene, OR: Pickwick, 2014.

Waltke, Bruce. "A Response." In *Dispensationalism, Israel and the Church: The Search for Definition*, edited by Craig A. Blaising and Darrell L. Bock, 347–59. Grand Rapids: Zondervan, 1992.

Watson, Ivan, et al. "Father Blames Israeli Military in Palestinian Teens' Deaths." *CNN*, May 22, 2014. https://edition.cnn.com/2014/05/22/world/meast/israel-west-bank-shooting.

Weisbrot, Mark and Robert Naiman. "Arash Norouzi Explains the 'Wiped Off the Map' Controversy—What Iran's President Never Said." *Huffington Post*, May 25, 2011. https://www.huffpost.com/entry/arash-norouzi-explains-th_b_39069.

Westerholm, Stephen. *Perspectives Old and New on Paul: The "Lutheran" Paul and His Critics*. Grand Rapids: Eerdmans, 2004.

White, Ben. *Israeli Apartheid: A Beginner's Guide*. 2nd ed. London: Pluto, 2014.

———. *Palestinians in Israel: Segregation, Discrimination and Democracy*. London: Pluto, 2012.

Wilsey, John D. *American Exceptionalism and Civil Religion: Reassessing the History of an Idea*. Downers Grove: InterVarsity, 2015.

Witte, John, Jr., and Frank S. Alexander, eds. *Christianity and Human Rights: An Introduction*. Cambridge: Cambridge University Press, 2010.

Wolfe, Patrick. *Settler Colonialism and the Transformation of Anthropology: The Politics and Poetics of an Ethnographic Event*. London: Cassell, 1999.

Wright, N. T. *The Climax of the Covenant*. Minneapolis: Fortress, 1992.

———. *Jesus and the Victory of God*. Minneapolis: Fortress, 1996.

"Ya'alon Says Troops in Nakba Day Killings Were in Danger, Acted as Needed." *Times of Israel*, May 20, 2014. https://www.timesofisrael.com/yaalon-says-troops-in-nakba-day-killings-were-in-danger-acted-as-needed/.

Yiftachel, Oren. "'Ethnocracy' and Its Discontents: Minorities, Protests, and the Israeli Polity." *Critical Inquiry* 26 (Summer 2000) 725–56.

———. *Ethnocracy: Land and Identity Politics in Israel/Palestine*. Philadelphia: University of Pennsylvania Press, 2006.

———. "Nation-State Law's Present Absentees." *Haaretz*, August 1, 2018. https://www.haaretz.com/misc/article-print-page/.premuim-nation-state-law-s-present-absentees-1.6336526.

Yoder, John Howard. *The Politics of Jesus*. Grand Rapids: Eerdmans, 1972.

———. *The Priestly Kingdom: Social Ethics as Gospel*. Notre Dame: Notre Dame University Press, 1982.

Zaretsky, Tuvya. "Israel the People." In *Israel, the Land and the People: An Evangelical Affirmation of God's Promises*, edited by H. Wayne House, 35–59. Grand Rapids: Kregel, 1998.

Zaru, Jean. *Occupied with Nonviolence: A Palestinian Woman Speaks*. Minneapolis: Fortress, 2008.

Zaspel, Fred Z., and James M. Hamilton Jr. "The Typological Future-Mass-Conversion View." In *Three Views on Israel and the Church: Perspectives on Romans 9–11*, edited by Jared Compton and Andrew David Naselli, 97–140. Grand Rapids: Kregel Academic, 2018.

Zavadsky, Katie. "It Turns Out That Hamas May Not Have Kidnapped and Killed the 3 Israeli Teens After All." *Intelligencer*, July 25, 2014. https://nymag.com/intelligencer/2014/07/hamas-didnt-kidnap-the-israeli-teens-after-all.html.

Zeitlin, Solomon. "The Names Hebrew, Jew, and Israel: A Historical Study." *Jewish Quarterly Review* 43 (April 1953) 365–79.

Zertal, Idith, and Adiva Eldar. *Lords of the Land: The War over Israel's Settlements in the Occupied Territories, 1967–2007*. Translated by Vivian Eden. New York: Nation, 2007.

Zonszein, Mairav. "Border Cop Arrested for Nakba Day Killing, Debunking IDF Tales." *+972 magazine*, November 12, 2014. https://www.972mag.com/border-cop-arrested-for-nakba-day-killing-debunking-idf-tales/98670/.

Subject Index

Note: Page numbers in **bold** type indicate a photograph.

Scripture Index

Milton Keynes UK
Ingram Content Group UK Ltd.
UKHW012154280923
429580UK00002B/7